The
DARK SIDE
of the FORCE

The
DARK SIDE
of the FORCE

A True Story of Corruption and
Murder in the LAPD

JAN GOLAB

THE ATLANTIC MONTHLY PRESS
NEW YORK
♦

Published simultaneously in Canada
Printed in the United States of America

Library of Congress Cataloging-in-Publication Data

Golab, Jan.
The dark side of the force: a true story of corruption and murder
in the LAPD / Jan Golab.
ISBN 0-87113-499-3
1. Police—California—Los Angeles—Complaints against—Case
studies. 2. Police corruption—California—Los Angeles—Case
studies. 3. Murder—California—Los Angeles—Case studies.
I. Title.
HV8148.L55G65   1993   364.1′523′0979494—dc20   92-47020

DESIGN BY LAURA HOUGH

The Atlantic Monthly Press
841 Broadway
New York, NY 10003

FIRST PRINTING

This is a true story, based on court documents and personal interviews. The names of some secondary characters have been altered or withheld to protect those people's privacy.

To my father, E.J.,

who inspired me to be a free spirit and to keep an open mind.

I lost him while writing this book.

May he rest in peace.

Contents

ix

Contents

Contents

The
DARK SIDE
of the FORCE

Prologue

Nightmare for the Chief

CHIEF GATES SAT AT HIS DESK, DUMBFOUNDED, FIDDLING WITH THE tape recorder, replaying portions of the tape over and over. He couldn't believe what he was hearing: an LAPD detective raving like a wild man about burglary and capering and murder for hire, about kidnapping, raping, and torturing a woman to make it look like a sex crime, about "knifing niggers" and "doing whores," about fragging commanding officers and committing atrocities in Vietnam, about how being a supercop was "the perfect cover."

"That's one of *our* guys?" Gates kept asking.

"Yes, Chief. One of ours."

It was 1:00 P.M. on Friday, July 8, 1983. LAPD chief Daryl F. Gates had spent the morning in his office at Parker Center closeted with IAD brass, federal agents, and the D.A. Apparently, two of his men had just committed the most heinous crime in LAPD history. A noon press conference had been called, and the Parker Center auditorium was packed with reporters and TV cameras. Chief Gates had kept them waiting for an hour. He just couldn't stop listening to the tape.

Gates had weathered a few scandals in his five years as the head of the Los Angeles Police Department, but they paled in comparison to this. And it would be another eight years before Rodney King.

Due to that infamous George Holliday videotape, the March 1991 King beating would gain worldwide attention and have profound impact on the LAPD. The resultant Christopher Commission, with its report of widespread racism and a "culture of brutality" in the LAPD, would serve as a formal indictment and lead

3

to Chief Gates's early "retirement." And the verdict from the King beating trial would ignite the worst race riots in U.S. history, perhaps changing L.A. forever.

But as in most "excessive force" cases, the actions of the officers involved in the Rodney King incident were not so very puzzling. The questions would lie in whether those actions were justified or inexcusable, legal or criminal, unprejudiced or racist, and whether the "siege mentality" that led to that beating was endemic to the department. Hard questions, but relatively clear questions.

The case sitting before Chief Gates now, however, was something else entirely. No criminal case involving the LAPD had been so hard to fathom, so chilling in its ramifications, as that of Detective Richard Ford and Officer Robert Von Villas.

These two decorated war heroes had served thirteen and fifteen impeccable years with the LAPD. Their records showed uncommon devotion to duty and public service. The stack of commendations the two had received lay inches thick on Gates's desk. These were truly two of L.A.'s finest. And, apparently, cold-blooded killers as well.

How had such exceptional cops fallen from grace? Or was it possible that they had never really been the good men, the heroes their records showed them to be? That those many years of working selflessly to protect and to serve had been nothing but a ruse?

This was not a simple case of greed or disillusionment or police burnout or what Gates's critics called the LAPD "cowboy" mentality. No, this one involved all of the above. It was lurid, complicated, and frightening. It involved that strain of horror that connects My Lai to Rodney King, those frightening dangers attendant on any granting of power and trust. The actions of these officers seemed to provide a startling insight into the Dark Side of the Force.

It was a tough pill for a proud chief to swallow. A pair of respected, award-winning LAPD veterans, pillars of the community, had been killing people and committing armed robbery and doing just about everything else under the sun that was illegal. How could this happen?

When the D.A. finally stood before a jury five years later, pleading for the death penalty to be imposed on two L.A. cops, he would refer to this unprecedented case as "every citizen's worst nightmare."

But right now it was Chief Gates's nightmare.

This was *Los Angeles;* this kind of thing didn't happen here. The LAPD had a reputation as the nation's cleanest police department. The home of "Dragnet" and "Adam-12" was the birthplace of the modern-day internal affairs division, created by Gates's mentor, Chief William Parker, back in the 1950s. Chief Parker, who established the hard-charging, paramilitary style of the LAPD, was one of

4

the most widely admired and imitated law-enforcement figures of this century. He established a fail-safe system of interdepartment checks and balances and saw to it that the LAPD could not become politicized and thus subject to the wholesale corruption that mars so many other big-city police departments.

Parker was a realist. "Even the LAPD has to recruit from the human race," he once said. Parker understood that the corruption of some individuals was inevitable, but he insisted that the corruption of a police force could—and must—be prevented, and he had seen to this with breathtaking fervor.

Thinking back on other LAPD scandals only served to remind Chief Gates of how clean the LAPD was. Most recently, the "Hollywood Burglars," a gang of patrol officers, had been caught stealing movies from video stores after tripping the burglar alarms. IAD had also nailed a couple of cops who were involved in sexual trysts with female Explorer Scouts. And then there was the "Jay Paul Affair" concerning a "red squad" cop who'd been compiling data on suspected "subversives." These were all big stories in L.A. Heck, back east, a cop who took some booty or harassed a commie now and then was just a regular guy. If he got caught, the story didn't even make the papers.

But L.A. wasn't like that. Sure, cops would always be involved in shootings that would have to be scrutinized, but no L.A. cop had ever been charged with premeditated murder. You could go all the way back through the LAPD's 107-year history, back to the days when Zorro rode herd on the ranchos and you couldn't find a "killer cop" in L.A.

Even back east, killer cops were rare. Most citizens, of course, didn't know this. Killer cops were such a common dramatic device in books, movies, and TV shows that people simply assumed it happened all the time. Clint Eastwood, Arnold Schwarzenegger, and Chuck Norris made movies about killer cops. Every TV cop show from "Hunter" to "Hill Street Blues" had succumbed, at least once, to that simple but effective dramatic twist at the end of an episode: the good guy—the cop—turns out to be the killer.

But Chief Gates knew that was fiction. Later, after five years of hearings and trials, the accumulation of some 80,000 transcript pages of testimony and a mountain of news clips, when the D.A. stood before a jury and banks of court-room TV cameras and declared "This just doesn't happen," Chief Gates would know he wasn't employing hyperbole. It had never happened—until now.

Nearly ten years later, when Daryl Gates sat down to write his best-selling autobiography, *Chief,* he would muse about the embarrassment he felt over those Hollywood cops stealing videotapes. He'd explore the particulars of the Jay Paul police intelligence scandal. He'd address accusations of LAPD bungling and cover-ups in the Marilyn Monroe and Bobby Kennedy investigations. He'd attempt to explain all those outrageous Gatesisms about how black people don't respond to choke holds like "normal" folk and how casual drug users ought to be shot. He'd even unburden his soul about his own son's long struggle with drug addiction. And, of course, he'd spill his guts about Rodney King.

But Chief Gates would not reflect upon the biggest investigation in the history of the LAPD's Internal Affairs Division. He wouldn't mention the unmentionable: L.A.'s killer cops. It was the case Chief Gates would choose to forget.

But on that sultry afternoon in 1983, the chief sat at his desk and thought about nothing but the case, about the waiting press conference. He thought about an unlikely hero—and victim—named Bruce Adams. Who would have thought that a troubled auto mechanic, a Vietnam vet, could uncover the worst case of corruption and criminality in the history of the LAPD? But most of all, he thought about having to explain it all to the citizens of Los Angeles. How could he tell them the impossible had happened?

The chief shook his head as he eyed the tape. "Let me hear that part about 'the perfect cover' just one more time."

1

Doc

BRUCE ADAMS SPENT HIS ENTIRE LUNCH BREAK PACING AROUND the shop. He had a weird feeling, something to do with the red can opener. Sure, he knew it was stupid. But every time he walked through the grungy shoe-box office at JJJ Automotive to pick up some paperwork, that red can opener crossed his field of vision. He'd see it—whether he wanted to or not—and sure enough, he'd get *antsy*.

Damn it, Adams thought. Not again.

It was one of those church keys everybody used before pop tops—aluminum coated with red plastic. It was hanging by a string on the wall next to the tiny fridge where the crew stashed their beer and sodas, right next to the tacked-up *Hustler* Honey of the Month. It was no big deal. For anyone else, that is.

Adams liked working at JJJ, a truck repair shop in North Hollywood. Wrenching on heavy trucks paid good money, and Bruce liked the occasional road work—going out to troubleshoot on big rigs broken down on the freeway. It was sort of like going out on a mission in Nam. There was an objective, a purpose. Terrain had to be covered quickly and strategically, costly equipment was at stake, and it was dangerous. Not dangerous like Nam, of course, but it made him feel useful, important. More than once his know-how and can-do marine attitude had saved the day for some hapless trucker. That was a good feeling. He didn't want to leave—or get fired—because of those antsy feelings again.

Adams had proven to be an ace mechanic during his six months at JJJ; they didn't keep him around because he looked like Mr. Goodwrench. Adams was a stressed-out Vietnam vet straight from central casting, a poster boy for posttraumatic stress disorder. He was anxious, nervous, paranoid—all shaggy around the edges. But Bruce would never cop to being a stress case. No sir. Those guys were scammers. Bums.

A man of medium height and build, Adams walked with a limp from the foot-long metal pin in his right leg. Scars from shrapnel wounds were visible on his face and chest. His straight dark hair always needed a trim. With his "Joisey" accent, seedy clothes, and distinctive limp, he resembled Ratso Rizzo, Dustin Hoffman's character in *Midnight Cowboy*. But instead of a high nasal twang, Adams spoke with a gravelly baritone that seemed to boom right from his chest.

Bruce was world-class nervous. He'd jump over a stack of tires—gimp leg and all—if you came up and startled him from behind. Guys at the shop thought this was funny until they learned he was just as likely to nail you with a right cross. His nerves weren't helped any by his constant coffee drinking. And he smoked worse than Mount St. Helens. His trembling hands fumbled constantly to light the Marlboros that dangled perpetually from his lips. The guys at the shop marveled at the way Bruce could perform any job, no matter how heavy, with a smoking butt wedged between his lips.

Although just after noon, it was already 105 degrees on this unseasonably hot spring day in 1981. Adams's leg acted up whenever the temperature slipped above ninety, so he was limping more than usual. He was drenched in sweat and grime. His grease-monkey jumpsuit was covered with so much oil it was more black than white. Somehow, you could still read his name where it was embroidered over his chest pocket. Being a big-rig mechanic was a dirty job on days like this. And now, on top of being as filthy and sweaty as a hog and having a leg that burned like it was covered with napalm, he was starting to get nervous again.

He was determined to put it out of his mind. No way, he vowed. Not again.

"Hey, Doc, how we doin' with the fuckin' tranny on that Road Ranger?" It was Johnson, the shop foreman, a big bald-headed bruiser, calling out from the doorway of the office.

"No problem, boss," Adams replied. He'd earned the nickname Doc—from his ability to fix anything mechanical—back when he was just a teenager. Yeah, it was no problem, he thought. That thirteen-speed RR transmission only weighed about a ton, and it was chewed up all to hell. He'd been trying to pull it all morning.

"That mother's been fuckin' with me," Adams yelled, "but I'm yankin' that cocksucker out of there right now. That mother is history." He lit up a Marlboro with a shaky fist as he lay down on his creeper and scooted beneath the truck.

"You've been fuckin' around under there all morning," Johnson needled. "Whataya doin', Doc? Bangin' the bone?"

"Hey listen, Jack," Adams growled, "if I pulled a boner under here this cab would be humpin' up and down on it like a Tijuana whore." Adams' deep chortle reverberated from under the truck and was met with hoots from the other grease jockeys standing around the bay.

"Yeah, maybe you should hump that tranny out," Johnson laughed. "Only you probably don't got a big enough tool."

"Right, cocksucker," Adams retorted. "You only *wish* you had my kinda tool. If I stuck my tool in that tranny, I'd pop that mother out like a fuckin' cherry—no problem."

Grease-shop repartee came easy to Adams. That was another nice thing about Triple J's. There weren't any blue-haired old ladies standing around waiting for you to fix the windshield-wiper fluid switch on their Mercedes. Only truckers with big greasy jobs. You didn't have to watch your language. A man could talk like a man. Like a *marine*.

Adams grabbed the transmission with both hands and started to shake it violently. His curses echoed from under the truck, to the amusement of the entire audience at Triple J's.

"Hey, Tommy," Adams huffed, "get under here and help me hold this motherfucker."

The mechanics' helper, a long-haired kid of nineteen, slid under the truck to lend a hand. Adams's head was engulfed in a cloud of cigarette smoke. The transmission, which was about halfway off the drive shaft, was propped up on a heavy hydraulic jack. Adams was shaking it back and forth like a man possessed, the sweat flowing down his face and dripping off his hair. He looked like he'd just been doused by a garden hose. In the background, the combined noise of compressors and hydraulic drills working at full blast had risen until it was deafening. The decibels danced off the concrete in a crescendo of violent *rat-a-tatt-tatt*s. The floor was vibrating. Suddenly, Adams stopped working and lay perfectly still. Tommy looked over and was frightened by what he saw.

Adams's face had turned a bright, glowing red. His chest was heaving up and down. He was hyperventilating. Tommy looked into the mechanic's eyes and could see he wasn't all there. "Bruce, are you all right?" he yelled.

Adams didn't hear him. He could hear his own heart, pounding like a drum, ready to kick though his chest. *No, not again.* He heard choppers. He felt the ground rumbling from a mortar attack. He heard explosions, distant echoing screams. His chest heaved up harder and harder as he gulped for air. His vision blurred as a collage of shadowy images swirled before him.

Just before he passed out, he saw something from his dreams, from his nightmares.

"Bruce, Bruce," Tommy continued to yell. Then he looked up in horror. The tranny was sliding off the vibrating jack. Tommy quickly shoved Bruce's creeper to one side as nearly a thousand pounds of metal came crashing to the shop floor between them.

Tommy slid out from under the truck and rushed around to the other side. He pulled Adams the rest of the way out. Bruce was unconscious, the blood drained from his ashy face.

"Holy shit!" Tommy cried. "Somebody call nine-one-one!"

Adams was delirious when he came to in the ambulance. I'm lucky, he thought. At least I got a medic flying with me back to base camp. "How bad is it, Doc?" he asked. "Where'd I get hit? How many of our guys are down?" He told the medic about what he'd seen. He told him about the blood on the can opener.

The Sepulveda Veterans Administration is located in Northridge, in the heart of the San Fernando Valley. The massive complex is spread across 164 acres of rolling manicured lawns dotted with palms, eucalyptus, and small lemon groves. Fairways from the bordering Mission Hills Golf Course enhance the relaxed, country club atmosphere. A dozen buildings from the 1950s lie scattered across the campuslike landscape, all sporting the same institutional boxlike orange brick exterior.

Shirley Adams and her two little girls arrived by cab. Julie, seven, had visited Daddy in the hospital before, but it was the first time for three-year-old Stacey. As they pulled up the horseshoe drive to the main hospital, Shirley was filled with dread. She didn't know if she could take any more. She knew that Marilyn, fourteen, and Eric, twelve, who were both in school, would be devastated if they had to move again.

Finally, they had a house. It was a cheap, nondescript clapboard rental in Van Nuys, but it was a house, a home, and it was theirs. If Bruce lost his job, they would again be reduced to living hand to mouth. They'd be staying again in grungy, roach-infested weekly rentals, fleabag motels with incongruous names like the Essex Arms or the Paradise. Such accommodations would be bearable, perhaps, if they were temporary, but for the Adams brood they had been part of a gypsy nightmare for nearly a decade.

With a wife and four kids to support and a troubled work history, Bruce was always struggling, one jump ahead of a wolf pack of creditors. Whenever they nipped too close to his heels, he would pull up stakes and move. For the past seven years the Adams family had been one step away from homeless. Whatever cheap rental they hoveled in, before long there was no phone, then no electricity, then no hot water. Shirley recalled having to heat water on a kitchen stove to give her baby a bath. She thought about the thyroid surgery she desperately needed but couldn't afford. About how the kids never saw a dentist. About how neighbors brought them bags of groceries to make sure they had food.

Please, God, Shirley prayed, not again.

A short woman just over five feet tall with red curly hair, Shirley would have been attractive except that she was forty pounds overweight. Her clothing was an ensemble of K mart specials—ill-fitting blue polyester pants with a simple red-and-white striped cotton top. One of her well-worn sandals had a broken thong and was held together by a piece of twine. But nothing was more pathetic than the look of fear etched on her face.

Shirley carried Stacey in her arms as Julie walked beside her up the steps to the main entrance. Once inside they walked to the check-in desk. Shirley had already decided not to see Bruce right away. She had also decided not to ask to see the doctor. She asked instead for the head of Social Services.

Social worker Dotty Smilgis, a pleasant, gray-haired matron in her sixties, had many years of experience dealing with veterans' wives, who were often as troubled as their husbands. She looked at Shirley Adams and knew she was in for a formidable tale of woe. Shirley, she suspected, was yet another insecure woman who was convinced she had no alternative but to stay in a perpetually troubled relationship with a sick man. She had four kids, she was out of shape, she was getting old—who else would want her? And even if there was any love left in the relationship, well, that could make things even more painful.

Despite the nightmare she'd been through with Bruce, Shirley really did love him. He was her man, for better or worse. From listening to Shirley, Dotty Smilgis learned that Bruce apparently did have his lovable qualities. Despite his nervous demeanor and inability to hold down a job, there were reasons why people liked Bruce. Shirley ticked them off in a sobbing litany. "He never looks for sympathy," Shirley explained. "He doesn't complain about his war wounds. He never whines about his disability. I've never heard him express anger or bitterness about Vietnam. He isn't afraid of hard work. He's always trying to better himself."

Still, Shirley admitted she put up with a lot of grief, like the fact that Bruce wouldn't marry her. Bruce claimed he couldn't because he'd been married before and the divorce had never been finalized and he couldn't find his ex-wife. He always had explanations for things like that. But after living together for seven years, Shirley had stopped bothering him about it. They were common-law now. Perhaps Bruce wasn't a great provider, but he had nevertheless become a father to the two children she brought to the relationship, as well as to their own two little girls. They were a family.

Bruce's biggest problem, Shirley admitted—aside from holding down a job—was holding on to money. He didn't drink or take drugs, but he loved to play the big shot whenever he got some cash in his pocket. And yes, he had a vice: cars and tools. Bruce was always sinking money into tricked-out dragsters that he worked on in his garage, on the lawn, out in the street—wherever he could. When they were flush, it wasn't uncommon for him to buy a vehicle—God knows how he got the loan—then customize it, adding new wheels, new uphol-stery, a new motor. Eventually, of course, he'd fall behind on the payments and the car would end up getting repossessed. Meanwhile, Shirley would need forty dollars for clothes for the kids and they wouldn't have it.

But it was hard to stop Bruce from working on his cars, Shirley said. He couldn't see why she minded him leaving parts strewn all over the lawn, the kitchen floor, throughout the house. Trying to change Bruce would be like asking him not to breathe. Through her tears, a smile creased her lips as she described Bruce's all-night wrenching sessions, the exhaust manifold she once found in the bathtub, the time a racing engine caught fire and he smothered it with her jacket. Her best jacket!

The social worker was amused, but only briefly. After questioning Shirley, Ms. Smilgis concluded that the Adamses' destitute condition was at least partly self-inflicted—an all-too-common instance of poverty exacerbated by stupidity. Even when Bruce was unemployed, they would collect nearly $2,000 a month in combined disability and welfare checks, yet they couldn't get it together to rent a house. Instead, they would stay in motels, paying exorbitant weekly rates. Typically, they would spend $260 a week for a motel dive when they could rent something much nicer for half as much—if they could only put together enough for a first month's rent and deposit. Bruce would rent a color TV for forty dollars a week when he could easily buy one for two hundred dollars. They could never keep bank accounts because they were always bouncing checks—so they spent a small fortune on check-cashing fees.

Ms. Smilgis felt sympathy tinged with rage when she heard such frustrating tales. The truth was that the poor paid penalties for being poor. They were like people caught in quicksand; the more they struggled, the deeper they sank. Working hard was not enough. You had to be smart and make the right deci-sions. Once a family was reduced to living from day to day, it was often impossible for them to stop.

The social worker didn't have the heart to lecture Shirley about handling household finances more responsibly. Not now, anyway. What Shirley needed right now was a shoulder to cry on.

"Please," Shirley implored, "couldn't you get somebody to talk to him?" Then—sure enough—Shirley clutched the woman in a desperate embrace as she broke down and sobbed.

2

Definitely One of Them

A HALF-DOZEN PHYSICIANS EXAMINED BRUCE ADAMS. IT TOOK THAT
many to convince him to stay in the hospital. Adams wanted to get up and leave
right away, almost as soon as he arrived. He insisted on returning some equipment and tools to his van, so he signed a release stating that he was leaving
against medical advice. He left for a few hours and then reluctantly returned for
five days of tests.

"I think maybe I've just been working too hard," Adams grumbled repeatedly, annoyed at all the fuss.

They ran a battery of tests—EKG, EEG, ultrasound, nuclear brain scan.
They couldn't find anything wrong with him.

Dr. Llorens Pembroke, a neurologist, along with a team of specialists,
reviewed the test findings and Adams's medical history. They didn't need to
confer for very long. Adams had previously undergone the same exhaustive tests
at three other V.A. hospitals and on each occasion they had found nothing. Nor
did Dr. Pembroke really need to review the report from Social Services, even
though it did give him cause to act with more conviction. Pembroke insisted that
Adams talk with Dr. Jefferson Davis, one of the V.A.'s psychiatrists. He sent
Adams over to building 25, which housed Mental Services, Psychiatry, Psychology, and Social Work.

Bruce Adams had never had any use for shrinks. The V.A. docs had been
trying to get him to see one ever since he came back from Nam. "I ain't crazy,"

Adams always insisted. He hadn't changed this refrain in a dozen years. Would a real marine talk to a shrink?

But he'd had enough. He'd go talk to this Dr. Davis guy just to make everybody happy. Get 'em off his back.

Adams thought Davis was too young to be a doctor, but Davis impressed him with his apparent experience with cases like his. He seemed to know all about Bruce's problems, about his attacks.

Dr. Davis almost started to lecture Adams about his smoking, but he stopped when he saw Bruce's trembling hands. Most patients who came into his office at least asked if it was all right if they smoked, but not this guy. He kept lighting up as if it was as unobjectionable as breathing. Davis scanned Adams's paperwork, which included standard forms and notes made by previous attending physicians: Bruce Edward Adams. Born Englewood, New Jersey, 5-4-48. Father, Charles Adams, truck driver and mechanic. Mother, housewife. One younger brother. Raised in small towns in Bergen County. Happy childhood. Teenage passion for building and racing dragsters. Joined marines at seventeen. Volunteered for Vietnam. Returned after two tours, 1969. Purple Heart, Bronze Star. Twice wounded. Eighteen months rehab in V.A.s mending from a series of operations on his leg. Granted 20-percent disability pension—about four hundred dollars a month.

"You volunteered for *two* tours in Nam?" Davis asked. Obviously, it wasn't really a question. He was simply making an observation.

"Yeah, I was gung-ho," said Adams.

Davis asked Adams if he had nightmares.

"I had them occasionally when I first got back from Nam, but that wasn't unusual. The doctors told me they'd go away in a year or two and I wouldn't have any problems. And they were right. I didn't have any trouble after I got out. I was in good shape mentally. I had my head on my shoulders." Adams paused and dragged on his cigarette. "It wasn't until years later I started getting this reaction, or whatever it is."

Adams ran through his post-Vietnam life for Davis—a restless haze of changing jobs and new locales. He moved to California in 1970 "because the [East Coast] weather was playing havoc with my war wounds." He'd wrenched at more than a dozen shops since then. Even when he liked his employers, he would eventually start feeling antsy and suddenly pick up stakes and change jobs for no apparent reason.

He met Shirley Pine at a Jaguar shop in Hollywood. She was working in the office. They started living together in 1974. They changed towns, addresses, and jobs continually for the next seven years—to New Jersey, then back to L.A., Arizona, then Redwood City near San Francisco. There, Bruce had his first major attack, which landed him in the V.A. at Palo Alto. "They gave me some Librium. Next day they ran tests—a full CAT scan, blood pressure, EKG—but they couldn't find nothin' wrong."

Back in L.A., around 1975, Bruce began having periods where he would get real jumpy. Sometimes he literally felt scratchy, as though a chemical were on his skin. One day, he was overcome by the worst headache he'd ever had in his life. It took two days for it to go away. Again, the doctors couldn't find anything wrong.

Before long Shirley had two baby girls in addition to her two kids from an earlier relationship and Bruce was supporting a family of six. They kept moving—to Santa Monica, then the San Fernando Valley. After a half-dozen more jobs, Bruce managed to open up his own shop for a while in 1979 called Doc's European Performance. It closed after he suffered an intense week-long attack. "I walked in one morning, opened up the shop, and boom: heavy breathing, my arms went numb, rapid heartbeat. I don't know what I saw or did that triggered it."

The incidents recurred over the next few years. They became so severe that Bruce invariably felt like he was having a heart attack: his face would turn as red as a hothouse tomato, his heart would pound as though it were going to kick through his chest, his hands and arms would turn numb, and he'd be incapacitated by excruciating headaches. The trigger for the attacks was a mystery; they could happen anytime, anywhere.

Adams also became agoraphobic—fearful of crowds. The strain on his family was severe. "Sometimes, we'll go to a restaurant and I'll go into an acute state of paranoia," Adams explained. "It's weird, because I've always been able to go anywhere with no problems. All of a sudden I'll get in a crowd and I'll start getting the sweats, hyperventilating. My stomach turns into a knot. I feel like I'm having a heart attack. A couple of times I've run to the hospital and they planted me up on all the machines to see what was wrong. They could never find anything."

Dr. Davis didn't beat around the bush. "Delayed stress syndrome. That's what you've got," he said.

For Dr. Davis, it wasn't a hard call. The pattern was unmistakable. Adams had had difficulty dealing with the simple stresses of everyday life ever since he came back from Nam, demonstrated by his zigzag itinerary and erratic work history. Typical. He'd been plagued by severe, inexplicable anxiety attacks. Like many Vietnam vets, he was largely unaware of PTSD (Posttraumatic stress disorder), which was not officially recognized by the medical community until 1980. Even now, in 1981, some doctors and much of the public viewed PTSD as a disability scam. But Davis knew how to spot a genuine case. He already knew that this patient's biggest problem was his refusal to admit he had one.

"You know, Bruce, this latest attack of yours almost cost you your life."

"Yeah, I heard about the tranny," Adams mumbled through a cloud of smoke.

Davis launched into a stern lecture on the hard realities of delayed stress syndrome. "One-half million of the three million American troops who served in Vietnam exhibit symptoms of PTSD," he explained. He paused, deliberately, for emphasis. "It's time you realize that you are definitely one of them." He told Adams that his attacks were most likely a slow-fuse reaction to trauma and combat. "This is serious," Davis admonished. "You need treatment. You can't just go home and forget about it until you have another attack."

Adams sighed as he blew smoke from deep inside his lungs.

For immediate relief from his antsyness, Davis gave Bruce a prescription for a daily five-milligram dose of Valium.

"I don't like those special drugs," Adams said. "If you eat the wrong things they can trigger an attack. I got heartburn and gas already from all the anxiety."

Davis shot Adams a hard stare. "Take the pills," he said.

The tranny incident and lecture from Dr. Davis finally convinced Adams that maybe he really did need to do something about his condition. He returned home, but rather than going back to work, he went on workmen's comp and enrolled in an on-the-job training program at the V.A. as a biomedical technician. He convinced himself that a career change was really what he needed—a chance to get his head out from under the hood. He began meeting with Davis for twice-weekly counseling sessions to work out the symptoms of delayed stress, which he now reluctantly accepted as the possible root of his problems.

Only a few V.A. hospitals had inpatient programs for PTSD in 1981, and those were still in the experimental stage. But the Sepulveda V.A. had a delayed stress encounter group that held weekly meetings. Dr. Davis warned Adams that they were gut-wrenching sessions, not for the faint of heart. But Adams had made rapid progress. He appeared to be gaining some insight into his problems. Eventually, Davis agreed that he should give the group a try.

It was a sunny Wednesday afternoon in the summer of 1981 when Bruce attended his first session. He steered his Chevy van up the winding drive to building 25, apprehensive but determined. He parked the van in the lot, taking in the swaying palms and the distant backdrop of the Santa Monica Mountains. The pleasant view gave Adams the willies. There was no escaping the comparison to landscapes he'd seen in Nam.

Adams strode up the walkway, trying hard to suppress his limp; his leg had been acting up again with the summer heat. A half-dozen men stood outside the doorway of building 25, smoking. Another sat in a wheelchair. Adams noticed that his useless legs were secured to the seat with silver duct tape.

A man in his late twenties dressed in jeans and sporting a dark beard and long hair approached Adams as he walked up the steps. "You must be Adams," he said.

"That's right."

"I'm Dr. Lopata. Dave."

Again, Adams was surprised by the doctor's youth. The V.A. gets the young ones, he thought. Lopata, the group's moderator, introduced Adams to a few of the men standing by the entrance. Some nodded, but none of them spoke. Lopata fidgeted with a clipboard he was carrying as he pulled Adams aside.

"Things might get rough in there today," he warned. "I've got two more cherries joining us."

Adams shrugged, not knowing what to say. He lit a cigarette.

"Are you taking your Valium?" Lopata asked.

"Yeah," said Adams. He tapped his shirt pocket, rattling the small plastic bottle of pills.

"Good," said Lopata as they walked through the doorway of building 25. "You brought your script with you. That's very good."

The cherry seated at the middle of the long folding table in the stark meeting room started to cry. The group erupted with laughter. "Fuck you, asshole," someone shouted above the din. The group pressed its vicious attack, badgering the new man as he tried to talk about Vietnam. It was hopeless. The regulars had already concluded that he was a goldbricker looking to get a disability pension for his alleged problem with delayed stress.

"Gee, thirty whole *days* in Nam," one of the men cracked. "As a supply sergeant!"

"Yeah, but they rocketed his base twice!" another laughed.

"Fuckin' asshole."

The other cherry was just as bad. Before long both men were unceremoniously driven from the room by the barrage of verbal abuse. The second cherry appeared to be heavily sedated. When he tried to get up from the table he collapsed into a heap on the floor, blubbering like a child. He dropped a small plastic bottle of pills, which flew across the floor. As he lunged to retrieve it, the group roared. No one offered him any help.

"Kiss off, sucker," someone yelled when he finally stumbled out the door.

Bruce Adams sat silently at the table. What a fun group of guys, he thought. After more than an hour in the room, he realized that no one had made eye contact with him. Just like being a cherry back in Nam, he figured. The troops were cold to new recruits. Nobody wanted to know you. They didn't want to get involved in case you wound up as so much chopped meat.

Dr. Lopata had opened the meeting by speaking briefly about the fight or flight syndrome, a problem for many suffering from delayed stress. He also addressed the difficulty of uncovering the sources of stress and listed ways of dealing with stress on a day-to-day basis, such as meditation, exercise, and biofeedback.

Lopata struck Adams as a hippy with all his mumbo jumbo about spiritual growth. After his initial speech, Lopata had thrown the meeting open to the group.

Adams didn't know what to think of this crew. First, there was a big black guy, Phil Jones, who talked about covert ops he'd done in Nam for the CIA. Adams got the impression Jones was a dope-smoking fool. Gil Durkin, a former marine sarge, also seemed strung out, but not necessarily on drugs. He was just weird, and not because of the war, Adams thought. Gil talked about how he relaxed by constructing model trains at his house in Orange County where he lived with his mom, about a graphic design course he was taking, and about how he really wanted to join a religious order and become a brother. Oh, brother, is right, Adams thought. Fuck this, I want to get healed, not listen to a bunch of wackos.

Jose Cardenas was a factory worker from Pacoima, a fat little Latino with a ninety-mile-an-hour hairdo swept back off his forehead and an accent right out of a Cheech and Chong movie. An asshole looking for a disability, Adams surmised. It didn't sound like he had it so bad in Nam. Another guy was just a total mess—lots of wounds, suicide attempts, a drug addict, unable to work, really, really lame. Who needs this?

But a couple of the guys seemed like they had their act together. Maybe he could learn something. The sharpest of the lot was Dick, a friendly guy about forty wearing a sharp suit, gold jewelry, and expensive cowboy boots. Dick had the voice of a TV newscaster, a gift for gab, and a twisted sense of humor. It was obvious that he was very popular. He was Mr. Personality, a streetwise bullshitter, the group's resident entertainer. A guy who knew how to laugh at everything—even death.

When it was Dick's turn to "share," he started out talking about stress management techniques he had tried, but somehow his spiel quickly became an off-beat examination of alcohol's effects on the intestines—farting in particular—and then segued into uproarious tales of his Saigon barroom adventures with an army buddy who was capable of farting at will, particularly in the faces of unsuspecting *mama sans,* and how this led to one particular red-light hooch-house fracas that, well, landed him in the brig. His story went on and on, but nobody seemed to mind, because he was really funny. With that mellow, smooth-as-honey voice and rambling shoot-from-the-hip delivery, this guy could enter-tain people for a living. It was no surprise his humor was appreciated by the group. These guys needed some comic relief.

Another man who spoke was Phillips, a former army lieutenant with a balding dome and gold wire-rimmed glasses. He told of hitting a mine while in an armored personnel carrier and being blown into a river. To this day, he explained, he harbored an unreasonable fear of drowning. Goldman, the man in the wheelchair, wore an old, crumpled Cincinnati Red baseball cap and a sleeve-less pullover that was making him sweat. He talked about how he couldn't stand to look at raw chicken—it made him think of bloody flesh and ravaged limbs in Vietnam. Butchered poultry, he concluded, was something he had to avoid, since it could bring on a stress attack.

Adams thought about the can opener at Triple J's. Had it triggered sub-conscious memories of Vietnam? As the regulars opened up about themselves, Adams found a lot to think about. Like himself, they were all hard-core combat vets. He could relate to their problems—sleepless nights, nightmares, anxiety, fear of crowds . . .

Adams sensed two different sides of the group. On one hand, the "group consciousness" was understanding and supportive. When one of the regulars broke down during his talk, no one got on his case. At the same time, bullshit of any kind was dealt with ruthlessly, and the taunts were often callous, some-times brutal.

Now, the group was poised to intimidate him like they had the other two cherries. Good fuckin' luck, Adams thought. He knew he belonged.

Adams quickly ran through his background, jumping ahead to boot camp at Parris Island in 1965. He mentioned that he had volunteered to go to Vietnam.

"Fuckin' gung-ho marine," hooted Phillips as he leaned back in his chair and scratched his balding head. Others laughed or shook their heads.

"Fuckin' A!" cried Clayton, a thin, dark-haired man who seemed to be the youngest in the group. He offered a friendly nod to Adams. "It's about time we got a few more marines in here with all these army maggots," he said. "Glad to have you here, Bruce. Don't pay any attention to these fuckin' maggots."

Adams nodded as he lit a cigarette. "I spent six months at the naval station at Guantánamo Bay in Cuba," he related. "I was trained in jungle warfare, demolition, reconnaissance, and as a weapons expert—automatic weapons, heavy mortars, rocket-powered grenades. I also received parachute and underwater demolition training, the same as the Green Berets, except I wasn't taught any foreign languages."

"John Fucking Wayne," Phillips snickered.

Adams ignored him. "I went to Nam in early sixty-seven as a private first class with First Force Recon, Charlie Company. My first op was Hastings up in the DMZ."

"Hastings!" Clayton exclaimed, obviously impressed. He had arrived in Nam too late to take part in the war's premier offensive. "Were you at Hamburger Hill?"

"Yeah, I was there," said Adams. "It was search and destroy. At one point my entire company was nearly wiped out, in just one night. We took rounds, mortars, rockets, frontal and side attacks. If it wasn't for marine air and Puff the Magic Dragon, our asses would've been done. But we held on till dawn, when we got some support. By then, there were only fifteen of us left out of a company of a hundred and fifty. We'd hit ten hard-core units of the Twenty-seventh NVA— seasoned regulars, not the rice-paddy bums. The operation went on some thirty-odd days. I can't remember the kill count, but I know we got up in the thousands. A lot of weapons were captured. The end result was that we slowed their forces from infiltrating down across the DMZ into South Vietnam and kept them from mounting a major offensive."

"Fuckin' A!" chimed Clayton.

"Yeah," chortled Phillips, sarcastically, "a regular fuckin' hero." Others in the group laughed.

Dr. Lopata waved an arm to silence the group. "Your record shows you received two Purple Hearts, three battle stars, and a number of combat action ribbons, that you were wounded twice and have a twenty-percent physical disability," he said.

"Yeah," said Adams, lighting a cigarette and staring over at Phillips. He knew he had to deal with him right away. "My first tour lasted seven months, until I was wounded outside Da Nang while with a CAG outfit, a combined action group. We were working with local militia and army troops. They'd put a platoon of marines in to train them."

"Fuckin' A," Clayton beamed. "Army maggots couldn't get their heads out of their assholes without a few marines to give instructions."

"Listen to this leatherneck horseshit!" Phillips scoffed as the room erupted in a chorus of hoots.

Adams sighed, exhaling a deep cloud of smoke as he continued to stare at

Phillips. He was all too familiar with interservice rivalries. He could handle it. "I was there three months," he continued, "training these guys, going on patrol, observing. We were on an island where we set up a bunch of LPs—listening posts. Our job was to resupply these people, to make sure batteries, water, and food were getting out to the different posts."

Adams paused again, dragging heavily on his cigarette. "The day I got wounded was a bad day for me, 'cause I'd lost my best friend. At three in the morning we started getting heavy probes—artillery, mortars. They were trying to run us off the island. We went out on patrol and we couldn't find my buddy's LP. He wasn't where he was supposed to be, according to the map coordinates. We went back to the base area and were getting ready to go on night patrol when a runner came in from his LP. My buddy had been trying to get water down by the river when they developed sniper fire. He got hit three times in the head. We assembled a small strike force to go out and see what we could do, but by the time we got there he was dead."

The group listened in a silence that was punctuated only by a steady communal stream of exhaled cigarette smoke. "What really pissed me off," Adams said, his voice now betraying a slight but discernible quiver, "was that this guy was well liked by everybody, but nobody in the platoon would volunteer to help carry his body back to the CP so it could be evacked."

Several members of the group nodded silently. Adams continued, his voice starting to crack. "The first thing my platoon sergeant said to me was, 'Don't pull Pancho off his face.' I said, 'Why?' He said, 'Because he ain't got no head.' I said, 'Well, that's my *buddy*.' So I pulled Pancho up and he had no face. Everything was gone. The whole right side of his head was blown out."

Adams continued quickly, as though anxious to move on. "That night, it was my team's turn to go out on an LP, and they hit us with artillery. I got hit in the head, face, shoulder, and chest. Shrapnel penetrated through my right cheek into my mouth. It tore my pectoralis major out on the left side and shattered my upper left arm. There was no way to get back except to walk. So I led the patrol back in, about a thousand meters. It was a three-hour wait for the chopper. They thought I was gone. I had a sucking chest wound, so they threw a piece of cellophane over it to keep the air from coming into the chest cavity. When they do that, it's just a matter of time."

Adams seemed to be over the hump now. His voice and hands began to steady. "But when the corpsman radioed for the medevac, he requested a doctor on board the chopper. I was lucky. Usually you didn't get one, but I had a doc who worked on me all the way back to Da Nang Battalion Aid Station. I probably wouldn't have made it without him.

"I was evacked to Clark Field in the Philippines, then to St. Albins Naval Hospital in New York. I convalesced for about four months. Then they sent me to Cherry Point, the North Carolina Marine Corps air station. Made me a rifle-range coach. I trained second-lieutenant pilots how to use forty-fives and M-sixteens. After sixty days, I requested orders back to Westpac in California and then back to Vietnam."

"Jesus Fuckin' Christ," Phillips sighed as he polished his glasses with a handkerchief. "A Chesty Puller type."

Adams bristled at the reference to the gung-ho Marine Corps hero of World War II. "Damn right," he said without hesitation. "I wanted to win that fuckin' war."

"Fuckin' A!" chimed Clayton, beaming.

"Was that always your attitude?" Dr. Lopata asked quickly.

"Yeah," said Adams. "When I went over, being a World War Two generation war baby, everything was the American flag and apple pie. There was a lot of patriotism then, but as the war progressed, patriotism just went down the fuckin' tubes. But our division, the First Marine Division, we had good morale. We had a reputation all the way from Guadalcanal. Tradition is very strong in the Marine Corps. Once you're a marine, you're never *not* a marine. They take care of their own."

"Whoop-de-do!" scoffed one of the wags.

"Hey, fuck you," Adams barked. "The marines is like a brotherhood. Once you're a member you're a member for life. They'll put a color guard on your grave at your funeral, give you a twenty-one-gun salute. That says something about that organization. You don't find that in the air force, army, or navy."

Adams was pissed now, and Dr. Lopata could see that the anger had a positive effect. It had steadied his hands, given him strength.

"The marines is where I became what I am," Adams continued. "It's where I learned how to deal with a lot of heavy situations. The American people might have lost the war, but not the guys who fought it. The marines can't lose a fucking war."

"Fuckin' A!" Clayton shouted. He pounded a fist on the table. "Fuckin' A!"

"Spare us the war-hero crap," Phillips mocked, pushing his wire-rims back up on his nose. "Nobody but an asshole or a nut case would volunteer for *two* tours in Nam."

"Hey, ease up, bro," Dick interrupted.

"What's it to you?" Phillips asked.

Dick, the smooth-talking funnyman, pulled a Marlboro from a pack in front of him on the table and adjusted the gold bracelet on his wrist. As he slowly lit the cigarette and exhaled, all eyes in the group watched him, waiting for his response. "Hey, I volunteered to go to Nam," he said. "Both times." He looked around the table and saw that everyone was looking at him. "Hey, I was a wild young kid with a boner. What was I supposed to do? Go to Disneyland?"

The group cracked up. Adams could feel the tension ease.

"Jesus," said Phillips, "the war heroes are coming out of the woodwork. You never fuckin' mentioned that before." He stared across the table at Dick.

"Well," Dick shrugged, "nobody ever fuckin' asked me." More laughter.

"Dick, I always knew you were all right," Clayton yelled. "Even if you were an army maggot!"

"So anyway," Dr. Lopata said, steering the group back to Adams, "you wanted to go back."

"Yeah, I wanted to go back," Adams continued, "and I did, April of sixty-seven. I went to Da Nang with a ground unit, a B-four corporal. Then I was sent back into the First Marine Division, First Battalion, which I was very happy about. It was the Hue City operation during the Tet offensive. It was like conventional warfare, house to house. Basically we attacked the city, and that was a big fuckin' city. They'd infiltrated God knows how many regiments and battalions into that place, and nobody knew where they were. They were hiding everywhere. You never knew who the enemy was. You could be walking down the street and get your head blown off by some kid.

"Then I was sent back up into the DMZ on Operation Prairie, which was just a constant change of territory. One month the Americans would have it, the next the VC or the NVA would take it. We'd strike, then they'd pull us out and put us someplace else. There was no method. You never knew where you were or where you were going, or where your next battle would be."

Adams shook his hair back from his eyes as he lit another cigarette. "Then I was transferred into the Twenty-seventh Marines, back to Da Nang, about fifteen k from where I was first hit, and that's where I got hit the second time.

"I was assigned to a Rough Rider outfit to ride security for convoys. I was up in the gun ring of a two-and-a-half-ton truck with a fifty-caliber. We came down a road and spotted another two-and-a-half-ton off in the rice paddy with its front end blown off and the driver staggering around. He said he hit a mine. I told our driver, 'Whoooaaa, slow it down, fella, where there's one there's another.' He said 'No, they just swept through it.'"

Adams paused, inhaling smoke deep into his lungs. "Evidently, either they missed it or there was a sapper out there who planted another one, because a hundred yards down the road we detonated an antitank mine with the right front wheel. The driver was killed. Six guys in the back of the truck were launched.

They were all killed. I was blown out of the truck. There was one other survivor, a black guy. The lower section of my right leg was totally shattered up to the kneecap. It was twisted around so my foot was pointed behind me. I was conscious for five or ten minutes and then I passed out.

"I came to five or six days later at the Italian aid station in Da Nang. They didn't know if they were going to save me or not. I had a concussion and was in shock. My temp was about a hundred and six. I didn't know who I was. I didn't know what happened. I didn't even know my own name. About two weeks later I started remembering.

"They flew me to the Twenty-second Surgical Hospital in Tokyo, where they performed an operation on my leg. They pinned it with a lottes nail that ran from the ankle to the knee, straight through what was left of the bone." Adams managed a nervous laugh. "I remember I was under a spinal, and the doc set up a mirror so I could watch him put the nail through my leg.

"Then they evacked me back to St. Albins in Long Island, where I spent seventeen months and had five more operations to repair my leg—bone grafts, impression plates, pulled the pin once and broke the leg. It bent so bad that it just bowed. The doctors I had were pretty good. The orthopedic surgeon, a Commander Nabaha, an Arab, he promised me I'd walk again—maybe with a brace or a cane, but he told me he'd get me up on two feet. The other doctors didn't think so. They were ready to hack it off at the knee. But that son of a gun kept his promise. He stuck with me."

"You were lucky," said Goldman as he squirmed slightly in his wheelchair and fingered the brim of his baseball cap.

"That's what I understand," said Adams.

"Were you under a lot of medication?" Dr. Lopata asked.

"Yeah," said Adams. "I was on Demerol for about eight months while they were doing all the operations." Adams knew what Lopata was getting at, so he continued. "But afterward they slowly decreased the dosage and brought me down and got me off it. I've never had a problem with drugs. I don't even drink."

Dr. Lopata arched an eyebrow. Nearly every member of the group was a practicing alcoholic. At least.

"Finally they sent me to the V.A. in Lake City, Florida, and then to the naval air station at Cecil Field in Jacksonville, where I was medically retired in August sixty-nine."

Lopata broke in. "Did you have any stress-related problems when you were discharged?" he asked.

"No, not really. Not then. I didn't start havin' these anxiety attacks until about ten years later. At first, I had nightmares for a while."

"What type of nightmares?" Lopata probed.

Adams emitted a deep sigh. "Violence."

"What type of violence?"

Adams pulled another cigarette from his pack and lit it from the tip of the one he was already smoking, even though it was only half gone. Reluctantly, he described the recurring nightmare that had most plagued him over the years. "During Hastings, my platoon came upon an enemy field hospital on Hill Eighty-one in the DMZ. We captured an NVA nurse. Somebody tied her down on the back of a two-and-a-half-ton truck. A bunch of guys raped her, then somebody grabbed a pop-up flare and stuck it up inside of her. It blew her head off."

His nightmare, Bruce explained, always ended the same way. "I'm standing there and I'm watching but I can't believe it. I don't know what to do. I can't move. Sometimes I wake up screaming." Adams also described his recurring vision of a bloody can opener. He suspected it was somehow related to this horrible scene.

"There were a lot of times when we got totally violent over there. We'd lose a man and not be able to figure out how we lost him, and, well, we'd just go over and burn down a village. Just torch the whole fuckin' place, maybe see if we could find out what was going on. And that would be orders from the platoon commander. The atrocities were phenomenal. There were times you'd almost get animalistic. Everybody you looked at was the enemy, and you didn't think of them as people. You'd lose a friend and you'd get upset and go on a rampage, terrorize 'em, burn 'em out, torture 'em. A lot of guys had a habit of shootin' a dude in his kneecaps and then just leavin' him there. Others would take guys up in a helicopter, toss one out to make them talk. That was common practice. Or walk up to one and just shoot him in front of the others and watch them all sing like a bunch of fuckin' canaries."

Adams paused. "But then, the Cong and NVA would castrate a guy and stuff his genitals in his mouth. It was a whole different world over there."

"Yeah, I used to gut-shoot 'em," said Dick, tapping down a cigarette on the cowboy boot arched across his knee. "I liked to watch 'em die slow." Dick's comment provoked a few uneasy titters.

"Asshole," said Phillips.

"Fuckin' A!" said Clayton.

"Everybody's got their favorite way," said Dick, displaying a twisted smile. "How about you, Adams?"

Adams looked at Dick. He didn't like where this was going. Dick was obviously just fooling around, but it kind of gave him the willies. "I never liked to waste ammo," said Adams. "I'd just as soon shoot 'em in the head."

"A gourd shooter," said Dick.

"Fuckin' asshole," said Phillips.

Lopata jumped in to steer things in a more constructive direction. "Did you get into the protest movement when you got back to the States?" he asked.

"No," said Adams. "I had a lot of animosity toward protesters when I first came back. It took a long time to get the whole story about what went down over there. But I never joined any fuckin' protests."

"Can you believe this?" cried Phillips. "He volunteers for two hitches in Nam, nearly eats it twice, winds up with a gimp fuckin' leg, a permanent disability, but then, when he gets home and finds out Uncle Sam was yankin' his chain—sent him over there for nothin'—he's still gung-ho fuckin' America. Now I'd say that's either stupid or crazy."

"Hey, ease up on the guy, bro," said Dick, waving a smoking Marlboro through the air. "He's not the only guy here who never protested against the war."

"Oh fuck," said Phillips as he looked at Dick. "You too?"

Dr. Lopata looked at his watch. "All right," he said, "that's enough for today. We'll pick it up again next week."

As the group began to disperse, Dr. Lopata walked up to Adams and patted him on the back. "You're gonna be all right, Bruce," he said.

Out in the hall, Adams leaned up against a wall and vacuumed down a Marlboro. His hands trembled, out of control. He felt drained, but he also felt good. It was as if a huge weight had been lifted from his shoulders. A dozen years after coming home from Nam, he sensed he had finally taken the first step toward putting the war behind him.

Members of the group gathered around Bruce before they started to leave. "Don't let these maggots get you down," Clayton told him, shaking his hand.

"Yeah, thanks," said Adams. He smiled. He really did feel better than he had in a long time.

"Yeah, bro, they're all a bunch of shitheads," said Dick.

"Yeah," said Phillips, "we're all assholes. And you, Adams, are a *flaming* asshole." He grinned and extended his hand. "So welcome to the group."

"Come on, Adams," said Dick. "Let's you and me go out and get a little taste."

"I don't drink," Adams said.

"Okay, then I'll buy ya some fuckin' coffee. Come on."

"Watch out for this guy," Phillips told Adams. "That's Dr. Death himself."

Adams looked at Dick, taking in the gold bracelet, expensive suit, and cowboy boots. Something about him didn't seem right. He was too slick, too calm and reserved, too together and successful looking for a stressed-out vet. But what the hell, he was in the mood for a few laughs. He really felt good. These meetings are going to be all right, he thought.

Dick pulled off his jacket as the two men walked out the door into the blazing afternoon sun. Adams noticed the military tattoo on Dick's left arm: a skull and crossbones with the words Death Before Dishonor. He also noticed that Dick was packing a piece, a .38, on his hip.

"What's this Dr. Death shit?" Adams laughed.

"Aw, that's just one of the handles I used to have back in Nam," Dick said. "Come on, we'll take my Caddy."

They walked to the lot and slid into Dick's white 1977 Fleetwood. It was parked next to a sign that warned golfers from the nearby country club not to park at the V.A. The radio came to life with country music as Dick fired the engine up.

"I'm getting fed up with this piece of shit," Dick laughed. "She needs to go into the shop. In fact, this fucking piece of shit always needs to go into the shop. Almost died on me up in Washington last week, towing the family around on vacation in the goddam motor home."

Adams shook his head. "What kind of work do you do?" he asked.

Dick laughed. "My name is Ford," he said, offering his hand across the seat to Adams. "Detective Richard Ford, Los Angeles Police Department."

3

Nice Guy

RICHARD FORD GROANED AS HE THRASHED ABOUT, TWISTING IN THE sheets, until his arm slammed with a metallic jolt and the pain in his wrist rocked him into consciousness. He wasn't fully awake—or released from his nightmare—until he heard the familiar jingle of the chain attached to his wrist. He looked up at the swaying silver links and bellowed a deep sigh. It was over. He felt the incessant pounding in his head and the familiar hangover fog as he reached across the bed with his free arm and discovered that Lillian was not there.

He fumbled for the keys on the nightstand, unlocked the handcuff on his wrist, and left it dangling from the headboard. He ran his hands through his hair and rubbed his eyes. He was covered with sweat. "Honey?" he called. "Lil?"

He sprang to his feet and nearly swooned from the rapid ascent. He clutched his throbbing temples as he shuffled across the bedroom floor to the large walk-in closet. Inside, he could see his wife. She was lying on the floor, in her nightgown, curled up next to the three dogs. One of the two large Dobermans lifted his head and sniffed at Dick as he peered inside. The Scotty wagged his tail.

Dick felt around in the blankets for the gun—a large magnum revolver. Lillian's elegant manicured fingers were still clutching the grip. He checked the safety as he softly stroked Lillian's hair. He could tell that she was heavily sedated. She would not awaken for some time.

I'm going to find him, he thought. So help me God, I'll find the son of a bitch who did this!

Dick walked over to the dresser and opened his briefcase. He juggled the plastic bottles, settling on a handful of Excedrin, some uppers, and a few of his wife's codeine tablets. Up, down, sideways—he did what he had to do. He could handle it.

He walked out into the hallway and passed three additional bedrooms. His mother-in-law, Lupe, was slowly dying of cancer in one of them. His teenage son, Richard Jr., whom he suspected was a stoner, was passed out in another. He stopped at the last, to peek in at Christina. He smiled as soon as he saw the sleeping four-year-old. Everything will be all right, he thought. It's time to do the job. He could handle it.

When he finished shaving, Dick picked up a stack of mail that was lying on the long bathroom counter. He flipped through the bills until he reached a fat envelope. It was from his mother, Lorine! He opened it, and out spilled photographs. Pictures of Lorine. Pictures of Lorine with Lillian. Pictures of Lorine with him and the kids.

Richard Ford almost came unglued. *What fucking nerve!* His eyes reflected a demonic gleam as he picked up a pair of nail clippers and began chopping at the photographs. *That fucking cunt! That fucking bitch! That fucking whore!* He continued until he had slashed and scissored a dozen images of Lorine into a flurry of glossy shards. *That bitch!*

He was still upset when he stepped outside into the morning light, but was immediately calmed by the wafting scent of night-blooming jasmine. He walked around the side of the house and stood quietly for a moment, inhaling the delicate fragrance. He understood their poetry; out of darkness yet sprang life! He breathed deep the smell of precious hope and happy endings. After a short, quiet moment, he walked back to the front of the house, past the two-car garage bulging with gardening tools, and down the driveway to his waiting Cadillac.

Like every morning, when Richard Ford exited his spacious white suburban Northridge ranch house, dressed in a tailored suit and carrying his black attaché case, he looked like any Valley businessman. He was handsome, about 5′ 10″, well built, and athletic. His sandy-colored hair was starting to recede at the temples, and like many in the LAPD fraternity, he sported a mustache. For Richard Ford, this served as a final holdover from his days as an undercover narcotics investigator, when he had cultivated a seedy appearance. The mustache, invariably bleached blond by the sun, gave him a rugged "Marlboro Man" look, as it stood out against a face usually tanned from weekend gardening, sitting around his backyard swimming pool, or occasional vacations in Mexico.

Dick started to back his Caddy down the drive, but stopped when he saw his neighbor Frank running toward him across the lawn. Dick rolled down his window.

"Hey, Dick, I wanted to thank you for taking care of my boy the other night," Frank said, out of breath.

"Aw, hi Frank. It was nothin'. We love the kid. Anytime." Dick beamed a warm smile. Frank's son was retarded, an infant in a boy's body. He was always welcome at the Ford house.

"And while I'm at it, Bill told me about what you did for his kid," Frank huffed. "You have no idea how grateful he is. He was at the end of his rope."

"I do what I can," Dick said. "I always try to be of service."

That was an understatement. Dick was always helping somebody out. Bill, another neighbor, had a teenage son who'd gotten picked up burglarizing a garage. Dick managed to straighten the kid out while keeping him out of jail. Dick worked the day shift as a burglary detective over at Devonshire Division.

His neighbors mostly knew Dick Ford as a warm, casual guy who liked to spend his off-duty hours in jeans and snakeskin cowboy boots, working around the house. Dick enjoyed country music and going out to an occasional concert, but he was a family man. He liked staying close to home. His neighbors would have been shocked to learn he was a stressed-out Vietnam vet undergoing treatment at the nearby V.A. Most were surprised when they learned he was a cop. He didn't have that hard-boiled vibe. His neighbor Bill always said, "That Dick Ford is the nicest guy you'd ever want to meet."

"See you Sunday," Dick said as he rolled out the drive.

"Right," said Frank. He and Dick went to church together. They were both active in the Christian ministry.

Shirley Adams knew something good would happen when Bruce joined the encounter group. Now he had a new best friend—a cop.

Shirley liked Detective Ford. He was such a nice man—and funny, too. Dick always stopped by the house to hang out with Bruce while he was working in the garage. They developed a quick rapport and were always laughing and joking around. Dick would come in and talk to Shirley while she was in the kitchen and tell funny stories, sometimes until the tears rolled down her cheeks. It was wonderful for Bruce to have such a good friend.

Truth was, some of Bruce's old acquaintances left a lot to be desired. Shirley suspected that some weren't exactly law-abiding. They were people on the fringe, often in trouble about something, like drugs or stolen auto parts or . . . who knows? And even the nice ones—well, they were usually motorheads. Dick was different. He was so interesting, so cultured. So respectable! He talked to her about his wife, Lillian, and their kids, about music and gardening, about his speaking engagements for the LAPD, about the birds and the night-blooming jasmine he loved so much.

Unlike Bruce, Dick didn't show any obvious signs of delayed stress. He wasn't intense, nervous, or morose. He seemed to be in control of his life, well-adjusted, even happy. He was a detective with a dozen years on the job, a proud homeowner, an active member of his church and the PTA, a man admired and respected throughout the community. Now this was someone who would be good for Bruce.

Shirley could tell that Dick really wanted to help her luckless husband. Dick was so warm and compassionate, so very Christian. He was always performing some service—counseling his fatherless nephew, caring for the retarded boy in the neighborhood, talking to some citizen who needed advice. It was hard for Shirley to think of Dick as a tough-guy cop. He didn't give that impression; he was such a nice guy.

Shirley met Lillian Ford when Dr. Lopata invited the PTSD wives to a meeting—sort of like an Al-Anon group. Lillian Ford, a second-generation Latina, was a petite, dark-skinned beauty with long dark hair and a voluptuous figure. She talked at the meetings about her love life with Dick. She said that he sometimes tied her to the bed. That bothered Shirley a bit. Lillian also mentioned that she'd been raped about six months ago while working as a bus driver for the RTD. She didn't provide a lot of details. She was very friendly, the kind of woman Shirley could see getting close with.

Eventually, the Fords invited them to their house for dinner. Shirley was envious. It was a lovely home, and Lillian was an immaculate housekeeper. There was a huge crystal chandelier in the dining room and plush upholstered furniture throughout the house. Their daughter, Chris, had a bedroom out of one of those house-beautiful magazines, all in yellow. Lillian was dressed to the nines, with manicured nails and a diamond ring that nearly covered her knuckle. They were wonderful hosts. Dick barbecued by the backyard pool, and he got so carried away telling stories that he burned everyone's dinner.

Even though Dick and Lillian seemed to have a perfect life, Shirley had learned from Bruce that appearances were deceiving. Detective Ford and Bruce had a lot in common. They could relate.

Richard Ford, like Bruce Adams, had been wounded twice during heavy combat action in Vietnam. A helicopter gunner, he was shot down twice and took some heavy shrapnel in his arm. His left elbow, like Adams's leg, was held together with a metal pin. Small shards of shrapnel were still embedded in his back. Ford's recurring violent nightmares were as bad as any of those experienced by other members of the group. He and Bruce joked around a lot, but their conversations were laced with dark humor.

"Sometimes I handcuff myself to the bed at night before I go to sleep," Ford told Adams.

"Oh yeah?"

"You know, so in case I wake up tryin' to kill Charlie, my old lady can get away before I do any major damage."

Adams laughed.

"Yeah, it wouldn't be real smooth if I did the bitch," said Ford. "You know, like by accident."

"Yeah," Adams laughed, "that might be hard to explain."

"Yeah, I can see me on the stand. The D.A. says, 'So tell us, Detective Ford, why did you kill your wife?' 'Well sir, because I thought she was some gook NVA whore, so I just fuckin' did her.' "

"Yeah," said Adams, "I get your drift. That wouldn't be too cool, man."

"No, not cool at all," said Ford.

Ford wouldn't talk about his childhood. He had grown up in Pico Rivera, a working-class town southeast of downtown L.A. He wasn't particularly close to his parents and practically never mentioned them. As far as he was concerned, his life didn't really start until 1957, when he joined the army at age seventeen. The army, and then later the LAPD—that was his family.

Ford did ten years in the army and had considered making it a career. He served in the presidential honor guard at Arlington Cemetery in Virginia, a prestige assignment. He served with the Signal Corps for two years in Japan and for as many years with an armored unit in Germany. He studied all areas of soldiering. He married once in the service, just before going to Europe, but dismissed that first coupling as a disaster.

Like Adams, he had volunteered for two tours in Vietnam. When he was finally discharged in 1968, he was an E7 staff sergeant, first class. Like Adams, he arrived home with a mixed bag of ribbons, medals, and wounds. At first, there were no problems with nightmares or stress.

He immediately signed up with the LAPD. He was already a leader of men, a soldier proven under fire; the LAPD was pleased to have him. He graduated from the academy with glowing recommendations.

After less than a year on the job, rookie officer Dick Ford was shot and nearly killed. Once, over beers at a bar after their Wednesday PTSD meeting, he told Adams about it.

"It was June 10, 1969. Me and my partner are on evening patrol in Central Division, on Olvera Street. You know, the historic L.A. pueblo settlement area in downtown L.A."

"Yeah, right," Adams nodded. "Beanerville for touristas."

"Right. So we're driving along and we see a young male Latin attempting to break into a vehicle. Naturally, being two of L.A.'s finest, we stop and arrest the fucker. After we get the perp cuffed and stuffed in the back of the black and white, I start writing up an FI card—a field interrogation card. Meanwhile, my partner is inspecting the tampered-with vehicle. Before I know it, another beaner comes out of nowhere and pounces on me. This guy's a monster. Short, but stocky, like a sumo wrestler. Apparently, the second perp was hiding behind some parked cars while we arrested his buddy. Next thing I know, we're rolling around in the middle of the fuckin' street. Somehow, this guy manages to pull my service revolver from my holster and he shoots me through the neck."

Ford lit up a fresh Marlboro. "I couldn't fucking believe it. I'm just back from two tours in Viet-fucking-nam. I survived being shot at by about a million gook Vietcong motherfuckers—rocket attacks, mortars, booby traps, you name it— and I get wasted by a greaseball car thief back in the USA. I'm lying on the street in downtown L.A., bleeding like a pig, dying.

"Somehow, I manage to pull out my backup, my thirty-two-caliber, and I fire one shot, wounding the assailant. That just pisses the guy off. Then my partner charges toward us, and the perp shoots him too, right through the groin. But my partner also gets off a shot—one round right through the heart. The fucker falls over dead right on top of me.

"So I'm waiting there—it seemed like hours—bleeding all over the pavement, listening for the sirens, with this huge dead prick on top of me."

Ford explained how the bullet passed through his shoulder and neck and missed his jugular by a hair. After just two months he was back on the streets. He still had nightmares about the shooting. Invariably, they ended the same way—with a feeling of overwhelming relief following the death of the perp.

It was a few months before Dick finally had Bruce work on his Caddy. Ford bitched constantly about the car. It had become a source of endless frustration to him and an ongoing joke with Bruce. After all, in the Valley, a man's car is more than transportation. It's a second home, the ultimate statement he makes about himself. Ford's Caddy shimmied and clanged, sputtered after the ignition was killed—it was a mess.

"I thought you weren't working as a mechanic anymore," Ford said sarcastically whenever Adams suggested he take a look at the car. "I thought you're gonna be a 'biomedical technician.' "

"Right," said Adams. "But I still make exceptions for preferred customers."

Ford brought his Caddy over to Adams's house in Van Nuys on a Sunday afternoon in late September. As was usual in the Valley, it was the hottest time of the year. Adams was working on a pickup out on the street when Ford pulled into his drive. Bruce was stripped to the waist, grease smeared across his arms and chest. Julie and Stacey were splashing in a little plastic pool in the front yard.

"You asked for it," Ford said, stepping out of his car with a six-pack in a paper bag. He looked over and smiled at the two little girls. "I don't know," said Ford. "Nobody can fix this lemon. It hasn't been straight since day one."

While Adams got to work, Ford went inside to say hello to Shirley. The house was a small two-bedroom, sparsely furnished, simple but cozy. Ford nearly tripped and fell as he walked through the living room.

"Hey Shirl," Ford yelled. "What the hell happened in here?"

Shirley came running from the kitchen. She gave Dick a hug and a peck on the cheek. "I asked my husband to clean the carpet," she explained. "Well, you know Bruce. He wouldn't rent a carpet shampooer—he's too smart for that. So he doused it with soap and hosed it down. The water went through the carpet and warped the floorboards."

Shirley looked at Dick and tried to keep a straight face. Then they both burst into laughter.

"Well, otherwise, how ya doin', Shirl?" Ford asked as they walked into the kitchen. Ford deposited his beer in the fridge.

"Oh, fine," Shirley answered. "Except for this damn water heater. How am I supposed to do dishes without hot water? The landlord says he won't replace it. Bruce keeps saying he'll get us a new one, but since he quit work, well . . ." She paused and quickly changed the subject. "How's Lilly?"

"She's fine," said Ford. "I think she's ready to go back to work." He walked over to the ancient water heater to take a look. He shook his head.

An hour later, Bruce came in. Dick was watching the Rams game. "All right, cowboy, why don't you take her for a spin," Adams said.

"You're done already?" Ford asked.

Ford got into his Caddy and drove it around the block. When he returned he was all smiles. "I don't believe it," he said. "She's really tits."

Adams laughed. "So whadjya expect? They don't call me Doc for nothin'."

"You know what, Adams," Ford said, "you've got a God-given gift. What are you doin' with this technician shit? You're a natural. Why abandon your profession?"

"I don't know," said Adams, wiping the grease and sweat from his arms. "There's a lot of stress being a mechanic. Everybody wants their work done yesterday. The boss is always breathin' down your back."

"Yeah," said Ford. "Well, what you need is your own shop."

"Well, that would be great, but . . ."

"I might be able to help you out."

Adams laughed. "Yeah, sure."

"No, I mean it," said Ford. "I got a partner, a real businessman. We might be able to work something out."

"Right," said Adams.

"Anyway," said Ford, "what can I give you for the work?" He reached for his pocket.

"Forget about it, partner," said Adams.

"Come on, let me give you somethin'."

"Nah, it was nothin'."

"Well, all right," said Ford.

An hour later, Bruce, Shirley, and the two little girls were cleaning up the kitchen table after dinner. They heard a knock on the door. It was Richard Ford. He walked into the living room and unloaded a pair of dolls from a paper bag. The girls squealed like it was Christmas.

"Come on, bro," said Ford. "I got somethin' out in the Caddy. You'll have to help me carry it in."

Bruce and Shirley looked at each other, then followed him out the door. Roped down in the trunk of Ford's Caddy was a huge rectangular box. A water heater.

"Come on," Ford said excitedly, "we can haul this sucker in there, pull out that antique, and replace it in no time."

"You fucker," Adams laughed.

"Oh, Dick," said Shirley.

Officer Richard Ford appeared to recover quickly after the 1969 shooting. He returned to his old job in Central Division, where he earned glowing reviews from his supervisors. He was "eager . . . enthusiastic . . . a take-charge officer . . . respected by all the men . . . mature and knowledgeable . . . conscientious . . . dedicated." He showed "outstanding enthusiasm and initiative" and "handled himself well in the field." During his first year on the force, it was discovered he had a special talent for PR, that he was "a good speaker who could interface extremely well with the public." It was also noted that he had a tendency "to blow his own horn." Translation: he was a bullshitter.

Ford moved to Vice in the early 1970s. He started out at Central Division's porno task force, tracking down smut peddlers. He moved on to beverage control enforcement, which gave him the opportunity to hang out with a higher grade of scum—downtown hoodlum bar owners. He got more rave reviews: "Maintains his composure under stress, . . . always reliable and dependable." Ford's talent as a raconteur also received its first note of appreciation. "His pleasant and witty personality has kept the unit laughing."

Ford transferred back to patrol and was quickly elevated to senior lead officer. He was praised for being gifted at "selling the basic [squad] car to the public. He deals exceptionally with the public and presents an excellent department image."

Unlike many cops, Richard Ford acted like a regular guy, someone who didn't feel superior because he was a police officer. Hence, citizens responded to him. Throughout his career, Ford's superiors would continually report that "he relates well to the public." Constant mention of this quality perhaps served unwittingly to illustrate a sad truth about the job: most cops *don't* relate well to the public.

But then, Richard Ford related well to everybody. He was a regular guy with the public, but back in the locker room, he could be the biggest cowboy there ever was. And when he worked undercover, he played bad guys so well it was scary. Other cops got goose bumps when they listened to recordings of Ford's conversations with slimeball suspects. He sounded exactly like one of them.

Fact was, Richard Ford was a natural actor. Although he never mentioned it, he had won the lead in his senior high school play, *Our Town,* and had turned down an offer to study at the Pasadena Playhouse in order to join the army. Fifteen years later, it gave him a kick to test his skills on tough undercover assignments.

Chief Daryl Gates would one day write in his biography, "Enormous detail goes into a drug-buying operation. First and foremost, the officer must be a superb con man. He must totally unlearn all police mannerisms and assume, as skillfully as any actor, an entirely new role. If he makes even the smallest slip, he's likely to lose his life."

Richard Ford made a perfect undercover cop. He could play a psycho scuzball with total conviction.

Ford progressed through Auto Theft and then Narcotics, where he continued to excel. He immersed himself in the study of narcotics. He became an expert on PCP and gave presentations on that growing menace to community groups around the city. He earned more rave reviews. He also developed an uncanny ability to deal with informants. Affecting a drug-culture persona was as simple for him as slipping on an old leather jacket—a talent that proved instrumental in many arrests.

He met Lillian Galvez Roeder at Central, where she worked as a records clerk. Richard and Lillian had a hot soap opera romance that quickly progressed to nuptials in 1972. Lillian had a son by a previous marriage. Dick adopted little Richard Junior and, by all accounts, loved him as his own. The couple bought a beautiful home in Northridge and then little Christina came along. Everyone agreed that Chris was the apple of Dick's eye. His friends and neighbors all noticed how "blissed-out" Dick was by family life. They all suspected that he craved a warmth and closeness he had been denied as a child.

Ford made investigator I (detective) in 1977 and shortly thereafter was transferred to Southwest Narcotics, an inner-city hellhole where his talents were badly needed. Again, his performance was exceptional. His supervisors, noting that "he expresses himself orally in an outstanding manner," trained Ford to handle roll call for uniformed personnel. He proved to be a natural, performing to raves from the peanut gallery.

Despite appearances, all was not well with Richard Ford—or at least that's what he told his boss. In November 1978, Ford went to Captain Matthew Hunt at Southwest Division and told him he was having problems—emotional problems, job problems, drinking problems, and motivational problems. He told Hunt that if he didn't get transferred off the streets of Southwest Division soon he would "end up shooting a coon."

This wasn't an unusual reaction for a guy who spent his working hours slithering around rathole dives consorting with Southwest Division scumbags. Most cops figured there was something wrong if you didn't eventually develop some problems. That's why the LAPD had police psychologists like Dr. Martin Reiser on the payroll.

A distinguished gray-haired civilian in his fifties, Dr. Reiser had worked for the LAPD for fifteen years and was considered one of the best police shrinks in the country. He made his living by listening to cops tell horror stories. They used to say that Reiser heard more hair-raising confessions than a Sicilian priest. Captain Hunt thought that Ford could probably use the doctor's services, so he sent him over to his office in downtown L.A. There, in a tranquil fourth-floor suite overlooking Chinatown, Richard Ford unburdened his soul.

"Something is going on inside of me that isn't right," Ford told Reiser. "I've been avoiding the issue for the past year, and it's starting to scare me. My lifestyle and attitudes are changing. I'm starting to identify with the hypes. I'm feeling sorry for them. I've been having some strong feelings lately—a desire to kill dope dealers."

Ford rambled through a gut-wrenching, disjointed monologue. He talked about his combat experience in Vietnam and how several of his friends had been killed in action. He told of flashbacks of Vietnam, nightmares, intrusive thoughts of violence, his difficulty sleeping. He explained that he had started drinking excessively on Sundays, that his family life was changing, that he felt depressed about going to work on Monday mornings, that he was getting sick over going to court, feeling that he couldn't win. He mentioned, just in passing, that he had been shot and nearly killed in the line of duty nine years before but that it was "no problem." Of course, he still had nightmares about that moment: the gun blast, the bullet ripping through his neck, the look on the perp's face as he too was shot. In his nightmare, just as in real life, he experienced the man's death as a relief.

Dr. Reiser had a problem with Ford's "no problem." Of course it was a problem. Getting shot and nearly killed is always a problem.

"Lately, I haven't been carrying my gun," Ford told Reiser. "I've been having suicidal thoughts, which is really weird, because I'm not a suicidal person."

Reiser later explained, "It was my impression that Detective Ford was experiencing a stress overload . . . that his reality testing was a little shaky . . . that he was a little bit loose in his thinking. I recommended a transfer to a low-stress, nonfield assignment out of Narcotics. I also recommended that he get additional counseling."

Heeding Reiser's recommendations, Captain Hunt had Ford transferred to a desk job out at Devonshire Division, a low-crime area in the San Fernando Valley. Ford requested Devonshire; its headquarters was located just a mile from his home in Northridge, a predominately white, upscale suburban community. Captain Hunt later wrote in his biannual evaluation of Ford, "The negative environment of the narcotics culture created a stress overload which had an adverse effect on Investigator Ford. He requested and was granted a transfer from Southwest Narcotics to a less dynamic area."

Ford saw Dr. Reiser again ten days after their initial meeting. He said he felt much better. Things were quieter and the people more professional at Devonshire. He wondered aloud about whether he would be assigned there permanently; he didn't like to make too many changes. He said it was like "a different world" because there wasn't as much pressure there. He was feeling 1,000 percent better. Ford continued to see Reiser for the next month and appeared to improve with each visit. After six sessions, Ford's stress level had been reduced considerably. He seemed to be functioning quite well. Dr. Reiser told him he could call for additional counseling on an as-needed basis.

Dr. Reiser wouldn't hear from Detective Ford for a couple of years. For a while, at least, things would go quite well at Devonshire Division, "a less dynamic area."

4

Club Dev

DEVONSHIRE DIVISION COVERED FORTY-FOUR SQUARE MILES OF OLD
and new suburbia in the western San Fernando Valley. The area was composed
almost entirely of upscale bedroom communities—Northridge, Chatsworth, Mission Hills, Granada Hills, and Porter Ranch Park. Compared to Southwest or
Central, it was a playground. It contained sprawling hectares of palatial landscaped estates, enclosed condo compounds with community swimming pools,
and nice suburban developments bearing names like Peppertree, Indian Springs,
and Saratoga Hills.

These communities were checkerboarded by tree-lined six-lane boulevards,
each of which led inexorably to a mall. This was, of course, the San Fernando
Valley, or just "the Valley," where shopping malls spontaneously combusted into
yuppie marketplaces, new-age town squares, and cultural phenomena—then
spread like blight across the land.

Although derided by the cultural elite, the Valley was clearly the home of
choice for mainstream Americans. It was suburbia's birthplace, where mass-
market tract housing—along with spectacular climate and scenery—had first
lured urban expatriates after the Big War. *Look* magazine dubbed it "America's
Suburb," and for half a century the gracious Valley lifestyle was the embodiment
of the American Dream. It was, according to a popular Gordon Jenkins song,
"Where the West begins and the sunset ends."

By the 1980s, however, the Valley had changed. It was no longer dotted with
orchards and olive groves and criss-crossed by dirt roads leading to truck farms

and chicken ranches. They'd been driven out with the bobcats and coyotes. Suburban sprawl was swallowing it up.

The *American Graffiti* scene of innocent suburban kids cruising Van Nuys or Ventura Boulevard would eventually give way to gangs and rampant drug abuse. Movie stars' ranches would be replaced by pop-star enclaves like Michael Jackson's private Encino zoo. By the end of the 1980s the area's population would top a million, and the once insular Valley would no longer be able to keep urban turmoil beyond its hills. Residents began to realize that they no longer knew their neighbors or felt a sense of community, that they were afraid to go out at night, that their once rural two-lane roads had transmogrified into booming boulevards reverberating with street noise and police sirens. Having accepted a longer commute as a trade-off for a bargain mortgage, residents would discover that it wasn't such a bargain. The freeways became jammed; the drive to L.A. was twice as long as it used to be. The life wasn't so great. City stress had followed them to America's suburb.

But when Richard Ford arrived at Devonshire Division in 1978, a cop couldn't find a better place to work. The western Valley was still home of the American Dream. There wasn't any street crime, largely because there wasn't any street life. People in these communities didn't hang out on the streets, they drove cars. Everywhere. A number of white, upscale, punk gangs had emerged by then, but they were Mickey Mouse compared to the hard-core inner-city Crips and Bloods.

Devonshire Division's headquarters was nestled in an idyllic setting. The modern, redbrick building was on Devonshire Boulevard at Etiwanda, adjacent to the rolling, pastoral confines of California State University–Northridge and Devonshire Downs racetrack. The Canyon Creek townhome complex, with its waterfalls and landscaped hills, was right across the street. This sylvan outpost was the very antithesis of the dilapidated inner-city station house surrounded by urban blight.

Shortly after Devonshire Division first opened in 1969, cops all over Los Angeles had dubbed it "Club Dev." For a cop, it was the top of the pyramid: the best division of the best police department in the country—quite possibly the world.

Cops at Club Dev were well trained, well equipped, and well paid. They operated the way idealistic police academy cadets imagined police were supposed to operate; that is, they actually did police work. While cops at Central or Southwest Division struggled to contain a parade of muggers and rapists and gangbangers and drug addicts and zoned-out recreational killers, hoping at best to move all the bodies and perhaps clear a case now and then, the boys at Club Dev actually served and protected the citizens of the Valley. They actually did follow up on cases and organized strategic attacks on major crime problems.

Of course, the biggest crime problem in the bedroom communities of Club Dev were residential burglaries committed by truant juveniles. Armed robberies got the manpower and attention other divisions gave to murders. Homicides? A handful every year, usually domestic cases easily cleared. Stories circulated in other divisions, some of them true, about how a Club Dev homicide detective might get sent out to answer a complaint about construction noise or a faulty traffic light.

Cops in places like Brooklyn, Boston, or Detroit often face diabolical knots of corruption, sometimes reaching to the very core of their departments. But this didn't happen in the LAPD, and especially not at Club Dev. Club Dev officers didn't need to do anything illegal to live the good life. For starters, they were paid extremely well. After ten years of normal advancement, an officer could make forty or fifty grand, depending on his overtime. And opportunities for picking up extra cash were everywhere.

The Valley was packed with gleaming high-tech corporations that were obsessed with security. Lucrative moonlighting gigs were there for the asking. A number of Devonshire cops even operated their own security firms on the side, providing rent-a-cops for office complexes, industrial parks, malls, banks, and swank residences.

And of course there were movie gigs. With a hundred TV shows being cranked out week after week, plus scores of feature films and commercials, they were always shooting something in the Valley. And every shot they took required police officers. All a cop had to do was stand around and wave tourists away from the cameras and trailers, or direct traffic, or ride a motorcycle up and down Ventura Boulevard all night showing off for a bunch of hot-to-trot starlets, or escort some movie star to a restaurant for dinner, or hang out and rap ballistics with the stuntmen—and he got paid outrageous movie bucks.

The Devonshire cops were also involved in more sophisticated pursuits. While most cops hassled with lowlifes, Club Dev cops were surrounded by yuppies, so it was hard to avoid stumbling on opportunities. Cops at Fort Apache, the Bronx, or the Alamo in Brooklyn traded war stories in the locker room and showed one another their bruises at the end of watch. Cops at Club Dev traded stock tips and scoops about bond issues or a zoning ordinance that was likely to affect real estate prices. Real estate was the drug of choice for most Valley residents. It seemed like everybody fell into dealing sooner or later. You couldn't help it. No matter how high, how ridiculous the prices became, they never dropped—at least not until the 1990s. The Valley was a far cry from Southwest Division.

It seemed an incontrovertible fact of life in the LAPD that division commanders were always boneheads. To make it to a top position you had to be a brown-nosing jerk. But not at Club Dev.

Captain Willard Vosfinder, who opened Club Dev in the late 1960s and became division commander, was an aberration. He was, by most accounts, a reasonable person, a leader of men, a fantastic guy. Nobody could figure out how he had wended his way through the LAPD's byzantine politics and somehow made captain.

Vosfinder established a warm and sane atmosphere and had a good rapport with his men. Under his leadership, the division set LAPD records for arrest and clearance rates. Everything ran smoothly and the troops developed tremendously high morale. Vosfinder's personable style became his legacy when he retired and was maintained by his successor, Captain Tom Osborne.

Understandably, Club Dev was top choice for most veteran LAPD officers. Guys with ten years on the job didn't want to work Central or Seventy-seventh or Southwest anymore; they wanted to be at Club Dev, the LAPD division with the lowest crime rate and practically no officer-involved shootings. And most L.A. cops, it seemed, lived in the Valley, regardless of where they worked in Los Angeles. The small far-west Valley community of Simi Valley, in particular, was renowned as a bedroom enclave for L.A. cops seeking affordable housing and a safe, crime-free atmosphere to raise their kids.

When Richard Ford arrived in 1978, Lieutenant Vern Higbee was officer in charge, the direct commanding officer of the troops at Club Dev. Higbee, whose linebacker physique seemed at odds with his sweet-tempered disposition, had so many applications from LAPD officers he had his pick of the department. Devonshire detectives, in particular, were hand-selected from eager applicants from around the city.

Club Dev detectives were a notoriously social group. They held regular weekend outings with their families—in the desert, at the beach, in the mountains. Their summer campout at McGrath State Beach, near Oxnard, was an annual blast. They had Christmas parties every year and regular summer barbecues. Every Friday night the Club Dev dicks retired to a nearby restaurant called the Plank House for booze and bonding.

But, contrary to their social image, Club Dev detectives didn't really spend all day hanging around movie sets, doing lunch, and playing golf. They handled a substantial amount of crime—particularly a high volume of burglaries scattered over a very wide area. Sure, it was nonviolent crime, mostly, but it was still crime. And they took their jobs seriously.

Lieutenant Vern Higbee had tried to fight Richard Ford's transfer into Devonshire Division. He didn't want somebody else's problems, but he wasn't given any choice. So, naturally, he turned the problem over to Ray Romero.

Detective Ray Romero, a stocky second-generation Mexican-American, had a reputation for being one of the most easy-going guys at Club Dev. Except for a two-year stint with IAD, he'd been at Devonshire since 1970. He was a detective III, working as burglary coordinator when Ford arrived.

Romero was too nice for his own good. Whenever there was a job nobody wanted—like breaking in a new recruit—he got the call. So Romero was handed the job of keeping an eye on Richard Ford.

Dr. Reiser had recommended that, for a while at least, Ford not be issued his service revolver. When Romero read that in the report, he marched right into Higbee's office. "What can I do with a guy if he can't have a gun?" he protested. "If he can't have a gun then he can't leave the station. He can't follow leads. He can't do a damn thing. I never had a guy without a gun before."

"Well, see what you can do," Higbee replied.

Romero didn't waste time on small talk with Dick Ford. "I guess the best thing for you to do is answer the phone. We'll just see how it goes."

Romero soon concluded that Ford was hopelessly lax about police procedurals. Whatever police work he'd learned at Central or Southwest, he hadn't learned his paperwork, that was certain. At Club Dev, they took that stuff seriously. Burglary detectives had to know how to conduct investigations from beginning to end: how to take cases through the court system, how to collect and store evidence properly, how to testify—stuff that slipped by cops at other divisions.

Still, Ford acted like the second coming of Jack Webb. And even though he was a nice guy, what a bullshitter he was. Romero was suspicious about Ford's "shoot a coon" story right from the start. Ford didn't strike Romero as a racist; they were usually easy to spot. Ford actually seemed pretty liberal—his wife was a Chicana, and there was nothing in his evaluation. And he didn't act like some stress case who was going to shoot the next perp he ran across.

Romero's suspicions were confirmed one day when he was in the storage room going through some old files. He was squatting on the floor, where he couldn't be seen, when he overheard a conversation between Ford and another cop who had stopped in from Southwest Division.

"Hey, Dick, how did you get out here?" the cop asked.

"Oh, hell," Ford laughed. "I went in and told Reiser I'd shoot some nigger if they didn't get me off the street. So they sent me out here."

Romero couldn't believe it. He marched straight into Higbee's office. "Let's get rid of that son of a bitch now," he insisted.

"We can't do that," said Higbee. "He's a pretty good guy, isn't he?"

Romero had to agree. "Yeah, but he's not a very good detective."

"Well, that's why we gave him to you, to work on him."

Doomed, thought Romero.

Despite his shortcomings, Detective Ford came to be liked by almost everyone at Club Dev. Though he would resume his full duties after a month, initially his days were spent logging reports and talking to burglary victims on the phone to see if there was anything more they could add to their stories. He may have lacked certain detective skills, but he made up for it in public relations. Invariably, Ford wound up shooting the breeze with victims and giving them advice, and citizens loved him for it.

The cops at Club Dev figured that Ford had missed his true calling. He should have been a Doberman breeder. Ford owned a few Dobies of his own and was so enthusiastic about promoting them it was believed he single-handedly caused a population explosion of the breed in Northridge. Ford's common refrain never failed to crack everybody up: "Well, ma'am, if you can't afford a burglar alarm, my advice is to get yourself the meanest dog in the world. Get a Doberman."

One day Ford had the squad room in tears as they listened to him give advice to a silver-haired old lady who walked into the station house to file a burglary report.

"But I have a dog that barks," the lady told him. "I have little Fluffy, my poodle."

"Lady, that isn't a dog," Detective Ford exclaimed, his golden newscaster voice echoing through the halls. "That's a football. Burglars love to kick 'em through a window. You want a Doberman. You want a Rottweiler. Now that's a dog."

"Fluffy? They would kick little Fluffy? Through a window? Oh my," the lady cried.

Ford's phone calls were supposed to be quickies, three to five minutes, enough to ask burglary victims if they had thought of anything they had left out of their report. But invariably, he'd be on the horn for half an hour. "That's right,

Mrs. Jones, a burglar alarm is a lot cleaner and you don't need to feed it, and deadbolts are a lot cheaper, but . . ."

Detective Ford had a grand old time chatting on the phone all day. What amazed everyone within earshot was the way he immediately assumed the role of the division's burglary expert. He wasn't on the desk for a week when he was overheard saying, "Yeah, I've been arresting these kids lately who've been kicking in back doors. That's the big MO in that area right now." Fact was, he hadn't even been out from behind his desk.

One of Ford's favorite raps went like this: "Mrs. Smith, I'm really sorry about that. Yes, I know it's terrible. We're living in a civilization now where you just can't trust anybody. You know, Mrs. Smith, from now on I don't want you to trust anybody. Don't even trust me. If you see me walking up your driveway, call the police. There are a lot of criminals out there and you never know—I might even be a criminal."

The guys at Club Dev couldn't believe his bullshit.

Ford also loved to rap about Vietnam, particularly the battlefield and barroom heroics of himself and a particular platoon buddy. These tales took on near-mythic grandeur. They were always saving each other's lives, either from the clutches of the VC or from those of some diseased whores. They were always gettings in fights while on R and R. Ford got demoted four times for marine bashing, he claimed, and he had a great story for each incident. His buddy, it seems, had a special talent for acts of grossness and an innate comic timing. He would hit on some babe in a bar, and if she didn't respond, would turn on cue and fart in her face. Ford had a theatrical ability to re-create this deft courting ritual, which raised howls in Club Dev's corridors.

Ford also told stories about all the women they had screwed, about the orgies they had engineered. But sometimes his stories turned heavy, like when he talked about fragging.

"You guys actually killed your COs over there?" someone would ask.

"Oh yeah, happened all the time," Ford would say. He knew guys who'd done it. He told others he'd done it.

Ford was really in his glory when he ran the weekly roll call, briefing fellow officers on various ongoing investigations. From day one Ford was the most popular roll-call detective with the boys on patrol. He raised the roof. There was something about his breezy style, his appreciation for the black humor of the job, his delight in gory details, that the street cowboys couldn't resist.

"We nabbed a disgusting character this morning," Ford told them at one Monday roll call.

"How disgusting was he?" the wags asked in unison.

"Well, hold on now and I'll tell you. This guy thinks he's a burglar, see, so he decides to climb though the air-conditioning duct over at the doctors' complex on Zelzah Avenue. Maybe cop some pharmaceuticals. Only problem is, he's got a fat ass. So he gets his big fat ass stuck in the air-conditioning duct all weekend—until we fished him out this morning. Forty-eight hours this guy is in the air-conditioning duct. So this clown eventually shit and pissed all over himself. And then it *froze*. He literally almost froze his *huevos* off!"

Between stories, Ford would work in something about the problems in each area, specific MOs or IDs to watch for. The only problem was, most of it was bullshit. It was stuff he'd heard about in other divisions, stuff that never happened. He sounded like a performer at the Improv or the Comedy Store. While the Club Dev detectives couldn't deny that Ford was popular with patrol, they generally agreed that he didn't know what the fuck he was talking about.

Most Club Dev detectives were understandably perplexed as they watched Ford become the division's most popular detective with citizens of the community. Ford could drop the street-cowboy persona and become a civic statesman and diplomat with the ease of adjusting his tie. He was an ace at handling domestic problems, like burglaries committed by estranged offspring. Ford would handle these cases deftly, speaking with all parties involved, patching up the family's communication channels, keeping their problems out of the courts. Before long, Ford's file became thick with letters of gratitude from citizens impressed by his thoughtful and compassionate handling of their affairs.

Detective Ford also took on speaking engagements. The Parthenia Street School Advisory Council wrote a letter stating their appreciation for his instructive and motivational talk on drugs and youth, noting "his obvious deep concern for parents and children." A letter from the Granada Hills Chamber of Commerce expressed appreciation for his crime-prevention seminar. A letter from the L.A. Housing Authority praised Officer Ford for suggesting and implementing a series of talks on crime against senior citizens. There was a letter sent to the Police Commission from Robert Farrell, councilman of the Eighth District, who noted the extraordinary assistance and advice received from Investigator Ford in their anti–angel dust [PCP] program.

Despite Ford's great popularity, Detective Romero found it necessary to give him a middling evaluation at the end of his first rating period. He pointed out, in a diplomatic way, that while Ford excelled at public relations, he was not very productive.

Ford was incredulous. "This is bullshit," he told Romero. "I'm the best detective in the world."

Romero contemplated this for a minute. Right there under his command was a man professing to be not merely a great detective, not simply the best detective at Club Dev or in the Los Angeles Police Department, but the best detective in the world. Yeah, him and Inspector Clouseau.

Still, Romero was ever the diplomat. "You know, Dick, you may be the best," he told him. "But you haven't done anything to show it. You haven't initiated any arrests. You're not putting anybody in jail. You haven't cleared any crime. You haven't recovered any goods. So what are you using as a scale?"

"I really know my job," Richard Ford insisted.

Ford and Romero worked a few stakeouts together, usually sitting on rooftops. Most burglars in Club Dev, other than the hypes and the juveniles, were sophisticated pros, and it could take weeks or months to catch them. When they did finally nab one, Ford had a way of dealing with him that Romero found revolting.

Ford would go into the interrogation room and treat the perp like he was some kind of celebrity. "You know, I'm a professional," Ford would tell the guy, "and I take pride in my work. And I consider you a professional. If you don't take pride in your work, well, you should, because you're really good. It took us a helluva long time to get you."

What really disgusted Romero was how convincing Ford was. Ford would stroke the hell out of the guy, and before long they'd be babbling like long-lost platoon buddies. Unfortunately, most of the information Ford would end up getting was crap.

"Dick, you sound just like that fucking asshole," Romero would complain. "Why are you lowering yourself?"

"Well, it's the only way I'm going to get any information," Ford insisted.

Ford also had a knack for scaring the hell out of the suburban teenagers they picked up, usually hypes or cocaine freaks who had turned to burglary. "Boy, do I feel sorry for you," Ford would tell them. "You'd better make a deal with us, 'cause once you get in the joint the Crips and Bloods are gonna buttfuck you so many times you're gonna start to like it." He'd relate outrageous stories, complete with gross, scatological details; before long, the kids would be in tears.

"You can't do things like that," Romero warned him. "It's against department policy. It's illegal to intimidate perps, for God's sake. What if this gets out?"

Sure enough, some of the teenage perps told their parents, and a few complained. But even more of them showed up at Club Dev to meet with Detective Ford and personally thank him for helping to reform their kids.

Doomed, Romero thought.

Although Ford seemed to be loved by one and all, Romero always had problems with him. "Everybody likes me," Romero would later explain. "You ask anybody and they'll say, 'Romero, he's a helluva nice guy.' That's because I really am. But Ford, he was a nice guy for his own advantage."

Ford was eventually teamed with a detective II named Mike Moen. Tall and thin, a deadpan, just-the-facts-ma'am type of detective, Moen was one of Devonshire's best. He and Richard Ford became the Odd Couple among Club Dev detectives. Moen found Ford likable but hard to work with. He didn't particularly like his penchant for bullshit and the way he talked about killing and the things he'd seen in Vietnam. Sometimes, Moen got the impression that Vietnam had robbed Ford of his respect for human life.

Moen felt it was obvious that Ford had scammed his way into Club Dev with his "shoot a coon" rap. He couldn't discount the possibility that Ford had succumbed to racial prejudice: it happened to a lot of cops. After a few years of picking up nothing but black perps, a guy gets an attitude. But this didn't seem to ring true with Dick.

Then again, Moen was never sure if he knew the real Richard Ford.

The most notorious criminal at Club Dev was a character the burglary unit had dubbed Casper, the Friendly Ghost. Casper was a celebrity in the San Fernando Valley. Almost weekly, the papers ran stories about his ethereal appearances, which served as a never-ending source of embarrassment to the burglary detectives at Club Dev.

Casper was a hot-prowl burglar, a sneak thief extraordinaire. He broke into homes in the middle of night while the occupants were in bed. As soon as he entered, usually through a kitchen window, he would prepare for a quick exit by unlocking all the doors. Then he would sneak through the house, heading for the master bedroom. He would steal jewelry off nightstands and wallets from pants pockets without disturbing the slumbering residents.

Casper pulled 286 known burglaries between 1976 and 1981, primarily in Northridge near Club Dev headquarters, and he was never caught. This was more than unusual, it was eerie. Hot prowlers always got caught eventually because theirs was such a high-risk crime. Club Dev detectives came to believe that Casper was one of the best thieves in the annals of crime.

There were a lot of unique things about Casper. He seemed to be very knowledgeable about police procedures. And it was almost as if the property he was stealing was really secondary to the thrill of the crime. A number of victims saw and confronted him, but he never resorted to violence. Rather, he simply disappeared into thin air. He was extremely agile and athletic. Victims reported that he could run like an antelope and leap over six-foot fences.

On many nights, Casper hit more than one house. Sometimes, after being confronted in one residence, he'd run out and do a few more in the same neighborhood—knowing the police were on the way. Casper seemed to enjoy playing cat and mouse.

One house Casper broke into belonged to a cop—a West-L.A. burglary detective who lived in Northridge. In addition to lifting his money and jewelry, Casper also copped his badge—but not for a keepsake. He placed it on the pavement in the middle of the cop's driveway, obviously his way of snickering at the LAPD.

Casper primarily took cash and jewels, but he would also steal some trademark item as a sign that he'd been there. For a while it was clocks. And unlike most hot prowlers, Casper took his time. He would go through a man's wallet, take the cash, then replace the wallet in the pants pocket where he'd found it. The playful burglar would often leave the shoulder strap of a woman's rifled purse slung over the knob of the front door.

There were a number of cases where Casper managed to get past watchdogs—including Dobermans. An owner would insist vociferously that there was no way Adolf would allow anyone to get into his yard, much less his house, without barking to wake the dead. And the bedroom? Impossible. Adolf slept at the foot of the bed! Still, there it was. Their wallets and purses rifled, their jewelry stolen, their alarm clock pilfered from under their noses, and Adolf never made a peep. Some Club Dev burglary dicks speculated that Casper knew how to hypnotize canines. He didn't drug 'em or poison 'em or shoot 'em. He certainly didn't just step over them. He had to be doing something.

A few partial prints were found once, but they couldn't be identified. A number of composite drawings were made—male Caucasian, early twenties. That was it.

Citizens were up in arms. They besieged the station house with complaints, pursued reporters, and saw to it that Casper was constantly in the news. Casper soon became the bane of the department. Club Dev did the only logical thing: they set up a special task force.

In most Divisions, special task forces are established only when the streets become unsafe even for drug dealers, when a rash of nude butchered young girls show up in back alley dumpsters, or when a swarm of former Cuban convicts suddenly moves into the neighborhood. At Club Dev, the target of the Special Problems Group was Casper, the Friendly Ghost.

The group came to be known as Kurowski's Raiders, because they were led by Bob Kurowski, a detective III who wanted Casper so badly he could taste it. Kurowski organized a team of about a dozen officers and detectives. They plotted

Casper's every conquest on a war map and tried to guess his next move. They rousted every potential snitch in the Valley. They set up stakeouts all over the area. On two occasions the task force actually caught Casper as he was leaving a residence. Well, they didn't actually catch him. They saw him making his exit, but when they gave chase, Casper vanished like a puff of smoke. They could never lay a finger on him.

After a while, with all the time they spent plotting Casper's demise and staking out neighborhoods, Kurowski's Raiders became like a subfraternity at Club Dev, going on social outings together. One infamous photograph shows thirteen Raiders grouped around a Jeep parked on a sandy rise in the scrub-brush terrain of the Simi Hills. The jeep has the name Desert Fox printed on the door. The Raiders are all decked out in fatigues and wield a small arsenal of weapons—rifles, shotguns, pistols, machine guns. Some wear spiked World War I German helmets. Draped atop the roof of the Jeep, in the middle of the group, is the zaftig, reclining profile of the lone female, Detective Linda Warren, decked out in knee-length leather boots and gripping an assault rifle. People who saw the eight by ten usually asked which Rambo movie it was from. This gang of Club Dev's finest looked ready to take on Afghanistan. It was just a goof—guys on the job having fun—but Casper would probably have died laughing if he ever saw it.

By 1982, a hundred thousand Club Dev man-hours had been spent in pursuit of Casper. It was estimated that he had snagged $100,000 in cash and $30,000 in jewelry in his 286 capers. But suddenly, the burglaries stopped. About a year later, Mike Moen received a call from investigators in Seattle. They had suddenly developed a very similar problem in the Puget Sound area and thought it might be the same suspect. The MOs on the burglaries matched exactly. Seattle police went through the same frustrations as the LAPD. By 1984, Casper had pulled over 330 burglaries in their city.

To this day, Casper has never been apprehended, and police in two divisions speak of him in reverent tones, marveling at his speed, silence, agility, and seeming omnipotence. To the boys at Club Dev, he remains the one who got away.

Aside from Casper, Club Dev got a steady diet of interesting professional burglaries, crimes with good MOs, not just smash and grabbers, that invited real police work. Another related crime that had become fashionable in the Valley was insurance fraud. Insurance companies, especially in California, had emerged as new-age villains. They were commonly viewed as legally sanctioned rip-off artists. A growing number of citizens considered insurance fraud a victimless crime and hence not really a crime at all.

Detectives Ford and Moen stumbled on a number of such cases. One time they handled a $30,000 residential burglary—stereos, TVs, guns, art, a coin collection—with no leads or suspect information. It was a C-3, a case that didn't look like it would go anywhere. About a month after the robbery, the two detectives were contacted by the insurance carrier, who sparked their curiosity. They went back to the house to take another look, only to discover it was up for sale. Ford and Moen posed as potential buyers and were walked through the house. There, in plain sight, were a number of items listed in the report as stolen. They proceeded to obtain a search warrant and recovered ninety percent of the items reported as missing—and prosecuted the owner for insurance fraud. Ford and Moen realized that if such a blundering and boldfaced rip-off nearly succeeded, there was no telling how many burglaries or car thefts were bogus. Insurance companies were indeed easy marks for anyone with criminal intent.

Ford and Moen didn't work together like partners in the traditional sense. Richard Ford preferred to work alone, so the men usually separated the tasks at hand. Ford often disappeared for hours at a time, out in the field by himself, and for a while Moen thought maybe he had a substance abuse problem. He never saw direct evidence, but Ford's attendance was terrible. And some mornings it was obvious his partner had had a bad night.

Vern Higbee had similar suspicions. One day he drove with Ford down to the police academy to qualify at the firing range. Ford spouted nonstop war stories about fragging incidents and other tales that reeked of bullshit. Ford said that when he was wounded in Vietnam, they drugged him up so much he felt he was addicted. Until then, Higbee had never felt that Ford had a drug or alcohol problem; now, he too began to wonder.

One thing Mike Moen knew for sure was that Richard Ford was a loner, a private man. Despite all his gab, he didn't reveal a lot about himself. He never talked about his parents or his childhood, and he kept his distance. Moen socialized with most Club Dev detectives—dinner and shows with the wives on weekends—but not with his partner.

Occasionally, there were exceptions. One night, about half a dozen detectives were working late at headquarters, wondering what to do about Casper, the Friendly Ghost. Romero suggested they call out for sandwiches.

"Hell no," said Ford. "Let's go to my house." He got on the phone. "Honey, I'm bringing some of the guys home."

By the time they arrived, Lillian had a major league spread waiting for them—mounds of luscious corned beef with a variety of cheeses and breads and an assortment of gourmet deli salads. Romero was taken aback by the lavishness of the spread and commented about the obvious expense.

"Oh, don't worry about it," Dick Ford said. "I've got money. Lillian's family has money."

Ford explained that Lillian's parents owned apartment buildings and were very generous to their daughter. Lillian worked as a bus driver for the RTD, and on top of that Dick still got a monthly disability check for five hundred bucks. So they could afford the fancy snakeskin cowboy boots he liked, the beautiful chandeliers in their home, the pool out back, the six-hundred-dollar exercise bike in the bedroom.

Romero had often wondered. Ford always seemed to have a wad of cash in his pocket, and he lived a bit high off the hog. Mike Moen also wasn't surprised to learn about Ford's finances. Moen, who ran his own security business on the side, had already figured that Ford, like almost everyone at Club Dev, had some type of extra income. It took a lot for a family to get by in the Valley.

5

I Can Handle It

THE CLUB DEV DICKS GENERALLY AGREED THAT RICHARD FORD HAD the sexiest wife in the department. Lillian Ford was *muy caliente,* with long dark hair, a voluptuous figure with large, full breasts, and a fiery temperament. As a standing joke around the station house, the guys would tell Ford, "If anything ever happens to you, dude, I'll be knocking on your door."

Ray Romero was charmed by Lillian, who, like himself, spoke fluent Spanish. She struck him as an exceptionally fine lady, an outstanding cook, the kind of woman who really knew how to take care of a man. No feminist, she was a woman who did what her man wanted her to do.

Lillian became a legend at Club Dev, and Dick didn't discourage it. He obliged drooling comrades with locker room tales of his and Lillian's incredible love life. He told them about how Lillian would do erotic dances for him, about how he would wake up in the middle of the night to find her giving him head, about doing it right on the floor the moment he got home.

Once, when Dick was taking a few vacation days, Ray Romero ran into him and Lillian at the local Bank of America.

"Hey, are you guys going anywhere on vacation?" Romero asked.

"No, we're not going anywhere," answered Lillian.

"So what have you been doing?" Romero asked.

Lillian smiled. "Oh, we've just been fucking all day."

Romero knew she was just saying that to play with him. But he also knew that was the kind of relationship they had. He figured that really was what they had been doing.

The DARK SIDE of the FORCE

*   *   *

According to their friends, Dick and Lillian's relationship was like one of those true love stories in a romance magazine. After eight years of marriage, they remained as passionate and devoted as teenagers. But on Thanksgiving night, November 27, 1980, their dream marriage turned into a nightmare.

Bus driver Lillian Ford was working the late shift because of the holiday. She was just finishing up her route for the evening. It was after midnight and her bus was empty when she picked up a passenger on Van Nuys Boulevard in Sherman Oaks. The young man, a Caucasian, about twenty-three, five foot ten, 150 pounds, with a blond ponytail and one black eye, pulled out a knife and held it to her throat. He forced the terrified woman to drive to a remote alley a few blocks away. Once there, Lillian was brutally beaten, robbed, raped, strangled, and left for dead.

When she was discovered by police an hour later, Lillian was in shock. "She was in pitiful condition and was barely able to tell us her story," said Sergeant Ted Hanson. "She must have been his prisoner for about forty-five minutes before he fled the scene."

Lillian had activated the silent electronic alarm on her bus, but apparently an error made by a dispatcher delayed the signal in reaching the LAPD. Had the police received it right away, they could have responded in minutes. Both newspapers and TV reported that the unnamed victim and her family were enraged by the incompetence of the RTD.

The public was spared the full horror of what happened to Lillian Ford. She was treated for a possible concussion, bruises, and shock at Van Nuys Hospital. Then she was transferred to St. Francis Hospital in Linwood, where she spent three days undergoing tests and emergency psychiatric evaluation. Dr. Frederick Hacker, a distinguished, gray-haired Austrian psychiatrist in his sixties, was confronted by a woman who was "absolutely devastated, a pitiful and terrible sight, whimpering like a baby with bursts of hysterical crying . . . crawling into herself, like a frightened animal or child, terribly regressed."

Lillian told Hacker the morbid details of the incident. Years later, Hacker would reveal these in courtroom testimony. According to Lillian, the assailant struck her with his fist just after he boarded the bus—then he pulled out a knife. She tried to jump out of the bus but he blocked her exit. She hit the hidden alarm and expected help to arrive at any moment. She felt she could fight off the assailant until help arrived, so she kept fighting throughout the episode. This only enraged her attacker. He pushed and kicked her numerous times, then tied her up with his belt, stripped her, and gagged her with her underwear. He pulled on her breasts and pubic hair, asking her how she liked it, then raped and sodomized her. When he was finished, he subjected her to prolonged and gruesome sexual torture. He stuck a hairbrush in her vagina and rectum. He pushed his fist into her rectum. He kept masturbating in front of her but couldn't climax.

The ordeal seemed to go on for an eternity and was so horrible that Lillian begged to be killed. Perhaps meaning to oblige her, the assailant choked her to unconsciousness. When he finally left, she revived and was able to untie herself and crawl under a seat of the bus. It was there that she was found sobbing by police.

Hacker diagnosed Lillian as suffering from an extreme case of PTSD. Lillian returned home but remained an invalid for some time. According to Hacker, her symptoms included "a total preoccupation with the event, self-loathing, an inability to function at all, regression. She was unable to control her bowels or bladder and slept crumpled up in the back of the closet. She had attacks of rage directed at her husband because efforts by police to find the perpetrator were inadequate. She carried two or three revolvers, ready to shoot anyone who might attack her. She was unable to perform any domestic duties or drive a car. She had tremendous nightmares, psychosomatic symptoms, tremendous rage and fear of repetition. . . . She had been an independent and self-assertive woman, but she became totally dependent, like an infant."

Dr. Hacker found Richard Ford to be "extremely loving and kind." Ford showed great patience and understanding. He pampered and babied Lillian. According to Hacker, Lillian "would no longer tolerate any sex" with her husband. Lillian told Hacker she developed terrible guilt about this, but she just couldn't have sex. She finally told her husband to "get yourself a girlfriend."

According to Hacker, Lillian's condition placed Richard Ford under a great deal of stress. "His own posttraumatic stress was greatly reinforced. He was having nightmares about Vietnam and feeling dissatisfaction with the LAPD. He felt that he hadn't adequately protected her or found the culprit. I saw him as a nice man, an ideal support and understanding husband, very patient. He stayed up with her all night long, cajoling her, getting her out of the closet. He was very kind to her. She was very grateful but also felt very guilty. She needed care every minute of the day, and the children needed care and so did the home. He did it without getting angry or upset. She said he was 'angelic,' and that she felt like a bitch.

"I've seen many marriages break up from the stress of such a thing. Many husbands despair and give up, but not in this case. His sexual frustration due to her total withdrawal was an added strain, but he never complained. He just asked me whether to keep babying her. He was very sympathetic. I sensed he had no subconscious hostility toward her, that he was authentic, caring, loving. He said he was going to get the rapist. He said it all the time—and he would get carried away with rage."

Christina Forbess, one of Lillian's best friends from childhood, also noticed how supportive Dick was after the rape. She visited Lillian and found Dick vacuuming the house, cooking meals, shopping, cleaning, taking care of the kids. At first, Lillian didn't want to see anybody. When she finally came over to Forbess's house, she had cut her hair and dyed it jet black.

"I'm trying to get the ugliness out of me," Lillian said. "I want to make a complete change." She was very nervous. She chain-smoked and had to clasp her hands on her lap to keep them from shaking.

Lillian's attack received substantial press coverage. Neither Lillian's nor Richard's names appeared in any of these stories; they had requested anonymity for the sake of their children, who were not told of the rape.

On February 10, 1981, Richard and Lillian Ford filed a $4.5-million civil lawsuit against the RTD, citing negligence that resulted in "rape, sodomy, torture, physical injury, mental injury and extreme emotional distress." The suit claimed that the RTD had negligently failed to summon the LAPD after Lillian had activated the bus's silent alarm.

Apparently, the dispatcher had at first presumed that the alarm had been activated accidentally, since it went off at the end of Lillian's run. The dispatcher first tried to locate Lillian's bus by telephoning the yard and having RTD workers search for it. Only after they had failed to find it did they activate the electronic tracking device. Had there not been this delay, the suit claimed, Lillian's brutal rape could have been prevented.

Richard Ford appeared at a press conference called by their attorney, Lawrence Drasin. Mr. Drasin did most of the talking. "She fought her attacker, thinking she was buying time," said Mr. Drasin. "The system, which was supposed to save her, actually caused her greater harm."

The suit was later dismissed by the California Supreme Court. The court ruled that since the plaintiff's injuries occurred on the job, any claims would have to be made through workmen's compensation. A workmen's comp claim filed by the Fords was later settled for $50,000.

While he was struggling to help Lillian, Dick was also caring for his mother-in-law, who had cancer, and was trying to keep an eye on his son, who was experimenting with drugs. He claimed he was also searching on his own for the rapist. He started drinking heavily and taking his wife's sedatives to sleep and his own prescribed amphetamines to stay awake. By May 1981, six months after the rape, Ford finally told Vern Higbee that he needed help. The stress was taking its toll. Higbee referred Ford back to Dr. Martin Reiser, with whom he met on June 1, 1981.

Ford unburdened himself to Reiser in a flood that spilled from one topic to the next. He told Reiser he was worse than before and was drinking more. His wife was seeing a shrink and having all kinds of problems. She cried frequently and screamed at the kids. She had nightmares, and slept in the closet with the dogs. He'd had no sex in six months. He had to clean the house and take care of the kids. One of his kids was using narcotics. His sister-in-law was having problems and he was trying to take care of her kids as well. His mother-in-law was living with them and was terminally ill with cancer. He was finding it harder and harder to cope.

Ford rambled on and on. He still thought about Vietnam and had weekly flashbacks and chronic headaches. He was thinking about suicide and homicide. The department was like his family, but he felt like he didn't make one iota of difference in the department or the world. No one cared anymore. There were no morals. The war had changed him. He'd had no friends since Vietnam. He was a freak. If he caught his wife's rapist he'd like to torture him for three or four days. He was taking some of his wife's codeine and doing "dangerous things."

Dr. Reiser concluded that Ford was suffering from deep depression and couldn't function properly at work. He recommended that Ford be placed on indefinite sick leave so he could seek further treatment. Reiser consulted with Vern Higbee, and together they concluded that, because of his problem with flashbacks about Vietnam, it might be best for Ford to seek treatment at the V.A. It would be five months before Detective Ford returned to active duty at Club Dev.

The resident psychiatrist at the V.A. was Dr. Gerald Motis, a former army officer who had served in Vietnam. Dr. Motis knew firsthand the unique horrors of the war. He knew how troops had often found it necessary to kill civilians, even women and children, because they couldn't distinguish them from the enemy. Motis had worked with the very worst PTSD cases, from unemployed vets living in cars to unapproachable "bush vets" living in caves in southern California. He'd seen many men with problems like Richard Ford's, and he immediately felt a great deal of compassion for the troubled cop.

Motis diagnosed Ford as suffering from an exacerbated case of PTSD. "He had all the primary symptoms. He was reexperiencing traumatic events through nightmares, intrusive thoughts, ruminations, daydreams. He was suffering from depression and anxiety. He was isolating himself from people, except for his family."

Ford, however, was reluctant to accept that he needed treatment. Like many members of the military or law enforcement fraternity, he was mired in a traditional macho trap. He'd recite a litany of horrors and stress-related problems, then conclude with that tired refrain: *But I can handle it.*

Of course he could handle it. He was a soldier *and* a cop. Sure, stress was a problem. But you lived with it. That's what you did. To admit otherwise was to destroy the GI Joe self-image you'd built up over two decades. And there were professional ramifications to consider as well. No cop wants to work with a stress case.

To Dr. Motis, it seemed this last consideration was the real source of Ford's denial. Dick Ford wasn't one of those dense macho types. He knew he had some problems. But he had an understandable fear that admitting to a stress problem might cost him his job.

Ford wouldn't even consider staying at the V.A. as an inpatient. He panicked when he saw the lockup unit. "I won't be locked up. I'm not going to stay here," he said with finality. Who would take care of his family? Dr. Motis and Dr. Lopata, Ford's therapist, recommended outpatient peer group therapy. They also arranged for a complete physical exam.

While going through Ford's medical history, Motis discovered something very interesting. He learned that Ford had already tried most of the medications normally prescribed for anxiety and depression. None had done any good. In some cases, as with Valium, the drugs had actually made him more irritable, hyperactive, tense, and depressed. Ford mentioned that he had taken amphetamines in the past, and they had actually helped. This gave Motis an idea. He gave Ford a prescription for Ritalin, a nervous-system stimulant most often used to treat children with attention deficit disorder. Although a stimulant, Ritalin has a calming effect on hyperactive youngsters. Sure enough, Ford's condition improved. Motis concluded that perhaps, while in Vietnam, Ford had sustained some minimal brain damage that was causing some of his problems.

Ford quickly assumed the role of de facto leader of Dr. Lopata's PTSD group. He was well liked and respected, easily the most articulate man in the group. Dr. Lopata found him to be generous and kind, willing to give to others— often, it seemed, to avoid dealing with his own problems. Ford may have initially joined the group to satisfy the LAPD, but he soon developed a genuine camaraderie with his fellow vets. Especially Bruce Adams, who joined the group a few months after Ford.

On the surface, Richard Ford and Bruce Adams seemed to have little in common. But the two men shared many experiences from the war and many similar PTSD problems. They had both been patriotic kids who joined the service at seventeen and volunteered to go to Vietnam. They had both seen intense combat, had both been wounded twice. They could relate in ways they couldn't with the other men. They called each other almost daily—whenever they had problems with delayed stress. Before long their mutual support system became the foundation of a strong friendship.

Ford, like Adams, frequently found himself sitting up at night staring out a window, or walking the floor, unable to sleep. They both had flashbacks to Vietnam and recognized similar triggers to anxiety attacks. The most common was the sound of an approaching helicopter. The arrival of an ambu-copter at the V.A. could set them both off, making them feel like they were back in the central highlands of Vietnam.

Richard Ford returned to Club Dev in October 1981, after five months' leave. Doctors Motis and Lopata wrote a letter recommending his return to duty: "At this time he has positive feeling about himself and we feel the likelihood of suicidal or homicidal behavior is minimal."

Many at Club Dev saw a dramatic change in Richard Ford. Harlene Settles, a civilian police service representative who worked the front desk, was one of Detective Ford's biggest fans. She always found him "pleasant, compassionate, very kind and honest with citizens at the desk." After the rape, however, she noticed that he became very quiet, "like a whupped puppy dog."

Sally Barnes, a shapely blond LAPD officer, had partnered with Ford for a short while at Club Dev and found him "very personable." But after the rape, he became "more restricted, not so outgoing, not so happy-go-lucky."

Ford began telling the other cops that he was on the track of Lillian's rapist. He frequently commented, "Don't worry, I've got people out there looking" or "I hope they find him before I do." He mentioned that he had somebody working for him and that he was also driving around at night looking for the perpetrator.

Ford later told Lieutenant Higbee that he had a friend from Vietnam who owed him a favor. This friend, he said, had identified and found the rapist in the Haight-Ashbury district of San Francisco. Supposedly, he was going to "do" the guy as a favor for Ford.

Higbee figured it was just bullshit. He told Ford that if he had any information, he should turn it over to the Van Nuys detectives who were handling the case, that he should "do it the right way."

Eventually, Ford told his partner, Mike Moen, that "the problem had been solved."

"What do you mean?" Moen asked.

"An old army buddy of mine located the suspect up in the Haight district in San Francisco," Ford said. "It's all been taken care of."

Moen assumed he was implying that the suspect had been killed, but he didn't take it seriously. He figured it was more BS from Dick Ford. Maybe it was just his way of coping with the fact that the perp had never been caught.

6

Partners

IN FEBRUARY 1982, ADAMS FELL INTO SOME TROUBLE WITH THE police. He was repairing a Chevy pickup for an acquaintance. LAPD officers from Van Nuys came to Adams's residence, impounded the vehicle, and informed Adams that he would be charged with receiving stolen property. They didn't arrest him, however, but told him they would give him some time to find the man who had allegedly brought him the stolen truck.

Adams called Richard Ford. "Whatever you do, don't cop to nothin'," Ford told him. "Don't say nothin', don't tell them nothin'. They gotta prove it." Ford told Adams not to worry, he'd help him take care of it.

Heeding Ford's counsel, Adams surrendered for booking three weeks later at Van Nuys Station. He told the officers he was unable to locate the man who had brought him the Chevy. Adams went to court with a public defender and told the same story. The case was dropped because the D.A. couldn't prove anything. Afterward, Ford told Adams he was proud of him for keeping his mouth shut—implying that Adams did in fact know the man's whereabouts.

Bruce Adams was not opposed to skirting the law to pick up a little extra cash. He was out of work, living on disability and workmen's comp, and he had six mouths to feed, so he didn't ask a lot of questions when somebody came to him with work. For a few months, Bruce took a night job as a driver for a prostitution service. One of the men in the PTSD group at the V.A. operated this clandestine escort service. It paid good money and it was kind of fun, driving hookers all over town, acting as their lookout and protector when they went in to party with their johns.

Richard Ford was intrigued by the escort service. He grilled Adams, wanting to know how the girls were recruited, how they found the tricks, the weekly net, everything about the operation.

The PTSD group was not the Boy Scouts. Many members, like Adams, did what they had to to get along. Hundreds of other vets were treated or hung out at the Sepulveda V.A. In some ways, it was like Nam. Anything was available—you just had to know who to ask. Drugs, girls, guns, hot merchandise like VCRs and color TVs—they were all passed around by the troops. The group served as a commercial network as well as a support group.

Adams continued to study biomedical engineering and electronics at the V.A. while he worked on cars at his home in Van Nuys. Before long, Richard Ford was bringing his cars for repairs and supplying Bruce with a steady stream of paying customers—other Club Dev cops.

According to Bruce Adams, his relationship with Richard Ford took a bizarre turn in November 1982 when Ford asked him to drive out to Colorado with him on a hunting trip. Adams enjoyed getting out in the country, and he liked to shoot. He'd often told Ford that one of his ways of relaxing was to go out in one of the canyons and shoot at rocks and squirrels.

Before they left, Adams fixed Ford's 1977 green-and-yellow woody Datsun station wagon. Adams had trouble getting parts, so he spent three weeks working on the car. He overhauled the engine, fixed the heater and air-conditioning. He wanted to replace the clutch, but Ford got impatient. "We're leaving Thursday night," Ford finally said. "We're going to Colorado."

"Okay," said Adams. He sensed something was up.

David Jimenez, a V.A. buddy who was homeless at the time, was crashing on Adams's couch. He would later claim that Bruce Adams knew the real purpose of the trip before he left.

On Friday at 4:00 A.M., Ford and Adams loaded their gear and .30-'06 deer rifles into the Datsun. "Dick, we'd better load the tool box in the back," Adams suggested. "There's some questions about the clutch."

"Nah," Ford scoffed. "It'll be okay."

Adams shrugged. He didn't want to start an argument. When he really got down with Dick, when they started tearing into each other, calling each other motherfuckers and what not, it inevitably turned comical. After a while, they'd look at each other and start laughing like a couple of grunts on leave in a Saigon whorehouse. Bruce wasn't ready to start up with his good buddy yet. They'd be going at it soon enough.

After Bruce and Dick had left town, Shirley Adams stopped by the Fords' house to visit Lillian. Lillian was back working again, and everything seemed fine. Over coffee, Shirley commented on how nice it was for Dick to ask Bruce to go hunting with him in Colorado. Lillian started to laugh. "Is that what they told you?" she cried. "Oh, Shirley, you're so naive!"

After they stopped for breakfast in Palmdale, Bruce took the wheel and Ford navigated while he scanned the radio for country music. For the next four days, Adams would get his fill of Waylon and Hank and Merle.

"Take the road to Vegas," Ford said as he punched the buttons.

Only problem was, they weren't anywhere near Interstate 15, the road to Vegas. Neither was paying much attention. Bruce got on Route 14 instead, and they wound up heading north, along the eastern slope of the Sierras. They were past Bishop, halfway to Tahoe, before they finally crossed over into Nevada.

About midway through Nevada, Ford reached over and handed Adams a billfold. Adams opened it up. It was a badge.

"What's this?" Adams asked.

"In case we get stopped," Ford explained. "You're an undercover narcotics cop out of L.A."

"Oh yeah, right," said Adams. What the fuck? he wondered.

While driving a mountain road through a state park, they decided to take a nature break. Bruce was taking a piss into some brush. All of a sudden Bruce heard gunshots—six rounds in a row. He jumped like a jackrabbit and pissed all over the Datsun.

It was only Ford, cappin' off rounds with his .38 service revolver. "Boy, this is fun," Dick said as he took aim and blasted away at a tall saguaro cactus. Ford handed Adams the revolver, and he capped off a few rounds too.

About seven that evening, going into Utah, they headed up a steep grade and Bruce felt the clutch starting to go. Ford sniffed the air. "What's that smell?" he asked.

"Gee, I don't know, Dick, what's it smell like to you? Burnt pancakes? It's the fuckin' clutch. I told you the goddam clutch was gonna go."

The nearest town was eighty miles away, and Bruce drove as fast as he could to keep the pressure off the clutch. Finally, they reached a little Mormon town that looked like it was straight out of the 1950s.

"Yeah, we can get you a clutch for a Datsun," the service station guy said. "But it's gonna take three days. It's gotta come out on a bus from Provo."

"Great," said Adams. "How far is Provo?"

"Oh, about a hundred miles. But it's all flat, just a few little hills. You can probably make it."

The hills proved to be little only when viewed from a great distance. Before long, smoke was pouring off the clutch. Adams managed to white-knuckle it for about an hour, until they reached a small town called Payson, twenty-seven miles outside Provo.

"Dick, I don't think we're gonna make it," Adams cried. "I can hardly pull the hill goin' into this little town." As they drove through the middle of Payson, Ford spotted a police car. "Stop the car!" he yelled. "I'll jump out and badge that motherfucker."

The next thing Adams knew he was following a black and white to the police station. Ford made the introductions. "I'm Detective Ford and this is Detective Adams," he told Payson's finest.

Holy shit, Adams thought, now I'm a detective. One of the cops he was introduced to was also named Adams. Bruce decided to let Ford do all the talking.

Suddenly, a 211 in progress came over the station house scrambler—suspects wearing ski masks with automatic weapons were taking down a grocery store. "Hey, you guys want to go along on this?" one of the Payson cops asked. Adams tried hard to light a cigarette without shaking as he looked at Ford. "Nah, we gotta figure out how we're gonna get to Boulder," Ford said.

One of the Payson cops called up a buddy who had a parts store. He got his friend to drive down to the station at one o'clock in the morning with a clutch assembly. Another cop found them a place to crash for a few hours. Then, at 5:00 A.M. another cop got somebody to open up the local Goodyear tire shop so Adams could use their lift and tools. Adams had the car ready by ten and they were back on the road to Colorado. It was none too soon for Adams. He was a nervous wreck, worrying about what would happen if they called L.A. to check on "Detective Adams."

"You boys in blue really take care of your own," Adams commented as they drove out of town. "It's like being in a goddam fraternity."

Ford laughed. "That's right, Doc. Law enforcement is the best fraternity there is. Whenever you're in a jam, you just flash the shield and your brothers take care of you."

Shortly after they crossed into Colorado, Ford dropped his bomb. He told Adams the real purpose of their expedition: they were going to purchase some automatic weapons. Adams had been a weapons expert in Vietnam and Ford wanted him to inspect the goods.

"We need the guns for a robbery at a jewelry show at the Century Plaza Hotel," Ford explained. "I've got a partner, another cop, who's also a Vietnam vet. He'll be the inside man. The take will be close to two million dollars—the biggest caper ever pulled in Los Angeles. That's how we're gonna open the auto shop. We need a guy like you, Bruce."

Adams remained silent. "You realize, Bruce, that you're in it now," Ford told him. He paused, letting this sink in. "If you open your mouth about this to anybody, you're dead."

Adams's heart began to pound. A lot of things about Detective Richard Ford suddenly made sense. Adams could tell that Ford was serious. He also knew that Ford had his .38 tucked inside his belt. Adams decided to play along. "What's my percentage of the take?" he asked.

"Equal partners, of course." Ford smiled.

They rolled into Boulder about eleven that night. Ford made a phone call from a Denny's restaurant, across the street from the hospital by the university. When he got back in the car he gave Adams directions toward Estes Park. They drove fifteen miles northwest of Boulder until they hit a dirt cutaway. Waiting for them a few yards off the highway was a man—a male Caucasian, about forty-five, five foot nine, 170 pounds, reddish brown hair and beard, slightly balding, a handlebar mustache. About twenty yards farther up the dirt road was a plain white Dodge half-ton van. Adams pegged it to be a 1977 or 1978 model.

Ford and Adams hopped out of the Datsun. The bearded man looked like he belonged in the mountains. He was wearing jeans with a western shirt and boots. He said his name was Steve. Adams figured him to be a vet—no question. Probably a bush vet, one of those wackos who couldn't hack civilization. Maybe even a mercenary. Ford and Adams followed Steve up the dirt road on foot. Steve opened the rear door of his van; lying in the back was a wooden box that Adams recognized as a 105-mm howitzer ammunition crate. Inside the crate were six Mac-10 machine guns—fully automatic, with silencers and loaded thirty-round ammo clips.

Adams wasn't dressed for the mountain fall. He shivered as he picked up the guns and looked them over. He fan-fired each of them, making sure they were fully operational. Each weapon had been equipped with a selector, which con verted it to fire as either an automatic or semiautomatic. He noticed that the conversion had been done by drilling in a locking cam in the receiver above the trigger; it appeared to be a professional job.

After Adams deemed the guns authentic, Ford pulled an envelope filled with cash from his leather jacket and handed it to Steve. Adams eyed the wad of fifties and hundreds and estimated it to be about five grand. Then Ford and Adams loaded the crate of Mac-10s into the Datsun, covered it with their sleeping bags, and took off. The whole exchange was smooth and businesslike. It lasted only minutes.

"Here, try some of these," Ford said as they got back on the road. He held out some pills.

"What's that?" Adams asked.

"Uppers."

"Uh, no thanks, not for me, no way," said Adams. Jesus. His hands were already shaking so badly he had to keep them fastened to the steering wheel while he struck the matches to light his cigarettes. Yeah, that was just what he needed. Some *speed*.

Ford laughed as he popped a couple of dexies into his mouth.

They took turns driving back to L.A. Adams wanted to go to sleep when Ford was driving, but he couldn't. For one thing, he was too afraid. Plus, Ford never shut his mouth long enough for him to grab a wink. Ford rattled on and on about the upcoming caper, about jewels and guns and fences . . .

"Yeah, partner, you and me are gonna make one helluva team," said Ford as he smoked Marlboros one for one with Adams. "This fuckin' trade show at the Century Plaza Hotel will be a piece of cake. It's gonna go down one, two, three. We got it all cased. My friend, Bob, worked security there the last couple of years. We'll go in together and take down the vault on the second floor. It's only guarded by two off-duty LAPD officers. That's the only security they got, other than roving patrol in the building. We're gonna send you in as a telephone man. Nobody will suspect a fuckin' thing, Adams. You'll be perfect. You're gonna have to knock out communications, create a fuckin' distraction, disrupt the phone lines and all the traffic lights in the area. We'll rent a van. Me and Bob will be wearing suits, you know, like jewelry salesmen. We're getting professional wigs and disguises—Bob's already got that wired. Bob figures there'll be a couple of million in jewels—easy—and we already got someone lined up for unloading the goods."

Ford sprinkled in a few cautionaries throughout his marathon rap. If Adams ever squealed they'd put him away. And if he tried to drop a dime on them, they'd find out about it. They had their hooks in at IAD. Any complaints would get back to them. "I've knocked people off before," Ford said. "It don't bother me at all."

They arrived in L.A. at 3:00 A.M. Monday morning, having been gone only four days. Ford dropped Adams off at his house and left.

Adams was tired, dirty, and stressed to the max. The cops would think he was crazy if he went to them with this story. But how could he go to the cops anyway? Ford and his "partner" *were* the cops—and cops took care of their own. He tried to forget about it. Maybe, he thought, this will be the end of it.

* * *

A few weeks after their return from Colorado, Ford brought Bob over to Adams's house in Van Nuys. "Meet your new partner," Ford told Adams. Ford had already told Bruce about Bob, whom he often referred to as "the Colonel" or "the Simi Valley Cowboy."

Officer Robert Von Villas, thirty-eight, was five foot ten, lean, handsome, and nearly half-bald, with dark wavy sidewalls accenting an expanded dome in front. His baldness actually made him look more distinguished. A full mustache added a rakish touch. Outfitted in the full regalia of an LAPD officer, he presented a striking figure. Hints of his German ancestry could be detected in his features and in his brilliant blue eyes, as well as in his aristocratic bearing and gate. To some, however, his air suggested arrogance.

In coming years, as Von Villas became something of a legend in southern California, citizens and newscasters alike would often pronounce his name as though he were Hispanic: *Von Ve-yas,* like Pancho Villa, with the double *l* spoken as a *y.* In fact, his name was pronounced with a hard *l:* Villas rhymed with Willis. He was not an *amigo,* he was a *Freund.* The Von, an aristocratic German prefix, should have been a tip-off. But in a city where Hispanics were rapidly becoming the predominant ethnic group, Anglos frequently went overboard in latinizing their pronunciations.

Von Villas projected an image of supreme competence and authority. His full eyebrows and furrowed brow gave him an aura of gravity—a man to be reckoned with. When dressed in a dark business suit he could appear somewhat sinister—like a Mafia lieutenant. Upon introduction, however, this formidable countenance gave way to broad smiles and an effervescent personality. People were quickly won over by his bubbly, impish quality and gift for conversation. He exuded enthusiasm, and his voice was clear and slightly high pitched. He was a talker, a natural salesman, a smoothie.

Everyone's first impression of Bob was that he was a hustler—no question about it. Most people saw this as a positive attribute. They found it admirable, entertaining, and quite often irresistible. Others—like Bruce Adams—found themselves on their guard.

Adams immediately pegged Von Villas for a con man, as cool and slippery as an ice cube on a summer day. But he was duly impressed by him nonetheless. Von Villas worked with juveniles at Devonshire Division, but he made it a point to let Adams know he was as much a businessman as he was a cop. He played the commodities market, dabbled in real estate, and owned pieces of a few businesses. He worked off-duty bodyguard and movie gigs. He bragged to Adams about a few scams he had in the works—selling interests in trust deeds to police widows and various complex insurance frauds and real estate development deals. Adams couldn't believe all the angles this guy was playing.

Von Villas was even more loquacious than Richard Ford. But while Ford just talked a good game, Von Villas seemed to have the smarts to follow through. He was a player, not a bullshitter. Adams could see why Ford called him the Colonel. Along with his hustler's instincts, Von Villas had the attitude and the mentality—as well as the appearance—of a top field marshal.

Over the next few weeks, Von Villas stopped by regularly at Adams's house while he was on patrol in his squad car. At first, his visits made Adams uncomfortable. He felt strange having a uniformed, spit-and-polish supercop hanging out in his garage. But Von Villas made sincere overtures of friendship and before long they were friends. Von Villas had Adams do some work on his Pontiac Grand Prix and on the new Camaro he had bought for one of his daughters. He steered additional business Adams's way, recommending him to some cop buddies at Club Dev. He gave Adams an old beater he had, a 1964 Oldsmobile, so Bruce could fix it up for Shirley.

Von Villas, like Ford, had been a sergeant in the army. He earned a Bronze Star for rescuing members of his platoon from a burning helicopter. The tip of one of his fingers had been diced by a fragmentation grenade. But unlike Richard Ford, he didn't like to talk about his experiences in Vietnam.

When he was off duty, Von Villas would usually arrive at Adams's house wearing cowboy boots, jeans, and a western shirt. He shared Richard Ford's passion for country music. And, like Ford, he flashed big rolls of cash, often five thousand dollars or more. He and Ford continued to promise Adams that they would bankroll him in an auto shop, just as soon as they had the financing.

Ford told Adams that the Century Plaza job had been pushed off but they had another caper coming up. One night Ford called Adams and asked him if he could find a license plate from another 1969 Pontiac that they could use on Von Villas's car. Ford told Adams they needed it for a jewelry heist. They had the place all reconned. They were just waiting for their professional wigs and disguises. "My fuckin' wig is gonna cost me two hundred and fifty dollars," Ford complained.

Adams didn't know what to believe. He felt like he was in the twilight zone. He told him he couldn't find a plate. He told him to go look in a junkyard.

Another evening Ford and Von Villas showed up at Adams's front door. Von Villas wanted to hear all about the escort service. He grilled Adams on the particulars of the operation.

"How much are they pulling in?" Von Villas asked.

"I don't know," said Adams. "I only worked there a couple of months. Maybe five grand a week."

"Do you think we can take down the operation?" Ford asked. "Do you think it's worth knocking this dude off?"

"I guess, I don't know," said Adams. He wondered what Ford really meant. He wasn't talking about offing the guy, was he? Nah, he thought. Taking down his operation didn't necessarily mean killing the guy.

"This guy ain't too slick," Adams said. "He's a loady. He's always sampling the stable, screwin' the women. Let me talk to this other guy who works there."

"Why don't I just go in and badge him," said Ford, "throw him in the back of the car, and take his ass out to the fuckin' desert. Then you can just run the place."

Oh shit, Adams thought.

Adams called around and found out that the guy who ran the service had recently overdosed and flipped out. He was in the lockup unit at the V.A., so he had taken himself out of the picture. Adams managed to acquire a list of the names and numbers of all the girls.

Later, Adams turned this list over to Von Villas. Adams sensed that Von Villas, who fancied himself a ladies' man, was as interested in the girls as he was in the business. Von Villas also grilled Adams about some other hookers he knew, Monique and Karen, girls he had met while working at an auto shop in Hollywood. Von Villas wanted to know how many hookers Adams could round up. He wanted to start his own escort service.

7

The Simi Valley Cowboy

ROBERT FULLER IS ONE OF THOSE HOLLYWOOD ACTORS EVERYONE seems to recognize, even if they don't know his name. Tall and lean as a rail, he has that leathered, Old West look found in so many Remington paintings—the quintessential trail boss. "I did every TV western there ever was," Fuller has said, "and back in 1958 there were twenty-five of them." Fuller became a star on "Laramie" in 1959 and then mosied on to "Wagon Train" in the 1960s, riding that celebrated trail for two years.

The Valley was once swarming with TV cowboys like Fuller. They drank and fought and caroused in little river-bottom country bars near the Burbank studios with the likes of Chuck Connors, Steve McQueen, and Richard Boone. But with the passing of the western, they became a dying breed.

Fuller, however, was a survivor. During the 1970s, he got out of the saddle to star in a contemporary firehouse drama, "Emergency!", which ran from 1972 to 1977. He wrangled in occasional feature films during the early 1980s and hosted his own outdoors show called "Fishing Fever," which was filmed in Florida and the Caribbean. Fuller was an avid hunter and fisherman, a man who appreciated good firearms, and an active member of the National Sports Foundation and the NRA. He also had a lifelong affinity for law enforcement that could be traced back to his childhood.

While growing up on the streets of Chicago, Fuller was inspired—perhaps saved—by Police Athletic League programs. After he came to Los Angeles, he forged tight bonds with the LAPD. He appeared regularly at PAL luncheons and served as master of ceremonies at LAPD Medal of Honor presentations. His beautiful home in Toluca Lake, near the Burbank studios, was a frequent hangout for local cops, who would stop by for some coffee and chitchat.

One day in the early 1970s, a uniformed patrol officer drove up to Fuller's house and knocked on his door. He introduced himself: Officer Robert Von Villas, North Hollywood Division. Officer Von Villas told Fuller he had some PAL benefit activities coming up and wondered if the actor would be willing to make an appearance. Fuller said sure. He committed himself to the PAL function and began what would become a long friendship.

Fuller had a big study where he and Von Villas would invariably retire. An avid gun collector, Fuller kept two huge gun cases on either side of the fireplace. Von Villas, who appreciated quality firearms, was impressed by this collection of shotguns, rifles, and pistols. Sharing a common love for guns, country music, horses, cowboy boots, Jack Webb, PAL, and police, Fuller and Von Villas passed many hours in animated conversation. Fuller's study also served as his trophy room and was cluttered with animals he had bagged around the world—Russian boar, sheep, antelope, deer, marlin. Von Villas wasn't a hunter, but he loved listening to Fuller recount his wilderness adventures.

Over the years, Fuller hosted a number of PAL luncheons for Von Villas, in North Hollywood and later at Club Dev. These were usually held at fine restaurants and were well attended by the business community. Fuller and other celebrities, like actor David Soul or local TV anchor Christine Lund, would sit up on a dais—along with Bob Von Villas. Mayor Tom Bradley, Chief Daryl Gates, and other civic VIPs would also make an appearance. The TV news teams would get clips for the five o'clock news.

Fuller was awed by Von Villas's PR abilities. He planned these events to perfection—seating, introductions, speeches and presentations, food and cocktails, the media. Von Villas always had a broad, sincere smile and was so zealous about PAL, so enthralled with his work, he simply overwhelmed anyone he encountered. It was easy for him to walk into a room of VIPs and convince them of the absolute necessity of volunteering their services. As a result, he had contacts everywhere—with other actors, sports celebrities, politicians, and the media. In fact, Von Villas was so good at PR, Fuller simply assumed he was an official public relations police officer. It seemed so obvious he never bothered to ask.

Fact was, Von Villas planned and organized and recruited for these events strictly on a volunteer basis. His position as a juvenile officer assigned to the school car involved a lot of PR work, but that wasn't his official job, just his avocation.

The DARK SIDE of the FORCE

Fuller thought Von Villas was top of the line. He was one helluva guy, a good husband and father, a cowboy, a conscientious cop, a very sharp police officer. "Just by the way he wore his uniform and carried and presented himself, you could tell he was an asset to the LAPD," Fuller explained.

Another one of Bob's stop-by-and-chat buddies was Christine Lund, one of L.A.'s most popular TV newscasters. A platinum blond blue-eyed beauty in her thirties, Lund had worked at KABC Channel 7 since 1973 and was credited with helping to bring the station to prominence.

Lund lived on an eight-acre Valley ranch that evoked the old Valley. She kept ducks, geese, chickens, dogs, horses, rabbits, and sheep—which she sheered herself. In fact, Lund was "addicted" to spinning yarn, an activity that gave her the same blissed-out buzz some folks got from yoga or meditation. She'd sit in her kitchen, spinning her heart away, looking like a Hollywood version of a frontier housewife, while Bob sat at the table drinking coffee. They'd chat up a storm.

Lund's pet social issue was domestic violence and child abuse. There wasn't much she didn't know about it. In fact, during the mid-1980s, when she got "burned out" with the news and took a four-year leave, she went to grad school to obtain a family counselor's license. So whenever Bob popped in and began talking about his kids, they'd often get into hours of passionate discussion. They shared their frustrations. Christine would complain about having to provide a slick, glib, superficial headline service as opposed to being able to really dig into issues. She'd complain about how meaningless her work seemed compared with that of counselors and social workers. Bob would vent his frustrations over seemingly insurmountable byzantine LAPD bureaucracy and politics.

Bob really knew and cared about kids. Christine was always happy to help him out when she could.

So was the actor David Soul. Bob met Soul while doing security on "Starsky and Hutch." Soul met lots of cops, but none ever impressed him like Bob Von Villas. This guy was really genuine. He was welcome to stop by and chat anytime.

Von Villas went out with his celebrity friends occasionally. He and Robert Fuller loved country music, so they'd take their wives out to dinner and a concert; Eddie Rabbitt, Kenny Rogers, Waylon and Willie. They shared a lot of laughs. Von Villas also knew when the best acts were playing at local clubs, like the Longhorn Saloon and the Palomino. When he was off duty, Von Villas dressed the way Fuller always dressed—western shirts, jeans, cowboy boots. For Bob

Von Villas, however, the cowboy motif was hardly just an affectation or a fashion statement. He actually owned and operated his own horse ranch.

Von Villas lived in Tapo Canyon in Simi Valley, about ten freeway minutes west of Devonshire Division. Simi offered a haven for suburban cowboys. Ringed by the Santa Monica Mountains to the south, the Sierra Madre foothills and Santa Susana Mountains to the north, and the pristine Simi Hills to the west, Simi Valley offered a vast wilderness playground for horsemen and off-roaders.

Back in the 1950s and 1960s, the rugged, undeveloped canyons of Simi and neighboring Chatsworth had served as the location for hundreds of westerns. Now, of course, the developers had taken over from the movie men. The hills were alive with development—everything from tract homes to mansions to presidential libraries. Simi Valley was widely regarded as the ultimate white-flight suburb. Every year it made the FBI's list of the safest towns in the nation. Perhaps for this reason it was also a renowned enclave for L.A. cops. By the end of the 1980s, nearly one fourth of the LAPD's 8,300-man force lived in Simi Valley. The housing was also affordable, and one could commute to L.A. (about forty-five minutes to downtown if traffic wasn't snarled). Simi Valley had everything a respectable suburbanite needed: new mega supermarkets, a Mann multiplex theater, lots of spacious parks and pretty houses. A restored Victorian ranch house stood near the town center in Strathearn Park as a reminder of the pre-1900 rancho era when Simi was first settled. Away from the town proper, amidst the rugged western landscapes, rustic suburban ranches provided an outlet for the commuter cowboys.

Von Villas moved to Simi in the early seventies, buying a popular "horse property"—a small ranch—and expanding it. The house was old, but Bob and Judy Von Villas turned it into a showplace worthy of a spread in *Town & Country*. Judy was quite a decorator. She had worked for furniture stores, and for a while she had her own business, the Blacksmith Shop, which featured wrought-iron furnishings. Adjacent to the house on their seven-acre spread were a barn and a corral, where they boarded nearly a dozen horses belonging to local residents.

Von Villas spent many of his off-duty hours feeding, grooming, and tending to the horses, as well as taking spectacular early dawn and evening rides through the breathtaking countryside. The Simi Hills were alive with glistening reddish sandstone outcroppings and skyscraping sedimentary rock formations that glistened at sunrise and sunset. The taller but rounder Santa Susana Mountains offered the peace and solace of a church. The terrain was still home to deer, hawks, owls, bobcats, coyotes, rattlesnakes, and over forty species of birds. On a clear day you could see all the way to the ocean.

Officer Von Villas had been involved in youth services throughout his police career. He worked with Explorer Scouts, boys age fourteen and up, and the Deputy Auxiliary Police (DAP), boys and girls under age fourteen. DAPs were given special badges that allowed them to go on organized outings with police volunteers. The officers, by virtue of their good example, would help teach the boys and girls to be good citizens. Von Villas often drove busloads of DAP kids to Disneyland or Dodgers games. He'd also get them involved in community projects, like recycling or setting up Christmas tree lots.

As with PAL, the key to such programs was personnel. Sports equipment or field trips were merely the bait used to get kids off the streets—or, in Club Dev's case, out of the malls. But the program was only effective if the kids developed a relationship with a proper role model, someone they could respect and look up to, someone who really cared about them. For street kids, or even advantaged kids with inattentive parents, such a relationship could make all the difference when it came to withstanding negative peer pressure.

Not every cop can fill such a role. Some could take a thousand children to a hundred ball games and never connect with a single kid. Other cops could connect with a whole busload as soon as they climbed aboard. Bob Von Villas was one of those cops who had that rare gift.

Club Dev established a J (juvenile) car to fight truancy in the mid-1970s, shortly after Von Villas transferred into the division. Von Villas was a natural choice for the job, and due largely to his efforts, the program was a huge success. It wasn't uncommon for the J car (or school car, as it was also known) to pick up three hundred truants in a week. Daytime burglary rates in Devonshire Division took a nosedive.

The J car's secondary purpose was to act as a liaison between the police and schools in the division. It was there that Von Villas truly shined. He loved the kids and they loved him. He knew how to reach them, to make them open up. He could talk to them without patronizing them. He really listened to what they had to say. He remembered all their names. He was hip, with-it, enthusiastic, a guy who was fun to be around. Whenever Officer Bob showed up on campus, the kids flocked to his side. And he was always available to any kid who wanted to talk.

One time on Halloween, Von Villas and his partner, Mike Arroyo, made the rounds of all the schools in the division wearing elaborate latex pig masks. They'd park in front of each school, sitting in the black and white, in full uniform, wearing pig heads. When the kids came out they nearly died of laughter. Officer Bob's sense of humor endeared him to all the kids.

The LAPD J-car program, in which Officer Von Villas was a pioneer, was basically the precursor of Drug Abuse Resistance Education, a program that spread nationwide in the mid-1980s. The J car was responsible for handling all crimes or disturbances at Chatsworth, Kennedy, and Granada Hills high schools and at half a dozen junior highs in the division. Whenever there was a problem, Officer Bob got the call. Von Villas became renowned for his ability to handle the most unruly kids. Once he saved a "jumper," pulling him off the high school's roof before the boy could commit suicide. He was also in great demand to give presentations in the classrooms. He would talk about the police, about how they weren't just there to harass kids but to make sure they had a safe environment. He'd talk about the role of police in government, about how you became a police officer, about peer pressure and the dangers of drugs—and he'd field questions on almost anything.

The kids responded to Officer Bob. They loved to hang out with him. While most uniformed cops couldn't get a high school kid even to talk to them, Von Villas could do that and more. He could extract information about burglaries and drug deals. And he was just as good at dealing with teachers and principals.

The brass at Club Dev were awed by Von Villas's performance. His job developed into a free-form operation based on trust—and the fact that he always produced results. His supervision was nil. Basically, Officer Von Villas was set free to do as he pleased.

Detective Ray Romero, like everyone at Club Dev, considered Von Villas an outstanding youth officer. Romero had the opportunity to observe him when he worked with the Explorer Scouts at the station house. He was amazed by the tremendous zeal he showed for his work. It was obvious that Von Villas loved those kids and that the kids all looked up to him. He was their idol.

Romero was even more impressed when he saw Von Villas in action out on the streets. Every year, there was a Christmas festival held by the Napa Street School in Northridge, which was located in Club Dev's only poor area. Von Villas tagged Romero to play a bilingual Santa Claus. Romero was surprised to see that Von Villas knew all the kids by name. He dealt with them as individuals. When he snapped his fingers, they'd run and do whatever he asked. And Von Villas had hustled up donations of food and gifts from local merchants. He did the same thing at Thanksgiving. Nobody could say no to him.

Romero would recall the time he took his wife and kids to a movie in Hollywood. While standing in front of the Pantages Theater, a big, yellow school bus pulled up to the curb. The doors opened, and there was Officer Bob in the driver's seat. He piled out, and a busload of kids followed him into the theater, happy as clams. Romero couldn't believe it. Von Villas looked just like the Pied Piper.

Romero found Von Villas to be a very conscientious officer. He always knew what to look for, the right questions to ask during an investigation. He was simply a top-flight policeman. The downside was that he was arrogant. He was a real gentleman with the public, but a lot of the other cops felt that he was insolent, a know-it-all, a guy with a superior attitude. He never hesitated, for example, to tell another cop he was making "a shitty arrest." Von Villas always knew more about proper police procedure than anyone else. He also had a bad habit of ignoring chain of command, of going over a supervisor's head if he couldn't get his way.

But the thing about Von Villas that most bothered Romero, and many others of Club Dev's finest, was his relentless hustling. That, and his related telephone addiction. Von Villas received more telephone calls than anyone else at Club Dev. Every supervisor he ever had found occasion to reprimand him about it. It was always somebody—his broker, business partners, girlfriends, kids, teachers, friends, God only knew who else. There were a dozen different places at the station where you could use a telephone, and Von Villas always seemed to be at one of them.

LAPD policy did not prohibit moonlighting. Largely, this was a legacy from an earlier era when L.A. cops had to work outside jobs to supplement the low department pay. While the money in the LAPD had gotten better, moonlighting was still accepted practice. Most of the older commanding officers had held side jobs all through their careers, so they hardly frowned on ambitious youngsters who continued the tradition. Club Dev's Lieutenant Higbee had worked side jobs for fifteen years. Ray Romero looked after numerous real estate interests. At Club Dev, if you needed someone to do brickwork, there was a guy who did masonry on the side. If you needed a roofer, there was a guy who ran his own roofing company. So nobody saw anything wrong with the fact that Bob Von Villas hustled outside work. The only problem with Bob was that it never seemed to stop.

Von Villas was always working off-duty bodyguard or security gigs—at private homes, malls, concerts, or movie sets. He was always trying to interest someone in a business partnership or real estate deal. And he always had a trunkload of goods he was peddling. Sunglasses, blenders, office supplies, watches, toys, hardware, sporting goods, kitchen utensils, bar lamps—you name it.

Von Villas was buddies with practically every merchant in the area, particularly those located near the division's schools. He'd make it a point to stop in, say hello, introduce himself, ask if they were having any problems, if there was anything he could do, and quickly charm his way into their hearts. Meanwhile, if they happened to have a case of those nifty coffee mugs they could let him have at wholesale, well, that would be just swell.

One time Von Villas went to the Schlitz brewery and told them that Club Dev was having a raffle and needed some prizes. They let him have a bunch of bar lights at wholesale, eight bucks a pop. Von Villas brought one into the station house, showed it around, and took orders. He eventually sold about twenty of them for fifteen bucks each. Inevitably, somebody later found out how much he had paid for them, and it got around. Things like this happened a number of times; after a while, a lot of the guys considered him a weasel.

The cops got used to Von Villas's constant wheeling and dealing. His phone conversations—about diamonds, gold, silver, pork bellies, a new subdivision or business venture—became part of Club Dev's audio landscape. He seemed to want everybody to know he was a successful businessman. When he was subdividing some land, he'd come into the station with his blueprints. He enjoyed all the props. If you asked him "How ya doing'?" Bob would light up and launch into a quick report: "Silver is up. I just made a thousand bucks!"

Once a year, Ray Romero hosted a meeting for burglary investigators from around the city, from Santa Monica to Lancaster, from Ventura County to Glendale. He called it the Mulholland North/South Meeting. Every police department and every LAPD division within gunshot of Mulholland Drive would attend. Romero needed doughnuts for all these burglary dicks, so he went to Von Villas, who got them wholesale from his personal doughnut hangout in Chatsworth. One year Romero met Von Villas at the shop to help him pick them up. There was Von Villas, acting the part of a benevolent king holding forth in his court. Everybody who came in knew him and gave him a warm greeting. The kids from Chatsworth High who hung out there fawned over him. The proprietors of the shop, a woman and her daughter, treated him like family.

But whatever you thought of Bob Von Villas, you had to admit he took good care of his own. If any of "his" merchants or businessmen ever had a situation—a noisy neighbor, a wayward child, a destructive tenant—Bob would take care of it. Many Club Dev cops who saw him in action were genuinely moved by his compassion and resolve. So even though he was a weasel, a lot of guys still admired him. Besides, anytime the division really did need something cheap or free—gifts for the Christmas raffle, food and drink for a picnic—Bob Von Villas, the division scrounger, was there to answer the call.

And then there was the matter of Sintic's widow. That was the real clincher for most of the guys at Club Dev. When they heard what Bobby had done for Linda, well, they didn't need to hear anything else.

Nick Sintic had been Club Dev's only fatality. He was shot and killed in 1976 during a robbery at the McDonald's at the corner of Devonshire and Reseda. He responded to a burglary call at six o'clock in the morning. He walked in through the front door very relaxed and nonchalant, figuring that at that hour it had to be a false alarm. Instead, he walked in on a hardened ex-con who had been pulling jobs at McDonald's restaurants all the way from Colorado. The guy blew Nick away as soon as he walked through the door. Then he barricaded himself in the restaurant and raped one of the female employees. When the SWAT team finally arrived the perp committed suicide. To this day, Sintic's picture still hangs on the wall in the entranceway at Club Dev.

Bob Von Villas was a good friend of Sintic and his wife, Linda. At the funeral, he was right at her side, comforting her. Over the years he became a surrogate father to Sintic's kids, who called him Uncle Bob. Every Christmas, he'd bring Linda, along with his wife, Judy, to all the Club Dev Christmas parties. He also helped Linda out financially. Nick Sintic didn't have any life insurance, so Linda had problems holding on to her house. Von Villas cut a deal with the bank to use his own good credit to help her refinance her home so she wouldn't lose it.

When word about this got around at Club Dev, the terms used to describe Von Villas sort of took on a different glow. Call him what you like—schemer, wheeler-dealer, sharpie—you had to smile now when you said it.

8

Officer Bob

JOE REINER WAS A NEW YORK COP FOR FIVE YEARS BEFORE HE moved west and joined the LAPD. He left the Big Apple in 1966 because he was appalled by the graft and corruption he encountered. "I got out of there just in the nick of time," he often said, referring to the scandals spurred by the Knapp Commission. "I got out of there clean."

Reiner looked and sounded like a streetwise New York cop. He was a handsome guy with dark hair, sturdy build, a New York accent, and an aggressive, outgoing personality. He was married to a Hollywood actress. He was slick but likable, a hustler, a people person, a guy who could pick up on strangers the moment he encountered them on the street.

Reiner was a sergeant at North Hollywood Division in 1972 when a new recruit named Bob Von Villas came under his immediate command. Reiner, ten years older than Von Villas, was immediately impressed by the sharp young officer, whom he affectionately called Bobby. Bobby was just like one of the kids he'd grown up with on the streets of New York; he had that innate street sense most L.A. kids simply didn't have. He also had an undeniable charisma. He could talk his way out of anything. He could talk his way into anything. Bobby just had a God-given talent for dealing with people. He was as sharp and quick-witted as they come.

After working with him over the next decade, Reiner would describe Von Villas as the most effective police officer he'd ever run across, either in New York or L.A. Von Villas would also become Reiner's best friend in the department.

But as capable as Bobby was, he was a wild one, a world-class hustler and philanderer—Reiner could see that right away. After knowing Bobby only a few weeks he warned him, "Don't ever tell me anything I can't tell the old man," meaning their captain. From that time on they had an agreement; Reiner asked no questions and Von Villas told him no lies. "I knew Bobby was doing things, minor things, that weren't according to the rules and regulations of the LAPD," Reiner later explained. "Particularly with women. He was a great womanizer. And I knew he was hustling outside work. But I didn't mind that. That was his nature."

Von Villas had tremendous confidence with women, and he also had an oversized sympathy for women who had been victimized by boyfriends or husbands. Bobby ran across many such victims through his police work and often talked them into hiring him as a bodyguard. Sometimes he'd talk his way into their beds. Occasionally, he did both.

Reiner accompanied Von Villas once on an off-duty job. Von Villas had met a woman who was being terrorized by an estranged boyfriend. "All we have to do is sit in her house for a while," Von Villas told Reiner. So they baby-sat her. Reiner left at two in the morning, but Von Villas stayed overnight.

"Bobby, how do you do it?" Reiner asked him the next day. "How do you get away with this stuff? One of these days Judy's gonna kill ya."

Despite his wild-dog ways, Von Villas was devoted to his wife and family. Every cop at Club Dev talked about his kids and bragged about their accomplishments, but none as much as Bob. He was very close to his two daughters, for a while serving as a coach of their swim team. He was always dragging out pictures of Michele and Shannon with their latest trophies and medals. One of the guys at the station made shadow boxes, so Von Villas brought in all their medals and had them mounted in beautiful custom-made holders. And he was crazy about Judy. He talked about her all the time. Sometimes he would start telling Reiner about how great she was in bed and Reiner would stop him. "Hey, that's your wife," he'd admonish him. "Don't talk to me about her, tell me about your girlfriends."

One time Reiner came across a beautiful young airline hostess from Hong Kong. Apparently, she had flown over to marry an American, but her fiancé got in a traffic accident and was in the hospital. When Reiner found her, she was stranded on a street corner in North Hollywood with no place to go. While she was telling Reiner her story, Von Villas drove by. Reiner directed him to drive her to the Mikado Hotel and help her get a room. "I don't want you spending the night with her," Reiner warned him. "Just take her there and leave."

Years later, when Reiner and Bobby had become close friends, Von Villas made a confession.

"Hey, Joe, you know I've never lied to you, so I gotta tell you this. Remember that girl? The Chinese girl?"

"Yeah. Don't tell me you went back to the hotel."

"Yeah, I went back."

"Don't tell me you had sex with her."

"Yeah, I did."

"Son of a bitch!"

By the mid-1970s, both Reiner and Von Villas had transferred to Club Dev. Their relationship continued to flourish, as did Von Villas's philandering. The bedroom communities of Club Dev were his happy hunting ground.

Von Villas was so smooth he could talk a woman into bed on the telephone. One time the guys at Club Dev heard him talking to a woman on the phone about her problems with her boyfriend. The conversation eventually turned very personal, and before long Von Villas asked her what she was wearing. "A black negligee? Well, let me ask you something," Bobby said. "How would you like a chance to seduce a policeman?"

The next thing they knew Bobby was out the door. After scoring with that line once, it became one of his favorites.

For a while Reiner was the officer in charge of the school car at Club Dev, which again put Von Villas under his command. Reiner found little need to give Bobby any direction. He was self-motivated, a go-getter, simply phenomenal at the job. There was nothing to do but turn him loose and watch him perform.

Reiner often accompanied Bobby on DAP field trips, riding along with him on the bus. They took kids everywhere—Dodger games, movies, the Magic Castle, Disneyland. Bobby always made the arrangements. He'd finagle special permits and access and discount rates—if not total freebies. The kids, aged nine through twelve, always had a great time. They thought Officer Bob was the greatest guy in the world. He knew how to keep kids happy, how to keep the action rolling. Sometimes, Reiner would just sit back and marvel at his gift.

Still, as his commanding officer, Reiner had occasion to chew his buddy out, especially about his tying up the damn telephone. Reiner also knew that whenever Bobby was out of his sight he was probably up to something. He was like a mischievous kid; as soon as he was out the door you knew he was getting in trouble. Not real trouble—just hustling work, discounts, deals, trying to pick up broads. Reiner didn't really want to catch him and spoil his fun. He kind of enjoyed Bobby's devilish streak. He was even drawn in by it on occasion.

Reiner and Von Villas worked a couple of punk rock concerts together at Devonshire Downs racetrack. The punkers were wild and had a lot of dope. Bobby had some tear gas and was like a little kid with a new toy. Whenever a group of punkers gave him some lip, he'd squirt their car full of tear gas. Then, after the concert, he'd point to all the cars he'd gassed, and he and Reiner would sit back and watch. The punkers would get in their cars, and a few seconds later, they'd start falling out on the ground, coughing and gasping for air—as Reiner and Von Villas broke into hysterics.

A lot of times the kids would be itching for a fight, and Reiner was more than ready to take them on. He liked to fight; that was his way. But Von Villas was a negotiator, and Reiner wound up learning a lot from him.

One of the biggest problems in the Club Dev communities was raucous *Risky Business*-type house parties thrown by teenagers and young adults. Somebody's parents would leave town for the weekend, word would spread all over the Valley, and four hundred kids would show up. Reiner developed his own strategy for handling these affairs.

Unlike Von Villas, Reiner was basically a cop from the old school. His inclination was always to send in the troops and bust some heads. The only problem was that you had to have a reason before you could crash into a house full of teenagers and start carting them off. So he came up with an ingenious plan. He'd send in a decoy—a lone police officer—to close down the party. When the kids laughed at this Lone Ranger, or attacked him, Reiner and his troops would charge down the hill and clear the place out.

This usually worked. Club Dev would receive a complaint, and Reiner would get on the radio and position his troops. He'd get all the squad cars and motorcycles together about a block away from the party. A lot of the cops loved these little soirees. With Reiner handling them, they knew there was probably going to be a fight, maybe a full-scale melee. One of the job's universal dark secrets is that many cops, like football players, enjoy a little violence. And in Los Angeles, where Chief Gates promoted a cowboy mentality, a little roughhousing was nearly always deemed acceptable, particularly with regard to drug busts or crowd control.

When he had about fifteen cowboys together, Reiner would select a "volunteer"—Bobby Von Villas—to drive up to the party and tell the kids to knock it off. Reiner always tagged Bobby because he was a hot dog who enjoyed being in the spotlight. Besides, he was so much fun to watch.

Von Villas would drive up to the house in a black and white, all alone, in full uniform, and would proceed through an elaborate ritual. Usually the stereo was blaring, hundreds of people were crawling through the house, kids were fornicating and pissing and puking on the lawn, guys were lying around out front drinking beer, raising hell, throwing bottles. Bobby would park right in front. He knew, of course, that another scout with a radio, usually Reiner, was watching him and that the Club Dev cowboys were waiting around the corner.

If anybody attacked him, the cops would sweep down like the cavalry and bust up the place.

As Von Villas stepped out of his car, his impeccable military bearing would immediately command attention. He'd walk around to the back of the black and white and open the trunk, taking out his helmet bag. Very slowly, as his audience grew, he'd unzip the bag, take out his riot helmet, and place it over his head. His motions would be exaggerated, slow and deliberate. He'd take his time adjusting the chin strap, making sure it fit just right. Next, he'd slowly reach back into the bag for his gloves. He'd pull them on slowly, tugging out each and every wrinkle. By now, the revelers would be thinking, Who the hell is this guy? What's he think one guy is gonna do? Von Villas would zip up his bag, carefully put it back, and close the trunk. Then he'd take his PR-42 baton out of his baton holster, put his keys away, straighten himself out like he was preparing for inspection, and march straight up to the front door. Sometimes he'd whistle a chipper little tune, as if he didn't have a care in the world.

"Good evening, ladies and gentlemen," Bobby would address the drunken crowd at the door. "Are you enjoying yourselves tonight?" He never spoke discourteously, never made derogatory or disparaging remarks, never used foul language or called anyone a bad name. The kids would wonder at this guy. Next, he'd gently press his way into the living room. "Excuse me, would you mind moving that bottle so I don't step on it?" he'd ask. When he found the host, he'd tell him, "I'm sorry, but we've received some calls, some complaints, and I'm afraid I'm going to have to ask you to close this party down."

The reaction, of course, would be laughter. This one guy was gonna close down the party? As Von Villas pressed his position, the laughter would turn to jeers, and before long somebody would throw something or push or jostle him out the door and slam it in his face. In moments, the Club Dev cavalry would charge around the corner, kick in the door, and crash through the house. A few kids would get their heads busted, many more would get carted off to jail, the house would get wrecked, and complaints would later be filed against the department. But the Club Dev cowboys had a wild and woolly time.

The only problem was that all too often, Von Villas was so damn good he succeeded in closing down the party all by himself. He'd keep talking, politely and respectfully, and before long he'd become everybody's buddy and they'd finally listen to him and do exactly as directed.

Afterward, the other guys would really get on his case. "What the hell did you do that for? We wanted to kick some ass!" they'd complain. So after a while, they wouldn't let Bobby do party patrol anymore. He ruined everything.

Von Villas always played the good cop. He always had a big smile on his face and treated everyone with respect. It was an unorthodox approach, but it worked; people he arrested often joked with him like he was an old friend. Reiner, on the other hand, was always getting into fights. He'd go on calls with Von Villas where they'd confront a perp, and Reiner would get attacked. Although he had far more experience, Reiner found himself learning a lot from Bobby.

Von Villas was a master at the art of generating voluntary compliance, or what some cops call "verbal judo." He could instantly read and redirect people; he didn't have to use force. He had presence of mind under pressure. He instinctively knew that police work was 98 percent verbal interaction. Unfortunately, the police academy only taught cops the other 2 percent of the job. The really important part—knowing how to talk to people—you either had or you didn't. Bobby had it.

Von Villas knew how to avoid expressions that could aggravate people in distress, like the vaguely threatening "Come here." Instead, he'd say, "Excuse me, I need to chat with you a second." He never put people on the defensive by deriding them with a "Don't you know any better?" Instead, he focused on the behavior, not the person: "I know that you know better, so tell me what happened." He used expressions of reassurance like "Let me see if I understand your position," followed by a restatement of the person's problem, which served to absorb and defuse his or her frustration so he could get them to act less destructively. And nobody ever doubted Officer Bob when he told someone, with genuine compassion at just the right moment, "It's going to be all right."

Von Villas knew that a cocked tongue was a dangerous weapon. He knew that the old-fashioned technique of ordering people around was often counterproductive, and he knew it long before most of the LAPD brass, who were still old-school military types. He knew that someday, when anachronisms like Chief Gates finally faded away, all cops would be like him.

Reiner and Von Villas never went to bars, which was unusual for a pair of cop buddies, but Von Villas wasn't a drinker. He and Reiner spent most of their time on social outings talking about business. Everything was business with Bobby, and Reiner kind of liked that. Bobby was constantly plotting and planning, buying commodities, talking about a development, thinking about how he could make a buck off something. A lot of the other guys called him a wheeler-dealer, but Reiner didn't see him that way. He saw him as a businessman. Everyone he knew who did business with Bobby always made out—including Reiner himself.

Reiner, who also lived in Simi Valley, started dabbling in real estate there in 1976. He knew property values, so when Von Villas came to him with a deal in 1978, he knew it was a winner. Bobby had befriended a contractor who owned a piece of prime property in Bell Canyon, a pricey new subdivision in the Simi Hills. All the lots were at least a half-acre, and all the front yard fences had to be white and in the western style. The contractor was maxed out and couldn't get the construction loan he needed to develop the land. Von Villas put together a deal with the contractor and Reiner. They each put $13,500 down for a one-third share. Bobby wrangled a construction loan, and they built a house and sold it instantly—each of them making $50,000 on the sale.

Reiner and Bobby immediately jumped into another deal. Von Villas knew a real estate agent, an ex-cop, who got them three apartment buildings in downtown L.A. for the bargain price of $80,000. They put $18,000 down and became slumlords. The idea was to hold on to the buildings for a while, fix them up a bit, and sell them at a big profit.

The apartments were in a bad neighborhood on East Seventy-second Street and were run-down and crammed with Mexicans. Reiner and Von Villas spent a lot of time together, driving all the way downtown every month to do some fix-up work and pick up the rent. They had an onsite manager who collected the rent in cash, because few tenants had checking accounts. Each month the manager would hand them a paper bag filled with three thousand dollars in bills. Reiner would walk out the door with his gun in hand, just under his jacket. Men would be sitting around on the steps, drinking beer, and they all knew the two gringos had the money. "God, Bobby, we're gonna get killed one of these days," Reiner complained after a few nerve-racking sessions.

They came up with a plan to provide some insurance against a robbery. They told their manager not to tell anyone they were cops. Instead, they had him spread the word they were Mafia, that they worked for a powerful family that was into drugs, prostitution, gambling, extortion—the works. Pretty soon it got around the complex, and, sure enough, nobody ever messed with Reiner and Von Villas. Indeed, when the two men dressed up in pin-striped business suits—which they made it a point to do—they looked the part. Reiner, with his stocky build, full head of dark, slicked-back hair, and thick New York accent, could have passed for a capo. And Von Villas, as long as he kept his mouth shut and kept a lid on the charm, could appear as forbidding as any syndicate button man.

As it turned out, they could have done without the charade, for Bobby quickly endeared himself to their tenants. Reiner couldn't believe all the compassion Von Villas had for them. Everything had to be brought up to proper living standards. Bobby took great pains to make sure the tenants were comfortable and their apartments were in good repair. Along the way, he learned a lot of hard lessons. Von Villas wanted his tenants to have wall-to-wall carpeting, so he'd pull some old carpet out of Dumpsters behind carpet stores and put it in. He didn't know that the standard drill among his tenants was to take a bucket of water with ammonia and throw it on the floor, which quickly ruined his decorating efforts. Every window in the units was broken out, so Bobby installed new Plexiglas. "Let's see them break that out," he told Reiner. Unfortunately, instead of washing the windows with soap and water, the tenants used kitchen cleanser and scratched them badly.

Whenever a tenant was short on rent, Bobby would work something out with him. He never belittled or threatened anyone, and damn if his nice-guy approach didn't work again, even in the ghetto. In the two years they owned the buildings, they were only stiffed for a hundred dollars. Reiner was convinced that their success was due totally to Bobby's good nature.

They sold the buildings after two years for $130,000, a $50,000 profit in addition to the two grand in rent they had been pocketing every month after expenses. The guys at Club Dev could say what they liked; Reiner liked doing business with Bobby Von Villas.

Reiner wanted to start other ventures, but things changed after Von Villas bought his ranch in Tapo Canyon in 1979. Reiner felt that it was the beginning of Bobby's downfall.

Von Villas was ecstatic when he got his ranch. Not only did he love living and working there with the horses in the beautiful wide-open spaces, but he was also convinced he could make a bundle doing a little development on the side. The way Bobby talked, you'd have thought he made the best land investment since Isaac Newton Van Nuys bought most of the Valley south of Roscoe Boulevard for $115,000 in 1869.

Von Villas spent two years trying to subdivide his property. He wanted to put in a cul-de-sac, build four houses, and make a quick hundred grand. The only problem was that the city council wouldn't let him subdivide. Time after time he met with the planning commissioners, but he could never persuade them. Von Villas had always been able to talk anybody into anything—but not this time. It was hard for him to swallow. Plus he had a $70,000 balloon payment to make on the ranch. If he didn't come up with the money by a certain date, he'd lose the property.

At one point, Von Villas asked Reiner and his wife to lend him $100,000. Reiner's wife had the money, but neither she nor Joe felt it was a good idea. It made Joe wonder how Bobby's deals were going. He knew Bobby had lost some money in commodities, which was a shame, because for a while he was up about thirty grand. Sugar was going up, and Bobby was making five hundred, a thousand a day on paper. Reiner would grab him and say, "Bobby, call your broker right now and tell him to sell!"

"No, one more day," Bobby always said.

Finally, in 1982 Von Villas lost his ranch. He managed to trade into another beautiful home in Simi Valley. There was nothing wrong with the new house. But it wasn't the ranch.

Bobby wasn't much fun after that. Reiner sensed that something was very wrong.

About the same time Bob Von Villas started having money problems, his natural inclination for hustling—both women and work—got him in trouble at Club Dev.

Lieutenant Higbee, like most cops at Devonshire, was impressed with Von Villas's extraordinary people skills, but he didn't entirely trust him. Working the J car gave Von Villas a lot of freedom, and Higbee knew that freedom could get a cop like Von Villas into trouble. One officer who had previously worked with Von Villas, Ron Skyvnick, had to be pulled from the J car because he took advantage of the minimal supervision and spent too much department time running his own business, a security firm in Simi Valley.

Higbee had good reason to worry about Von Villas. Everybody knew Von Villas could make brass if he wanted to, but he had made a deliberate decision not to advance beyond policeman II. He considered working with juveniles to be his calling. The J car assignment also allowed him the freedom to pursue his personal business ventures. Von Villas had no intention of getting himself promoted out of his dream job.

Unfortunately, Von Villas wasn't entirely discreet about his on-the-job hustling. One of his common ploys was to review police reports about assaults against women. He'd call up the victim and offer his services as an off-duty bodyguard. He would arrange a meeting with the woman and invariably wind up with a personal-security job, which often also landed him in bed with his client.

It was perhaps inevitable that Lieutenant Higbee would learn of one of these liaisons, and he did in November 1982. Higbee gave Von Villas a two-week suspension, effective in January 1983. He also told Von Villas he would be pulled from the J car so he could be placed under tighter departmental supervision.

Higbee reminded Von Villas that the school car wasn't meant as a permanent assignment. Perhaps Von Villas wasn't interested in advancement, but other men in the department were, and they could benefit from serving a term of duty there.

Von Villas protested vociferously, claiming—rightly so—that no one in the division could match his qualifications for the job. The J car was more than an assignment to him; it was his vocation. But Higbee held his ground.

Before long, Higbee was barraged by letters of protest. Irate teachers and principals wrote and told him what a gifted and dedicated man Bob Von Villas was, about the tremendous impact he had on the kids. A pair of teachers from Chatsworth High were so upset they showed up at Club Dev and barged into Higbee's office and demanded that Von Villas be reassigned to the school car.

One of these was Shirley Hess, a local social studies teacher who taught the Youth and Law Program, a special curriculum designed to improve relations between young people and the judicial system. Her classes studied the role of police in government, held mock trials, and brought in speakers. Von Villas frequently came on his day off to talk to her classes or to play the Police Patrol game, which gave students the chance to react the way they thought the police would react to a particular situation. Because of Officer Von Villas, it was a rave success.

Hess told Higbee how Von Villas put in many hours of his own time counseling troubled youths. "He is a very special person on our campus," Hess told Higbee. "He always treats children with dignity and respect. The students all like him, but they say, 'Are all policemen like him, though?' " As far as Shirley Hess was concerned, they all damn well should be like Officer Bob Von Villas. She was so mad at Higbee she wrote a letter to Chief Gates and started a petition. Higbee wasn't about to tell her he was pulling Von Villas from the J car for diddling some gal he met through his police work, but he was tempted.

Many people noticed a dramatic change in Bobby after he was removed from duty as a youth officer. He was bitter and continued to insist that the department was blind, that the LAPD didn't appreciate him. "They have no right to do this to me," he told Ray Romero shortly after he was pulled from the J car and put back on regular patrol.

"Bob, you've got to be kidding," Romero said. He tried to make Von Villas understand that the department couldn't tolerate the flagrant indiscretion of using police files to solicit work. And other things.

But Bobby didn't see it that way. He spent a lot of time visiting with his friend and sympathetic ear, Christine Lund. While the newscaster sat at her spinning wheel, the disillusioned cop railed for hours about the uncaring, insensitive, myopic, archaic LAPD.

Officer Bob couldn't accept the fact that they just didn't seem to give a damn about the kids.

9

Trouble

HOLLYWOOD COSMETOLOGIST AND CUSTOM WIG MAKER DARLIS Chefalo had seen it all during her long career. She had worked on the lot at Columbia and Universal and as a staffer and freelancer for dozens of TV shows. She had groomed innumerable movie and TV stars—on and off the set—and developed the look for all manner of freaks, from space aliens to dummy Charlie McCarthy.

Like most industry veterans, Chefalo had developed the requisite sense of humor and world-weary appreciation for the bizarre. It would be hard to shock Darlis with a request. The raspy-voiced redhead would simply laugh and say, "All right, deary. Tell me again about the new you that you have in mind." Nonetheless, she would never forget Dick and Bob, a pair of "federal agents" who were sent to her by Jack Stone in the fall of 1982.

Stone was doing a favor for his actor buddy Robert Fuller. According to Stone, the two feds needed professional disguises to go undercover. Fuller had wanted Stone, the best makeup man in the business, to help them out. Unfortunately, Stone couldn't do the job—he was going into the hospital to be treated for cancer—so he recommended his colleague Darlis Chefalo instead. Jack Stone had advised the agents that he thought their plan was risky, for even the very best makeup job can usually be detected. It's one thing to fool the camera, another entirely to fool a murderous *narcotraficante* sitting across the table from you at a drug deal. But they went ahead and made an appointment to meet Chefalo.

When they arrived at her house in Hollywood, Dick and Bob didn't give Chefalo any last names. They seemed pleasant—even upbeat—like they were enjoying themselves. "We're going to work an undercover operation," Dick told her. "We want to look older, like fifty-year-old Mexican drug dealers."

"Yeah," said Bob. "I want to look dissipated. Really wasted."

Chefalo fit them for wigs, helping them select color swatches of synthetic hair that matched the phony beards that had already been supplied by Jack Stone.

When Dick and Bob came back on November 18 to pick up their custom-made salt-and-pepper wigs, Chefalo spent a few hours showing them how to apply makeup. It was a Friday afternoon, and the boys were in a party mood. Chefalo poured drinks and joked with them as she went about her work, explaining what she was doing as she went along. She used dark brown makeup, ash gold, shades thirty to thirty-six, and both light and dark Egyptian. She had to color Dick's light eyelashes. Although she assured him that many Mexicans have blue eyes, he insisted on hiding his behind dark glasses to best achieve the desired effect.

Bob wanted his complexion even darker. She showed him how to use the different pencils, brushes, sponges, and stipple. She applied their beards, one mustache (on Dick), and both wigs and schooled them in the use of liquid adhesives. At their request, she also showed them how to apply spray-on scars.

Before their very eyes, Dick and Bob were transformed into a pair of *muy malos hombres*. They really got a kick out of it. They polished off nearly a fifth of Crown Royal while Chefalo practiced her art, laughing and cracking jokes like a couple of marines on R and R.

When Chefalo was finally done, they paid her in cash for the wigs, about $250 apiece, a real bargain considering they were worth as much as $700. Stone had inveigled Darlis into giving them to the guys at just a little more than cost. She tried to write them a receipt, but Dick snatched the paper from her hand. "You never saw us," he said.

"Won't you be getting reimbursed?" she asked.

"Naw, we don't need any records," Dick said. "The department won't pay. Just keep your mouth shut."

Well, Chefalo thought, whatever. But it struck her as strange. "Sit back down so I can take off your makeup," she directed.

"No, leave it on," Dick and Bob both chimed. They were still mugging before the large bank of wardrobe mirrors, laughing, cutting up. They really enjoyed their transformation into bad-ass desperadoes. Plus, they were loaded.

Chefalo figured the two feds probably wanted to try to pick up girls in some sleazy bar while wearing their new disguises. Or fool some of their friends—a lot of clients liked to do that. Well, she shrugged, it takes all kinds.

Northridge Fashion Plaza, located just a mile from Devonshire Division headquarters, is a large, upscale shopping mall typical of those found in the San Fernando Valley. The area is well patrolled by private security officers and by cops from Club Dev. It's not a place generally targeted by professional holdup men. Nonetheless, on the evening of November 22, 1982, a pair of armed robbers boldly walked into the Schaffer and Sons jewelry store on the second floor and made off with $200,000 in gems, primarily loose diamonds.

Eyewitnesses described the two men as having dark complexions with salt and pepper hair and beards. While one of the men stationed himself outside as a lookout, the other entered the store just moments before it was about to close for the night. He was a male Caucasian in his forties, dark skinned, about six feet tall, wearing a black overcoat. The man walked up to one of the display cases and placed a brown attaché case on top of it. He was very calm. "Good evening, ladies," he said cordially, addressing the three female employees of the store. Then he reached into the attaché case and pulled out a large-caliber revolver. One of the ladies noticed that he was wearing surgical gloves and that he had an unnaturally ruddy complexion, possibly from makeup.

The man then ushered the three women to the restroom in the back of the store, where he tied them up and gagged two of them with duct tape. By the time they managed to free themselves, some forty minutes later, the thieves were gone. They had looted the drawers and display cases, then carefully placed the leather coverings over them—just like the employees did each evening—to make the store look like it had been properly closed for the night.

A mall security guard actually confronted one of the men inside the store while he was covering the display cases. The man came to the door and spoke to him, asking, "Is there anything I can do for you?" The man's calm, assured reply convinced the guard that he was a store manager and that nothing was amiss.

A few minutes later, a pair of shoppers saw two men with dark complexions and dark salt and pepper hair and beards "acting strange" in the parking lot outside the mall. One of them was peeling off a pair of surgical gloves.

The day after the robbery, Detective Ray Romero sat down at his desk and read the police report. "Hey, this really sounds like some ex-cons," he exclaimed to some of the guys hanging around his office. "And if it's not ex-cons," he laughed, "then it must be cops. I mean, look at all this cop talk."

Romero noted that the armed perpetrator had instructed the victims to "put your hands behind your back, palms together" before he taped them up. Romero found that interesting—it was the exact command officers learned at the LAPD police academy. The perp had also told the three ladies that his partner was monitoring a Rover police radio so they would know if any cops were in the area.

The 1982 Club Dev Christmas party was held at Granada Hills Golf Course on December 9. Bob Von Villas arrived not only with his wife, Judy, but with Linda Sintic and another police widow, Joyce Reynolds.

Bob brought Linda and Joyce with him to a lot of Club Dev social gatherings. He made it a point to make sure they knew about these events and that they had transportation. Bob Von Villas knew how important it was to them.

At first, when a cop's wife loses her husband, she gets an outpouring of comfort and support. The other cops and their wives are always there to help any way they can—making funeral arrangements, taking care of the kids, helping out with finances. But eventually, people stop coming around and the widow feels like she not only lost her husband but her friends as well. She no longer has a social life, because for cops, social life always involves other cops and their wives. Von Villas knew this and he saw to it that Joyce and Linda got invited to division picnics, barbecues, and all the other social gatherings of the Club Dev police family. Most of the time he simply picked them up and brought them along.

Bob and Joyce had become like brother and sister. Bob had become godfather to Joyce's daughter Julie, who had spent years in the DAPs going on field trips with Bob. When Bob had the ranch, Julie would come out to ride, and she was always welcome at the Von Villas house. Bob had become her replacement father.

Bob and Joyce danced together at the Christmas gala, and Joyce filled Bob in about Julie. She was a grown woman now. In fact, she was getting married the day after Christmas. They talked about the arrangements for the small wedding reception Joyce planned at her home, and Bob volunteered to serve as bartender.

Joyce also told Bob how Julie was upset about having to leave her job. The boy she was marrying lived in Montana and she planned to move there with him after the honeymoon. Julie worked as a medical technician at an allergy testing lab in Reseda and had grown very fond of her boss, Dr. Ogilvie. So had Joyce, who met with Julie and Dr. Ogilvie frequently at the lab and for lunch.

Dr. Jan Ogilvie, a black woman in her late thirties, was very fond of Julie, and she paid and treated her well. But Ogilvie was going through a horrible and complicated divorce from her husband, a white man named Thomas Weed, who was her partner at the lab. Tom Weed was verbally abusive and treated Julie like a child. Julie hated him. She would be happy not to see him anymore but sad about leaving Dr. Ogilvie.

Bob listened attentively, as he always did, and then he shared with Joyce some of his own frustrations about his upcoming two-week suspension and his being taken out of the J car. "I'm tired of being an honest cop," Bob told Joyce. "I get in as much trouble being honest as I would if I were dirty. If you hear of any jobs I can do for money, let me know. There isn't any job I wouldn't do for money, including murder. I'll do anything for money."

Great debate would one day ensue over whether this conversation actually took place as Joyce Reynolds claimed. And if it had, was Von Villas serious? Being facetious? Or simply venting his frustration?

In mid-December Mike Moen threw a blowout Christmas party for Devonshire detectives at his Chatsworth home—an event that had become the traditional follow-up to the official Club Dev bash. Invariably, some sixty cops, wives, dates, and assorted friends of the department would party late into the night. Although these soirees often turned a bit wild according to the standards of a quiet bedroom community like Chatsworth, for some reason Moen's neighbors never complained.

Although Bob Von Villas wasn't a detective, he was always invited to Moen's parties. Moen's 1982 Yule bash was the first time most Club Dev dicks first became aware that Richard Ford and Bob Von Villas had become buddies. The two new "partners" made quite an impression when they arrived that night.

Ray Romero was in Moen's dining room, picking at the buffet, when he looked out the window and saw Dick Ford and Bob Von Villas walking up to the house, accompanied by their wives. The two cops were dressed to kill and strutting like roosters. They both sported fancy new ten-gallon hats cocked across their foreheads, spanking new cowboy shirts, and expensive new snakeskin boots. As they came up the walkway they snickered and shared a few muffled jokes. Something about the way they were laughing made Romero uneasy.

Ford and Von Villas were fashionably late—the last to arrive, in fact—and they made a grand entrance. "Jesus Christ, you guys really look sharp!" Romero exclaimed. He watched the two men strut through the kitchen and den, showing off their new threads, enjoying the hoots from the guys. He listened as they bragged about the great deals they'd gotten on their new hats and boots. They really made a rakish pair, and Lillian and Judy were probably the two best-looking wives in the department. Lillian Ford was dressed to the nines and flashing cleavage, as well as a sparkling new diamond ring. Judy Von Villas was draped in a fur. To some of the guys, it seemed a bit much. The two beautiful, giddy couples were really showing off—and enjoying it.

Later that evening as Ray Romero was walking to his car, he realized what had bothered him earlier. "Those guys were laughing at us," Romero told his wife. "Ford and Von Villas think we're all a bunch of squares. Dumb shits. They think they're hipper and smarter than everybody else."

Dr. Ogilvie had caught the latest California craze. Health-obsessed yuppies were eager to plunk down $345 for a complete battery of citotoxic and RAST and GGT enzyme blood tests so they could be counseled about the reaction of their bodies to different foods and potential allergy-provoking materials. The Ford/ Kennedy Medical Laboratory was pleased to oblige. The lab's name had no real significance—Dr. Ogilvie had chosen it because it sounded reputable. Indeed, the lab was so successful—to the tune of about $15,000 per month in net profits— that Dr. Ogilvie had just opened a second one in Costa Mesa. Phoenix would be next.

Only in her late thirties, Dr. Ogilvie was a respected and successful PhD and lab clinician, an intelligent, knowledgeable, and affluent businesswoman. An avid feminist and a voracious socializer, she made the rounds of practically every professional women's meeting in L.A. She dined with important people—council-men, physicians, financiers. She was also voluptuous, sexy, and vivacious. She felt she had it made.

The only problem was her husband.

Jan Ogilvie had married Thomas Weed in Las Vegas in November 1981, just months after she opened the lab. She and Tom made a strange couple. She was an intellectual, a professional black woman; he was a white-bread salesman jock. He was about fifty, a new arrival to L.A. from Toronto who had suddenly become Mr. Southern California, always tanned and fit, sporting boating clothes and a new curly blond wig.

Thomas Weed had accompanied Ogilvie to allergy clinic seminars in Boston and Wyoming, and he began working at the lab as an administrator, handling payroll, budgets, advertising, and employee benefits. But three months after their wedding, the marriage went sour. They broke up for the first time in January 1982, when Weed moved out of their Woodland Hills home and into an apartment complex in Northridge. Ogilvie eventually moved to a house in Canoga Park. After that, they struggled through a turbulent on-again, off-again relationship until it ended for good and they began divorce proceedings in October 1982.

Despite their personal problems, Weed continued to work at the lab; he was still her legal partner. Ogilvie had started the business with an investment of $23,000 of her money; Tom had contributed about $1,200 worth of art and plants. Initially, Ogilvie had no written or verbal agreement with Weed about ownership of the lab. But in January 1982, when they first separated, she signed an agreement granting Weed 35 percent of the business. She claimed that Tom had beaten her into signing the contract.

Now that they were divorcing, she had filed a lawsuit contesting the agreement. The divorce quickly degenerated into a quagmire of emotional disputes and legal countersuits. The pair frequently engaged in screaming matches in which they pushed and shoved each other, and Dr. Ogilvie was weary of all the verbal and physical abuse. Finally, one of their late-night confrontations turned violent and Tom beat her up. The Polaroids taken of Jan by her neighbor showed her with black eyes, a swollen mouth, and bruises on her face.

Nearly all of Jan's twelve female employees at the lab became entangled in the ongoing Weed/Ogilvie civil war. One of Dr. Ogilvie's favorites was a twenty-year-old medical technician named Julie Rabold. Dr. Ogilvie felt a motherly instinct toward Julie; Tom Weed often took his anger out on her because she was "Jan's little girl." Tom was drinking at the office now, so his abuse often turned ugly.

Julie's mother, Joyce Reynolds, often visited the lab and went to lunch with the gang. At one of these lunches in the fall of 1982, Dr. Ogilvie was distraught about her marital problems. Weed was harassing her, starting fights, embarrassing her in front of the employees, contradicting her directives. While spilling her tale of woe, Julie Rabold joked, "Why don't you just hire a hit man and get rid of him?" Everybody had laughed.

Dr. Ogilvie's relationship with Weed continued to deteriorate. The screaming matches turned increasingly violent. During one, Tom struck her in the chest, kicked her in the back, and shut the door on her arm. Dr. Ogilvie filed a police report on October 19, 1982. A month later, after another fracas, Weed went on the offensive and filed charges against her after she slapped him in the face. In December they went at it again and Weed threw a heavy ledger book at her. One of the women in the office called the police and they came and took Tom Weed away.

Julie told Dr. Ogilvie that she had a friend, a cop over at Devonshire Division, who could help her "take care of" Tom Weed. In mid-December, at a restaurant called Wolfies in Reseda, Joyce Reynolds told her the same thing. Dr. Ogilvie was getting tired, worn down. Her lawyer, Mr. Brot, wasn't making any progress with a settlement. She broke down and sobbed.

10

The Shop

BOB VON VILLAS STOPPED BY UNEXPECTEDLY TO SEE BRUCE ADAMS one evening in mid-December. As Bob pulled up Adams's driveway and got out of his Pontiac, he saw Bruce in his garage working on a car. "Come here, Doc, I want to show you something," said Von Villas.

The cop opened his trunk and pulled out a shoe box. He laughed as he showed Adams the contents. It was filled with small manila envelopes—bindles of loose diamonds. The diamonds had been categorized. Each bindle was marked to indicate carat, brilliance, shape, type of stone, and low and high appraisal of value.

"What's this?" Adams asked.

"Oh, I sold some property and took these as partial payment," Von Villas said. "I want to get some stuff."

"Yeah?"

"I want some stereo speakers, seat covers, stuff for my Pontiac. I figured maybe you could get it for me for some diamonds." Von Villas knew Adams was tight with the assistant manager of an auto parts store. He gave Adams his shopping list. Bruce told him he'd look into it.

Von Villas pulled out a big wad of cash. He peeled off five hundred dollars and handed it to Adams. "I want you to find a location," he said.

"A location for what?"

"For the auto shop. Use this for the deposit." Von Villas also explained that he wanted to start an escort service and run it out of a back room at the shop.

Adams thought hard as he took a heavy pull on his Marlboro. It would be nice to have his own shop. He knew a lot of people in the Valley who would bring him their business. He could do pretty well. Maybe he could live with this arrangement. Ford and Von Villas wanted to use him as a front for an escort service? He could live with that.

Besides he couldn't say no. They might not trust him to keep quiet. He'd have to get out of town—or go straight to the police. And how could he do that? These guys were the police.

Adams laughed as he stuffed the five C-notes in his pocket. "So, partner, where do you think we should set up shop?"

"I was thinking Chatsworth," said Von Villas. "Somewhere between my place in Simi and division headquarters. That would make it easy for me to stop by before and after work. Same for Dickie. And if we keep it close enough, we can bring you plenty of work out of Devonshire."

Bruce found a location on Owensmouth Avenue in Chatsworth, a small unit that was part of an L-shaped industrial minicomplex. It had a bay area large enough for three cars, plenty of parking spaces out front, and a small office. It was nothing special; just perfect for a mechanic going out on his own. And it was totally inconspicuous.

Chatsworth was perhaps the last town in the Valley to retain its rural character. Founded in 1880 and named after Chatsworth, England, it still had many vegetable patches, orchards, and horse ranches. But the subdivisions were growing, crowding out the horses and felling the lines of eucalyptus that had once served as windbreaks for farms. Chatsworth was also in the throes of massive office construction, primarily for the high-tech firms that were flocking to the area. Chatsworth was going the way of the Valley, but it wasn't there yet. It still had some beautiful country.

The shop on Owensmouth was just a few blocks east of Chatsworth Park, home of the Devil's Slide Trail and those great western movie rock formations. Stony Point, another famous backdrop for movies, was a few blocks north. The shop was just a few blocks south of Devonshire Street. If you traveled east just a few miles, Devonshire took you right to Club Dev headquarters in Northridge; if you went west, Devonshire would take you to the winding Santa Susana Pass Road and into Simi Valley.

After he found the spot for the shop, Adams took Von Villas over to meet his buddy Charlie at an auto parts shop in Van Nuys. He introduced Von Villas as "my new partner." Von Villas shopped for the stuff he wanted while Adams picked out things he needed for the new shop. As luck would have it, Charlie wanted to give his wife a diamond for Christmas. He told Bruce to come back after eight that evening, when the manager would be gone, so they could make a deal.

Von Villas gave Adams an envelope with three diamonds in it worth about $1,200, which Bruce later turned over to Charlie. He got everything his new partner wanted—two SX 300 Sparkomatic automobile receivers/equalizers (list two hundred dollars each), eight Sparkomatic six-by-nine inch four-way speakers (one hundred dollars a pair), two five-inch round Sparkomatic speakers (eighty dollars a pair), a set of brown sheepskin seat covers for a 1969 Pontiac Grand Prix and a set of black sheepskin seat covers for a 1974 Camaro (thirty dollars per seat), and an AC-Delco speedometer cable for the Grand Prix (twenty-two dollars).

Adams and Von Villas spent the next few days running around town getting what they needed for the shop. Again, Von Villas traded diamonds, making deals for a truckload of office furniture, a tool kit, and the air compressor Bruce needed for his pneumatic tools.

Von Villas came up with the name for the shop: International Automotive of Chatsworth. He also decided on a couple of names for their prostitution racket: Classy Ladies and Classy Coeds.

Shirley Adams didn't like the vibes she got from Bob Von Villas. Unlike Richard Ford, who was warm and affable, Bob seemed cold and calculating. She knew he wasn't getting involved with her husband out of friendship. Bruce told her that Bob was just an investor, a wheeler-dealer looking for a tax dodge. Like Ford, he'd be able to steer a lot of Club Dev business his way. Bruce painted a very nice picture of the venture; he'd be a part owner, plus he'd pull down a regular salary.

Still, the idea of Bruce going into business with two cops didn't sit right with Shirley. She knew Bruce would end up the workhorse. His silent partners weren't going to get their hands dirty. She argued with Bruce about it, but he insisted the shop would give them a better life.

Shirley's intuition proved right almost from the start. Christmas approached, but Bruce's regular salary failed to materialize. Von Villas controlled the company checkbook and he immediately began cutting Bruce's salary and withholding payments, always with excuses about waiting until business got going at the shop. An ongoing dance had begun. Bruce would complain to Ford. Dick would talk to Bob. Bob would finally loosen the purse strings.

The Fords invited Bruce and Shirley over to their house for Christmas. Lillian's family was there and Lillian put out a huge buffet dinner. Dick was the generous and gracious host. The Fords bought presents for each of the Adamses' little girls, and they gave Marilyn and Eric twenty dollars each.

Shirley could see how Dick's daughter, Christina, was the apple of his eye. She was a sweet, well-mannered girl who went to Catholic school. Dick considered her religious schooling extremely important and insisted on going to church with her every Sunday.

As Bruce and Shirley were leaving, Dick gave Shirley a kiss and slipped a hundred-dollar bill into her hand. "Buy some more stuff for the kids for Christmas," he said.

Mike Moen soon became convinced that something was going on between Ford and Von Villas. He'd see Ford on the phone at Club Dev, sitting at his desk, while Von Villas was on the phone across the squad room. He could tell they were talking to each other. Moen assumed they were using the phones to avoid a reprimand for discussing private business on the job. When Ford finally told him about his partnership with Von Villas, Moen told him to be careful.

"I know, I know," said Ford.

When Ray Romero heard that Ford was in business with Von Villas, he took the detective aside and offered him some advice. "Man, you better watch yourself. That guy'll screw you."

"Nah, I know how to handle him," Ford replied.

Right before Christmas, Von Villas asked a number of the guys at Club Dev if they were interested in buying some diamonds. They made wonderful gifts, great investments, and he could get them a great deal. Most of the guys shook their heads and laughed. Good old Bobby, the division scrounger. One week he's pushing sugar futures, the next it's silver or Bell Canyon condos or office products or lube jobs at his new auto shop. So now he's got diamonds.

According to at least one source, Richard Ford was also trying to unload some diamonds. Something about a relative of Lillian's in Mexico who died and left them a bunch of jewelry. He was also shopping around for a car for his nephew, and some of the guys helped him out.

"Diamonds is where it's at," Von Villas told Ray Romero. "You hold on to them for ten years and they'll go way up. And you keep it away from the IRS."

Romero in particular thought it was a little strange that Bobby was suddenly peddling diamonds. Only a month before, Von Villas had asked Ray to loan him ten thousand dollars. Bobby told him he had some money coming soon on a deal, that he'd pay him 25 percent interest. Romero and his wife had made some wise real estate investments over the years, and Von Villas knew they had the capital. But Romero's wife hadn't gone for it.

So now Von Villas was walking around with a pouch full of diamonds in his attaché case. "Where the hell did you get diamonds from?" Romero asked. "You don't have any money."

"Oh, I borrowed some money and I got some money from my property," Von Villas said.

Romero shrugged. Bobby always had a story. Like everybody else at Club Dev, he'd given up trying to keep track of all his angles. Romero had been through it before. Like the time when Bobby had wanted to know how to set up a life insurance policy on the sly.

Romero's father had died a few months back and Ray had gotten stuck with the funeral bill. Afterward, he realized that the same thing would happen when his mother and mother-in-law passed away, so he decided to get some insurance. But Romero didn't want to tell his mother or his wife's mother about it. He figured he'd get two small life insurance policies, just enough to cover funeral costs, and not say anything. But after making some phone calls, he discovered he couldn't do it. You had to tell the party you were insuring, because they had to sign the papers. Romero had done some private investigations for an insurance company, so he knew the right people to ask. He eventually became somewhat of an expert on the subject.

When Von Villas heard about what Romero was trying to do, he approached him for some advice. "I'm giving a loan to some gal and I want to get a life insurance policy on her, but I don't want her to know about it," Bobby told him.

"You can't do it," Romero said. "For one thing, she has to take a medical."

"You see," Von Villas explained, "I got this gal who almost owns this house but she's getting ready to lose it and the first notice is twenty-five thousand. I'm going to buy it off her and she's going to repay me."

Romero didn't really want to hear about it. Von Villas always had some woman he was trying to help out, like Linda Sintic or Joyce Reynolds. This one was someone named Joany.

Initially, the plan was for Ford and Von Villas to handle the girls. But they quickly realized that two of Club Dev's finest would need a buffer. It was Bruce Adams who ended up running the service. Before long, Adams was working around the clock; fixing cars by day, chauffeuring hookers all over town at night.

Von Villas had information on a slew of prostitutes that he had pilfered from police records at Club Dev. He had the complete file on a recently closed escort service that had been the largest in the Valley. Von Villas always carried a classy brown leather attaché case which had his initials, RAVV, stenciled on it in gold letters. One day he pulled out a five- to ten-page police department computer printout of names, booking numbers, and offenses charged for several prostitutes. He had mug shots, fingerprint cards, even addresses and phone numbers. He was anxious to solicit many of these girls, as well as some of those from Star Modeling, the service Adams had previously worked for.

Von Villas was more than just an eager businessman. He fancied himself a playboy and anticipated that his new venture would come with a few perks. However, Bobby figured he couldn't exactly be up-front with these girls about what he did for a living. So he devised a scheme whereby he would present Adams as the operator while he played the role of the wise guy backer.

The first recruit, at Von Villas's insistence, was Monique, a working girl who had been a regular with Star Modeling. Von Villas had the hots for her in a big way. A knockout blonde in her late twenties, Monique had been working the hotels by the airport for about five years. Adams found her to be "a decent chick," not a typical street whore. He set up a dinner meeting with Monique and Bob just after New Year's at the Jolly Roger restaurant near LAX.

Von Villas came on strong, flashing a big wad of bills, playing the high roller. He told Monique that his new service was offering standard terms—a $45 per hour "modeling fee" plus 20 percent of any tips she received went to the service. Since the "model" generally got $150 on top of the fee, she wound up with at least $120 per session. But he also told her he was offering a special incentive program for girls who brought in new customers—perks and bonuses like clothing, free trips to Mexico, and regular free doctor's checkups. He told Monique he'd even buy her a car.

Halfway through dinner, Bob excused himself to make a phone call. The moment he was out of range, Monique turned to Adams. "This guy's either Mafia or he's a cop," she said. Adams nearly spit out his iced tea. "Yeah," Adams said. "He's with the mob." He wasn't about to explain how the guy bankrolling his new prostitution service was Officer Bob, LAPD supercop, hero to youths and parents alike throughout the San Fernando Valley.

"Yeah, that's what I figured," Monique repeated. "Either that or a cop."

Later, when they walked out to the parking lot, Von Villas stopped and stationed himself up against a big shiny new Cadillac. He acted like the Caddy was his, pulling out his keys as he and Monique said their good-byes.

After Monique jiggled off to find her own ride, Adams stared at Von Villas. "What are you doin'?" Bruce exclaimed.

"Oh nothing," said Von Villas. "I just want her to think we've got some class."

Since the night was still young, Von Villas and Adams got into Bob's Pontiac and drove to Hollywood. Von Villas propositioned a dozen hookers, trying to recruit them. Watching Von Villas in action, Adams laughed so hard he almost choked on his cigarette smoke. Bobby would jump out of the car and start telling the girls about this great new escort service. He'd tell them about profit-sharing programs, benefits, paid vacations. These Sunset Strip sirens looked at him like he was crazy. Some just laughed. Only in L.A.!

But Bobby was undaunted. The two entrepreneurs followed a guy in a white Chevy Capri with Montana plates who had picked up and then dropped off a hooker. Bob jumped out and badged the trick, threatening to bust him, leveraging him until he got as much information as he could about the girl. Then he went after the hooker and tried to use his knowledge to impress her. Naturally, he only succeeded in broadcasting that he was a cop and scaring the hell out of her.

The two erstwhile wise guys cruised Hollywood on a few more nights, producing the same results—zip city as far as recruitment, side-splitting free entertainment for Adams. One time, Bobby actually stopped a working girl and made his pitch about incentives and benefits packages while he was still in his *police uniform.* "What is this?" the girl laughed. "Am I on 'Candid Camera'?" Adams nearly died of apoplexy as he sat watching from the car.

As the two spent more time together, Adams became dazzled by his new partner's intrepid hustling. He also was bewildered by his blizzard of bullshit. One hundred and fifty angles all the time—trading on the commodities market, developing real estate, hawking diamonds and stereos from the trunk of his car, plotting various insurance scams, selling interests in bogus trust deeds to police widows, setting up an escort service, and hustling hookers on the street. And all the while maintaining his impeccable bearing and image as an LAPD supercop. Officer Bob.

Monique finally helped Adams get the service rolling by recruiting a few other girls. Adams placed some ads in the *Hollywood Free Press,* a skin tabloid, and they were in business. The first week he had to use the names Fantasy Ladies and Star Modeling because somebody was already using Classy Ladies. Basically, they were all the same—a picture of some half-naked babe on the telephone with the caption "Call me!"

By now, Richard Ford had become the security man in the partnership. Having once been an undercover vice cop, Ford had a solid knowledge of the law regarding solicitation. His job was to make sure the girls knew how to avoid entrapment.

Whenever a new girl was hired, Ford would call up the service, posing as a trick, and get her on the phone. He would try to get the girl to say something she shouldn't, like, "Yeah, sure, I'll give you a blow job for fifty bucks." Hookers who'd been around knew better than to make incriminating statements. They knew the time-honored code employed between whore and trick. But vice cops were wily; they had ways of getting the girls to slip up. Ford made sure they passed muster. If they didn't, he'd instruct Adams to give them a little lesson in safe hookerspeak.

The service needed a reliable person to answer the phones and set up appointments. Obviously, it wouldn't hurt if it was a lady with a sexy voice. Von Villas had a perfect candidate, a friend named Joan Loguercio.

Loguercio, a thirty-seven-year-old mother of three, had known Officer Bob for nearly a year. She had met him when he came to her house in Granada Hills to take a report on her teenage boy, Joey, who had run away from home. She thought Bob Von Villas was the greatest. He seemed genuinely concerned for her welfare, and he was great with her kids, particularly Joey. He really helped straighten him out. Officer Bob would stop by frequently just to visit. He put the moves on her at first, but Joany wasn't interested, so they settled into a close friendship instead.

Joany was going through a long and bitter divorce. Her estranged husband was no longer providing any financial support. Having no skills besides that of a homemaker, she had little luck on the job market, and she needed money desperately to keep from losing her house. A minimum-wage job simply wouldn't cut it. Joany did have one asset, however. She was a looker—a willowy, dark-haired woman with a good body and dark olive skin. And she liked to dance.

Joany took a few waitress jobs and eventually began dancing at the Honey-bee Club in Reseda, where she was an exotic bikini dancer. She later moved on to a string of topless and all nude go-go bars in the Valley. The work wasn't entirely to her liking, but the tips were great. Still, making the transition from housewife to professional exhibitionist wasn't easy. She needed supportive friends—and Officer Bob was one of the best. He wasn't judgmental, even though he was a cop. He even understood when Joany admitted to him that she had turned a few tricks. She had no intention of turning pro, mind you, but a few offers had come her way that she simply found too good to refuse.

Von Villas told Joany he knew a guy, a wise guy from back east named Bruce Adams, who needed some help setting up an escort service. "I know you're strapped for bucks," he told her. "This sounds like a pretty good deal. You might as well try it." He set up a lunch meeting between her and Bruce at the El Presidente restaurant in Granada Hills.

With his gruff baritone, Jersey accent, and street-smart talk, Adams had no trouble playing a hood. He'd play that role for all the girls, although his shabby wardrobe, shaky hands, and gritty fingernails gave some of them pause. Joany and Bruce hit it off right away, talking about times they'd had growing up in the New York area.

Joany started work immediately, manning the phones and setting up appointments for the Classy Ladies Out-Call Service. She never knew Von Villas owned the business. That's the way he wanted it.

When Detective Ford called up to check her out, he cut her off after about three minutes and told her to put Bruce on the line.

"Oh, you know Bruce?"

"Yeah, I know Bruce."

Ford told Adams to give the lady some instruction. "This dingbat gives me enough in three minutes to send us all to the joint!" Ford laughed. "Where the hell did Bob find her?"

Later, when Ford saw Joany at the shop, he thought she was kinda cute.

The white brick building at 9835 Owensmouth had a corrugated aluminum roof. Outside the rolling garage bay door—the only entrance—were a pair of large metal Dumpsters. Across from the gravel driveway was a small house with a thirty-five-foot Chris-Craft dry-docked outside. The two businesses on either side were strictly day concerns; it was rare that anyone else was around at night.

A door and a sliding window connected the service bay area to a small office. Inside the office was a sofa along the wall, a filing cabinet, and a desk facing out so that customers could sit in front of it and watch Adams total up the bad news on the adding machine. A second service desk, with another phone, faced the far wall. It was close quarters, one in which phone conversations could be easily overheard.

The escort service was set up in a back room that had a sign on the door that read Engine Clean Room. They put in a desk, telephones, a TV, and a small bed, where Adams would often collapse after his eighteen-hour days at the garage and escort service.

The girls, usually four or five, would start to arrive around four o'clock and work out of the office. After about a month, Von Villas started to get nervous about that. Adams couldn't figure out why; he was only servicing about half the private vehicles owned by Devonshire Division cops. On any given afternoon, four or five officers from Devonshire Division were likely to be hanging around waiting for their cars. Whenever one of the boys from Club Dev commented about the arrival of some too-hot babe, Adams would grab his crotch and laugh. "Yeah, I been doing some work on her rear end. A major lube job." What the hell.

The boys from Club Dev understood that nobody walked in L.A.—not even *streetwalkers*. Somebody had to fix their rides.

But after about a month, Von Villas got really nervous, so they moved Classy Ladies to 7252 Remet in Canoga Park, about ten minutes away and just outside the Devonshire boundary in West Valley Division. It was an upstairs corner office in a six-unit complex with a stairway and outer balcony, like a motel. The room, which went for $550 a month, was tiny, sedate. The other units were occupied by daytime self-employed office types—accountants and travel agents. Von Villas instructed Adams to rent the office under the name Star Imports and tell the landlord they'd be there nights making calls to England.

Adams would work at International Automotive till about seven, then head over to supervise the service. Joany or Monique would usually handle the phones. Some girls would hang out at the office, while others would wait by their phones at home. Adams would pick them up and take them to their tricks.

Adams would walk up to the door with the girl, just so the john knew she was being escorted. That way, they wouldn't try to stiff the girls or do anything funny. It also put the girls at ease knowing somebody was watching their backs—and it made them more inclined to turn over 20 percent of their tips like they were supposed to.

Adams didn't have any problems. He wasn't big and he had a gimp leg, but he could be intimidating. If a john tried to pass a check or hemmed and hawed about payment, Adams didn't screw around. "I want the cash and I want it now," he'd bark in his gravely baritone. He'd slide into his Vietnam-vet-from-hell persona; it wasn't a terrible stretch. The john would look at Bruce's bulging eyes and wild, shaky hands and pull out his wallet. Of course, the johns could pay with MasterCard or Visa, which they would launder through International Automotive.

Bruce Adams and Joany Loguercio quickly developed a flirtatious friendship. Joany was from the Bronx, and Adams had a lot of wild tales to share about his experiences there. Adams had grown up across the river in Englewood, New Jersey, and had torn through the streets of the Bronx as a hot-rodding teenager. After Vietnam, he'd been stationed with the military police at St. Albins in Long Island, where for a while he pulled duty as a foot chaser, someone who runs down AWOLs. The job took him all over the East Coast and up to the Canadian border, but he spent most of his time in the wilds of Brooklyn, Queens, the Bronx, and Manhattan. A lot of grunts were going AWOL back in 1970, some just to have a few nights out on the big town. So Adams had been around.

Adams soon realized that Joany had led a more sheltered life. She had married and run off to L.A. when she was still in her teens. For twenty years she had been a mother and a Valley housewife. Her husband, Ron, had owned a used car lot. She was a sweet lady, but at times she could be an airhead. She occasionally talked about wanting to turn tricks like the other girls, but Adams did his best to discourage her. Adams thought if Joany turned hooker, she'd probably get herself killed. She was too naive.

Adams found Loguercio's flirtation with "the life" amusing, since she was very religious and could quote chapter and verse from the Bible. Joany was a lapsed Jehovah's Witness, but she spoke frequently of her desire to "get back to her religion." As they worked together scheduling and delivering hookers, Joany would try to talk Bruce into joining the Jehovah's Witnesses with her.

Joany really loved to dance. For her, it was a physical and mental release that made all her troubles disappear for a while. The fact that she got paid to do it made it even better. After a while, she got used to being practically nude in public. But the places where she danced—the Candy Cat, the Batman Club, the Honeybee—were pretty rough joints, almost biker bars.

When they first started working together, Joany had goaded Bruce to come out and see her dance. He wasn't interested. After they became tight, Bruce decided to do it just to embarrass her. He had a road call near her club one afternoon, so he stopped in. He sat down in the front row. Joany came out onstage and started dancing in the near altogether. She looked down and saw Bruce, who looked up at her and smiled. From the look on her face, he thought she'd fall off the dance floor. Bruce just got up and headed out the door.

Joany called him later that night. "You son of a bitch!" she yelled. "You surprised the hell out of me!"

"Don't worry," Bruce laughed. "I won't ever do it again."

Joany had a boyfriend, Frank, a tow-truck driver who would drink and rough her up from time to time. After a few of these fights, Adams had warned Frank not to lay a hand on her again, but to no avail. One day Bruce was fixing the water pump on Joany's Camaro when Frank came storming into the shop, half-bagged, and started yelling and pushing Joany around. Bruce heard the commotion, and when he came in and saw Frank shoving Joany against the wall, he went nuts. He dragged Frank out by the scruff of his neck and threw him into his tow truck. Bruce adhered to an inviolable John Wayne ethic. "I don't care what kind of woman it is," he'd say. "Even if she's a whore, there's never a reason for a man to beat up on a woman."

Joany had other boyfriends, all low-life macho dudes who liked to beat up on women. One of them was a Puerto Rican body builder who thumped her pretty bad one night. Bruce couldn't understand it. Joany would cry on his shoulder and he'd get steamed. "What are you doing with these assholes?" he'd yell. "Where do you dig them up? You're not a bad-looking lady. You got a great personality, you got a nice body. What are doing going out with this scum?"

Frank moved in with Joany for a while, but it seemed obvious to Bruce that she didn't really love him. She just needed somebody to help pay the rent. She took in a number of boarders to help make ends meet. Her house was like a 1960s crash pad, with strange people coming and going at all hours.

Joany lived like a hippie because she was a hippie. She loved to smoke dope. Bruce quickly learned that there were only three things in life important to Joany: her kids, her house, and a never-ending supply of weed. Bruce hadn't whiffed so much secondary pot smoke since he was in Nam. Whenever he'd take her out for coffee, the first thing she'd do after climbing in his van was fire up a joint. Bruce would have to roll down his window to keep from choking. He'd smoked some in Nam, but he'd had no use for it since he'd come back to the States. Getting stoned was a great way of inviting a panic attack.

Bruce and Joany started spending a lot of time together. They went out a lot for coffee, and Joany often hung around at the shop, where Adams usually slept. She had Adams over to her house for dinner, and Bruce became close with her son Joey. He also met Joany's older son and daughter and her father, a mason and stonecutter, who was living with her. Joany's mother had died of cancer at the age of forty; Joany would tell Bruce that she was convinced she'd also meet an early end.

During the winter, Joany loved to just sit in front of her fireplace and talk. She also liked to drive out to the beach and watch the waves. She talked Bruce away from the shop on a few occasions; eventually, they had a brief affair.

11

Crazy Business

FORD AND VON VILLAS STOPPED BY INTERNATIONAL AUTOMOTIVE every day. Much to Adams's dismay, the shop became their clubhouse and capering headquarters. When Bruce wasn't hauling hookers or fixing cars owned by cops, he got dragged into one crazy scheme after another.

Von Villas's suspension went into effect on January 11, 1983, and for the next two weeks he spent nearly every day at the shop. The Simi Valley Cowboy moseyed around in his jeans and boots, playing country music on the radio and making calls from the office. Adams shook his head and laughed as he listened to Bob chatting up movie stars, hookers, business partners, and jewelers. Between calls, he did some work on his cars. First, he put the sheepskin seat covers and new speedometer cable in his Poncho. Then he started putting a stereo system into the 1974 Camaro he'd bought for his daughter, Michele, who had just turned seventeen. Bruce almost died watching him install it. Bob spent a whole day wrestling with it, asking Bruce a question every five minutes. When he was finished, the speakers were rattling and the holes in the upholstery were all out of wack.

But Bruce didn't really realize what a pair of cowboys he'd partnered up with until the van caper. Bob had a blue 1979 Dodge van in pretty fair condition. But seeing as he had some time on his hands, he decided to trash it and run an insurance scam.

Adams wound up spending most of a day and an entire evening at the shop helping Ford and Von Villas strip the van. While they were working, Bob Von

Villas called and reported the van as stolen. He also reported that he had two gun cases in the back worth about a grand each. (A cop buddy of Bob's who did cabinetwork on the side had given him a receipt for some phantom gun cases.)

They did a complete number on the van, removing the seats, hood, bumpers, dashboard, stereo, interior tables and chairs, drive shaft, transmission, and most of the engine. Adams couldn't believe how much fun these guys were having. They were drinking beer, having a swell old time. Von Villas took a ball-peen hammer and beat the carburetor off the top of the engine and broke the intake manifold, laughing his ass off the whole time. Ford pulled the transmission without first taking out the torque converter, and nine quarts of tranny oil spilled all over everybody and onto Adams's garage floor. Bruce started cussing like a marine; Dick and Bob laughed like they were at the Comedy Store.

By one in the morning they'd cannibalized the van. Adams hooked it up to his old Chevy pickup and they towed it out Fallbrook Road to Chatsworth Reservoir, which sat in a remote area of sagebrush hills and rock outcroppings. It was a common dumping ground for Valley rip and strip boys. Von Villas sat on a milk crate in the empty van while he steered it behind the pickup; Ford drove behind both of them in his Datsun wagon to act as a chase car or blocker car. If they encountered an officer of the law, Detective Ford would badge the officer, talk some cop talk, explain how he was on some undercover job, and send him on his way.

Ford and Von Villas acted like they were going to a party. They didn't have a care in the world. The shield would take care of everything.

When they got to the middle of nowhere and were surrounded by nothing but starlit sky, they rolled the van off the side of the road. The two tipsy cops started bashing the van, laughing like kids. The radio in Ford's Datsun rattled with country tunes. Ford grabbed a rock and threw it through the right-hand van window. Von Villas hefted a huge concrete block and chucked it through the windshield. Adams couldn't believe these guys. But what the hell—he didn't wanna miss out on the fun. He backed his pickup into the van a couple of times, knocking it with his heavy diamond towing bumper, adding a few nifty crinkles to the ravaged Dodge.

Ford, who was still covered with tranny fluid, was running around like some juvenile delinquent, smearing grease all over the van, leaving his fingerprints big as life up and down the sides.

"Jesus Christ, what the fuck are you doin'?" Adams growled. "You got your prints all over the fuckin' thing."

"Don't worry about it, bro," Ford laughed. "They can't match any prints. Not unless they got a suspect."

"Whatever you say, partner," said Adams. "You're the fucking detective."

Von Villas, meanwhile, was wearing rubber surgical gloves, which seemed strange to Adams. It was Bob's van. What was he worried about? His prints were supposed to be all over it.

Von Villas had reconned the job beforehand, and they planned to leave the van just inside Ventura County. He didn't want the case coming back to Devonshire Division or the L.A. sheriffs. But apparently he had his map upside down, because a Devonshire Division patrol unit spotted the van just a few hours after they dumped it—five hundred yards short of the Ventura County line.

But it was no problem. Nobody suspected Officer Bob. Von Villas later collected about four grand for the van and another two for the invisible gun cabinets. On top of that, they scammed the insurance company on storage. When they called and asked Bob where to tow the van, he told them International Automotive. Adams proceeded to hammer them with ten days of inside storage charges, which is how long it took for the adjuster to show up and declare the van a total loss.

If the insurance guy had ever looked, he could have found all the van's parts lying around the shop. But who would suspect that the parts of a stripped vehicle would be sitting right next to its recovered shell? And who would suspect a cop?

Meanwhile, International Automotive was getting lousy with cops. Adams put in shocks and a carburetor on a Volkswagen Rabbit for Damien Lewis, one of Ford's ex-partners, a real straight arrow who was a preacher in a nondenominational church. He put a radiator, shocks, and cruise control in a four-wheel-drive Cherokee for a cop named Bannister. He stayed up all night putting a new camshaft in a Fleetwood Cadillac for Officer Glenn Bedford, who also owned a brand-new five-speed Z/28 Camaro 305, which Adams also worked on. Another one of Von Villas's good Club Dev buddies, Ron Skyvnick, had a Jaguar XJ6 and a Mercedes 450SEL, which Adams also fixed. (Needless to say, Skyvnick had a pretty successful security business going on the side.)

Between the capering Colonel and his enforcer, Dr. Death, the out-call hookers, and all the Club Dev cowboys, Adams had days when he felt like the ringmaster at Barnum and Bailey Circus. Like the time Officer Muzinski almost murdered his Pinto.

It was around five in the afternoon, and Bruce was trying to finish up on three vehicles at once. One belonged to a "Classy Lady" who came in with three friends who all looked like Madonna wannabes. Joany was there as well, getting ready to start work for the night. Three other customers were screaming for their cars; two of them were from Club Dev's finest, and they started partying with the girls in the bay area after somebody went out for beer and pizza.

Bruce was just stepping around a double pepperoni and sausage to get a better angle on a catalytic converter he was trying to yank when he heard a tire squeal from hell. He looked up and a blue Pinto was skidding up the drive. It came to a jarring halt just in front of the bay door, and out tumbled an officer in police blues. He did a slick stuntman tuck and roll and came up with his service revolver aimed at the Pinto. He pulled back the hammer on his .38 and crouched in combat mode like Dirty Harry.

It was Officer Ed Muzinski, a two-striper, a Vietnam vet, a 101st Airborne crazy and Club Dev compadre of Bob Von Villas.

"Fix the fucking thing." Muzinski yelled.

Adams limped over and tried to talk the crazed cop out of committing assault on his car. "What's wrong?" Bruce asked. He could tell by the look in Muzinski's eye that the man was ready to blow the defenseless Pinto away.

"I don't know." Muzinski shouted. "Just fix it. Or I swear to God, I'll kill it."

Adams looked behind the Pinto and noticed a black and white had followed Muzinski up the drive. A couple of cops inside the squad were laughing like hyenas. Behind him in the bay the girls were squealing like a gaggle of lit-up debutantes at a beer bash. Adams dropped his ratchet wrench and wound his way through the empties and pizza boxes and drunk chicks and car-killing cops and scattered auto parts and limped into the office to find his Valium and a fresh pack of Marlboros.

Another time, Von Villas found a nice-looking lady in distress whose car had stalled out during a rainstorm. So he used his squad car to push her to International Automotive. While his head was stuck under the hood, Bruce heard her gushing over Officer Bob.

"Oh, you're such a kind police officer," she cooed.

"Yes, ma'am," Bobby smiled. "I protect and I serve."

At the shop, Adams would often overhear Ford and Von Villas discussing capers they had in mind. They talked about knocking off the gate receipts from the Renaissance Faire out in Agoura, of pulling a major tire heist out of a warehouse. "It'd be easy," said Detective Ford. "You fill up a big van, back the motherfucker into the shop, unload it, and close the door. Then you run a special on Avon tires."

One day, Ford took Adams with him down to Century City to recon the Century Plaza Hotel, where he and Von Villas were allegedly going to take down the big jewelry show. He showed Bruce the PBX systems he'd have to knock out while he and Bob went in with automatic weapons. The need for advanced weaponry, Ford explained, was purely psychological. "Cops and security guards have all seen pistols before," he told Adams. "But if you stick a sophisticated automatic weapon with a silencer into a cop's face, he's intimidated. He thinks, These guys are pros, they're serious, these guys will kill me, I better do what they say. If you pull a thirty-eight there's always some guy who's gonna try to be a hero."

Ford told Adams stories about taking down dope dealers and other scumbags when he worked Southwest Division. One time, he caught a dope dealer with some money and he tried to rip him off. But the dealer jumped him, and Ford ended up stabbing him. He implied that he killed the guy. Ford was also injured in the fight, and he holed up for a while in Hollywood with a hooker/stripper named Venus. Ford still saw Venus from time to time. Adams took calls from her at the shop.

Another time, when they were all at the shop, Ford started bitching about how Bob had left him in the lurch on some jewelry caper. From what Adams was able to gather, the cops had taken down a jewelry store, somewhere in a mall Von Villas had worked foot patrol, so he had it all reconned. Apparently, Von Villas had waited outside while Ford went in and took down the store by himself. Ford started talking down Von Villas, like he was pissed because he hadn't come in and helped him. "That son of a bitch almost got me killed!" Ford complained. "I should have shot his ass."

Adams heard lots of stories about the jewelry store heist. At first they told him it was somewhere in Orange County. Later, they told him it was in the Valley.

Adams and Ford also got into heavy discussions about the war. Sometimes they'd get going and start talking just like a couple of grunts back in Nam, blistering the ears of everyone around. One time Adams told Ford about the time he had to fix a transport vehicle in the middle of a mortar barrage. So Ford launched into a story about his chopper duty with James Hollingsworth, the legendary First Infantry commander.

"Pressure? You want fuckin' pressure? Try being door gunner on the command ship of General James Fucking Hollingsworth," Ford cried. "Old Holly was a hard driver. We flew around the clock—no sleep, no daylight, no maintenance. The whole fuckin' chopper would be falling apart. We don't even know if we can make it back to base. Holly says, 'Some of my boys down there are hurt, let's get 'em.' This is the commander of six fuckin' battalions. He wants to risk his life and ours, the whole op, to pick up some grunts. Somebody in the crew would make a suggestion: 'General, shouldn't we wait for a medivac?' Oh no, says Holly, that'll take too long. Those are my boys down there.

"So we go flyin' through the jungle like the Lone Fuckin' Ranger. We're dodging hundred-and-twenty-millimeter mortar rounds. There's a hundred and one NVA all over the fuckin' place. I'm blastin' these rice heads with my sixty-millimeter like target practice. We swoop down, scoop up a bunch of kids. They're all fucked up. We're limping back to base, I'm trying to spray gooks out the door while I'm tying fuckin' tourniquets. We get back to base, God knows how, and we go right up again to recon one of the fronts. Then Holly spots a weak line in their defense and calls up some gunships to break through. But would he wait? Hell fuckin' no. Not Holly. He wants to charge in, get it started. So next thing you know we're flying right into enemy fire again, in the fucking command ship.

"Old Holly, boy, he was fuckin' nuts. He was one helluva commander. He was the best."

"Oh yeah?" Adams growled. "Flyin' them Hueys was pansy patrol compared to what went down in Hue. Did I tell you about the time . . ."

Adams found it strange that Von Villas never jumped into any of their mad sessions about Vietnam. It was a rare vet who could listen to combat talk without telling some of his own stories. From talking to Ford, Adams knew Bob had seen some heavy combat. He'd been wounded, gotten a Purple Heart, a Bronze Star, the whole nine yards. But Bob never talked about Nam. In fact, he never talked about anything but business. He never talked about his parents, where he was from, his background, nothing. The Colonel was tight jawed about his past.

But Dick Ford wasn't an open book either. Adams asked him about his folks a couple of times and all he got was dirty looks. One time Ford mentioned that he had lived in Nevada for a while as a kid, but when Adams asked him about it he clammed up. But at least Ford had a sense of humor and could joke around. The only time Adams saw a smile on the Colonel's face was when he was talking about money.

Before his new partnership, Adams had been making progress in dealing with his delayed stress, but the pressure at the shop set him way back. He was just one mechanic with a helper or two, but Von Villas expected him to perform like a whole crew, or a magician. And when something went wrong, it became an ordeal. A cop would come in with a Mickey Mouse cruise-control package, have him install it, then complain like hell to Bob when it didn't work properly. And Adams would catch shit from Officer Bob. To make it worse, Ford and Von Villas played an ongoing game with Adams. Von Villas would tell Bruce that Ford was mad because somebody's car wasn't ready. Bruce would talk to Dick, who'd say, "Nah, I ain't mad at you."

After his suspension was lifted, Von Villas continued to stop by the shop

116

three or four times a day to deliver his daily battle plans to Adams. It wasn't long before Bruce realized that "his" shop was being operated according to military code. Von Villas was the CO, Ford was second in command, and he was the grunt.

Shirley Adams worked in the office for a while after the shop first opened. She did the paperwork and handled the customers, calming them down when their cars weren't ready as promised, which was most of the time. One afternoon while going through the desk she found a spiral notebook with a list of girls' names in it. Next to each name was the woman's age, hair color, and other descriptive tidbits.

She asked Bruce about it and he told her, "That's Bob's. Don't get into Bob's stuff."

Shirley had a jealous streak. She knew there were a lot of legitimate women customers at any garage, but this list wasn't your normal customer roster, and it troubled her. Especially since Bruce had started coming home for dinner, changing out of his greasy clothes, getting dressed up, and heading back out with his briefcase for what he said were "business meetings." He never told her about the escort service.

Shirley was also suspicious about the number of phone calls she took from Joan Loguercio, who always wanted to talk to Bruce. Her husband always had an explanation. He was working on her car. She was a friend of Bob's and she couldn't reach him so she had to give Bruce a message. Shirley accepted this—for the time being.

Shirley met Joany at the shop a few times and thought she was nice, but she didn't like the way she looked at Bruce. And she wasn't pleased when she learned what she did for a living. Joany asked Shirley a lot of questions about Bruce— how long they'd been married, about their kids, and so on. It made Shirley very uncomfortable.

Judy Von Villas and Lillian Ford also stopped by the shop on a few occasions. Shirley couldn't help but notice that they both seemed to wear a lot of jewelry, including some expensive diamond rings. Lillian had a real doozie; the stone looked as big as her knuckle.

Shirley thought that Judy was a snob, that Bob and Judy looked down their noses at Bruce. As far as she was concerned, Bob and Judy made a perfect pair. The only thing about them that seemed genuine was their devotion to their kids. Shirley had to give them that. There was no denying Bob's pride in his two girls. He'd practically glow when he talked about them. One of his daughters, he said, was such a good swimmer she might try out for the Olympics.

Bob would come in every day to handle the books and the money and make all the bank deposits. Sometimes he'd ask Shirley to leave the office and wait out in the garage while he made a phone call. Bob hated to part with money; Shirley often had to pester him to cut loose Bruce's meager paycheck. After a while Bob told Shirley that she didn't have to come to work anymore; Joan Loguercio would be coming in to handle the office.

Detective Mike Moen, Ford's partner, had a Ford pickup that was misfiring, and he brought it in to have Bruce take a look. Adams told him his truck needed a complete overhaul, but Moen didn't trust him. Maybe he'd been a cop too long, but Adams just didn't look like the kind of guy he wanted to have working on his car. Moen thought he was a dirtbag—like some perp he would interview in jail. He was dirty, long-haired, unkempt, and real nervous. Moen questioned his honesty and ability. The shop seemed like a little hole in the wall. It was dirty and disorganized, and Adams's "help" didn't look like they knew what they were doing. Moen couldn't understand why Richard Ford would ever want to invest in such a place. He told Adams he'd bring the truck back later, but instead he took it to the Ford service center.

Shirley had a girlfriend whose husband worked with Bruce at the shop for all of three days. When the guy told his wife about what was going on, she made him get out. Hookers? Cops? A chopped-up van? Trading diamonds for tools? The lady in question really liked Shirley, but Bruce, as far as she was concerned, was a total sleaze, a man with no morals. God only knew what he would do. He'd sold Shirley a whole bill of goods about this wonderful shop, about how they would have insurance and all that. What a crock.

The final straw came when she heard some business about Bruce blackening out the windows on a rented van. "That's not what mechanics do," she told her husband. "Get the hell out of there."

Ford and Von Villas closed down the escort service after six weeks, even though it had netted them about twenty-five grand by Adams's estimate. They decided it was too conspicuous, too risky. This was a relief to Bruce, who was going nuts trying to run two businesses around the clock and explain his continual absence from home to Shirley.

But the adventures of Dick and Bob continued. One afternoon in late January when International Automotive was in its usual state of chaos, Bruce took a phone call from a woman named Jan who wanted to talk to Bob Von Villas.

Before he hung up the extension, Adams overheard a snippet of dialogue: "I want it done while I'm out of town," Jan said. "I'll be in Texas for two weeks. I want it taken care of then."

Adams didn't know what to make of it until he walked back into the office a few minutes later. Von Villas smiled as he dialed Richard Ford. "I got a job, maybe you can get in on this, Bruce," Von Villas said. When Ford answered the phone, Von Villas said, "Hey, I got a job for you. I know a woman who wants her husband knocked off. I'll give you her phone numbers tomorrow. You make an appointment to get the money and the information about the vic and start planning the hit. Do you want Adams to go with you?" With that, Von Villas handed the phone to Bruce.

"What's this all about?" Adams asked.

"Never mind," Ford said to Adams. "I don't need you on this, Bruce. Tell Bob I work alone."

On February 18, Von Villas called Bruce at nine in the morning. "I have a job for you." Here we go, thought Bruce. It was just like being back in the Marine Corps. Every morning there was a muster and a morning report and morning orders. "I want you to rent me a van," Von Villas instructed. "A one-ton with no windows, no markings, a rear seat, filled with fuel. I'll call back in two hours."

Bruce called around. The only van he could get had windows in the rear door. He called and told Von Villas.

"What can we do so you can't see into 'em?" Bob asked.

"I guess I could tint 'em," Adams suggested.

"Great," said Von Villas. "Get some tint and blacken 'em out. Get 'em as black as you can so nobody can see into the van."

Adams rented the van and got some spray window tint and blackened the windows.

Von Villas pulled in around four that afternoon, parked his Grand Prix, and rushed off in the van. "I'm in a hurry," he said. "I'm late to pick up Dicky."

Adams didn't see the two cops until the next day. The van rolled into International Automotive about noon. Dick and Bob piled out looking tired, grubby, unshaven—like they'd been on an all-night stakeout. They were covered with dust, and so was the van, as if they'd been out driving in the desert. Adams found a matchbook inside the van from a restaurant that he would later recall as being in Bakersfield or San Bernardino.

About a week later, in the office at the shop, Adams saw Von Villas hand Ford an envelope. It was stuffed with about ten grand in cash. "Here's your bonus, Dicky," Von Villas said. Ford laughed as he walked out the door.

Later, Ford told Adams they'd hit a man named Tom Weed and that

"Weed's bones are bleaching out in the desert." Ford also mentioned that nobody would ever identify Weed from his dental records, because he'd put a shotgun in the man's mouth and blown most of his head off. The way Ford talked, it sounded like a load of bullshit, but Adams really didn't know what to believe.

At the urging of Von Villas, Ford used most of his windfall to invest in corn futures. A few weeks later, the corn market hit the skids and tumbled to an all-time low. Von Villas reacted like it was the crash of 1929, running back and forth between the station and shop, stopping at pay phones along the way, desperately trying to reach his broker to tell him to sell before he was wiped out. He got to him too late. He and Ford lost almost their whole investment.

Ford was furious, ranting and raving about Bob and his stupid schemes. Von Villas avoided Ford for about a week and didn't return his calls. After they were speaking again, Ford never let him hear the end of it.

In March 1983, Von Villas recruited Adams into another insurance caper, involving a cop buddy named Geary Cade, the woodworker who had given Von Villas the receipt for the phantom gun cabinets. The Colonel had gone to high school with Cade, who now worked at Pacific Division out at the beach. Cade called Bob at the shop and asked what it would cost to change the wheel bearings on his 1977 Honda Accord. The car was a lemon and was nickel and diming him to death. Von Villas relayed Bruce's estimate—three hundred dollars—then made a suggestion: "Why don't you just do an insurance job like we did on my van?"

Geary Cade had fallen on hard times. He'd made a bad real estate investment and lost his shirt—at least that's what he told everybody. It wasn't a secret that Cade liked to play the ponies. He'd just gone through a bankruptcy and was getting back on his feet, so Bobby's idea about an insurance scam sounded pretty good.

The plot was hatched on Friday, March 18, 1983. Von Villas called Adams at California Moving and Storage in Van Nuys, where Bruce was doing a brake job on a trailer. He gave him Cade's address and the first six characters of his license plate. Adams was in a work-bay area, so he wrote down the information—12600 Braddock, BLW 960—by scratching it onto the side of a Coke machine with a pen. Von Villas told him that Ford would meet him at the shop around six that evening.

"Trash the seats," Von Villas said. "Make it look like some kids took it for a joyride and dumped it." He told Adams he'd pay him $250.

Adams met Richard Ford at the shop and they drove to Santa Monica in Ford's Datsun wagon. It was dark, raining, and it took them two hours to find Cade's apartment. Down the street was Cade's blue 1977 Honda Accord. Adams opened the unlocked car, and, as instructed, reached under the mat and found the key.

Ford drove ahead, serving as the blocker car. If a cop should stop Adams, Ford would pull over, badge the guy, and send him on his way. It would be a piece of cake. Again, they were shielded.

As they drove north on the San Diego Freeway, Adams kicked in the dash, ripped out the wiring, and broke the heater controls. He tossed his cigarette butts into the backseat and let them smolder in the upholstery. They turned off on Route 118, the Simi Valley Freeway, and went east to Pacoima Canyon in the Los Angeles National Forest. Once there, they drove to a remote area just past the reservoir and the Angels Crest Shooting Range. They parked and Ford joined Adams as they wreaked havoc on the interior of the car. Ford had a screwdriver that he used to rip up the right front bucket seat.

Adams was even more nervous than usual, mostly because of his ongoing hassles with Von Villas at the shop. The thought crossed his mind that Bob might be setting him up for a grand theft rap. When Ford got out of the car, Adams opened the glove box and looked at the registration. He was somewhat relieved when he saw that the car was indeed registered to Geary Cade.

Adams drove the Honda up a muddy dirt road at forty miles an hour, hit the brakes, and let the Honda slide off into a cliffside embankment. It was about ten at night, pitch-dark, and he almost misjudged the maneuver and went over the edge. Ford cursed and laughed as they both got out and rocked the car over the cliff, watching it crash and tumble some fifty feet down.

Ford later told Von Villas, "Nobody will ever find it. We dumped it about three hundred feet down a ridge."

Geary Cade didn't "notice" his car was missing the next day, because he went to the track with a friend. On Sunday he "discovered" it was gone and filed a report.

The police had already found the car. Cade received an insurance settlement of $1,600. Von Villas later paid Adams fifty bucks. He told Adams he'd invest the other two hundred dollars in the shop.

As summer approached, the relationship between Adams and Von Villas deteriorated rapidly. Von Villas, a meticulous businessman, was constantly interfering in the way Bruce was running the shop. He put pressure on Adams to highball his prices. Adams didn't like the way Von Villas treated some of his long-time customers. Bob's arrogance drove some of them out the door. Von Villas was unhappy with Adams's work and didn't like the way shop funds always seemed to disappear. He was convinced that Adams was stealing from the business. It also drove him nuts when he learned that Adams and Joan Loguercio had a brief affair. Adams enjoyed flinging that in his face.

Von Villas also argued with Bruce about his hot-rodding. Bruce had a motorcycle he would ride through the canyons to unwind, and he spent a lot of time souping it up. Adams also bought a race car and worked on it at the shop. It was a street-class Chevy Nova 350 LT1 with 50:50 Dontov racing cams, 4:88 gears, and dual quads. He'd spend most of his Friday nights prepping it, then take it out to drag strips in Bakersfield or Pomona on Saturdays. Von Villas thought it took too much of Bruce's time. Bruce also wanted to turn the business into a performance shop, a plan Von Villas wanted no part of. And when Von Villas found out that Bruce had talked to a local councilman about setting up a clinic for street racers at the shop, he really went ballistic.

Back in 1969, when Bruce was still young and stupid, he had crashed a Formula Barracuda into some parked cars while traveling 120 miles an hour in a street race on a wet road. He wound up with some stitches and cracked ribs, but he knew he'd been lucky. There were lots of kids killing themselves on Mulholland Drive and other Valley dragways, and Bruce figured a sanctioned racing clinic could help prevent some deaths. But Von Villas absolutely didn't want him to do anything that would involve local politicians or give the shop a community profile.

The relationship between the two men got so bad that Adams and Von Villas finally agreed that Bruce would buy Bob out of the auto shop. He started searching for a new investor and finally found one in Bill Mayhew.

Adams had gone through a string of helpers, most of them young, irresponsible dropouts who hadn't lasted more than a few days. But he finally found Mayhew, who lasted a few months. Mayhew was twenty-two, a skinny hippie-type kid with long blond hair who was living with his father-in-law in Thousand Oaks. He'd gone through a training program and was a decent mechanic for a young kid. And he wasn't a goof-off, which was all Adams could ask.

For a few weeks, Mayhew moonlighted at a job set up by Adams and Richard Ford. Ford called Adams one day and asked if he knew any dirtbag characters—long-haired hippie drug types—who could be used for an under-cover job. Mike Moen's security firm had a client, an electronics firm in Simi Valley, that suspected some drug abuse among night-shift workers. Adams brought Mayhew down to meet Moen, who placed the kid as the night janitor so he could see what was going on. After a few weeks, they made some arrests and Mayhew was gone. The only problem was that his cover was blown, and he had some angry people looking for him.

Adams was putting in long hours at the shop, and he knew it wasn't going to get any easier if he ever wanted to buy out his two partners. Mayhew knew the situation and offered to buy in with Bruce. He said that his father-in-law would give him some money to invest in the business. After some discussion, Adams agreed to give him a quarter share in the business for $2,500, which he hoped would be enough for him to buy out Ford and Von Villas.

Adams received a $2,500 check from Mayhew dated May 31, 1983. Later, he would claim that he cashed the check and immediately gave the cash to Von Villas, who had never given him a receipt. Von Villas would insist that Adams never gave him the money.

Whatever their arrangement, Ford and Von Villas continued to use the shop as their base of operations. On May 25, Von Villas instructed Adams to drive down to the El Toro marine base in Orange County to pick up a weapons shipment. Adams was supposed to meet a Latin male in a white Dodge van near the Sand Canyon Avenue gate. He would have a case of CS grenades, a case of smoke grenades, an M79 grenade launcher, two bandoliers of M79 white phosphorous rounds, and two bandoliers of M79 high-explosive rounds.

Adams refused. He'd had enough. He told Von Villas it was too risky and he wouldn't do it.

Von Villas became enraged. "If you don't pick up those weapons," he told Adams, "I'll have you killed."

Adams held his ground. But now he knew he was in deep trouble. He knew Ford and Von Villas would kill him if they suspected him of going to the cops. And by refusing to get more involved in their capers, he had no doubt made them suspicious.

Adams was convinced that the LAPD would treat him like a raving maniac if he went to them with his story about the extracurricular activities of two of L.A.'s finest, but he had to do something. For a while, he thought maybe he should just pack up and disappear.

12

The HollywoodLand Motel

AFTER THE DEMISE OF CLASSY LADIES OUT-CALL SERVICE, JOAN LO-
guercio continued to dance at a variety of go-go bars and strip joints. She also
worked as a barmaid at a club called the Candy Cat. Eventually, she ended up
at the Venus Faire on Lankershim Boulevard in North Hollywood.

One of the best-known porno palaces in Los Angeles, the Venus Faire was
a combination adult bookstore and "Live New York Style Nude Dance Theater."
For four bucks an hour—and far more in substantial tips from customers—girls
at the Venus Faire danced nude on a small stage surrounded by individual
booths. Men sat in these and watched the girls through little plastic windows.
The dancers could see them and would perform at particular angles for their
benefit. The men, in turn, would show their appreciation by slipping money to
the performers through little slots above their windows.

Some of the girls at the Venus Faire were professional porno queens,
"actresses" who made triple-X movies. The Valley, with its bottomless pool of
aspiring starlets and actors, had become the porno capital of the world. Some of
the female stars of this genre performed at the Venus Faire, and they put on quite
a show. They danced. They got down on all fours and humped to the music. They
fondled and played with props, like vibrators and dildos, or performed in tandem,
caressing each other and simulating lesbian sex to excite their customers.

Most of this action was way out of Joany's league. She wouldn't engage in
anything so explicit. She wouldn't use props or do any simulated couplings with
the other girls. She danced nude—period. Surprisingly, Joany still hustled nearly

as many tips as the raunchier acts. Enough patrons, apparently, appreciated a more demure presentation.

On a hot night in early June, Joany was dancing nude onstage, rather dispiritedly, counting the hours till the end of her shift. Although the Venus Faire was a relatively clean establishment compared to its dilapidated, foul-smelling Forty-second Street counterparts, the triple-X atmosphere and sleazy clients could be depressing if she let it get to her. Joany had to work at keeping herself up. She needed to remind herself, frequently, that there were far worse ways to make a living, that dancing nude was easy money, that she endured little compared to real working girls.

But it was a slow night and Joany was bored. The meager tips slipping through the slots were hardly enough to support three kids, or to lift her spirits.

Then a hand reached out from one of the slots and waved a twenty dollar bill, along with a note. Joany snapped them up and gave the patron a big smile. She read the note: "I'd like to see your pussy up close. You really turn me on."

Joany peered into the booth and was immediately impressed: a graying, handsome, middle-aged gentleman dressed in an expensive-looking suit and tie. Maybe tonight won't be such a bust after all, Joany thought. She danced in front of the customer's window, giving him a private show.

After just a few minutes, the gentleman tipped her again. A hundred dollar bill! This guy was definitely making her night.

Suddenly, Joany really felt like dancing. She started getting into it. As suspected, she'd hooked herself a good one. Before long the fingers poked out another C-note, along with another message: "I'd like to see you this Friday night. Give me your phone number." The note was signed Dr. A.

However grateful, Joany was not inclined to give out her phone number. She shouted to Dr. A. so that he could hear her above the music and through the Plexiglas partition. "I have to work Friday night. And I can't give you my number. I have a boyfriend and he wouldn't like that. If you want, give me your number and I'll call you."

This was Joany's standard line. It was partly true, in that Frank was still her on-again, off-again boyfriend. But this brush-off was also designed to avoid crushing the ego of a customer with an outright rejection—and thus losing tips—while at the same time protecting herself from weirdos.

"I'll make it very worth your while if you don't work Friday night," the man shouted from inside his booth. "I'm a very busy man. I'm from out of town and I travel a lot. You wouldn't be able to get hold of me."

He has a nice voice, Joany thought, a real smooth, friendly way about him. And his story rang true. He looked like a busy, important man, and he did have money. It was a judgment call. Joany's instincts told her she could take a chance on this guy. She slipped him her phone number and told him to call her in the morning, when her boyfriend wouldn't be there.

Dr. A. passed her another hundred dollar bill. Joany smiled at him as she took it. That was the nice thing about this job, she thought. Even on a bad night things could turn around pretty quick. She'd picked up $320 in just twenty minutes.

The doctor called her the next morning. His name was Dr. Anderson. He told Joany that nobody turned him on the way she did. He told her he'd been in an automobile accident and crushed his groin. As a result, it was very rare that he got sexually aroused. He would pay anything to be with her. He said he'd give her a thousand dollars. He asked her to meet him at the HollywoodLand Motel in Studio City on Friday night. He told her to get the room and he'd call to find out the room number so he wouldn't have to go to the desk. This request made Joany a little apprehensive. She told Dr. Anderson to call her back the next day and she'd let him know.

A grand for a night's work sounded pretty good to Joany, but turning tricks, no matter how upscale, still made her nervous. She decided to call up her good friend, Bob Von Villas, and ask him what he thought about it.

"It sounds pretty good," Bob told her, "but let me check out this Dr. Anderson for you."

That's what Joany was hoping Bob would do. Bob was great when it came to finding out about people. His connections in the Valley were so good he could get the lowdown on anybody. She'd seen him do it before. Of course, he also had access to police files, which he never hesitated to use.

Joany could always count on him. He had literally saved her from losing her house. Her divorce had been finalized and she either had to pay her ex $15,000 for his interest in the home or sell it. Bob talked to his mortgage broker, Gayl West, and tried to get Joany another loan, but he didn't have any success. So he came up with a last-minute plan to save her.

Bob arranged to buy her house outright, and then he put it back in her name. He spent most of April making the arrangements. Then, in May, he suggested they get a joint mortgage insurance policy for $100,000. That way, if anything happened to either of them, the payments on the house would be taken care of. Her kids would be secure.

Bob thought of everything. All Joany had had to do was take a medical exam and sign the papers, which she did on May 23 when she'd met Bob at Ciscos, the Mexican family restaurant across the street from the Devonshire station.

After the house incident, Joany knew she could trust Bob to look out for her. She could rely on him to make sure Dr. Anderson wasn't a creep. Bob called Joany back later that day. He told her he ran a check on the doctor and he looked pretty good. In fact, he looked like he could be the answer to Joany's problems. He was indeed a big-shot M.D., the head of a pharmaceutical company. He had all kinds of money.

Joany said she was worried about all that business about reserving the room and waiting for him. "Oh, he's probably just the type of person who's very lonely and wants to feel like he's coming home to someone," Bob told her. "That's probably why he wants you to be waiting in the room for him. A lot of guys are like that."

"What if he wants to do something kinky?" Joany asked. That was her other main concern. There were a lot of weirdos running around, and she didn't go for all that freaky stuff.

"Then you tell him to get lost," Bob laughed. "Just tell him you're not into that. It looks pretty good to me. I'd go for it."

Dr. Anderson called back and Joany agreed to meet him, but he called back later and said he had to cancel. His mother was sick and he had to fly to Philadelphia. He phoned a few weeks later and they set a new date.

Dr. Anderson made all kinds of promises to Joany on the phone. He told her he would pay her bills for her. He said he would give her anything she needed. When she mentioned her recent problems with her ex-husband and the house, Dr. Anderson told her he'd write out a check for $20,000 to pay off her bills.

That sounded way too good to be true, but Joany didn't mind listening. And Dr. Anderson said something else that put her at ease. "You know, I'm kind of old-fashioned and I don't go for whips and chains and other stuff," he told her.

The HollywoodLand Motel was a 1950s-era two-story-with-balcony that had started to go to seed. It had the requisite pool, A/C, and color TV, but its only real asset was a Studio City location on Cahuenga Boulevard, just across the Hollywood Freeway from Universal Studios.

Despite its age, it remained a good choice for tourists on a budget. It was just a block from freeway exits and the Universal Studio attractions, and it was midway between Hollywood and the Valley. Going north, Cahuenga turned into Ventura Boulevard, the Valley's glitzy grand concourse. To the south, Cahuenga unloaded right into the heart of Hollywood.

But tourists were no longer the primary denizens of the HollywoodLand Motel. It now served mostly as a temporary home to Tinseltown transients—

aspiring actors, writers, musicians, dancers, cameramen, studio technicians, wardrobe and makeup artists, and, of course, "players"—the ubiquitous deal-making producers. It was a good place from which to hustle up a day job, find an agent, and look for more permanent lodging.

The motel was also home to many new arrivals from distant lands, every-thing from Cambodian boat people to Central American political refugees. Los Angeles had usurped New York as the port of entry for the new wave of immigrants in the 1980s, and Hollywood had become the new Ellis Island. According to a survey taken in the early 1980s, 90 percent of the students at Hollywood High School had been born in foreign countries. The HollywoodLand Motel reflected this trend. In fact, it was now owned and operated by Chinese immigrants.

The HollywoodLand Motel was also known as a time-honored roosting post for Hollywood hookers. Ladies of the night went unnoticed among the motel's motley residents. Nobody in Hollywood could tell the difference between a whore and a starlet anymore. They all looked the same.

Joan Loguercio met Dr. Anderson in room 24 at the HollywoodLand Motel on the evening of June 17. Joany was such a novice she registered under her own name. Despite the drab trappings of the nondescript, box-shaped room, it wasn't a low-rent rendezvous. When Dr. Anderson showed up at nine-thirty, an hour after Joany, he immediately pulled out a big wad of cash, about two grand in hundreds and fifties and twenties, and handed it over to her.

"No woman ever turned me on the way you do," gushed Dr. Anderson. Well, well, Joany thought. She smiled as she stashed the wad in her purse.

Dr. Anderson carried a black attaché case. He opened it and started rum-maging through an assortment of pills—uppers, downers, inbetweeners—de-scribing each as he went along. Joany wasn't into pills, but Dr. Anderson said she'd like them. He said he worked a lot and now he just wanted to relax and have a good time. He was taking the pills and he wanted her to have a good time with him. Joany figured this meant that he wanted to have an all-night sexathon. She was willing to please, so she swallowed three uppers with a vodka and orange juice, also supplied by Dr. Anderson. Then she started rolling up a few joints.

They chatted for a while and Dr. Anderson asked Joany about her family and talked about his own. He seemed like a nice, caring guy. He talked about visiting his sick mother in Philadelphia. He also told her he was very wealthy and he wanted to help her out of her troubled financial situation. He told her he would write her a check for $20,000. Joany didn't know what to make of that. He also talked about taking her on a trip to Las Vegas at a later date.

Before long they started to undress, and Dr. Anderson took off his wig. Joany had thought it was a wig, so it didn't surprise her, but it did seem strange that he had a full head of hair underneath. He wasn't bald, only receding a bit.

Suddenly, Dr. Anderson seemed to change. He no longer acted like the proper gentleman she had been talking to. Instead, he began to act like a tough-talking, hip street person.

Joany's apprehension increased as they started to have sex. This Dr. Anderson really knew his way around under the sheets. She felt like she was with some porno stud, not a conservative physician with a sick mother in Philadelphia. But Joany was stoned, her head was floating, and turning tricks was still new to her. She tried to stop thinking, to stop worrying, to stop being paranoid.

They had sex twice and Joany also gave Dr. Anderson some head. Despite the uppers, by two in the morning Joany was exhausted. "Let's go to sleep for a while," she suggested.

"Okay," said Dr. Anderson.

But he was restless. He kept looking at his watch, at the drapes covering the windows. "Are those the motel's lights or is that daylight already?" he asked.

"I don't know," Joany mumbled from her pillow.

Dr. Anderson got out of bed, pulled the drapes aside, and looked out the window. It was still dark. He came back to bed, lay down, and closed his eyes. Joany thought he was going to sleep, but he didn't. He looked at his watch again, and Joany got her first good look at his arm. Dr. Anderson had a tattoo, a skull and crossbones. Awfully strange for a doctor, Joany thought. She wondered again about the wig.

Before long, the doctor started making moves again. But just as they started rolling, Dr. Anderson stopped and got out of bed. He walked over to the dresser where he had placed his attaché case. "I've got to get some Rolaids," he said.

It took him a long time to find them. When he finally came back to the bed, he told Joany to lie down on her stomach.

"Put your hands underneath," he said. "Masturbate for me."

Joany was hesitant, but she complied. Then he got on top of her, straddling her thighs. She felt one of his hands between her legs, like he was trying to have intercourse with her from behind, trying to move his penis into position. Then she heard a snapping sound behind her—like a piece of elastic.

Joany turned around and looked up at Dr. Anderson. He had his hand in the air and it was coming down at her head just as she turned around. There was something in his hand. It was dark, about the size of his palm.

Joany immediately bucked and twisted around so she was facing him. "I don't feel good," she said, and she slid out from under him and into a crouch. Dr. Anderson quickly slid his hand beneath the covers. Joany tried to see what he was hiding, but he wouldn't show her. She jumped out of bed.

"I have to go," she said. "I feel sick."

129

As she scrambled around the bed, picking up her things, Dr. Anderson kept moving his hand underneath the covers. He tried to get her to lie back down.

"C'mon, Joany, what's the matter?" he said.

He seemed concerned about her queasiness and offered her a drink of orange juice. Joany grabbed the glass and took a sip. As she did, she leaned over his chest and felt around on the bed, trying to find the hidden object, but he continued to move it away.

Joany panicked. Now, finally, she was certain her mind wasn't playing tricks. She felt real danger. She threw her clothes on.

"Relax, Joany, you'll be okay," said Dr. Anderson.

Joany reached into her purse and yanked out the wad of cash he had given her. She grabbed about half of it and shoved it back at him.

"You don't want my money?" he asked, shocked.

"No, I don't want your money. I have to leave."

Dr. Anderson started counting what she had given him. "Well, okay," he said. "I guess you can keep the rest."

Joany was already out the door, flying down the stairway to the parking lot. When she got home at about three in the morning she counted up her cash. She had about a thousand dollars. It wasn't worth it, Joany thought. She was trembling, scared to death.

Joany tried to contact Bob Von Villas the next day but she couldn't reach him. She left a message and he called back two days later. Joany told him the whole story. "I think Dr. Anderson was trying to kill me," she said.

"Oh, no, I don't think so," Bob said. He told her she was probably just being paranoid. She was new to all this.

"What about that thing he had in his hand?" she cried.

"It was probably just a vibrator or something and he just didn't want you to see it."

Joan wasn't buying it.

"If he calls, do you think you'll see him again?" Bob asked.

"No way," said Joany.

During the next week, Bob called a few times and asked Joany what her schedule was, he wanted to get together for a drink. He asked what hours she was working at the Venus Faire and the Candy Cat, when she got off work. He also asked about Frank—when he was around, when he was gone. It was like he wanted an entire rundown of her schedule.

"Why don't you come see me at the Candy Cat on Thursday night," Joany suggested.

"No, not the Candy Cat," Bob said. "I'm known there. A lot of people know me."

After a number of these conversations, alarms started to go off in Joany's head. She couldn't believe what she was thinking.

13

Confidential Informant

"DO YOU THINK THAT'S OUR MAN?" AGENT SAM ODDO ASKED AS HE pulled the unmarked sedan into the parking lot.

Oddo's partner, Mario Fontana, chuckled quietly as he climbed out of the shotgun seat. Agent Oddo, always with the jokes, he thought.

Of course it was their man. Pacing back and forth in front of the coffee shop was a white male, medium height and build, mid-thirties, with dark hair and a gimp leg. He was dressed in navy blue grease-stained work pants and a white, short-sleeved shirt that was also smeared with oil and grease. The name Bruce was embossed on the shirt above the left pocket next to a logo that read International Automotive.

Bruce looked like something you might yank out of a long-abandoned car wreck—mangled, greasy, dirty, unshaven, unwashed, unkempt, and scared to death. He looked like he'd bolt any minute and get run down in the heavy traffic. Everytime a car pulled into the parking lot, his head swiveled 180 degrees, snapping like a slingshot. His eyes scoured the lot relentlessly.

Agents Oddo and Fontana didn't know what to expect from the potential informant. He'd called their office and insisted that he had to talk to some feds. Bruce wouldn't elaborate on the phone. "Okay, we'll go talk to the guy," Oddo told the secretary who fielded the call.

So here they were, strolling up to the Carrows restaurant on Reseda Boulevard in Northridge. It was four o'clock in the afternoon, June 21, 1983.

Like most federal agents, Oddo and Fontana didn't look like feds. It was a hot summer day and they were dressed in jeans, sneakers, and T-shirts. Bruce eyeballed them as they approached the entrance to the restaurant. Finally, he darted up to them and blurted, "Are you the guys I'm supposed to meet?"

Perhaps it was cruel, but Agent Oddo couldn't resist playing with him a little bit. "Well, that depends," he answered slyly, "on just who you're supposed to meet."

"Are you from ATF?" Bruce whispered.

"Yeah, we are," said Oddo.

"Oh good, I need to talk to you," Bruce said excitedly. "I really need to talk to you."

"Fine, let's go inside."

"I got a lot to tell you," Bruce rattled nervously as he limped to a table. "A whole lot of good stuff."

Bruce insisted on a booth with a view of the street. He slid into a corner, his back against the wall, giving himself a full view of the entrance, the other tables in the coffee shop, and the street out front. Oddo and Fontana exchanged knowing looks as they sat down. It seemed likely that Bruce was a few cards short of a full deck. But they would try to keep open minds. It was part of the job.

The two feds started by trying to get Bruce to relax. God, he was nervous. He smoked incessantly, and every few minutes they went through the ordeal of having to watch him try to steady his hands so he could light a match.

"What really got my attention," Agent Oddo later recalled, "was that this guy was so nervous he was literally spilling his drink. He couldn't bring the glass to his mouth without spilling it all over himself and all over the table. We kept having to wipe it up. The glass was filled with ice and it was just rattling all over the place. That really made me think. It's rare to encounter someone that nervous. Someone who's being deceptive doesn't usually take on that type of demeanor."

"This is real sensitive," Bruce told them straight away. "I got a couple of bad actors that are L.A. cops."

"So why are are you coming to us?" Oddo asked. "LAPD has an internal affairs division."

Bruce jolted out of his seat and gripped the table with both hands, shaking it like a pinball machine. "NO, NO!" he cried. His words shot out like a burst from an automatic. "They told me if I went to IAD they had their hooks in there and they'd know about it in minutes, and once they found out I'd be pushin' up daisies."

Just as the words were out of his mouth, Bruce spotted a black and white cruising past the coffee shop. "That's them!" he cried. "I'll bet that's them right now!" He was frantic, about to come apart.

"Wait a minute, Bruce," Oddo implored. "How do you know that's them? And even if it is, how are they gonna know who we are? You could say we're some old friends from back east."

"Oh yeah. That's right," said Bruce. Oddo's logic had a calming effect.

"Okay, okay," Oddo reassured, grasping Bruce by the arm and settling him back into the booth. "So you have a good reason for not going to the LAPD. But I'm still curious—why did you call us?"

Bruce launched into a tale about a trip he'd taken with an LAPD detective to purchase some machine guns. Yeah, all right, that fell under the bailiwick of the Bureau of Alcohol, Tobacco and Firearms, or ATF. Agents Oddo and Fontana were interested now. Bruce's story spilled out in a rush—insurance fraud, some crazy stuff about running hookers from an auto shop, stolen vehicles, loose diamonds, confidence scams, armed robbery, and murder for hire.

As Bruce told it, he had a couple of business partners who were L.A. cops. Respected, beloved, award-winning LAPD veterans, regular pillars of the community. And they were killing people and doing just about everything else under the sun that was illegal. But Bruce couldn't go to the cops, you see, because these guys were the cops. Nobody at the LAPD would believe him, anyway; cops in L.A. didn't do stuff like that. And if he did go to LAPD, word of his attempted snitch would get back to his partners and they would kill him. But he couldn't keep quiet anymore, you see, he had to tell somebody . . .

Oddo, who was in his early thirties, had been with ATF for eight years, but he'd started out as a Chicago cop, so he was familiar enough with police corruption. Fontana, who was ten years older and hailed from Detroit, had also encountered his share of rogue cops. But never in Los Angeles.

Oddo and Fontana knew that the LAPD had a rep for being the cleanest police department in the United States. "When I was in the police academy, all we saw were films from the LAPD," Oddo recalled. "They never had any kind of continual record of police corruption—unlike some cities back east. I was under the impression they ran a pretty clean house."

So Oddo and Fontana knew that Bruce's story couldn't be kosher. It was impossible. Despite the widespread public perception that "it happened all the time," no LAPD cop had ever been nailed for murder. Bruce must be crazy. Otherwise, Agent Oddo realized, it would mean that after being in town for just three months, he had stumbled upon the worst case of corruption in LAPD history. This was so unlikely as to be comical, he concluded.

Still, Oddo couldn't shake a gnawing feeling in his gut. "This guy not only made the call," Oddo later explained, "but he went that one step further and was willing to meet with us. Most informants, especially those who inform on police,

just call and leave anonymous tips. And if someone gives you fraudulent information, they usually won't identify themselves, and for sure they don't want to
meet you. Bruce met with us and told us his name. He exposed himself to us. We
saw what kind of vehicle he drove. He told us where his business was. He gave
us his phone number. He showed us his driver's license. He gave us a whole
personal history on himself. And everything that we asked, he answered. He
didn't evade any of our questions. I asked him if he'd be willing to take a
lie-detector test, and he said he had no problem with that. All of this was very
unusual."

Agent Oddo told Bruce his story was worth looking into. "You've got to
understand, it's not that we distrust your information. But we'll need to check a
lot of this out."

"Go ahead, check it out," said Bruce. "Just don't tell anybody at the LAPD."
The fear in his eyes spoke volumes.

Out in the parking lot, Agent Fontana rubbed the large iced tea stain on his
shirt as he walked toward the nondenominational sedan. "Probably just a nut
case," he said.

"Yeah. Probably," said Agent Oddo.

After his June 21 meeting with Bruce Adams at Carrows, Agent Sam Oddo
wrote up a confidential report and conferred with ATF brass. They too found it
difficult to believe that this confidential informant was playing with a full load.
But they agreed that it had to be checked out; if Adams was telling the truth,
people could get hurt.

The first order of business was to have Adams take a polygraph test. Oddo
arranged to pick Adams up and bring him in for questioning just a few days after
their initial meeting.

The Federal Building in downtown L.A. is at 300 North Los Angeles Street,
just across the street from the Los Angeles Mall and south of LAPD headquarters
at Parker Center. While Adams was taking his polygraph, Agent Oddo talked
with two detectives from the Internal Affairs Division of the LAPD. Detectives
Roger Fox and John Fruge had walked down the street after receiving a call from
Agent Oddo.

Despite Adams's pleas not to contact the police, Agent Oddo had no choice.
Because Bruce's allegations involved members of the LAPD, the LAPD had to be
notified. It was policy.

When Agent Oddo apprised Fox and Fruge of Adams's charges, the two
detectives were incredulous. They listened attentively but didn't buy a word of

it. They helped Oddo draw up some questions for the polygraph examiner, figuring that the whole matter would soon be dismissed.

The examiner found Adams a tough read. Bruce was on Valium for his PTSD, and the effects of the medication had to be taken into consideration. And throughout the test, as questions were being asked and answered, Bruce kept taking deep breaths and exhaling slowly, as he'd been taught to do when he felt stressed. His increasing agitation made it particularly difficult to gauge his truthfulness.

The test results were inconclusive, but the examiner felt that Adams was "leaning toward the truth." On a scale from one to ten, with zero being total deception and ten absolute truth, Bruce clocked in at about six.

This put Oddo in a tough spot. He could neither dismiss Adams out of hand nor assume he was telling the truth. ATF would have to try to corroborate his story. That would probably mean having to convince him to wear a wire. And trusting the LAPD.

LAPD sergeant Roger Fox wanted to have at Adams right away, but Oddo held him at bay. Oddo knew the meeting had to be handled delicately or Adams might freak out. Bruce was on the verge of a major stress attack just being at ATF. If Oddo waltzed in with two LAPD detectives, they might have to call the men in white coats to scrape Bruce off the wall.

Oddo felt he was establishing a rapport with Bruce. He had spoken with him by phone a number of times since their first meeting and sensed he was comfortable confiding in him. But now, it was time for Oddo to lay it on the line—without losing his informant.

"The polygraph was inconclusive," Oddo told Adams. "Now, that doesn't mean I don't believe you, Bruce. But you have to realize the information you're providing is extremely sensitive. I'll take this information, but I'll have to check it out."

"Go ahead, check it out," Adams growled, miffed over the "inconclusive." "Just don't tell the LAPD."

"Bruce, you gotta understand the severity of the crimes you're alleging against these officers. And you have to understand that we've worked with the LAPD in the past many, many times before. We've established what I consider a very good rapport with that department. As a result, I've gotten to know some of these officers on a one-to-one basis. We know which of these officers we can trust. And at some point, you need to trust our judgment."

Adams let out a deep, loud sigh. "You didn't tell on me, did you?" he asked.

Oddo read volumes in Adams's sigh. He read fear, but he also sensed a creeping acceptance, perhaps resignation, that somebody else would have to get involved. Agent Oddo pressed on, delicately but firmly. "Bruce, you have to understand that they have to be involved."

Bruce lit up a cigarette. He was shaking a little bit more than usual, but Oddo felt him softening. "Remember what I told you," Adams said.

"Bruce, you have to understand our position. From a standpoint of policy, from a standpoint of properly investigating this, there has to be some involvement of the LAPD here."

"Well, can you trust anybody over there?" Adams asked.

"Hey, if I introduce you to some LAPD officers they're going to keep everything you say in the strictest confidence."

"Well, if you can assure me . . . But you've got to provide protection for me and my family."

"If that's necessary, we will." Oddo assured Adams that ATF would go to any lengths to keep his family out of harm's way.

"Well, all right," said Bruce. "Then I'll talk to someone."

Agent Oddo was taken aback. He hadn't expected Bruce to come around that quick. So Oddo made a few phone calls, hemmed and hawed around awhile—but not long enough to give Bruce too much time to think—then walked into the next room where Roger Fox was waiting and brought him in to meet Bruce.

Fox ran Adams through his story again. Agent Oddo was relieved to have him involved. Right from the start, the advantages were obvious. Fox had background information on Ford and Von Villas from their LAPD packages. He could immediately verify that Ford and Von Villas were indeed police officers at Devonshire Division, that Ford was a burglary detective and Von Villas a patrol officer—as Adams had described. Adams at least had his background facts right.

But that didn't mean anything. There was nothing in Ford's or Von Villas's file to indicate any hint of corruption or wrongdoing. After a cursory look at their records, Fox could see that these were good officers. There were some minor disciplinary problems, like those found in any package, but nothing to even hint at the type of criminal behavior Adams was describing.

Sergeant Fox talked privately with Agent Oddo after they were through interviewing Adams. "Do you think this guy is all there?" Fox asked.

"Well, Roger, to tell you the truth, I don't know," Oddo answered.

Fox was far more cynical. He thought Adams was a lying piece of scum, a small-time hood, a punk.

Oddo had to admit Adams could be off-putting, and he sensed this had something to do with Fox's reaction. Bruce acted cocky, like a tough guy, a typical East Coast hood. And he dressed like one as well. But being from back east, Oddo had more of an open mind. He had grown up in a neighborhood where lots of guys talked the talk and walked the walk. He knew it wasn't necessarily indicative of criminality. Acting like a wise guy was just part of the cultural conditioning. Oddo knew that a lot of California guys in the LAPD, who weren't entirely familiar with this style, were turned off by it.

Nonetheless, Oddo, like Fox, felt that Adams's story had to be checked out. They agreed to run a parallel investigation, keeping each other apprised of their findings.

Oddo wasn't able to confirm Adams's story about guns in Colorado. Bruce didn't have a name, license plate number, or weapons serial numbers that could be checked out—just a story about some guy on the side of the road near Estes Park. They could subpoena Richard Ford's credit card records to show he'd bought gas in Colorado, but that still wouldn't prove anything about guns. Oddo figured the best and only way to prove anything was to catch Ford and Von Villas in the act.

"Look, Bruce, what you're telling me is a lot of what happened in the past, and in order to establish your credibility and make our case we'll have to corroborate this information. The best way to do it is to record it live as it's coming out of their mouths."

Bruce looked at him and said, "Well, I'll wear a wire."

"Okay, but if you want us to introduce somebody undercover instead, we can probably do that, too."

Bruce told Agent Oddo that would be tough. Ford and Von Villas checked everybody out very carefully. Maybe the feds could do it, but it would take time. If a situation arose, he'd be willing to wear a wire. Bruce told Oddo that Von Villas had been bugging him since the end of May about making a trip to El Toro to pick up some guns. Oddo told him that if a deal like that came down to let him know and he would get him a wire.

After the interview, Agent Oddo drove Bruce back to International Automotive, dropping him off in an alley a few blocks away where nobody could see them. Once again, Oddo assured Adams that his family would be taken care of. Nothing would ever happen to them. For the next two weeks Adams lived in fear, terrified that word of his snitch would get back to Ford and Von Villas.

14

Wires

JOAN LOGUERCIO ENDURED TWO WEEKS OF SLEEPLESS NIGHTS FRET-
ting about Dr. Anderson. She pondered the wig and tattoo, the pills and wad of
cash and the unseen horror hidden beneath the covers at the HollywoodLand
Motel. She worried about an insurance policy and strange inquiries from Officer
Bob. Finally, on July 6, 1983, Joany called her friend, Bruce Adams, and told him
about the incident with Dr. Anderson. She was frightened, tearful. "Bruce, I think
somebody is trying to kill me!" she sobbed. "You don't think it could be Bob?"

Joany felt embarrassed at even suggesting this. Sure, Bob Von Villas was
the beneficiary on her $100,000 life insurance policy. But he was a friend. And
he was a cop. Still, she had this horrible nagging feeling. Perhaps Bruce, the
street-smart wise guy, her former boss and lover, a friend whom she felt she could
trust, could reassure her. Maybe he could set her straight.

Adams immediately suspected what was going on, but he didn't want to
frighten her. "Nah, Joany, whadaya mean? There must be some other explanation. Why don't you meet me tonight for dinner and let's talk." They made
arrangements to meet at the Greek Gardens on Rinaldi in Granada Hills.

As soon as Adams got off the phone he called Agent Oddo at ATF. Adams
had been in contact with Oddo almost daily since their initial meeting, but the
conversations hadn't amounted to much. Adams had also met with Fox and
Fruge from the LAPD, telling them everything he knew about Ford and Von
Villas. But at this point, neither ATF nor the LAPD had been able to corroborate
any of Adams's allegations, and Adams had been unable to provide them with

an opportunity to observe criminal activity for themselves. But during this phone call, Adams was nearly frantic. "I think something big is going down," Adams barked to Oddo. "I want you out there with me tonight." He couldn't explain because he was at the shop, but his urgency got through to Oddo.

Agent Oddo met Adams in a shopping center parking lot on Tampa Avenue near the 118 freeway. While Oddo wired Adams up, Bruce explained who Joany was and what he might hear from her. Oddo then followed him to the Greek Gardens restaurant in his nondenominational sedan. The technical conditions were ideal for a wire. Because Bruce and Joany would both be in fixed locations, it would be easy for Oddo to sit in his car in the parking lot and listen to their conversation on his monitor as he recorded it.

Oddo gave Bruce a few perfunctory instructions. "What you want to do, Bruce, is let her do most of the talking. The worst thing you can do is interrupt while she's trying to tell you something because she might lose her train of thought or close up and then you won't get that conversation back. So if she starts to run at the mouth, just let her go."

Bruce had no trouble with that. Over some wine and scaloppine, Joany ran through the whole story about Dr. Anderson. Adams kept quiet except to crack a few jokes to cool her out. Joany was distraught and Bruce didn't want her to break down or panic. He tried to make light of it all, to reassure her that she wasn't in any danger.

But Bruce Adams knew how serious it was. He knew who Dr. Anderson was—even before Joany described the skull and crossbones tattoo on his right arm. It was Detective Richard Ford. Ford had told him about using a wig on previous capers. And Dr. Anderson was the alias Ford often used when he called up to do security checks on the girls at the escort service. Adams couldn't believe the name hadn't rung a bell with Joany, but in fact she'd never been introduced to him, and if she'd seen him at the shop she'd have paid him no more attention than she did any other customer.

When Joany related the part about Dr. Anderson being on top of her and coming down with something from behind, about turning just in time and twisting away, Adams had to fight to contain himself. She had no *idea* how lucky she was. She'd been in the clutches of "Dr. Death" himself, and somehow lived to tell about it. Adams couldn't figure out why.

Bruce wanted to lean over the table and grab Joany and shake her. He wanted to scream, You stupid airhead! Do you realize you almost got yourself killed! Do you have any idea how close you came to being dead fucking meat! But Bruce didn't do that. He smiled. He joked.

Despite Adams's attempts at levity, Joany finished her tale in tears. "I don't want to die, Bruce," she cried. "Please help me. I don't want to die."

"Don't worry, Joany," Adams reassured her. "You're not going to die. I promise you. I'll do something."

"But what?"

"Don't worry," Bruce said. "I'll think of something."

But it wasn't just Dr. Anderson that had Joany so spooked, she explained. It was Bob, too. Thinking back, Joany realized that many of the concerns she had expressed to Bob about her liaison with Dr. Anderson were later addressed by the doctor himself. She had told Bob she was afraid Dr. Anderson might be kinky; Dr. Anderson had told her he was old-fashioned. Bob told her the john probably wanted her to get the room because he wanted to feel like he was coming home to someone; Dr. Anderson had made a similar remark. And Bob knew she needed money and was worried about her bills; Dr. Anderson had offered her a lot of money and said he would even write out a check so she could pay off her bills. "It's like whatever I said to Bob, Dr. Anderson would be saying back to me," Joany explained.

Then there was the insurance policy. Joany had gotten anxious about that situation and decided she wanted to talk to the broker to see if she could make her kids the beneficiaries, or maybe even cancel the policy. But she didn't know who the broker was. She had talked to him once on the phone but couldn't remember his name, because Bob had handled everything. So she called Bob and asked him who the broker was. He said he didn't know; the name and number were in his locker at Devonshire Division. He said he'd get back to her, but he never did.

And then, Joany explained to Bruce, after she told Bob about what happened with Dr. Anderson, he kept calling and asking her odd questions about her schedule.

Adams felt like a louse as he tried to make Joany think she was just being paranoid. "Trust me, Joany," he said. "You've got nothing to worry about."

At one point Adams excused himself to get a pack of cigarettes. He quickly stepped out the front door of the restaurant and addressed the parking lot. "Are you getting this?" he cried.

Agent Oddo, sitting in the ND sedan with his monitor, waved a hand out the window and nodded yes. Adams walked back in and resumed his conversation with Joany.

After dinner, Joany was afraid to drive home alone. Bruce agreed to follow her in his van just to make sure she was safe. Bruce was all excited as he limped rapidly toward his van, craning his head to look for Agent Oddo. "Sam, Sam, did you hear that, Sam?" Bruce kept repeating, knowing he was still wired. "Boy, we really got some good stuff on tape!" Agent Oddo smiled as he listened and watched Bruce scan the parking lot looking for him.

Oddo followed Bruce to Joany's house. As he drove, the agent contemplated what he had heard. It seemed unlikely that Adams had orchestrated this meeting. If this was a setup, Joan Loguercio was one hell of an actress. During the course of the dinner, she'd plunged through the whole spectrum of emotions, from tears to laughter, flirtatious giggling to guilt-ridden introspection, fond reminiscence to panicked speculation. Oddo knew real fear when he heard it, and Joany's was unmistakable. And her nervous, sometimes awkward responses to Adams's attempts at levity and reassurance also rang very true.

Agent Oddo was feeling somewhat reassured about Bruce, but he was also confused. It was obvious from the conversation that Joany knew Von Villas quite well and was concerned about the insurance policy and all, but what was this Dr. Anderson bit? What was the connection? It was the first question Oddo asked Adams when they met for doughnuts and coffee right after he dropped off Loguercio.

"That's Ford," Adams exclaimed. "That's his fake name. He goes by Dr. Anderson. And the skull and crossbones—he's got that tattooed right on his arm." Adams hadn't told Oddo about Dr. Anderson before. Now he explained it all—the wig, his use of that name when he did a security check of girls at the escort service.

The pieces of the puzzle began to fall in place. Oddo could sense Adams's relief at having finally delivered some corroboration of his story about Ford and Von Villas. But Agent Oddo realized he still didn't have much of anything, just the wild stories of Adams and a woman who'd come out of nowhere. He had to get some real corroboration. He had to get something from Ford and Von Villas.

"Bruce, you have to realize that if what you're telling me is true, when this all comes down, it'll get so much attention you won't believe it. It will be under so much scrutiny that everything will have to be checked and double-checked and triple-checked. This is something like this city has probably never seen, and hopefully will never see again."

Oddo gave Adams a quick rundown about the LAPD, about its rep for honesty and professionalism. "When this thing hits," Oddo said, "the people involved in the investigation better have their shit together, because they're going to be put to the test." Oddo knew that if the case ever moved to trial, he would end up on the witness stand being grilled on every minute detail of his investigation. And that, he told Adams, would be nothing compared to what his informant would have to endure.

"Tomorrow morning," Oddo said, "I need you to wear a wire on Ford and Von Villas. Can you handle that, Bruce?"

Agent Oddo didn't have to tell Bruce it would be dangerous, that his life would be on the line, but Adams knew it was just a matter of time before Ford and Von Villas finished the job on Joany. There wasn't any time to get further corroboration. He realized that if he wanted to save her, and himself, *he* would have to take down L.A.'s killer cops.

The tremble in Adams's hands wasn't so bad as he lit up a cigarette, but a deep sigh spilled out with his exhaled smoke. "Yeah, I think I can handle it," he said.

Sam Oddo met Adams at eight the next morning at a safe, prearranged location. As he wired Bruce up again, he lectured him thoroughly on the laws regarding entrapment. "You have to make sure the idea is coming from them and not from you," Oddo stressed. "It should be obvious to anybody who listens to the tape that the idea did not initiate with the informant, that you never 'planted the seed,' as they say in the law, because then you're starting to border on entrapment. Cases have been lost by the government because of that. It's an issue the defense frequently will raise, especially if they don't have anything else to defend their client."

Bruce was silent, distant. He was thinking about his nightmare.

"Do you read me, Bruce?"

Adams came out of the haze. "Yes sir," he responded. "Loud and clear."

They drove in their separate vehicles to International Automotive, arriving about eight-thirty. Oddo scouted a perfect location for monitoring and surveillance. North of the shop there was a large open field that ended at another street. By parking on that street, Oddo could use binoculars to see right into the entrance of the shop. He was also able to park his ND sedan right next to a pay phone, which would prove invaluable.

Bruce went into the shop and they tested the wire. The transmission was clear and Oddo's view was good enough to make out Bruce's facial expressions when he stood in the entranceway. Von Villas wasn't due in for another hour, so Oddo called Bruce on the phone and told him to turn off the wire to save the batteries.

Oddo called again in a half-hour. "Have you heard anything?" he asked.

"Yeah," said Bruce. "Von Villas called. He's on his way down."

"Turn on the wire and make sure it's working."

Bruce turned on the wire. "Okay, everything's working fine," said Oddo. He hung up the phone and got back into position in the ND sedan.

Bruce called up Joany and told her not to worry about anything, reinforcing his assurances from the previous night. Joany told him she was afraid to go to work that day at the Venus Faire, and Bruce told her to go anyway. "Don't worry, I'll have somebody watching out for you."

Before long Von Villas pulled up in his Pontiac. Oddo recognized him immediately from Adams's descriptions and LAPD photographs. As Oddo watched the cop get out and walk into the shop, he heard interference coming across the wire. It wasn't working the way it should be.

Von Villas and Adams left immediately in Von Villas's Grand Prix. Oddo wasn't alarmed; Adams had told him they would be going to pick up a vehicle that belonged to Bunny, one of Bob's girlfriends. About fifteen minutes later they returned. Bob was driving a red Firebird that belonged to Bunny's son. Adams drove Bob's car.

Adams and Von Villas went into the shop, but all Oddo could hear on the monitor was static. After a few minutes he went to the pay phone and called up the shop. "Bruce, did you turn that thing on?" Oddo asked.

"Yeah, yeah," said Bruce.

"It's not working properly," said Oddo.

"Well, what do you want me to do? He's here right now."

Oddo told Bruce to go to the bathroom and take a look at the wire and see if something was disconnected or if he might have hit the off switch by mistake.

Bruce left and then returned to the phone. He told Oddo everything looked the way it was supposed to. Oddo asked him if there was any way he could leave and come meet him. Adams said no.

"Well, as long as you've done your best to insure that you're following the instructions I gave you, then there's nothing else we can do," said Oddo. "Just do your best."

The transmission was sporadic and Oddo only picked up slivers of conversation. It went in and out, like something wasn't properly connected. Eventually, it went dead. He got nothing.

A few minutes later a man arrived in a plain four-door Plymouth with an antenna on the trunk. Oddo pegged it as an unmarked police car. Oddo knew it was Ford from Adams's descriptions and photographs. The car pulled right up to the front of the shop and Ford got out and went inside.

A few minutes later, Ford and Von Villas stepped outside, without Adams. Oddo watched as they talked for about five minutes. Then they went back inside and Oddo didn't see or hear anything for another ten minutes. Finally, both Ford and Von Villas left the shop.

Oddo went to the phone and called Bruce. "What happened?"

"You better pull out all stops," Bruce said. "These guys are going to take Joany down tonight."

"What do you mean?" Oddo asked.

"They're going to kill her tonight. I'm supposed to go with them. Me and Ford. We're picking her up when she gets off work."

Oddo couldn't believe it. "Is there any way you can meet me at my office and we can get this all down?"

"Yeah. I can close up in less than an hour and meet you back at your office."

Before he left, Oddo called in an alert to ATF headquarters; he'd just been advised by a confidential informant that two LAPD officers were planning to murder a woman named Joan Loguercio tonight at midnight when she got off work at the Venus Faire porno theater in North Hollywood. It was close to noon when he made the call. They had twelve hours.

When Adams arrived at the ATF Valley offices at the Van Nuys Federal Building, Oddo checked Adams's wire. The connection was very loose. Bruce didn't know how it had happened. Oddo told him it could have been caused by any of a number of things. Maybe Bruce caught the wire inside his armpit while he was turning or lifting something.

Adams explained what had gone down at the shop. When he got back from picking up the Firebird, he confronted Von Villas about Loguercio. "What's this Dr. Anderson shit?" he said. "You guys are getting sloppy. That Dr. Anderson routine is getting old."

Von Villas acted like he didn't know what Bruce was talking about. Adams told him he had talked to Loguercio, that she was scared—and ready to cancel the insurance policy. "What's this shit about you got a policy on her?"

"It's just for the house," Von Villas said.

"Well, that broad's gonna cancel the policy," Adams told him. "That broad's wise to you."

At this point, Von Villas got on the phone and called Richard Ford and told him to get over to the shop. When Ford arrived, Von Villas took him outside to talk.

Adams had no idea what was said outside, but when they walked back in, they copped to the whole plot. Von Villas told Adams he'd pay him $12,500 if he'd help them get Loguercio tonight. "She won't go anywhere with us," Von Villas said. "You're the only one she trusts."

Adams told them he'd do it.

"But she's got to go tonight," emphasized Von Villas. "She's got to be dead tonight." He was worried that she'd cancel the insurance policy.

Von Villas told Adams to get on the phone right away and set it up. He and Ford watched while Adams dialed Joany's number.

Bruce spent about five minutes engaged in small talk with Joany. Von Villas stood next to him, writing notes. The first one said "$12,500 *each*," a reference to what he had offered to pay Adams and Ford. Apparently, Bob felt that Adams might not have understood he would be getting $12,500 just for himself, that he wouldn't have to split it with Ford. The second note read: "Find out how much Frank knows." Von Villas was worried that Joany had mentioned her suspicions to her boyfriend. The last note read: "Meet me tonight. Late. Maybe motel?" Apparently, Bob thought it might be a good idea for Adams to suggest another tryst.

After his dinner with Joany the previous night, Bruce didn't have to come up with anything. Joany trusted him. "Whadaya say I meet you tonight after work and we go out for a drink, or maybe some coffee," he said. Joany said that would be fine. She told him to pick her up at midnight at the Venus Faire.

15

Firestorm

AGENT ODDO WAS NERVOUS. HE HAD THE WHOLE DAMN VAN NUYS bureau of ATF on alert, mobilizing to take down some killer cops, but the only evidence he really had was the word of a confidential informant, a sleazy Vietnam stress-case he'd known about three weeks, and the wild tale of a hysterical, perhaps paranoid nude exotic dancer/hooker.

"Bruce, we've got a problem," Oddo had explained after Adams related what had transpired at the shop. "Nothing came out on the wire. I'm not blaming you and I'm not blaming me. Maybe it was just faulty equipment. But what we need to do is at least get a recorded conversation so we can establish certain facts."

Oddo decided to have Adams telephone both Ford and Von Villas to apprise them of his progress in preparing for the hit. Adams claimed that they had directed him to find a good place to dump Loguercio's body—somewhere in Hollywood Division, where homicide detectives were too inundated with cases to follow up on a dead hooker. Adams was also supposed to get some carpet or other material to put in the back of his van for Ford to hide under. Ford had mentioned he had some drugs they could give to Loguercio to knock her out. The plan was to then rape and torture her to make it look like a sex crime. These were juicy little details; Oddo wanted to get Ford and Von Villas talking about them on tape.

Oddo and his partner, Mario Fontana, brought in Deputy District Attorney Robert Jorgensen to listen in and make sure everything was done properly. With the phone wired and tape recorders running, Adams sat at Oddo's desk and called up Club Dev at 3:09 P.M.

147

"This is Ford."

"Hello, Ford," said Bruce.

"Hi, whadaya doin'?"

"Nothing much," answered Bruce. "I got a location."

"Oh good, where?"

"Okay. On Mulholland, east of Outpost Drive. It's perfect. It swings into a big alcove and it can't be seen from the road."

"All right."

"Can you talk?"

"No."

"Oh, okay."

"No, no way. Okay . . ."

"Was I to understand that I'm supposed to get twelve or ten?" Adams asked. He was referring to his payment.

"Twelve," said Ford.

"Twelve," Adams repeated.

"Yeah, we're both the same."

"Both the same."

"Right."

Ford had to go. He told Adams he'd meet him at the shop at eight o'clock.

It wasn't much, but Agent Oddo's apprehension eased considerably. At 3:19 P.M., Adams called Von Villas at his home in Simi Valley. Von Villas was just getting over the flu and had gone home for the day. The phone was answered by one of his daughters, who said he was asleep. However, Von Villas picked up on the extension in his bedroom. Adams began by explaining his progress on Bunny's Firebird—that it had an exhaust leak and needed a new alternator. Then he said, "Okay, I also found the location."

"Okay, okay," said Von Villas. "Do you have carpet in the back of your van? Ah, behind, ah, there's always carpet behind . . . Damn, I can't think of the place. It's on Chatsworth."

"One of the carpet stores?"

"Yeah. We'll . . . ," Von Villas stammered, "get rid of this carpet. That's right after."

"Fire it up or what?"

"Aw, no, just go throw it in somebody's Dipsy Dumpster."

"I'll just stuff it in a Dumpster."

"And just put in a new piece."

"Okay. Ah, she is kind of kinky, man. Like I said, she's really getting squirrelly." Bruce was referring to Loguercio.

"Ah, you haven't talked to her since, have you?"

"No, uhn uh. But . . ."

"Okay, that's all right," said Von Villas. "Yeah, it will be taken care of. It will be over with tonight. Just ah, that's all there is to it, so, ah, make sure you have a full tank of gas."

"Need a full tank of fuel," said Adams.

"Put supreme in."

"Okay," said Adams. "This will square us, right?"

"Oh, more than that. I'll owe you. I mean, as far as, ah . . ." Von Villas paused a moment. "Yeah, yeah, yeah. It'll be squaring us plus." He was referring to what Adams had to pay him to buy him out of the shop.

"Plus."

"Yeah."

"Figure I'll come out with nine or ten?" asked Adams.

"Ah, at least nine."

"At least nine."

"Yeah, and the only reason for the other is, we've gotta . . . it's just the stupid machine," said Von Villas, referring to the air compressor at the shop. "What we might do is, ah, I'm thinkin' I'll keep three. And you give me the payment book."

"Okay, and then you'll just pay off the machine."

"And I'll make the payments for the next three years. All right. That way, there—because it's in my name."

"Yeah, true."

"That's the only thing I'm concerned about," said Von Villas.

"All right."

"And so, actually, yeah, it'll end up, you'll end up with about ninety-five and zero."

"About ninety-five and zero."

"Yeah, there you go. Like I said, both balances will be cut and if Ford's ah—Ford will be out about three thou. I'll give him his three thou." Ford and Von Villas had each invested about three thousand dollars in the shop.

"Okay."

"So he's going to be happy all the way around."

"All right."

"Okay."

"Any ideas what we should do with the, uh, remains?" Adams asked.

Von Villas emitted a loud sigh.

"Dump 'em? Just leave them to find, huh?" asked Adams.

"Yeah, yeah, ah, yeah. I'll ah, I'm gonna have a discussion with Dickie around five o'clock and run over the final details and then you two will get together and then . . ."

"Yeah, because I called him and told him I found a location."

"Okay, yeah that's great. All right, let's, on the Firebird now . . ."

The two men discussed a number of problems with the Firebird. "I can't believe she paid eighty-nine dollars for that battery," Von Villas said. "She bought it out of a gas station."

"Well, yeah, they rip you off out of a gas station," said Adams. "Anyway, Mulholland east of Outpost Drive, that's Hollywood, right? It's east of La Brea and north of Sunset."

"So it's on the south side of Mulholland?"

"Yeah, it's like . . ."

"Way down."

"Yeah, it's like a . . ."

"Quarter of a mile."

"It's three miles off Outpost, down east of Outpost Drive."

"Is it on Mulholland?"

"It's on Mulholland, but there's a helluva alcove in there, with a lot of trees."

"Okay, it's gotta be on the south side," said Von Villas.

"It's on the south side."

"Yeah."

"Okay."

"They might even be, ah, might even be . . ."

"Sheriffs?"

"I don't know. I'll have to take a look," said Von Villas, yawning. "It's not too far from . . ."

"It's about four miles from the Hollywood Freeway, up in the canyon."

"Yeah, that sounds great, uh, that, uh, what about ah . . . That's not too far from the location, though? Half an hour drive?"

"From her?"

"Yeah."

"Nah, it's about a twenty-minute drive."

"Okay. Just make sure that, ah, the vehicle is in good shape."

"Yeah, it's in good shape. I'll make sure I got a full tank of fuel and everything else so we can boogie out of there when it's done. Alrighty?"

"Yeah, that should do it. All right, so, ah, okay, there's no rush on the Firebird. Just try to keep it from getting banged up over there."

They talked more about the shop, about Von Villas's flu. Then Adams said, "What do you figure, before we can get paid?"

"Ah, I don't know. We're hoping within sixty days, which is a long time. But I can . . ."

"Well, if I can get a little, you know, financial support if I need it from somewhere."

"Yeah, ah, if I know there's not going to be any hassles or anything, then I've got a friend that'll give me some money for ninety days."

"Oh, okay."

"And then I'll give each of you some."

"Yeah, 'cause I'd like to have a little freedom of mind," said Adams. "You know, I just mean, it's not the point of doing this. It's my shop is starting to bother me. Because I put a lot of time and money into it, you know."

"Yeah, I know the time, I know the time. Yeah, I know people are breathing down your neck too."

They talked more about the shop, Adams's attempts to get other loans, the motor mounts on Bob's Pontiac—a job Von Villas said he needed done by Saturday night.

"It'll be ready to go," said Adams.

"Okay, now the only other thing would be the van preparation," said Von Villas, yawning again. "That's all, just make sure that van's in good running shape and I'm gonna mention it to Dickie."

"Okay."

"And as a matter of fact, if that carpet's already all screwed up, ah . . . why don't you strip it out of there and get a new piece?"

"All right."

"It won't take you, ah—any carpet store usually has something out back. You shouldn't have any problem, and the Dipsy Dumpster's out back. There's one on Zelzah and Chatsworth, to the rear alley. You turn right and you'll see. You'll see the Dipsy Dumpster."

"Okay."

"And he's always got some, even if you used a rubber pad."

"Yeah, foam rubber or something like that."

"Yeah! As a matter of fact, you might grab a couple of pieces and ah, that way there . . ."

"It'd save the carpet. No evidence."

"Yeah, yeah. Well it'll also give, ah, Dickie a place to be."

"Yeah, for sure. That way he could cover up underneath the foam padding."

"Come on in, Shannon," Von Villas said, talking to his daughter. Then to Adams, "Yeah, yeah. And that's about it."

"Okay, partner," said Adams.

"Okay, talk to you tomorrow."

"Right. Have a good day," said Adams.

Agent Oddo was not only relieved, he was ecstatic. This conversation really cemented things. Von Villas had brought up the details—the same details Adams had given to the Feds. Oddo's doubts about the reality of this caper were put to rest. He shifted into overdrive.

A major mobilization by a federal law enforcement agency is a sight to behold. Federal agents are accustomed to operating on short notice under life or death pressure. When the decision is made to move on dangerous suspects, particularly when lives hang in the balance, the entire agency clicks into war-room mode. Agents are called in off the streets and yanked from vacations, emergency strategy sessions are conducted at fever pitch, battle plans distributed, and before you can say "J. Edgar Hoover," an army of agents has been briefed, armed, equipped, coordinated, and mobilized.

This operation would prove doubly awesome, since it also involved the LAPD Internal Affairs Division, the model for all such divisions throughout the country. It was regarded in law enforcement circles with the same respect soldiers have for the Green Berets. The LAPD were overzealous, perhaps, but they were still the best.

This joint ATF/IAD operation, one of the largest Los Angeles had ever seen, would employ rolling communications and surveillance support vehicles, helicopters, dozens of squad cars and ND sedans manned by highly trained, well-armed troops, and an army of undercover agents. Within one hour of arriving at the ATF offices, Bruce Adams found himself in the eye of a firestorm, a military-precise whirlwind operation large and sophisticated enough to take down a small island dictator.

Despite this overwhelming support, Agent Oddo knew that Adams would be in harm's way. He proceeded to prepare his front-line soldier for the ordeal ahead. First, he delivered Adams's Chevy van to ATF's bug experts to have it wired. There would be no fuck-ups, no broken wires, no missed transmissions during this midnight ride.

The decision was made to keep Loguercio in the dark, lest she panic and upset the entire operation. But Agent Oddo would not allow her to be endangered in any way. Adams would have to shoulder all the risks. A team of undercover ATF and IAD agents were commissioned to disguise themselves as perverts and lonely businessmen and were quickly dispatched to the Venus Faire, where they spent the next eight hours keeping their eyes glued to a naked Joan Loguercio. It was tough duty, but somebody had to do it.

When preparations were complete, Oddo drove Adams back to International Automotive so he could instruct his helpers and have them close up the shop. At around six-thirty Oddo drove Bruce over to his house in Van Nuys. When they walked into the house, Shirley noticed that Bruce was really nervous, far worse than usual.

Shirley knew Bruce had been pretty stressed out lately. She knew he was trying to buy out Dick and Bob at the shop. Just a few nights before, Bruce had told her that he was at his wits' end and he didn't know what to do, that he wanted to run away and never come back. He was a nervous wreck; he could barely sleep. He told her that Bob had threatened him, but Shirley just assumed he meant with a lawsuit, or financially, that it was just some partnership disagreement, that Bob wanted more money. Shirley had no idea what was really going on. Bruce had always intentionally kept her in the dark about his partners' activities. Now it was time for her to be enlightened.

"Shirl, this is Sam," Bruce said. "I've got to take a shower. Then me and Sam have to go somewhere." Bruce left them together and jumped in the shower.

Bruce had mentioned to Shirley that he'd been hanging out lately with a guy named Sam, an old war buddy.

Sam Oddo strode across the warped floorboards of the Adams's living room to the dining room table and sat Shirley down. First, he explained that he wasn't an old war buddy; he was a federal agent, and Bruce was working with him on an extremely delicate and sensitive matter as a confidential informant. Then he dropped the bomb.

"Your husband is working with me on an undercover operation tonight that could be very dangerous," Oddo calmly explained. "The fact is, your whole family may be in danger. I want you to start packing your bags. You and your entire family are getting out of town. Immediately." Oddo decided to be completely honest. "Grab everything that's important to you. Chances are you'll never be coming back here again."

Shirley's heart nearly stopped.

Agent Oddo knew what lay ahead for the Adams family. So did Bruce. If the operation worked as planned, Bruce would be spending a few years, at least, in hiding. If it didn't work, he'd probably be dead. Either way, his business was history. His life as a San Fernando Valley auto mechanic was history. His entire life, at least as he had known it, was history.

Oddo was kick-starting their new life. He gave Shirley about ten seconds for the news to sink in, but he didn't want to give her time to go into shock. "Mrs. Adams," Oddo said gently, "I really need for you to get up and start packing right away."

Shirley suddenly let loose a flood of questions, and as Oddo had feared, she became hysterical. She started sobbing, "Oh please, don't let anything happen to him!" Oddo put his arm around her as her chest heaved and the tears flowed. "Don't worry, Mrs. Adams. We're going to take good care of Bruce. And we're also going to protect you and your family. Now please start gathering some of your things. We don't have much time."

As Bruce got dressed and Shirley packed, weeping as she filled their suitcases, two more ATF agents arrived and began turning the Adams home into an operations/communications center. Their walkie-talkies crackled continuously with messages from the units in the field. They brought in a sophisticated radio system and set it up on the dining room table. Shirley couldn't help but notice the huge guns holstered on their hips. She cried and cried.

Agent Oddo told her to send the two little girls away for the night. Shirley called some friends and arranged for them to pick up Julie and Stacey right away.

Eric, the Adams's teenager, was also sent to stay with a friend. Marilyn, the oldest daughter, refused to leave. One of the ATF agents told her, "Okay, fine, you want to stay here, that's up to you."

He knew she would clear out soon enough.

Oddo finally told the distraught woman to just grab what she could carry and leave everything else. "We'll get it later," Oddo said. "It will all be taken care of."

Oddo and Adams drove back to ATF headquarters. At Oddo's request, Adams made one more call to Detective Ford at Devonshire Division. It was 7:27 P.M. The phone was wired.

"Hey, guy, I'm runnin' a little late," said Adams.

"Okay, I'll meet you there at nine," said Ford.

"We, ah, we can take a ride by there. We're goin' to have to check out those places anyhow, guy, so we know what we're gonna do."

"That's no problem," said Ford.

"You already got it covered?"

"No, I ain't got it covered."

"Oh."

Ford laughed. "I just don't worry about it. I don't fuckin' worry about it, you know."

"You fuckin' maniac."

"It's like takin' candy from a baby, that's all," said Ford.

"I know, but . . ."

"No. No problem."

"All right. Do you want me to make it nine o'clock then?"

"Yeah, 'cause it's not even fuckin' dark yet."

"Yeah, I know, it's still daylight out," said Adams. "And I'd like to eat and have some time with my kids."

"Yeah, make it nine. I'll meet you at the shop at nine."

"Okay, kid."

"Okay, so it ain't gonna be no big fuckin' thing."

"Yeah, quick and . . ."

"It's gonna be like taking candy from a baby," said Ford.

"Yeah. Quick and easy."

"Yeah, it won't be any problem. If you get a chance, pick up a bottle of anything. Or, do you have a long-stem bottle?"

"Yeah."

"Good, 'cause I . . ."

"How about some Cella lambrusco?" said Adams. "That's what I used to drink and that's what we used to drink when we used to go out."

"Oh, it doesn't matter, 'cause—you ain't gonna get it down with that any-way. What I've got is six Tuinals, thirty milligrams. It's gonna knock her out, bang."

"Solid. And the rest is fuckin' easy."

"Yeah, the rest is easy," said Ford. "Otherwise we would have a big fight, a continuous big goddam fight."

"Yeah."

"Yeah. But we gotta get it down her throat, that's the problem, okay?"

"That's no problem. Just grab her by the nose and by the chin and jerk her jaws open."

"Yeah, we need somethin' to pour it in and make sure most of it gets in, though."

"Oh, that's no problem."

"Okay."

"That's it, partner," said Adams.

"Okay, we'll see you at nine," said Ford.

Downstairs in ATF's garage, Adams's van was wired and ready to go. Two microphones had been implanted in the ceiling just above the visors. ATF electronics experts were confident that Ford would never find them. They had also made sure to render the van's radio inoperative, so there would be no music to interfere with transmission of their conversation.

A half-dozen ATF and IAD agents convened a final operations meeting with Adams. They gave him explicit instructions, telling him exactly where they wanted him to park the van in front of the Venus Faire. He was told how numerous undercover teams would be listening to him at all times, as well as following him as long as they could without being spotted. They questioned Adams about what weapons Ford would most likely be packing. "He may carry his issue weapon," Adams told them, "and he carries a twenty-two derringer all the time in his pocket—a North American five-shot. It's enough to do good damage if you're sitting right next to somebody."

"You got a piece on you?" one of the agents asked.

"No," said Adams. "You wanna loan me one?"

They refused to supply him with a gun. "Just do as we tell you and it'll be all right," they told him. Bruce couldn't believe this. It was just like being in the marines all over again. Just do as you're told. Easy for them to say. Meanwhile, he was the grunt who had to go in and face Charlie. It was *his* life on the line.

One of the agents asked Bruce if he was scared.

"Nah, I ain't scared," said Bruce. What the hell was he supposed to say? The truth? That he was fuckin' terrified? He knew if Ford discovered the wire, or got suspicious, he wouldn't hesitate to kill him. Adams figured that Detective Ford, his good buddy from the Sepulveda V.A., was probably planning to kill him anyway after they killed Loguercio. Ford had bragged to him about jobs like this he'd done before. He'd bragged to him about fragging officers in the army. Adams was going eyeball to eyeball with Dr. Death himself. Why the fuck should he be scared?

Bruce stashed a commando knife in his boot. Just in case.

Agent Oddo rode with Bruce in the wired van. As they pulled out of ATF headquarters, they were followed by a fleet of vans and ND sedans filled with agents who were listening to them on their monitors, making a last-minute check of their equipment. Then, one at a time, they took off in different directions.

"Don't worry," Oddo kept reassuring Bruce. "You'll be in our sights all the way. Somebody will always be able to see you. Just be careful. Watch what you say. Don't worry about your family. I'll have men watching them. When this is over, I'll get protection for you and the family. Nothing's gonna happen. Everything is gonna go off fine. Remember everything we talked about . . ."

Bruce listened quietly as he drove and smoked, trying to convince himself that there was nothing to worry about. He wasn't just worried about Richard Ford—he was worried about himself. Could he handle it? Could he take the stress? What if he had an attack? What if he got agoraphobic and freaked out? Bruce wasn't taking any Valium. He didn't want to be calm. He wanted to be hyperalert. Could he really handle this?

Adams was so distracted by his own thoughts that he wasn't paying attention to his driving. Suddenly, the flashing lights of a police car began blinking right behind him. A regular LAPD patrol unit—totally unaware of the operation—had caught him rolling through a stop sign. Agent Oddo couldn't believe it. He jumped out and badged the unwitting patrol officer. So did about five other agents who were following in unmarked vehicles.

"We're federal agents," Oddo barked at the officer as he flipped his badge. "You are ruining an operation. Go on, get the hell out of here. This man is working with us."

The patrol cop looked at the swarm of feds who suddenly engulfed him, flashing Treasury badges, and figured he'd just interrupted an operation designed to prevent a presidential assassination. Ronald Reagan must be in town, he figured, probably heading back to Van Nuys or Burbank airport after spending Fourth of July up at Rancho Cielo. What else could it be? The cop got back into his black and white and took off.

16

The Dark Side of the Force

THE WAR HAD BEEN OVER FOR MORE THAN A DECADE, BUT BRUCE Adams and Richard Ford both felt like they were going out on an operation in Vietnam. It was 9:00 P.M., July 7, 1983, when they rendezvoused at International Automotive.

"If there's an investigation going down," Ford told Adams, "nothing's gonna happen. If they start leaning on you, you say nothing. If they take you down they can only hold you forty-eight hours. They might be able to file a case but they can't prove it. In order to file, they have to have some kind of fucking evidence.

"All right," Detective Ford continued, "the way I see it, it'll be chop, chop, chop. The next thing is, we cruise down to Hollywood . . . go down the alley and dump the body."

"Yeah," said Adams as he lit up a cigarette, "we'll just dump her out of the fuckin' van."

The two men piled into Adams's powder blue 1974 Chevy van. Detective Ford immediately looked in back. "You guys got enough shit in there for me to cover up with?"

"Yeah," said Adams. "Where's your attaché case? Near my feet?" Adams knew Ford had a "homicide kit" in his attaché.

"Yeah, somewhere there."

"Okay, I got blankets up the ass," said Adams. "Uniforms up the ass. Stuff like that, you know."

"It comes apart and the world comes to an end," said Ford.

"Oh fuck," said Adams.

Richard Ford was dressed in an old jeans jacket and cowboy boots. He knew it would get messy. His manner was cold, efficient. As Adams put the van in gear and pulled out of the drive, Ford proceeded to check out the interior—windows, doors, seat pull-backs—fiddling with everything, making sure it all worked.

Adams was nervous. "What are you looking for?" he asked. His heart pounded. Was Ford looking for a wire?

"I'm just showing terrain appreciation. Remember that?"

"Oh, yeah," said Adams.

"It's a military operation," said Ford. "Okay, let's get some fuckin' gas."

Jump-off point wasn't for another three hours: midnight, when Loguercio ended her shift at the Venus Faire. This gave Ford and Adams plenty of time to plot, rehearse, reconnoiter, pump each other up—and chain-smoke packs of Marlboros. Just like they had in Nam.

The plan was for Ford to lie hidden under the blankets in the back of the van. When Loguercio got in at midnight, it would be good-bye Joany.

"Okay, after the first half-block you have to hit the brakes," Ford explained. "You reach and grab her. Now, the only thing I'm going to have control of is her throat."

"Right," said Adams as he steered the van up Tampa Avenue toward the Simi Valley Freeway.

"The only thing I'm trying to do is stop her from fuckin' hollerin', okay?"

"All right."

"Grab her, hit her one, tie her up. Stuff a fuckin' rag in her mouth . . . The first thing is to come back and help me gag her."

"All right."

"Open her mouth wide and down her fuckin' throat . . . flip her over on her stomach and tie her hands behind her back and tie her hands to her legs. What I want to do while we have her in back . . ."

"Find out how many people know [that somebody's trying to kill her]," Adams interrupted.

"Yeah, find out everything you can find out," said Ford. "The way I'm gonna do that is the same way we interrogated Charlie. Number one, you have to rip me off for a thousand-plus dollars [the money Ford gave her at the HollywoodLand Motel]. Number two, there's a contract on your ass, twenty-five thousand fuckin' dollars, by a dude by the name of Bob Von Villas. Okay?"

"Yeah."

"And old Bruce and I here are splitting twelve thousand dollars each. Now she can make a deal with us, then we can turn the fuckin' tables around here and take old fuckin' Bob Von Villas out."

"I like that," said Adams.

"If you suck us and fuck us real good, then we can make a deal with you. That way . . ." Ford paused and lit a cigarette. "Every human being, as you well know, when they're dying, is looking for something to hope for."

"Yeah, it's like a ray of hope," said Adams.

"That'll make her easier to deal with," said Ford.

"Yeah, she'll be more controllable," said Adams.

"Now," Ford continued, talking quickly as if he were high on speed, "we'll hold her head back and give her this fuckin' Tuinal. These are big fuckin' Tuinal. Two should knock her down, or four should make her a blob of shit."

"Yeah."

"It should be obvious to the fuckin' police what happened," Ford explained. "A fuckin' sex fiend doped her up, tortured her, and killed her. They do that all the time. That's why I need a long-stemmed bottle to push her fuckin' mouth open."

"And shove it in."

"And shove it down her fuckin' throat so that shit gets down her fucking throat. Then about thirty minutes later she'll belong to us. Now, the next part is, she has to be fucked up, right? So it's gotta look like she's been up there dancing her ass off, as in the past, she's been dating. She made a date tonight with somebody. The guy who picked her up was a fuckin' sex fiend, took her out some fucking place, doped her up, fucked her, tortured her fucking ass, buttfucked her, just fucked her up, okay?"

"All right."

"Fucked her body up, beat the shit out of her, ended up fucking killing her and dumped her in a fuckin' alley in Hollywood. So the whole thing is supposed to look like it was a sex crime."

"Yeah, like a sex crime," said Adams.

"Wham, bam, thank you, ma'am," said Ford. "That's twenty-five thou even. That'll give us twelve thou each."

Adams lit a cigarette, eyes on the road. "Boy, I'll tell you what, you don't know what that is going to be like, kid."

"I sure fuckin' do," said Ford. "I know what it's like. I am so far in fuckin' debt, I've got bills coming out of fucking bills. That's in *this* caper. The next caper is going to be in August. I'm going after those fuckin' diamonds."

"What, the Jewelry Mart?"

"The Jewelry Mart."

"I thought that fucking thing was dead."

"Well, it was dead," said Ford, "but I'm going to rebirth it."

"All three of us are going in—you, me, Von Villas, all right?" Adams said.

Ford paused for a moment, thoughtfully dragging on his cigarette. "I didn't want to do that before," he said. "Bob is a partner and you're a partner. I tolerate Bob, but I don't particularly like the fucker. Okay, he's a good con man, a good bullshit artist, and I think he'll hold up his weight. But when the chips are down I'm really nervous about my back. You know, if the shit hits the fan, I got to have a right hand—somebody that's not afraid to zip a fucking magazine up someone's ass."

"I can take care of that, pal."

"Bob is good for talking," Ford continued, "he's a good businessman, a good organizer, but I need a third man. As long as you're coming in on this, it's going to make it perfect. It's going to make it like the Mafia, like small organized crime. When this thing goes down, you have to remember it's going to be the biggest fuckin' caper that's hit this goddam city in probably the last hundred years."

"I know," said Adams.

Detective Ford continued to talk, spitting out plans for future heists, plotting all the details: entry, knocking out power sources, getaway vehicles, weapons, fencing. For one operation, he planned to cut through the roof of a jewelry store and use the Jaws of Life to open a safe.

"Yeah, you make about a one-half-inch crack in the safe," Ford explained. "You take the fireman's Jaws of Life and crank that motherfucker up. You'll have to modify the muffler system on it, Bruce, to keep it quiet. Plug that motherfucker in the back of the safe, and it'll peel that fuckin' door like a goddam skin on a goddam orange."

While Ford babbled on, Adams turned south on 405, the San Diego Freeway. As he passed the Devonshire Street exit, he gazed off to his right and took in the huge complex and grounds of the Sepulveda V.A. where he had met Richard Ford.

Sitting next to him, Ford was still talking a mile a minute. "I've been capering alone for years," he explained, "but when you caper alone, you're limited to what you can or can't do."

"True," said Adams.

"As far as killing assholes, I'll just do it for fuckin' kicks," Ford said. "Instead of being depressed, going out and shooting at fuckin' rocks and squirrels, I go down south and shoot niggers. I think it's fun—but I'd rather get paid for it."

"Yeah, it makes it a little more meaningful," Adams agreed.

"Anyway, on the fucking broad," said Ford. "I don't think she's going to be any difficulty at all once I get her hooked."

"She's dead," said Adams.

"Yeah, I'm going to need some help to get her ass tied up before we cruise off into the fucking sunset."

Ford explained to Adams how he tried to dose Loguercio at the Hollywood-Land Motel by putting Tuinal inside some black mollies, a kind of speed. "The fucking broad wouldn't take any black mollies. If I could have gotten the black mollies down her, I could have taken her out in the fucking motel."

"Well, I got my Valiums," said Adams. "I could dose her with Valium."

"Valium are too slow. Fucking Tuinal will knock her fucking out, the strongest sedative made right there."

"Is it?"

"That's it, man."

"I thought Thorazine was."

"That's the top of the motherfucking line right there. That shit'll knock your dick in the dirt."

Adams laughed.

"There's short-acting, mild-acting, long-acting. That's short-acting, that motherfucker will knock you out in fifteen minutes. Whop, gone boy! You know what—I'll stick that fucker down her throat and in thirty minutes she won't know what her fuckin' name is. One of those will put you to sleep right now. Two of those motherfuckers will knock you out. You get fuckin' dizzy, whoa! Man, three of them fuckers will turn you into a blob of shit. That's why we need the bottle, so we can jam it down her throat."

"Doesn't fuckin' Lankershim Boulevard cross over here? At Victory Boulevard?" Adams asked.

"No, you should go off on Sherman Way," said Ford.

"We just went under Sherman Way."

"Ah, you should have got off there."

"We'll swing up Victory and come back."

Adams hoped that mentioning the cross streets was helping the agents tailing them.

Adams exited from the freeway and headed into North Hollywood, the Valley's center city. It was a weird mix of Mexicans and sleaze, Adams thought. The Mexicans worked in sweat shops, garages, and industrial parks, while struggling actors and writers were attracted by the relatively affordable housing near Burbank and the Universal City studios. Those with steady jobs could afford digs in the more upscale Studio City or Sherman Oaks. It wasn't surprising that in recent years North Hollywood had become the porn capital of the world. Aspiring actresses had to eat, and producers in the booming X-rated videocassette industry knew where to set up shop.

The Venus Faire was the best of a half-dozen porno shops located on a half-mile-long section of Lankershim Boulevard, just south of the famous Palomino Club.

A black and white cruised past the van, causing Adams's heart to pound through his chest. What the fuck are they doing? he thought.

"If we get stopped by the police," Ford said, "let me get out and handle it."

"All right," said Adams. He relaxed as he realized that the passing squad car was probably not part of the feds' operation.

"If we get stopped by the man, what we're doing is working an off-duty job, we're working surveillance," Ford explained. "We've got a fucked-up vehicle here, which is fucking everything up and I'll badge 'em and get rid of 'em."

"That's why I'm driving the speed limit and stuff, so they don't stop us," said Adams, lighting a cigarette.

"Just keep going cool . . ."

"Even more so, after we get the bitch in the van. I think we'll take fucking Oxnard [Boulevard] over."

"Before I drug this bitch, I want to be able to talk to her for a fucking while . . ."

"That broad is running scared, man," said Adams. "I mean, she is fucking double paranoid . . ."

"Ah fuck, that broad's had it, that fucking broad's over the hill. She's not a bad fuck, but she gives lousy fucking head."

"Tell me about it!"

"Pissed me off."

"She doesn't even give head, man," Adams laughed. "I don't even know what the fuck you call it, but I wouldn't call it getting a good fucking head job."

"Lousy fucking head," said Ford. "She's not a bad fuck though."

Adams realized they were off course and made a few turns to get them headed in the right direction. "I gotta make a U-turn here on Oxnard," said Adams.

"Did you bring any gloves?" Ford asked.

"No."

"You really come prepared, don't you?"

"What the fuck, I ain't going in no fucking building."

"No," Ford exclaimed, "you're going to punch this bitch's fucking head with your hand."

"Sure."

"You're going to look good tomorrow morning with fucking teeth marks in your hands."

"All right, I'll get a pair of fucking gloves."

"No, you don't need to. I got 'em," said Ford, motioning to his attaché case.

Adams wasn't surprised that Ford had an extra pair. Ford referred to his briefcase as "the homicide kit." He had everything in there—a gun, two daggers, a garrote, nylon rope, ski masks, gloves, an assortment of drugs, Vaseline.

"I need a fucking six-pack or two," said Ford.

"What do you want?"

"Ah, tall cans, Budweiser."

"Tall cans, sixteen-ounce?"

"Yeah."

"Fucking redneck."

"I'm going to love her like the VC that loved about half my platoon," Ford said.

"Yeah, I got it."

"If I can only find an NVA nurse."

"Yeah, you got it . . . Fucking NVA nurse—ah, man, that's righteous," said Adams.

"Did I ever tell you about the time," Adams and Ford chimed in unison. They looked at each other and broke up laughing.

"Let me tell you about fucking NVA nurses," Ford said, all excited. "Fuck, man, we just fucked that fucking bitch. Oh shit, man, we buttfucked that whore, fucked her in the mouth, fucked her for about two days. She got so good that you'd just walk up to her and she'd open her fucking mouth and her head went back."

Adams laughed.

"Then it got better when her tongue got all fuckin' swollen and her eyes were closed."

"They were shiners, huh?"

"This other one was one of the finest-looking fucking women I've ever seen in my life," Ford exclaimed.

"Yeah!"

"We were on patrol for about a month, horny as a motherfucker, up to our ass in swamp water. Fuckin' sampan come down, we laid there, right in the middle of our fucking ambush, didn't know for sure if it was friendly or NVA. Being United States Army troops, anything in the way gets dusted."

"You got it," said Adams.

"We wasted that motherfucker away, boy, just fucking wasted that bitch, that motherfucker—it didn't even have time to sink, it just disintegrated, the motherfucker just disintegrated, went *blop, blop* . . . After it all goes down it gets quiet. A guy's with an M79 with a shotgun round, I hear some splashing, I hear *bop-pow,* and everybody cuts loose, *rapt, tat, tat, tat."*

Adams laughed. "Everybody cuts loose. I've never seen it fail."

"And what he did was this fucking bitch lying on this fucking bank, some way or another lived. She came out of the water, crawling up the bank. He swung around, took her head right off her fucking shoulders."

"No shit."

"We dragged her fucking body up and she was the most beautiful fucking body. I don't know what her face looked like but her fucking body was beautiful. Over there I would have fucked the bitch anyway."

Adams laughed.

"Before she got cold, anyway," said Ford.

"You got it, boy," Adams laughed. "Take that last roll, motherfucker."

"You know what, he almost got his ass kicked," Ford said. "Everybody was on his ass: you stupid motherfucking asshole, prick, cocksucker, why the fuck don't you look where you shoot? There was a piece of fucking ass for the whole goddam platoon."

Ford was silent for a while. Then he began to go over plans for how they would kill Loguercio.

"If she doesn't want to go in the fucking van with you, go in her fucking car," Ford explained. "Go out and have a drink, relax. Give her a sad story when you get back. Say, 'Come on, you got to see my fucking van, you got to see how cherry that motherfucker is inside, it's got a fucking bar and shit.' You silly savage."

Adams laughed.

"When she gets there, take a quick look behind you and just push that fucking bitch in and I'll snatch her by the fucking head and drag her in and you follow me in and close the door behind you. Then tie her ass up, hop behind the wheel, and off we go, away in the fucking sunset."

"Got you covered, pal."

"But either way, she's got to go *tonight,"* Ford stressed.

"No shit, man."

"If she doesn't go tonight, we're dead."

"Yeah."

"She's not going to go cancel that policy."

"Tell me about it."

Ford picked a lighter up off the dash and lit a Marlboro. "I got too fucking far in the hole, man, and I need the fucking money. Twelve grand will make it better. It won't make it right, but it will make it fucking better."

"Well, twelve grand will damn near put me back on top."

"The body's got to be found," said Ford. "It's got to be identified. The fucking insurance company will probably take thirty to sixty days, so we got some time, we got to hang on."

"Yeah, but Bob said he was gonna come across with some bucks for us."

"Did he? Good. I'll take whatever the fuck I can get," said Ford. "I had to go to the credit union today to get fifteen fucking hundred dollars to pay my fucking bills and to buy that fucking engine for that piece of shit [Cadillac]. Money's tight. The only way you're gonna get it is to take it."

As Adams pulled onto Lankershim Boulevard and headed toward the Venus Faire, Ford started explaining why he hadn't killed Loguercio during their rendezvous at the HollywoodLand Motel. The problem, he said, was that the motel proprietor, a "Chinaman," hassled him on his way into the motel. Apparently the man had noticed that Dr. Anderson's eyebrows weren't the same color as his hair, or something, because he'd stopped him and questioned him like he thought he was a burglar. Because he'd been ID'd, Ford couldn't leave the body in the motel. He had to change his plan and try to kill her without any traces of blood or signs of a struggle and then carry her body out to her car.

"There wasn't supposed to be any MO," Ford explained. "It was supposed to be wham-bam-thank-you-ma'am. But everything fucking came apart."

"Yeah, that's what I figured," said Adams.

"I went back to my briefcase, told her I was—"

Adams laughed. "Told her you were getting your Rolaids."

"—getting a T-shirt . . . carried the T-shirt like I was wiping my dick off with it. Evidently she didn't see me wipe my dick off, and that would have been cool. Inside the T-shirt I had my garrote, the fucking choke, and I was telling her to lay down flat on her stomach, because I couldn't get a hard-on, I wanted her to masturbate for me, put her hands underneath."

"Uh huh. You'd have control."

"With me on top I'd have control, step up around the fucking neck, and wham-bam-thank-you-ma'am."

"Fuck her."

"But the fucking bitch got all fucking paranoid, so she evidently saw me go to the briefcase and didn't fucking see the T-shirt and thought I came back with a fucking gun or knife, some fucking thing."

Adams laughed.

"From that point on she was fucking noncooperative," said Ford. "You know, she wanted to get the fuck out of Dodge."

Adams pulled up to the Venus Faire, a two-story building with numerous signs painted on its white brick exterior: "Live New York Style Nude Dance Theater," "Adult Books & Movies," and "Open 24 Hours."

"Okay, let's see if her fucking car is there," said Adams, breaking to a slow cruise. "Yeah, there it is."

"Where?"

"Right there, the Camaro."

Adams parked in a dark place on a side street down the block from the Venus Faire and the two men began to rehearse. Ford got in back and started crawling around under the blankets to see if Adams could see him from the front seat. Adams laughed as Ford waddled around on all fours. "I can see you," Adams chuckled. "C'mon, man, we're supposed to be fucking professionals."

"Yeah, we're about as professional as dog shit," said Ford.

Adams laughed.

"Okay, walk outside and see what you fucking see," said Ford. "I'll cover up again."

Adams got out of the van and walked around, peering into the windows. Then he got back in. "Nothing, not a fucking thing, all I see is rear doors. You're covered up real well."

With Ford acting as director, the two men went through the motions of dragging Loguercio over the seat into the back, punching her, tying her up, and gagging her.

"Okay, that's location number one," said Ford. "Now we drive away. Go ahead, drive away."

"Okay, we drive away," said Adams. He fired up the engine and pulled out into the street.

"I love it! I love it!" Ford exclaimed. "We're gonna get you tonight, Charlie!"

Adams laughed.

The two men decided they didn't need to recon Hollywood for a place to dump Loguercio's body. "We don't have to necessarily do her in Hollywood," said Ford. "We just have to unload her in Hollywood. We can cover her up with the fucking blankets. Dumping her body is the last fucking problem . . . The next thing we need is a fucking place to park."

"Okay," said Adams.

"My wife, by the way, thinks I'm taking out a fucking asshole," said Ford.

"Okay."

"That you and I are going to do it together tonight and we're going to get paid seven to ten thousand, we don't know how much for sure, and we're supposed to beat the fuck out of him to a point where he ends up in the hospital. That's what she thinks."

"Okay, we're supposed to do him but not *do* him," said Adams. "Just make him fucking righteous. In other words, teach him a lesson."

"That's right."

Adams slowed down as he and Ford peered down a long, dark alley. "Nice and dark down there," said Ford. "I love it!"

"What's it remind you of?" Adams asked.

"An ops, in Nam."

A few minutes later, Adams pulled the van into a liquor store parking lot. Ford told him to get a six-pack of Bud for himself and some Michelob Light in bottles, with the long neck, for Loguercio. While Adams went in to buy the beer, Ford arranged the blankets and his tie-downs—nylon cords—in the back.

Adams was doing okay until he walked up to the counter and tried to fish some bills out of his pocket. Suddenly his hands were shaking like a jackhammer. The clerk, an Asian, finally reached out and pulled some bills out of Bruce's shaking hands. He stared at Adams and said, "You all right?"

"Yeah, yeah," said Bruce. "And gimme four packs of Marlboro reds."

Adams stuffed the change in his pants pocket and grabbed the paper grocery bag with both arms, hugging it close to his chest. He tried to maintain a slow, casual gait as he walked out into the parking lot. He acted cool, because he knew that could make him be cool. This is just like Nam, he told himself. Stay cool or die. Stay cool or die. He repeated this mantra to himself as he walked. When he climbed back into the van, he handed the bag to Ford and clutched the steering wheel to steady his hands.

17

Dr. Death

"DRINKING AND DRIVING OBVIOUSLY IS AGAINST THE FUCKING LAW," observed Detective Ford as he popped the top on a Bud while Adams steered the van out of the lot.

"Yeah, unless you drink and drive with a fuckin' Pepsi," said Adams.

"Perfect bottles here," said Ford, holding up a Michelob.

"You get it down far enough," Adams laughed, "and fuck, man, I bet you'll give one hell of a deep throat, like that chick you were telling me about that you were training with the banana."

"Tacha Cowa Rose."

"Yeah, Tacha Cowa Rose."

"Your fucking dick would have fell off," Ford laughed. "I'm going to have to tell this bitch tonight, the reason you're fucking dying is you give lousy fucking head. Leave me erected! That bitch gives such bad fucking head she shouldn't be alive in this world."

Adams laughed.

The two men began scouting for a location where they could take Loguercio and "do" her after they had tied her up. "Someplace we can have some privacy, no cops around," said Ford.

"Get our nuts off a couple times," Adams said. "You going to let her suck your dick again?"

"I don't think so," Ford laughed. "She might bite."

Adams laughed. "I'm going to take a right on Vanowen, go down towards

169

the [Burbank] airport. There's gotta be a whole bunch of fucking industrial in there."

Adams was familiar with the area; it was near Triple J's, where he used to work. He found a section of streets lined with warehouses and factories, slowing to look down a dead end into an industrial park. At first it looked good, but then he had second thoughts. "I don't like the idea we got no fuckin' way out. If the fucking man comes down the street, we're gone, he thinks it's a fucking B and E. Turns out to be a heavy caper, man."

Ford laughed. "What do you call this fucking body, bro?"

"Well, shit."

"First fucking degree," Ford laughed. "You're going to the fucking chair. You're going to be fucking fried!"

Adams lit another cigarette. "I thought they did away with the death penalty in California."

"Not under unusual circumstances."

"Oh."

"Like premeditation."

"Planned murder, yeah," said Adams.

"You know, like having some fucking bitch you not only kidnapped but you fucking tortured to fucking death."

"And then killed her."

"And then fucking killed . . ."

"Yeah, okay." said Adams. "Don't go any fucking further, man. I catch your fucking drift. No, we don't need that at all."

Adams pulled into a gas station, then pulled out and kept driving when he noticed that the attendants were Asians. "Ah, you motherfucker, I ain't buying no fucking gas from no fucking gooks, that's for sure." Adams coughed. Ford burped his approval.

"What would be wrong with dropping her off up this way, man?" Adams asked. "The motherfuckers would think a fucking beaner picked up on her, man. Throw it off on the Mexicans."

"Is this Hollywood Division?"

"This is North Hollywood."

"I want Hollywood Division," Ford insisted. "They're buried in fucking homicides."

"Are they?"

"Ah, fuckin' buried."

"Yeah, okay, that's the reason."

"You know, in Devonshire, the motherfuckers get two homicides a year and they get all year to investigate; fucking Hollywood gets whores, knockovers. I met one at the D.A.'s office the other day—a Hollywood homicide detective. He was saying, 'Them fucking whores, motherfucking cocksuckers, I hate even to investigate them motherfucking bitches.' Anyway, let's get some fucking gas. All we need to do is run out of gas."

"All right."

"That bitch is using all my good fucking dope," Ford laughed as he tried to dissolve the Tuinal in a Michelob Light. "I hope to fuck she appreciates this."

Adams laughed. "I wonder how much money she's going to have in fucking tips on her tonight."

"Fucking bitch," said Ford. "I popped for about three hundred fucking dollars."

"You handed her a note, with three hundreds and a twenty?"

"Yeah."

"When I heard that I knew who the fuck it was."

"I had to make an impression on that fucking bitch," Ford explained. "She wouldn't go out with me for five dollars and twenty-seven cents."

Adams laughed.

"Fucking Dr. Anderson failed again," Ford said.

"Dr. Anderson, Dr. Death," Adams laughed.

"Dr. Anderson, Dr. Death. Fucking got to change my MO. I'll tell you, I'm going back to be the fucking Professor. That used to be my name in Nam."

"What, the Professor?"

"Yeah, the Professor. The Professor or Dr. Death."

"Fucking Dr. Anderson. I almost choked on my fucking scaloppine when I heard that," Adams laughed.

"Why? Worked before. Do you know how many fucking dead bitches there are out there on Dr. Anderson?"

Adams laughed. "Probably."

"Fucking whores and shit."

"I have no idea."

"I got five grand for one fucking whore . . . Fucking pimp wanted her, and the fucking whore got herself a fucking gorilla for a boyfriend."

"No shit."

"Yeah, but Dr. Anderson got that fucking bitch."

Adams laughed.

"Dr. Anderson, the gynecologist."

"Yeah, right."

"I forgot how many fucking Tuinals I put in here now."

"Fuck, what are you worried about?"

"I don't want her to die on the Tuinals," Ford explained. "They'll say why in the fuck did this motherfucker die on the fucking Tuinals and then someone fucking tortures the fucking shit out of her? How the fuck do you torture a dead person, you know what I mean?"

"You'd have to be some real fucking asshole to do it. Yeah," said Adams as he pulled into a gas station. When he finished pumping gas and got back into the van, Ford was still stirring his beer and Tuinal cocktail. "Very scientific, homicide," said Ford, staring diabolically at the bottle. "Got to do this fucking scientific, get this shit organized . . ."

Adams laughed as he steered the van out on the street.

"We don't need that fancy shit. We just do it the old-fashioned good old American way. Kill that motherfucker!"

Adams laughed.

"Now how do you get this shit to break down? What the fuck happens when you mix beer with it?"

"It'll probably blow up in our fucking faces," Adams said.

"No, alcohol adds to it."

"Okay, rocket scientist."

"Two Tuinals plus twelve ounces of alcohol is like four Tuinals."

"Don't fuck up and drink the wrong bottle, asshole."

Ford laughed. "Yeah, wouldn't that be a trip!"

"That's all I need," Adams laughed, "is you laid out, laughing. Oh shit!"

Ford looked at Adams. "I didn't know you could handle this fucking shit."

"Who me? I told you, motherfucker, I'm crazy," said Adams. "I only look dumb."

"I'm not talking about being dumb," said Ford. "It has nothing to do with dumb. It has to do with morality, with fucking guts, intestinal fortitude and all those other fucking adjectives—"

Suddenly, a black and white sped past them. "Go get 'em, baby!" Ford cried. "Go get that motherfucker!"

"Burbank police. Shit," said Adams.

Ford laughed. "Go right by two homicide suspects, dumb fucker."

Adams laughed.

"Could've had yourself a big number. You could have been a fucking hero, arresting an LAPD police detective and his Vietnam psycho cohort."

Adams laughed.

"Kidnap, mutilation—terrifying motherfuckers, boy."

Adams laughed.

"We got to fuck the bitch up, man. It's gotta look like the motherfucker who got hold of her was a sex maniac."

"Like death warmed over," said Adams.

After another black and white passed the van. Adams decided to change directions. "Fuckin' North Hollywood is a pain in the ass place anyway. It's just like Tucson. Fucking sin city."

Ford went back to talking about his encounter with Loguercio at the motel. "She handed me the fucking wad back and it looked like the same fucking size, but she gave me the wad with the twenties, not the fucking hundreds. She got about a grand. Pissed me off to the max. And I'm trying to go on vacation, and I ain't got no fucking money anyway."

Adams laughed.

"So I put everything on the motherfucking cards—you know what I mean, charge all that shit. Now I owe Bank of America, American Express, Visa, MasterCharge, Union Seventy-six, Exxon, and probably some-fucking-body else, Sears and Roebuck, Penneys, my fucking soul, because this fucking whore didn't cooperate."

Adams laughed.

"This broad's got fucking problems. As a matter of fact, we should probably get a reward for getting rid of this motherfucker."

Adams laughed.

They continued driving until they found a spot in an industrial park suitable for doing Loguercio: a dark corner along the wall of a secluded building. Adams pulled the van over, parked, and turned off the engine. For the next fifteen minutes they chain-smoked and talked, going over their plans again and again, debating details, like whether they should tie Loguercio's hands first or her feet first.

Ford finally said he had to take a piss. "Hey, Bruce, I'm going to take a little quick recon and see what the fuck's out there and if I can get out of this fucking one-thirteen." He got out and closed the door.

Alone in the van, Adams started to panic. Was Ford getting wise? "What's a one-thirteen?" Adams cried out loud. "What the hell is a one-thirteen?" Adams thought it might be cop lingo for a set-up. He thought maybe Ford was about to pull out his service revolver and blow him away. Then, after a minute of heart-racing terror, Adams realized that one-thirteen was army talk for an armored personnel carrier. Ford was just being funny. Adams didn't catch on right away because in the marines they referred to it as a one-one-three. Then he calmed himself by taking a deep breath. "I hope you guys are getting all this," he whispered softly. Another hour of terror and this nightmare would finally be over, he thought. One way or another.

Ford got back in the van. He explained to Adams what their story would be if any police or security guards tried to roust them. "We're having a fucking meet here and you're an informant. You work for Detective Ward."

"Ward, okay."

Having found their killing ground, they headed back to the Venus Faire. When they arrived at the theater ten minutes later, Adams found a place on a side street around the corner and parked the van. Again they ran through the game plan. "You figure you got a good thirty seconds or so before she even begins to regain any kind of fucking reasoning of what happened to her," said Adams. "And by that time, it's all over with, baby. Tied up and gagged."

"Yeah," said Ford, "then go back to the location. Stuff antibiotic down her throat. Got to save this bitch's life, you know."

"Yeah, right," Adams laughed. "Try to cure her fucking dose of herpes of the throat."

"One hell of a way to make a fucking living, ain't it?"

"Tell me about it."

"Beats the shit out of working," Ford said. "Making ten, twelve grand every time I do this fucking shit. I used to do it for Uncle Sam for eighty bucks a month."

"Yeah, but we still got to work. The fucking head honcho, the Colonel, he's got two privates to go out and do his dirty fucking work."

"He's lucky," said Ford. "He's real fuckin' lucky I don't make a fucking deal with the bitch. Do his fucking ass a double-double-cross."

"Only trouble is, this bitch might not pay off."

"Ah, this fucking broad's got problems Bob ain't," said Ford. "Bob knows better cause Bob knows I'd kill him. He knows fucking well I would. I would, you know. I don't like to be fucked. I really don't like to be fucked."

"Nobody does, pal."

"Yeah, but I ain't nobody."

"I know you ain't nobody."

"You know I don't mind killing motherfuckers," Ford said. "It don't bother me fucking at all. I like to watch 'em die, anyway. It never ceases to amaze me the expressions on people's faces when, especially a nigger, when you stick a twelve-inch blade right into his fucking liver and the motherfucker is going 'haw!' "

Adams laughed.

" 'Say, you remember me, motherfucker? Yeah, uh huh. You don't remember me, do you?' "

Adams laughed.

" ' 'Cause I don't even know your fuckin' ass.' There used to be a nigger motherfucker that I don't like, keep mouthing on the fucking street all night."

"Yeah."

"A big asshole acting like his shit don't stink, talking about motherfucker thinking he's bad, motherfucker kick your ass, kill you fucking dead mother-fucker."

Adams laughed.

"Ain't no fucking guy that's ever fucked me that's alive."

Adams laughed.

"In Vietnam, I think I invented fragging."

"Fucking shit birds."

"I killed personally four fucking lieutenants and one captain."

Adams laughed.

" 'Lieutenant, you know what, you killed your last fucking man, you know what I mean?

" 'You are a dipshit, cock-fucking asshole,' " Ford screamed. " 'I have more respect for the NVA than I do for your ass. I have more respect for a gook in a fucking rice paddy. All you are is a fucking NVA in disguise. You know what I mean, you're probably a fucking mole.' "

"Fucking asshole."

Ford looked at the potion he was preparing in the beer bottle. "This just won't fucking dissolve," he said. "This just stays in powder form."

"Oh, wow, man."

"It don't matter as long as it gets down her throat."

Ford went back to explaining what happened at the HollywoodLand Motel. "So I pulled a couple of hours and I came up with an idea, okay. I can't leave the fucking body in the motel, but what stops me from taking this fucking bitch's car keys, throwing her fucking ass in the dead of fucking night, carrying her fucking ass out to the fucking car, throwing her in the fucking trunk, and drive off into the fucking sunset?

"I decided to go with plan B, so I couldn't fucking shoot the bitch. If I stabbed her, I was going to leave fucking blood all over the fucking motel . . . Foul play would be obvious. There's no way you can stab a motherfucker without some fucking blood. The only method left was to fucking strangle her . . ."

Once again, they rehearsed yanking Loguercio over the seat into the back. They debated whether to use parachute cord or nylons to tie her. Ford decided on nylons.

A motorcycle cop suddenly sped past the parked van. "Is that a cop on his bike and shit?" Ford asked.

"How the fuck do I know?" Adams said nervously. "You're the one that's been on the force for two hundred years."

"Yeah, but I work Detectives' Squad."

"Yeah, I know, you don't work the—"

"The crime-ridden areas," said Ford.

"Yeah, Devonshire's getting real fucking bad I understand," said Adams sarcastically.

"Yeah, I know," said Ford. "But I'm going to clean it up."

Adams laughed, choking on cigarette smoke. "Oh, right. You're another fucking Dirty Harry!"

"No, I'm gonna get the neighborhood watch organized," said Ford matter-of-factly. "For promotion, and maybe political purposes down the road."

"That and cover," said Adams.

"Yeah, I wouldn't be suspected," said Ford. "Good old Detective Ford, loved by one and all. Nice guy all around."

"Yeah," said Adams, laughing. "That would be Dr. Death, Mr. fucking Killer himself."

"Best cover in the world is when everybody thinks you're a nice guy. Everybody thinks you're a fucking sweetheart. Meanwhile, you ought to see my fucking victims, kid. They think the sun rises and sets on my ass."

Adams laughed. "What they can remember."

"Bob's done the same thing, 'cause Bob's a good PR man . . ."

"Right," said Adams.

"I'm supposed to call him when it's over," said Ford. "Let the telephone ring three times. That means it's okay. If it rings four times or more, it means big trouble. I ought to just let it ring four or five times."

"Shake his shitter up," Adams laughed. "Keep him up all night."

"The bitch got away and we tried to fucking kill her and she ran right into the fucking arms of the cops and we split and we're on our way to Mexico."

"Tijuana, somewhere. We'll be eating some fucking tacos."

"If you have a chance before you leave, give my family a call. Will you tell them I'm in fucking deep shit?"

Adams laughed. "Have him stop by my house and tell my old lady I won't be back in the country for a while."

"One thing's for sure, we can't fucking blow this," Ford said. "We got to do this fucking thing right, 'cause I have no intention of going to the fucking joint and getting buttfucked by two hundred and seventy-five people, man."

"Yeah, there'll be a lot of motherfuckers up there looking for you, boy," Adams said. "I don't even want to think about that."

"Ugh!"

"Dick, no problem. You crack me up, Ford. This is going to be a fucking piece of cake. It should go down one, two, three."

"It should be," said Ford. "It will have its fucking moments, no doubt about it."

Adams lit another cigarette. "The biggest point in our favor is the element of surprise," he said. "Look how it was when you walked in on Charlie. Catch that motherfucker with his pants down. That motherfucker takes twenty minutes to get his shit organized. Those fucking rice heads be running all over the fucking place. Beautiful targets, man."

"If she gets away, we're going to the fucking joint, man," Ford exclaimed, now pumped to a fever pitch. "This fucking bitch, even if we got to club her to death, any-fucking-thing, she's got to go."

"Right."

"If I get my hands on her, she ain't going no-fucking-where, boy. She ain't putting my ass in the fucking joint."

Adams laughed.

"All would have been cool if that fucking Chinaman wouldn't have been [at the motel]. She'd been fucking butched over right from the get go. I was going to do her right away. I was going to fuck her and fucking do her right there. Just fucking do her fucking ass. I was going to slice her fucking ass up. She wouldn't know what fucking hit her. But that fucking gook standing out there, telling me I'm a fucking burglar, and I said to myself when I got to the room, You know, if it had to happen, it had to be a fucking gook."

"Gook," said Adams.

"I swear to God, that guy was a fucking Vietnamese too, you know what I mean? Looked like a Vietcong motherfucker, and I'm saying, Isn't this a bitch! Twelve fucking years later."

Adams laughed, coughed.

"A guy trying to make an honest buck, you know, and a fucking gook is out here fucking me up again. I ought to take this motherfucker out and his fucking gook NVA old lady."

Adams laughed, coughed.

"Don't fucking gag to death," said Ford.

"You got me laughing so hard, I can hardly see straight, fucker."

"Yeah, life in the big city can be a motherfucker, you know," said Ford.

"This is like waiting for the fucking jump off," said Adams, referring to the moment before battle in Vietnam.

"That's exactly it," said Ford.

"But this is a newer type situation."

Ford looked at his watch. "Twenty fucking minutes. Dum de dum dum," he hummed, sing-songing the theme from "Dragnet." "Fuck, I ain't going!" he screamed in mock terror, as though he were a frightened grunt in Vietnam. "Goddam you, I can't take it no longer. I ain't going with you, motherfucker!"

Adams laughed and picked up on the refrain. "I can't walk. I just sprained both my motherfuckin' ankles."

"Fuck you. Lay here, motherfucker!"

"Die, motherfucker!"

"A fucking regiment behind us! Yeah, I'm coming."

"Carry your ass, shit fool!"

"As long as you're going to stay here," Ford laughed, "you might as well give me your fucking ammo. It ain't doing you no good. You're fucking bait. You're fucking dead-ass shit. You want me to tell your old lady you said to give me fucking head before you died?"

Adams laughed.

Ford picked a lighter up off the seat. "I hope this fucking thing's got fire left in it."

"It better have. We'll probably end up smoking a carton of fucking cigarettes between us tonight."

"We got to burn this fucking broad, too. That should be good."

"Cigarette burns."

"Always good," said Ford. "Every fucking broad has got cigarette burns. I guess the fucking pimps get off on that shit . . . At least, you know, I consider myself a really nice guy—I'm going to use narcotics."

"Try to ease some of the pain," said Adams.

"Well, it's not that, really. It's not that I'm a humane motherfucker. It's just that with all that fucking pain, she'll be really jumping around."

"Yeah, making a lot of noise. There'd be no control."

"If we don't get her tonight, we're fucked. She won't go with any of us anymore. Plus she tried calling that fucking insurance agent. And I need the fucking money, boy, you know what I mean? I'd do it for a fuckin' grand, let alone twelve."

Adams laughed.

"For twelve grand I'll do her and her fucking old man and the fucking kids, burn down her fucking house, dig up her fucking grandmother, stab *that* bitch once or twice."

Adams laughed.

"Fucking credit union and the fucking second I have on the fucking house. By the time I get done paying my bills, I don't eat."

"Shit, I heard that."

"It sucks. Twelve grand won't make the fucking world, but it'll sure be a big fucking help." Ford looked at his watch again and stared out the window into the darkness. "The quiet before the storm," he said.

"Yeah, the lull. I think they call it the lull before the storm," said Adams. "What you think about it, partner?"

"I don't want to think about it, partner."

"What you think about, man?"

"This ain't shit," said Adams.

"This ain't nothing. One skukey-ass fucking broad."

"Compared to a regiment of NVA."

"Yeah, fucking twenty fucking screaming gooks, with fucking AKs and shit and RPGs trying to take your fucking ass out . . ."

Adams lit another cigarette. "This is a fucking party."

Ford burped. "This is fucking ridiculous. We'll probably get in fucking trouble for this kind of shit, you know what I mean?"

Adams opened the door and got out. He slipped on a large camouflage-print hat that Ford had given him. It covered most of his head and part of his face, so he couldn't be ID'd. "I'll be back shortly, hopefully," he said.

"Hopefully," echoed Ford.

Adams closed the door. Ford climbed in the back and got under the blankets.

A few minutes passed. Outside the van, Detective Supervisor Martin Dorner from the LAPD's Special Investigations Squad approached the vehicle with his gun drawn. Dorner was backed up by Detective Henry Cadena and a dozen other SIS troops.

"Ford!" Dorner yelled.

"Yeah?" Ford answered from inside the van.

"Come out with your hands up!"

Ford stalled a few moments. Then reality hit like a brick. "That's the end of that caper," he said.

*   *   *

The van was surrounded by cops; there were twenty-eight units within a block. An LAPD chopper closed in and flooded the area with light. A dozen uniformed officers charged out of a liquor store across the street from the Venus Faire and stationed themselves around the vehicle, weapons drawn. When Ford slowly emerged, some of the troops thought he made a move for his pocket. The clack of slamming shotgun chambers echoed down the street. But Detective Ford knew better than to resist, and he quickly assumed the position. The cops entered the van and immediately found his homicide kit and Tuinal potion.

Two undercover cops, disguised as lowlifes, were waiting for Bruce Adams at the door of the Venus Faire. One of them was wearing an ear jack and a fake cast and sling, which held a transmitter.

"Mr. Adams, police officers," said one of the undercover cops, flashing his badge.

Bruce grabbed him by the arm and yanked him off the sidewalk and threw him into the middle of Lankershim Boulevard. The other cop grabbed Adams and slammed him into the wall in front of the Venus Faire. Adams unloaded a barrage of body punches. "You motherfucker!" Adams howled. "You son of a bitch! You ain't takin' me in!"

A crowd spilled out of the Venus Faire when they heard the commotion. Adams continued to scuffle and scream as cops swarmed over him. Down at the corner about twenty yards away, Richard Ford was getting frisked by a small army. Both he and Adams were slammed to the pavement and cuffed.

The area was blocked off by a half-dozen squad cars, their lights blinking blue and red. The chopper moved in close and hovered just overhead, aiming its searing high-beam spotlights at the two perpetrators. The beat of the whirling blades was accompanied by a symphony of crackling police radios.

Inside the Venus Faire, Joan Loguercio was approached by two men who had been eyeballing her all night. They identified themselves as SIS agents and explained they had just foiled a murder plot against her. She'd need to come in with them to make a statement. She was told that the men who had planned to kill her were Richard Ford, Robert Von Villas, and Bruce Adams; they would need to ask her what she knew about these three men.

Joany was in shock. When she walked out into the commotion in front of the Venus Faire, she saw Bruce Adams being driven away in the back of a black and white. She started to sob.

Ford and Adams were driven to the Federal Building in Van Nuys in separate vehicles. LAPD Internal Affairs investigators, who rode with Detective Ford, tried to squeeze him for information. Ford didn't say a word.

Jan Golab

The Van Nuys Federal Building is a modern, gleaming white eight-story office center. The ATF offices were swarming with feds and LAPD officials, as well as a team from the D.A.'s office, headed by Deputy District Attorney Robert Jorgensen. A mad scramble was in process to write up reports, issue warrants, and interrogate the perps; Jorgensen was there to make sure everything was done by the book.

Ford was already in one of the third-floor interrogation rooms when Adams came up in the elevator. When the sliding door opened, Adams bolted and ran down the hallway into a large office area and smashed into a desk, knocking it over with a thunderous crash. "You dumb-ass motherfuckers, you stupid sons of bitches," he screamed. "I ain't done nothin'! Prove it, mother-fuckers!"

About a dozen agents and LAPD officers pulled their service revolvers and trained them on Adams. With the camouflage hat pulled down over Adams's head, many didn't know it was their informant; some thought it might be Von Villas. A couple of cops almost blew Adams away.

About five guys dragged Adams, kicking and screaming, down the hall to a large back room. They shoved him in and closed the door. Standing at the far end of the room, along with a couple of ATF agents, was Joan Loguercio, terrified, dazed, confused.

Agent Mario Fontana walked up to Adams and smiled as he unlocked his cuffs. "Well, Bruce," he said, "can I get you a cup of coffee?"

Joan Loguercio went completely over the edge. "You motherfucker!" she screeched. "That son of a bitch just tried to kill me! Why the hell are you taking off his handcuffs?" Tears streamed down her face as she began to sob uncontrollably.

Agent Fontana grasped Joany by the arms and gave her a gentle shake. "Ma'am, this man just saved your life."

Fontana quickly explained how Bruce had tipped them off, about how he had risked his life to ride with Detective Ford in a wired van. Joany began to sob even harder. She rushed over to Bruce and he wrapped her in his arms.

"It's all right, Joany," Bruce said. "It's over now."

Bruce Adams would endure many attacks on his character and credibility in coming years, but as far as Agents Fontana and Oddo were concerned, he deserved a medal. His performance under fire had been something to behold. And having instructed him to go down hard after his arrest to maintain his cover with Richard Ford, they felt he had put on a convincing show. But right now there was no time for celebration.

They still had to pick up Von Villas. A separate team was now mobilizing to take down the Colonel. Adams told them how Ford was supposed to signal Bob that the op was a success with a three-ring phone call. One of the SIS guys made the call.

An hour later, a division of squad cars with bullhorns and SIS sharpshooters, along with a chopper spilling floodlights, descended on the Simi Valley home of Bob Von Villas. Bobby looked like a little kid at Christmas, running from window to window in his pajamas, looking at all the lights. Only the expression on his face wasn't one of wonderment and joy.

At 2:00 A.M., Ford, Adams, and Loguercio were driven downtown in separate vehicles to LAPD headquarters at Parker Center. Von Villas, handcuffed and still in his pajama top, arrived about an hour later. The three perps were taken up to IAD for questioning. The doors connecting their adjoining rooms were opened and closed as interrogators came and went, so Adams, Ford, and Von Villas could periodically see and hear one another. Each was once again read his rights.

"You have the right to remain silent—"

"Shove it up your ass!" Adams growled.

"If you choose not to remain silent—"

"Go fuck yourself, asshole!"

"If you do not have an attorney—"

"Get me a fuckin' mouthpiece," Adams barked. "I got nothin' to say to you fucking people."

Adams was maintaining his cover in order to buy time for himself and his family. Travel and protection had to be arranged. The idea was to get the Adams family out of town before Ford or Von Villas figured out Bruce was a snitch. Investigators tried to question Ford and Von Villas, but the two cops refused to speak until they had conferred with their attorneys.

After questioning, the cops took them all downstairs to book them for conspiracy to commit murder and attempted murder. Adams kept his act up while he was fingerprinted and photographed.

"What's your name?"

"Fuck you!" Adams spat at the booking sergeant. "You talkin' to me, boy?"

Von Villas was watching from the corridor. He looked at Adams and winked. Bruce took it as a show of support. Ford, meanwhile, was in a daze, like he was nodding out. Adams wondered if maybe he had drunk some of the Tuinal potion before he'd gotten out of the van. Bruce noticed some abrasions on Ford's face. Later, some LAPD guys told Adams that Ford had needed some "encouragement" to hug the pavement, so he'd gotten roughed up just a bit.

After booking, the three men were split up. Adams was taken to a retaining cell on the opposite side of Parker Center. From there, he was released.

Adams left LAPD headquarters with Loguercio in the back of a black and white. Joany was really upset. Not only had somebody tried to kill her, not only had she been dragged downtown in the middle of the night for questioning, but some damn SIS accountant had taken back all of her tip money, claiming it was evidence.

"I was dancin' my ass off for those creepy bastards all night long!" Joany cried, indignant. "They got the show of their life. And they take back my tips!"

As Joany rattled on, complaining about the cheap sons of bitches in the LAPD, Adams started to laugh. Pretty soon Joany was giggling, too. God, they needed a little levity. Bruce marveled at his near-steady hand as he lit up a cigarette.

They took Joany back to her car and escorted her home, where officers were already stationed to provide her with around-the-clock protection. Adams then drove with two LAPD detectives in a police pickup truck to International Automotive, where they loaded up the remaining parts from Von Villas's scuttled van. By the time they'd collected this evidence it was nearly sunrise. Adams then left with a team of agents who drove him up the coast to Ventura, where they checked into a motel. It was the first day of his new life as a "protected witness."

18

L.A.'s Killer Cops

AFTER HOURS OF STEWING OVER THE TAPES OF ADAMS AND FORD'S conversation in the wired van, LAPD chief Daryl Gates finally arrived at a packed news conference in the Parker Center auditorium. He explained to the waiting crowd that two veteran police officers, Detective Richard Ford, age forty-three, and Officer Robert Von Villas, thirty-eight, along with a Chatsworth auto shop owner, Bruce Adams, thirty-five, had been arrested early that morning for plotting to kill a San Fernando Valley woman in order to collect on a $100,000 insurance policy. He told reporters that two of the men had been outside a North Hollywood nude-entertainment club where the intended victim was working. "She was about three minutes away from being murdered," Gates said.

That day, Ford and Von Villas were the top story on the TV news. Shirley Adams, who was staying with friends, decided to call Lillian Ford. She played dumb, like she didn't know anything, like she was on the verge of hysterics. Lillian was calm when she answered the phone, which caught Shirley by surprise. Still, she poured on the tears. "Lillian, how could they do this to us?" she asked.

"How could who do what?" asked Lillian.

"How could the guys do something like that—try to kill someone!"

"Well, maybe because they do care for us."

"Well, that's it. I've had it," Shirley sobbed. "If that's what he wants to do, then fine, he can just stay in jail. I'm taking the children and I'm going to Chicago to stay with my family there."

184

"Well, let me know how you're doing," Lillian said. Shirley couldn't believe how calm she sounded.

On Saturday, the headlines read "Policemen Arrested in Murder Plot" and "2 LAPD Officers Held in Plot to Kill Woman." Some of the initial reports stated that the $100,000 in insurance money was earmarked to bankroll a suspected gun-running operation that was being investigated by federal agents. Scott Revell, operator of the Venus Faire, was quoted by reporters as saying that when detectives told the "unidentified intended victim" of the arrests, "she almost fainted." The *Daily News* ran a sidebar on Richard Ford titled "Arrested Officer Has Distinguished Record." The article stated: "Throughout the LAPD, officers reacted to the arrests in stunned disbelief." One former partner called Ford "a helluva policeman."

Lieutenant Dan Cooke, longtime LAPD spokesman, told reporters there had never been a case like this to hit the police force, "nor do I ever hope to hear of one again." Devonshire captain Edward Washington said that everyone in his division "was just kind of numb" after hearing of the arrests.

The initial press reports identified Bruce Adams as one of the perpetrators, but his cover held for less than two days. The TV news swarmed all over the story. One tenant at the Owensmouth complex told reporters he saw Adams at International Automotive with police after the bust. Adams wasn't arrested; he was the informant. By then, Ford and Von Villas were communicating with their wives by phone, and they learned of Adams's betrayal. Bruce was furious with the media, feeling they had placed his family in jeopardy.

Lurid details of the murder plot soon flowed into newspapers and TV reports. Over the coming weeks and months—and for the next six years—the media would piece together the facts of the case from interviews, released court documents, and the testimony of the ongoing parade of witnesses at Ford's and Von Villas's hearings and trials. Despite what seemed to be overwhelming evidence, the prosecutor faced a challenging case. The defendants would maintain their innocence to the end and many friends would stand fast in their public support. Ultimately, Ford and Von Villas would present a troubling yet plausible defense. What appeared to be an open and shut case would take on more twists and turns than a corkscrew roller-coaster.

During the first week after the arrests, Deputy D.A. Robert Jorgensen told reporters that Ford and Von Villas "methodically planned to drug and torture their victim to make her death appear to be a sex murder." The public heard about nylon cords, daggers, ski masks, drugs, possible robberies, and a prostitution ring. They saw a headline that blared "2 Officers Reportedly Bragged of Earlier Murder." Ford and Von Villas soon became known as L.A.'s killer cops.

Ford and Von Villas were arraigned on July 12 on one count each of conspiracy to commit murder, attempted murder, attempting to administer stupefying drugs, and carrying concealed weapons. They both pled not guilty on all counts. Municipal judge Michael A. Tynan denied bail after Deputy D.A. Jorgensen argued that their release would endanger the lives of the intended victim and the state's key informant. "They are a pair of cunning desperadoes masquerading as police officers," Jorgensen declared.

A July 13 account of the arraignment by *Los Angeles Times* reporters Larry Stammer and Joel Sappell noted that "as Jorgensen recited the accusations against them, the two officers exchanged unbelieving grins and shook their heads in disbelief." The headline read, "Officers Plotted to Torture Victim to Death, D.A. Says."

On July 28, the *Los Angeles Times* reported the details of the Loguercio insurance policy. Allstate insurance agent Ray Ossenkop explained that Von Villas was able to take out a $100,000 life insurance policy on Loguercio by saying that it was needed so he could get a loan to save her house from foreclosure. Although the loan never materialized, the policy went into effect a month before the attempt on her life. Ossenkop also stated that Von Villas offered to pay the entire $680 annual premium on the term policy and that the agent had never met Loguercio because "I ran everything to [Von Villas]. He did all the legwork."

On July 29 it was reported that Ford and Von Villas would be charged with the robbery of a Northridge jewelry store of gems valued somewhere between $100,000 and $200,000. Ensuing reports would cite a value as high as $240,000.

On August 6, the *Times,* having reached Joan Loguercio for an interview, described her sordid HollywoodLand Motel encounter with a Dr. Roy Anderson. The headline read "Woman Tells of Earlier Murder Try."

Ford and Von Villas were arraigned on August 12 on ten charges stemming from the Schaffer and Sons jewelry heist. Entering court in blue county-jail jumpsuits, they both pled not guilty to all charges. A preliminary hearing on all thirteen felony counts was set for September 26. Three hours of taped conversations—"the van tapes"—were turned over to defense attorneys Jack Stone (Von Villas) and Richard Lasting (Ford). "Policemen Deny Robbery Charges" declared the next day's headlines.

On August 16, two LAPD investigators who had been assigned to aid defense attorneys went to interview Bruce Adams at his Van Nuys home. Sergeant Darryl Mounger and Detective Paul Marks, who were dressed in plain clothes, pulled up to Adams's house in a Mercedes. Adams, who was no longer staying at the house, was there with his son, Eric, to retrieve some personal items.

Bruce didn't know the two men and he feared for his life, so he told his son to stand ready in the house with a rifle while he walked outside. Adams was satisfied once the officers identified themselves, and he motioned his son away.

A few weeks later, defense attorney Richard Lasting would charge that the incident had amounted to assault on police officers with a deadly weapon and he called for an investigation. Lasting claimed that IAD was covering up the incident to protect Adams's credibility as a witness against Ford and Von Villas. It was the first volley in what would become a protracted campaign to discredit Bruce Adams.

On September 26, Bruce Adams emerged from hiding to testify for the first time at a preliminary hearing before municipal judge Michael T. Sauer. According to the *Times*'s Larry Stammer, "The mustachioed Adams, who wore a dark purple shirt, white coat and brown tie, told the court the two officers intended to drug, torture and murder the woman, then dump her body in a Hollywood alley so that she would appear to be 'just another whore' killed in Hollywood." Adams also described the homicide kit with its "military combat-type daggers." His picture, in which he pretty much looked like a hood, ran with the piece.

Arnie Friedman's account in the *Daily News* stated, "Following his testimony Monday, Jack R. Stone, Von Villas' attorney, referred to Adams' version as 'seedy and surreptitious.' He referred to Adams' appearance in a tan sports coat and maroon shirt with a wide brown and white dotted tie. 'He looks like a seedy character,' said Stone of Adams, who was placed on probation for two years in 1980 after he pleaded no contest to a misdemeanor charge of issuing a check for $950 with insufficient funds."

The testimony continued the next day, when Joan Loguercio appeared and described her HollywoodLand Motel tryst with Dr. Anderson. "Woman Details 2 Officers Alleged Death Plot Ruse" the *Times* headline blared, accompanied by a photo of the dark-haired Joany that made her appear rather hard and severe. The *Daily News* account reported that "Ford glared briefly at Loguercio after she entered the courtroom of Los Angeles Municipal Judge Michael T. Sauer late Tuesday. The dark-haired woman, wearing a knee-length skirt with blouse and jacket, testified she first saw Ford in June while working at the Venus Faire nude entertainment club in North Hollywood."

On September 28 Joany continued her testimony, describing how she and Ford had been drinking vodka, smoking marijuana, and taking pills in the motel room before he allegedly tried to kill her. "I seen his hand up in the air coming down on me. I heard a sound like elastic, a snapping sound. I immediately turned around and jumped up. Whatever he had in his hands he tried to hide it in the covers."

Loguercio also testified that previously, while she had been having trouble with her husband in a divorce, Von Villas had told her, "Well, I know someone who would kill your husband for ten thousand dollars," but she hadn't taken him up on the offer.

Under cross-examination by Ford's attorney, Richard Lasting, Loguercio denied ever having a sexual relationship with Adams or Von Villas. She denied engaging in acts of prostitution with customers she met at the Venus Faire. She also denied that she had ever told Adams or anyone else that she thought her ex-husband or her boyfriend Frank might be trying to have her killed. By implying that she had, Lasting obviously wanted to portray her as paranoid. Lasting also asked, "Did Dr. Anderson ever suggest a particular exotic routine for you to perform?"

"No," answered Loguercio.

Obviously, Lasting was implying that he had. But just how that would figure in Ford's defense was a mystery—for now. Loguercio then stated that she had told Scott (the Venus Faire proprietor) and a number of friends that she thought Bob was trying to have her killed.

Jack Stone, attorney for Von Villas (and no relation to the makeup artist), asked Loguercio, "You were seeing and dating Bruce Adams at one point, weren't you?"

"Not really dating him, no," she answered.

"Didn't Frank and Adams get in a fight because of you?"

"No."

"Weren't you in the habit of picking up Adams after work? Wouldn't the two of you go out?"

"No, he was putting a stereo in my car. I used to go to the garage to have him work on my car."

"Wasn't Adams living in the shop for a while?"

"Yes."

"Did he ask to live with you?"

"No."

On September 29, the court heard testimony from victims of the Schaffer and Sons robbery and from Hollywood makeup artist Darlis Chefalo. The September 30 *Los Angeles Times* story was headlined "2 Officers Reportedly Got Disguises." As this increasingly bizarre case unfolded in the courts, a clipping of that story would later become an important piece of evidence submitted at Ford and Von Villas's capital trial for the murder of Thomas Weed.

Jan Golab

After the two cops were denounced in Assistant D.A. Jorgensen's closing arguments as "traitors to the Los Angeles Police Department," Judge Michael T. Sauer ordered on September 30 that Ford and Von Villas stand trial for robbery, conspiracy, and attempted murder in superior court. He scheduled the trial for November 17. According to a report the next day in the *Los Angeles Times,* "Sauer also vehemently denied defense motions to release the defendants on bail, declaring that he had been shocked at their behavior in the face of 'sordid testimony' and grave charges against them. 'At times they joked and laughed as if this was the funniest game show on television,' Sauer declared as Ford and Von Villas stood before him in silence."

Angered by one of the defense attorney's characterization of the defendants as "decorated Vietnam veterans who had served their country in war and their community as police officers," prosecutor Robert Jorgensen read from the van tape transcript. "Good old Detective Ford, loved by one and all. Nice guy all around. Best cover in the world is when everybody thinks you're a nice guy. Everybody thinks you're a sweetheart. Meanwhile, you ought to see my victims, kid. They think the sun rises and sets on my ass."

On their long and winding road through the California judicial system, L.A.'s killer cops never would make bail.

19

Call Out the Dogs

AFTER THE ARREST, BRUCE ADAMS UNDERWENT A THOROUGH DE-
briefing by LAPD's Internal Affairs Division. IAD wanted to hear everything
about Ford and Von Villas. Over the next few years, Bruce would go over his
story again and again. For the first few months, while he lived mostly in cheap
motels up and down the Ventura County coast, Adams was interviewed almost
daily.

"These guys were going crazy," Adams told investigators. "They were
planning caper after caper, a half a dozen at one time—the out-call, a jewelry
store, Cade's car, Von Villas's van, Loguercio, Tom Weed, El Toro gun ship-
ments, the Renaissance Faire, the Century City gem show—and those are just
what I knew about. God knows what I didn't know about."

Bob Jorgensen, a tall man in his late thirties with graying hair and glasses,
was present at many of these initial debriefings. Adams immediately liked
Jorgensen. He struck him as a real hawk, a hard-charging D.A. who went for the
throat. And he didn't miss a trick. Neither did IAD's Sergeant Roger Fox and his
partner, Detective John Fruge, who ran Adams through his story upside down
and sideways, exploring every turn of his troubling tale.

One of the prosecution's first priorities was to shore up the Loguercio case
with corroborating evidence. While Adams was running through his account of
the "broken-wire" meeting with Ford and Von Villas on the morning before the
arrests, he described again how Von Villas had him call up Loguercio so he could
arrange to pick her up after work. Bruce next described how Von Villas had

written him some notes and passed them to him while he was on the phone. Fox and Jorgensen looked at each other and their eyes lit up like headlights.

Moments later Adams found himself racing down the Ventura Freeway back to Chatsworth with Fox and Jorgensen. When they got to International Automotive they found that the office had been cleaned up; everything had been thrown away. Oh well, Bruce thought. But Roger Fox was already out front peeking in the Dumpster. It was loaded with garbage—greasy auto parts and oil cans and busted fan belts and radiator hoses and moldy pizza and sandwiches and a blizzard of paperwork. Fox, a trim, athletic man in his thirties, took off his jacket, rolled up his sleeves, and leaped into the morass. Adams, Jorgensen, and Fruge paced around the parking lot for the next hour while Fox waded through the garbage, examining every scrap.

Sure enough, Fox found the evidence—three notes in Von Villas's handwriting: "$12,500 *each*," "Find out how much Frank knows," and "Meet me tonight. Late. Maybe motel?"

The gang erupted in cheers when Fox fished out the goods. The notes helped verify a crucial part of Adams's story.

Adams was impressed. Working with these guys wasn't going to be so bad, he figured. Roger Fox was also warming to their partnership. When he'd first met Adams after the lie-detector test, he thought he was slime. Now, Roger had to admit that appearances weren't everything. Agent Sam Oddo had apparently been right about his informant.

It was to be a long, detailed investigation, and eventually a teamlike camaraderie really did develop. Fox and Fruge, along with Jorgensen, listened intently as Adams went over his months of stories about Ford and Von Villas. Jorgensen didn't seem to care how obscure the detail—he wanted to hear all about it, and then he went after it. Former U.S. Marine Bruce Adams really appreciated his hard-charging aggressiveness. Bruce also liked the close-to-the-vest manner in which Jorgensen handled the press; he didn't leak a scrap of information he didn't want to.

It became apparent early in the investigation that IAD wasn't screwing around. The dogs had been called out on Ford and Von Villas, and no stone would be left unturned. When IAD got a tip from a jailhouse informant that Richard Ford had allegedly mentioned something about burying some automatic weapons in a field, Bruce was again called out to the shop. This time he found a whole crew of earthmovers and backhoes and bulldozers ripping up the lot next to the shop. The guys were all wearing helmets from the L.A. Department of Water and Power, but they were really LAPD. Sergeant Fox was standing ready with his warrant.

Adams watched as they dug up every inch of the lot looking for the Colorado Mac-10s. They never would find them. Agent Sam Oddo and the boys at ATF were able to confirm Adams's story about a 211 in progress and an officer named Adams at the Payson, Utah, police station. Gas receipts confirmed that Adams and Ford had indeed made a trip to Colorado. But no guns.

Interviews with Loguercio and Monique, as well as rent, phone, and sex-tabloid ad receipts, confirmed Adams's story about the escort service. But Jorgensen and IAD weren't real interested in that. They were on the trail of bigger game.

An ongoing string of warrants was issued to search the homes, cars, desks, lockers, and other personal property of Ford and Von Villas. Investigators returned to the cops' homes numerous times with new warrants covering expanded territory. Meanwhile, practically everybody who ever knew Ford or Von Villas was interviewed. The investigation by IAD would grow to be one of the largest and most comprehensive in the history of the department.

Adams was impressed watching these guys operate. LAPD, and particularly IAD, were efficient, thorough, top-notch professionals. But they also had their bureaucracy, their hallowed, inviolable procedures, which eventually proved troublesome to him. These guys reminded him of the military—for better and for worse. He could understand how Ford and Von Villas had developed a love-hate relationship with their LAPD family.

Among the most incriminating evidence uncovered in the investigation were twenty diamonds found in Bob Von Villas's attaché case. Fox and Fruge grilled Adams on what he'd heard about a jewelry store heist. All he knew was that it was someplace where Von Villas had once worked foot patrol and that Ford had mentioned that they had used professional disguises.

On July 14, a week after the bust, Fox had taken a call and then interviewed a Hollywood makeup artist named Darlis Chefalo. Chefalo had seen L.A.'s killer cops on TV and immediately realized they were Dick and Bob, the two guys she had made disguises for.

Fox and Fruge ran through all the possibilities and finally came across the Northridge Schaffer and Sons robbery of November 22, 1982. Von Villas had once worked security patrol at the mall. Fox noticed that two of the victims mentioned that the perp who came inside might have been wearing a wig and makeup. The report also indicated that the robber had used "cop talk" while subduing the victims and that he had told them that his partner outside was monitoring a police radio. A check of records at Club Dev came up with the *coup de grâce*. At the end of his watch on the afternoon before the robbery, Officer Bob Von Villas "forgot" to turn in his Rover police radio. Further checks showed that it was the only time in his career that he had ever made this oversight.

But the big enchilada was this business about a murder for hire. Adams went over and over the phone conversation he had overheard. A woman named Jan wanted her husband killed. They had Bruce rent a van and black out the windows. Later, Bruce saw Von Villas hand Ford his "bonus." Adams later learned that the victim's name was Tom Weed. Ford told him, "Weed's bones are bleaching out in the desert."

IAD contacted Detective James Lewis, who was handling the missing person investigation of a Thomas Weed. Weed had simply disappeared without a trace from his apartment on February 23, 1983. His car was found abandoned in a parking lot at the Los Angeles International Airport a few days later. Lewis had begun to suspect foul play.

Fox and Fruge and Detectives Bill Gailey and Harry Eddo began putting the pieces of the Weed puzzle together. Weed's estranged wife was a black woman named Janie Elmira Ogilvie. Dr. Ogilvie operated a blood-testing laboratory, the ownership of which had become a matter of dispute in her divorce proceedings against Tom Weed. It turned out that one of Ogilvie's employees was a young girl named Julie Rabold Kanoske, whose mother was a police widow named Joyce Reynolds—a good friend of Bob Von Villas. Julie, in fact, considered Bob her godfather.

One of the pieces of paper seized from Bob Von Villas's Pontiac Grand Prix the day of his arrest was a bank deposit slip. On the back of the slip, written in Von Villas's script, was the name Jan Ogilvie followed by three phone numbers and the words "Ros Res."

A week later, an investigator serving a warrant at the Von Villas home saw Judy Von Villas stuffing some papers in her purse. He seized those papers, one of which had Jan Ogilvie's phone number written on it, along with a note that read, "Close friend, Mr. Ory in jail, *emergency,* police might have #, don't worry, need loan $30,000, will be paid back, no blackmail. Pay phone. Joyce."

Who the hell was Mr. Ory?

Sergeant Fox interviewed Jan Ogilvie on August 2, 1983, less than a month after the arrests of Ford and Von Villas. Ogilvie insisted, as she had to Detective Lewis, that Weed was either with family in Canada or had taken off for Mexico.

But one night a while later, Fox and Fruge were grilling Adams at IAD's offices on the third floor at Parker Center. They had many of these marathon sessions. They'd browbeat Adams like defense attorneys, picking away at his story, knowing that it would, eventually, need to weather an excruciating pounding.

Fox and Fruge played a number of tapes for Adams, and Bruce identified

Ogilvie's voice as that of the woman he had overheard on the phone at the shop. Ogilvie had a distinctive voice—very refined, with proper diction, impeccable English—as Adams had previously described. He had also told them there was no way to tell from her voice if she was black or white. Adams wasn't surprised to learn she preferred to be called Dr. Ogilvie and that she had a PhD.

After Adams's positive ID, Fox and Fruge went back and leaned on Ogilvie, but she stuck to her testimony. It would take the IAD a while to crack her case.

"I believe Ford did Weed himself," said Adams, explaining his theory about Weed's disappearance. "I think they probably used that rented van to stake him out, to observe his place of residence, as well as to recon a place in the desert to bury the remains. That's why they were all full of dust when they came back. Maybe they even dug the hole. Ford talked about taking a guy out with a small-caliber handgun, like a twenty-two, at close range. I think he waited until Weed came home that night and either badged the guy or shoved a piece in his ribs and walked him to his car. Then he had him drive to a prearranged destination and dusted him. He probably had him kneel on the ground and put one round through the back of his head. Then he used the shotgun to blow away his dental work."

Marlboro red cigarette butts, Richard Ford's brand, had been found in Weed's car. Tom Weed was a nonsmoker.

IAD would go on numerous wild goose chases sparked by tips on the whereabouts of Tom Weed's body. Once, Detectives Bill Gailey and Harry Eddo took Adams, along with some picks and shovels, out to some rough country in the far west valley by the old Spahn ranch, where Charlie Manson had lived. Twenty-five feet off the road was a fairly fresh mound of dirt that somebody suspected might be a grave. They dug but found nothing. This exercise would be repeated many times in coming years. Ultimately, however, the cops would have to make the case on the Thomas Weed murder the hard way—without a body.

Before he agreed to take down Ford and Von Villas, Adams had been led to believe that he would be placed in a witness protection program, that the LAPD would ensure the safety of himself and his family and provide the funds to help them get settled in a new place. As it turned out, little help ever materialized.

After the bust, federal agents escorted the Adams family to Ventura County for a weekend. Then they gave Bruce $150 and left him on his own. Adams lived hand to mouth for about two months, traveling up and down the coast, picking up odd jobs in towns from Ventura to Santa Barbara. Meanwhile, investigators shadowed Bruce so they could pump him for information, but they provided little in the way of material assistance.

After the Adams family lived like gypsies for two months, the LAPD finally agreed to put them in a witness protection program. But the LAPD refused to help him change his identity or move out of state or find a cover in some new profession. They helped him find a house to rent in Orange County, but their financial assistance was negligible—a few hundred here, a few hundred there. "Bruce went to Disneyland," the guys at IAD would say. But no enchanted life was in store for the Adams family.

Bruce got a job at a local auto shop almost immediately. But when his employer found out who he was, he was fired. It would become a recurring pattern. The guys from IAD or ATF or the D.A.'s office would show up at work to ask him some questions and out the door he'd go. Or he'd get subpoenaed to appear at a hearing and would have to ask for time off. Most often, he couldn't even tell his employer how long he would be away—maybe a day, maybe a week, maybe longer. Adams was let go by one employer who told him, "I'm afraid somebody's going to come by and throw a bomb in here."

Bruce and Shirley eventually lost their two oldest kids, Marilyn and Eric, who permanently relocated with friends. They lost nearly everything they owned that was of any value. Items disappeared from their Van Nuys home or were never returned to them as promised. Bruce simply had to write off his business. On top of that, most items left at International Automotive were looted. His 1974 Chevy Nova dragster was cannibalized, and although he learned through a friend who was responsible, the LAPD pressured him not to press charges; he would have to appear in court and it would create unwanted publicity.

The worst blow came when Adams got into a dispute with an employer who claimed Bruce was stealing money from him and confiscated his tools—worth about eight thousand dollars. Bruce swore the allegations were false, that the estranged employer actually owed him back wages, but the LAPD refused to get involved. Without his tools, Bruce couldn't find work on his own, and that had always been his safety net. Even when unemployed, he'd always been able to hustle up work through friends or on the street, but without tools he was out of luck. When he got fired from a job just before Christmas 1984 and was facing eviction, Adams put in a call for help to the LAPD. He was told there was nothing they could do.

Unlike most informants, Adams never made a deal with the D.A. He didn't exchange his information for immunity from prosecution. He wasn't coerced into talking to get himself off the hook. He readily admitted to his own minor criminal involvements because he wanted to get Ford and Von Villas out of his life, to see them put away. While this gave him fantastic credibility by informant standards and made him a relatively good witness for the D.A., the D.A., in turn, was under no obligation to do anything for him. Adams would probably have been better off if he had committed a major crime and been coerced into making a deal. That way he could have obtained a guarantee of help and protection.

Hoping to bring attention to his plight, Bruce Adams finally decided to go public by granting a few interviews in which he described how he had been lost in a bungle of bureaucratic red tape. "At first I dealt with a Sergeant Fox and Detective Fruge in Internal Affairs," Adams explained. "I have the utmost praise for these gentlemen. Then, as the case progressed into the second set of indictments and the whole Ogilvie thing, they changed it over to Major Crimes Investigative Section. They pulled Fox and Fruge out of IAD and sent them in different directions. All of a sudden, the guys I was dealing with weren't there. The last investigator I talked to told me, 'I don't deal with you. You're not one of my people. Fuck you.' Their attitude has been 'Don't be bothering us.' One IAD officer told me, 'Well, since you can't hold down a job, go on welfare.' Meanwhile, I put my life on the line for that operation. Without me it never would have gone down.

"The D.A.'s office never returned my phone calls. They only want to hear from me when they need me. So I stopped trying. If I hassled them too much, they'd probably put me under protective custody—which means throwing me in jail. I can understand why so many people think twice about being a witness.

"I can't go on like this. I'm up against the ropes," he concluded.

Adams could only speculate why the LAPD had treated him the way it had. "Because of me, two cops got burned," he said. "That could have something to do with it." The other possibility, he suggested, was that the LAPD was simply incompetent. "A number of cops in Major Crimes admitted to me that they just don't know how to handle a witness protection program," he said.

Adams's desperate ploy was somewhat effective. After the appearance of a feature story in the March 1985 issue of *Hustler* magazine (including much of the X-rated dialogue from the van tapes) and subsequent attention in the L.A. press—most notably a powerful front page story by *Herald-Examiner* columnist Gordon Dillow—Adams was finally relocated by the LAPD. However, he still only received minimal assistance in moving out of state and establishing a new identity. And today, he and his family are on their own.

The hard reality is that the LAPD doesn't have the same resources for a witness protection program as the federal government. Federal programs provide for relocation, a new identity, and substantial financial assistance; the LAPD rarely provides more than protection for court appearances. Witnesses in federal programs can receive hundreds of thousands of dollars over long periods of time; Adams received a total of seven thousand dollars from the LAPD to help him support a wife and four kids while on the run.

The LAPD also couldn't assuage Adam's ongoing fear of retaliation. Adams was notified as early as August 1983, a month after the bust, of alleged jailhouse talk about Ford and Von Villas plotting to have him killed. In April 1984, Adams's eighty-five-year-old grandfather was brutally murdered and mutilated in New Jersey. Authorities suspected a burglar; Bruce Adams wasn't so sure. The case was never solved. And in December 1984, Bill Mayhew, the would-be partner who allegedly witnessed the financial transaction between Adams and Von Villas that transferred ownership of the shop, was found dead, along with his girlfriend, lying facedown in a field in Wichita, Kansas, a bullet through his head. Once again, authorities found no evidence that the case was related to the killer cops; once again, Adams wasn't so sure. He wanted a new identity and a fresh start—as promised. "I'm walking around like I used to walk around in Nam," he told Gordon Dillow of the *Herald-Examiner*. "I'm looking over my shoulder twenty-four hours a day, seven days a week."

By the time IAD was finished with Adams, he had been through the wringer. After all, the purpose of IAD is not just to expose rotten cops, but also to protect good cops who are falsely accused. The perception that would later arise during the Rodney King affair—that the LAPD was lax in investigating its own officers—was arguably true when it came to complaints about excessive force. But when it came to clear-cut criminal activity—such as armed robbery or murder for hire—LAPD's Internal Affairs Division had a reputation for being ruthless, perhaps even overzealous. Both the accusers and the accused in the Ford–Von Villas case were held up to extraordinary scrutiny. Numerous sources in LAPD's Internal Affairs Division, including Captain Don Vincent, who headed IAD during the investigation, and department spokesman Commander William Booth, all concurred: however painful and difficult it was to believe, however hard they tried to prove otherwise, Adams's story appeared basically true.

Still, many of Adams's assertions couldn't be corroborated, so his character and credibility would prove crucial during the trial. This presented a problem for the prosecution, as Adams's work and personal histories were troublesome. Perhaps delayed stress could explain his ongoing difficulty with employers, his trouble holding down jobs and paying bills, the bad check charge against him in 1980. On the other hand, it was also possible—and it certainly would be so argued by the defense—that it was simply Bruce's nature to be shifty, irresponsible, and at times dishonest.

Investigators who worked the case painted a portrait of Bruce Adams like that of many confidential informants. While his story rang basically true and much of the information he presented could be verified, much of it could not. The missing pieces were troublesome because Adams couldn't be relied on to be entirely honest. One investigator recalled how while all the information Adams gave him about the case checked out, Adams would lie to him about personal things. The investigator loaned Adams some money to buy a car and never got it back, instead getting one tall tale after another. One time Adams told him that his house had burned down—but it hadn't. Many people who "loaned" Adams money had a similar experience.

Bruce Adams presented a dilemma because he simply didn't fit society's standard image of a hero. The fact that he did something heroic didn't change that he was kind of sleazy. And the fact that he was kind of sleazy didn't change the fact that he had done something heroic.

Many officers at Club Dev lived in fear of getting caught in the billowing IAD investigation of Ford and Von Villas. IAD was determined to ferret out anyone who was remotely involved in capers with the two rogue cops. Chief Gates shuddered at the thought that IAD might uncover evidence of widespread corruption, but it would be far more damaging to overlook such evidence and have it surface later, either on its own or as the result of scrutiny by the press. Gates and IAD were determined that the LAPD would clean its own house.

When Lieutenant Higbee called the troops together at roll call the morning of the arrests and told them what had happened, the Club Dev cowboys were stunned. Nobody for a moment believed that Ford and Von Villas were capable of such crimes.

A group of detectives who were up at a Lake Crowley cabin cut their weekend fishing trip short after one of the guys picked up a newspaper at the bait shop. Once they saw the front page pictures and headlines, nobody could think about trout.

A lot of cops who worked with Ford and Von Villas would later mention how devoted the two cops were to their families. This seemed to make the allegations against them so much more unthinkable. "Every policeman has opportunities to steal or do something dishonest," Lieutenant Higbee explained. "One of the things that always kept me from doing anything like that is my family. What would my son or my daughter think of me? I can't understand, a guy like Von Villas, who thought as much as he did about his daughters . . ." Higbee's disbelief was shared by the other officers at Club Dev.

For Higbee and Detective Ray Romero, the news was especially troubling. They were supervisors, and neither of them had any idea what was going on. The IAD nutbusters would want to know why. And poor Mike Moen—he knew the moment he got the news that he'd be in the hot seat and that all the guys would be wondering about him. After all, he'd been Dick Ford's partner. Everyone would assume he knew something. Even though he was clean, he knew IAD would probably be scrutinizing and second-guessing his past cases for years. It didn't turn out that bad—but close.

As the IAD investigation ballooned, it began to disrupt the division. Before long, everybody at Club Dev was convinced the IAD bloodhounds were after him. And just because they were paranoid, that didn't mean IAD wasn't out to get them. Because it was.

IAD had a team working insurance fraud, another working guns, another on jewelry and diamonds, another on Loguercio, another on Jan Ogilvie, another looking for Thomas Weed. Some Club Dev cops got quizzed by a half-dozen different guys in the course of the investigation.

Before long every cop at Club Dev was ruminating about evidence and roiling with suspicions. Every day, some worried-to-death cop would walk into Higbee's office to tell him some trivial thing Ford or Von Villas had said. "Should I call IAD and tell them?" Pretty soon it seemed like everybody recalled some incident that now made him wonder. Like the time Ford laughed at one of his jokes. Or the time he didn't. Or the time Von Villas came in with some blue-prints—and the next day he didn't. Or the time he took an apricot danish instead of the usual chocolate doughnut.

Imaginations ran wild. For a while, a rumor circulated at Club Dev that Ford and Von Villas planned to kill two policemen. Speculation raged through the division as to who were the likely targets. Smart money was on Romero and another CO named Crawford, the two guys at Club Dev who had given Ford and Von Villas a hard time.

Fact was, Ford and Von Villas had kept to themselves, and as hard as IAD tried, they could find nothing that connected any other Club Dev officer to the pair's alleged crimes. Still, it's a general rule that innocent people get hurt whenever IAD conducts a hard-nosed investigation. Better to come down too hard than not hard enough, the thinking goes. And this case was no exception.

When IAD investigates an officer suspected of committing a crime—any crime—it proceeds as though it were investigating a homicide. They not only grill the subject of the investigation mercilessly, they also talk to family, friends, neighbors, and acquaintances. They subpoena and seize records. They research past associations. Even if the guy is the cleanest cop on earth, he endures a grueling ordeal, with everything he's ever done held up to scrutiny. Sometimes it gets ridiculous. And for some guys, it just gets to be too much. After getting hung out to dry by IAD, a lot of guys lose their desire to be cops.

One of the unfortunates in this case was Brian Leslie, the first officer assigned to the Northridge jewelry heist. Many months after the robbery, Leslie routinely disposed of some evidence—after consulting with his superiors—because he felt it was a dead-end case. Later, when IAD decided Ford and Von Villas were the hold-up men, they figured that maybe Leslie was in on it. Leslie was eventually accused of conducting an improper investigation and was ordered to appear before a Board of Rights inquiry. He was also passed over for a long-overdue promotion. Rather than go through the inquiry, which can be as draining as any trial, Leslie simply retired. He'd put in his twenty years. He sold his Simi Valley home and moved up to Mariposa County and started a construction business.

The guys at Club Dev felt that Leslie had gotten the shaft. They considered him to be one of the best—as pure as the driven snow. If he hadn't investigated the robbery properly, his supervisor should have kicked it back to him. IAD had no evidence that he knew Ford or Von Villas were involved. Leslie had simply been in the wrong place at the wrong time.

The other guy who got squeezed was watch commander Joe Reiner—best friend, supervisor, and business partner of Bob Von Villas. Bobby was listed in Joe's squad on the morning he was arrested. When Reiner discovered Bobby wasn't there during roll call, he told one of the guys to give him a call. It wasn't at all like Bobby to be late. But then, another sergeant came up and pulled Reiner aside. "I got something to tell you, Joe. Bobby was arrested last night."

"That's impossible," said Reiner. "Bobby doesn't even drink." Whenever Reiner heard that a cop was arrested, he automatically assumed it was for DUI.

"No, this was serious."

When Reiner heard the story about Loguercio and the Venus Faire and Ford with his homicide kit in the back of a van and Bobby's house being invaded by helicopters and SIS, he swooned. He immediately knew he was in deep shit.

Reiner was close to Bobby. He knew IAD would soon be fitting him for a set of thumbscrews. Reiner immediately walked into the office of Club Dev captain Ed Washington. Reiner and Washington were buddies. They drank beers together on the shores of Lake Mojave. "I just heard about Bobby and I want to tell you, Ed, I didn't know a damn thing about it," Reiner said.

"We'll find out," said Washington, giving him an icy stare.

Over the next year, Reiner was subjected to so much scrutiny that he eventually cracked under the pressure. His long career as a police officer ended when he finally blew up one day and punched Captain Washington.

Reiner retired from the force and joined Ron Skyvnick's security firm. Skyvnick, a former partner of Von Villas, owned and operated the firm that handled security for the Renaissance Faire. He had also decided to leave the department after the investigation had begun.

The world-famous Southern California Renaissance Faire, the granddaddy of other such fairs around the country, was robbed of $35,000 in gate proceeds on June 13, 1983, about a month before Ford and Von Villas were arrested. A gang of four surprised a security guard as he was depositing the day's receipts in a night depository box at a Valley bank. The perps badly bungled the job, as they got to the guard after he had already deposited $190,000. They only got his last bag of cash.

Naturally, IAD went nuts when Adams told them he had overheard Ford and Von Villas planning such a caper. The fact that Skyvnick, Von Villas's former partner and good friend, handled the fair's security just seemed like too much of a coincidence. IAD put so much heat on Skyvnick he finally decided to just call it a wrap. He quit the department and devoted all his time to the security business.

IAD never did uncover any wrongdoing on Skyvnick's part. In fact, the four perpetrators of the Faire heist were all later caught, tried, convicted, and sent to prison. None of them ever implicated Ford, Von Villas, Skyvnick, or any other police officers. Nevertheless, stories would persist for many years that L.A.'s killer cops were the guys who pulled that job at the Renaissance Faire.

But then, Ford and Von Villas were about to become urban legends. They'd eventually get blamed for everything but the invasion of the killer bees up at Ronald Reagan's ranch.

Many officers eventually transferred or were reassigned out of Devonshire Division. A lot of new guys came in, and the social atmosphere changed completely. Most cops said that Devonshire Division would never be the same again. Club Dev was history.

20

L.A. Law

CITIZENS FROM OUT OF STATE OFTEN FIND CALIFORNIA'S JUSTICE
system rather curious. They are perplexed by year-long trials that could be
dispatched in a few months back home. And they are baffled by the likes of the
McMartin trial, which, at four years and change, became the longest criminal trial
in U.S. history. After all, how could the case of an alleged nursery school
pervert—who was eventually found not guilty—take up more time, fill more
transcript pages, than the Nuremberg or Watergate trials?

What's more amazing is that the public doesn't know the half of it. California courts can reduce even sensational trials to tedious proceedings, testing the
attention span of both the media and the public. Even headline cases like McMartin aren't reported on every day. With the Rodney King beating trial, at three
months a relative blip in the California legal system, the public finally saw
gavel-to-gavel coverage, only to discover how dull most days of a "sensational"
trial can be.

For every high-profile case there are dozens of year-long legal proceedings
that get attention only when they start and finish. And the public rarely hears
about the additional years spent on hearings, motions, continuances, and appeals.
A California trial is usually just the tip of the legal iceberg.

The credit (or blame) for this plodding system is the subject of much debate.
Some lay it at the doorstep of former California Supreme Court justice Rose Bird,
an appointee of then-Governor Jerry Brown. Before being recalled by a special
voter referendum in 1986, Bird made a number of rulings beneficial to defendants

202

that greatly slowed the system. Others say it's unfair to blame Rose Bird entirely and point to the lawyers' legislature in California, which has long taken care of its own. The system was streamlined somewhat in 1990 when voters overwhelmingly passed the Speedy Trials Initiative. Still, the California judicial system retains the consistency of an off-shore oil slick.

The killer cops extravaganza, which occurred entirely at the system's most cumbersome period in the 1980s, was a textbook case of wretched or blessed excess—depending on one's point of view. *The People vs. Richard Ford and Robert Von Villas* would eventually cost the taxpayers somewhere in the neighborhood of $8 to $10 million. Before it was over, the People would witness the mother of all internal LAPD investigations, two years of motions, evidentiary hearings, and grand jury testimony, a grab-bag assortment of delays and continuances, a nine-month preliminary hearing, more continuances and evidentiary hearings, followed by two dramatic nine-month-long trials. The matter of Ford and Von Villas wouldn't be settled until 1989, six years after their arrests. And even then, some would argue it still wasn't finished. Those who expected the killer cops to be an open and shut case were in for a lot of surprises.

That first preliminary hearing, after which Ford and Von Villas were ordered to stand trial, was merely the opening bell of a fifteen-round heavyweight fight. At a new bail hearing on December 19, Judge Robert T. Altman, who would deny the defense motion for bail, was presented with documents that suggested Von Villas may have tried to set up a former business partner the same way he did Loguercio. Von Villas had invested $20,000 in a tile business with a man named Edward Ricky Summers and had obtained a life insurance policy on Summers to protect his investment. Summers told authorities that after the business folded, Von Villas maintained the policy, and Summers heard of a possible plot on his life. Summers also related that Von Villas once told him it was "easy to make a person into an accident."

The prosecution also introduced incriminating information received from jailhouse informants. Ford and Von Villas had allegedly both expressed an interest in having each other killed, and Von Villas had allegedly offered $30,000 to one informant if he would assassinate Bruce Adams or kidnap his son to keep him from testifying. Ford and Von Villas were also allegedly trying to arrange Adams's demise through directions being relayed to their wives. Both Lillian Ford and Judy Von Villas appeared in court to deny these charges.

Ford and Von Villas were being held in the special high-power unit at the L.A. County Jail, where they were not exposed to the general inmate population. Still, inmates came forward claiming to have overheard their incriminating conversations. Even though such "information" was notoriously unreliable, Assistant D.A. Jorgensen used it to obtain a warrant to bug the jailhouse conversations of Ford and Von Villas. This warrant, and its subsequent results, would become the subject of a crucial legal and ethical dispute. The California Supreme Court had, in 1982, restricted the monitoring of prisoners for the purpose of gathering evidence. The only legitimate reason for such eavesdropping, the court had ruled, was to maintain security and protect the public. This situation was deemed to qualify.

The warrant did not yield any evidence of attempts being made on Adams's life. But it did result in the taping of a conversation that appeared to implicate Ford and Von Villas in the murder of Thomas Weed.

On the morning of December 20, 1983, the day after she had attended her husband's bail hearing, Lillian Ford found a team of LAPD investigators at her door. They had a warrant to search and seize a broad range of items, primarily papers and financial records. The investigators tore through the Ford house, seizing everything they could find, including many of Lillian's most personal letters from her husband. Understandably, she was quite upset. After the police left, she got in her car and drove downtown to visit Richard Ford at the L.A. County Jail. There, she questioned him about the possible purpose of the seizures.

Because the warrant had been issued "to protect the public," the conversation between husband and wife was taped. However, the technician had some difficulties that resulted in large silent gaps on the tape. Much of it came out one-sided; one couldn't hear the questions to which Richard Ford was responding. With the commotion and voices of other prisoners in the background, the dialogue was also spotty and difficult to decipher. Lillian frequently had to shout because the phones used to speak through the Plexiglas partition that separated them were not working properly. Sometimes she couldn't be heard at all.

This recorded conversation would later prove to be as troubling as it appeared to be incriminating, a bone of strident contention. Prosecutors would argue that it was the talk of a guilty man. Defense attorneys would insist that it was simply the conversation of a confused, innocent couple, fearful of being framed, who were trying to figure out what the heck LAPD investigators were looking for.

RICHARD FORD: So who was there? They all came, huh?
LILLIAN FORD: Okay, ready? [reading from the search warrant] Our house was searched. Bob Von Villas's house was searched. The garage, Datsun, Toyota, Pontiac, Camaro, the person of Judy Von Villas.
RICHARD: They're going to search her?

LILLIAN: They searched her.

[eleven seconds unintelligible]

RICHARD: No way to tie me to it.

[five seconds unintelligible]

RICHARD: What can I say?

[thirty-one seconds unintelligible]

LILLIAN: [reading from search warrant] Seventy-nine Mercedes-Benz, Mazda, offices of Shell Oil Company, Bank of America Northridge, Santa Clarita Bank, Oldsmobile station wagon, World Savings and Loan Association, deposit slips. [paper rustling] Huh?

RICHARD: Thirty. The twenty.

[eighteen seconds unintelligible]

RICHARD: That stuff . . . hot [?] I think. It's the only thing I can think of. No, that's not . . . [unintelligible] Let me see the dates. Is that the right dates?

LILLIAN: What?

RICHARD: Is that the right dates? April fifth through June fifth?

LILLIAN: [eight seconds unintelligible]

RICHARD: I've never talked to her.

LILLIAN: [eight seconds unintelligible]

RICHARD: That's just trying [machine noise] to show the money. They're trying to see where the money went to.

[five seconds unintelligible]

LILLIAN: I don't know.

RICHARD: I'll have it upstairs.

LILLIAN: I don't think it'll be there when you get back.

RICHARD: Did I ever use the Shell card?

LILLIAN: I don't know.

RICHARD: How long we had that?

LILLIAN: Not long. About a year.

[eight-second gap]

RICHARD: We didn't put any money in the bank, did we? [three-and-a-half-second gap] Did we pay anything off?

LILLIAN: [seven seconds unintelligible]

RICHARD: What the hell did we do with it? What did we do with it?

LILLIAN: [unintelligible]

RICHARD: Good. Good, there's no connection to me there. There's nothing there that connects me.

[two minutes of gaps, unintelligible]

RICHARD: Don't worry about it. Hey, you can't change nothing, honey. They're fishing.

LILLIAN: [unintelligible, conversation about the phone]

RICHARD: Don't worry about it. So they are all gone now, huh?

LILLIAN: What?

RICHARD: Did they give you a hard time?

LILLIAN: No. There was one Internal Affairs officer, the rest were Robbery/Homicide. It was a woman. There was a woman there too. She read all the letters. The folder of bills, I kept it next to the bed. It's [?] filled with my letters. She went through every one. I must have had six to nine months. I must have had about two thousand pages. I don't remember. [unintelligible]

RICHARD: I can't remember either. I don't think I said anything about that though.

LILLIAN: No, ah.

RICHARD: About the book? About the what?

LILLIAN: The what?

RICHARD: Did they get those?

[half-minute gap, unintelligible]

RICHARD: I love you.

LILLIAN: I love you too.

RICHARD: It's all we got left. [laughter] Don't worry about it, Momma. You know, it's just one more charge. Huh? [machine noise] How you gonna prove it?

[twenty-three seconds noise, unintelligible]

LILLIAN: [unintelligible] I thought I'd get down to you right away.

RICHARD: There's nooooo body. [twenty-second gap] The only thing that worries me is the gas.

LILLIAN: What?

RICHARD: The Shell credit card.

LILLIAN: [unintelligible] Why? That bother you?

RICHARD: Yeah, I don't know if I got gas. Don't remember. [unintelligible] They go through our bills?

[twenty-four seconds unintelligible]

RICHARD: Anyway, we can't talk. See, what's today, Tuesday? I'll be calling you again Thursday. Come see me tomorrow, maybe the phones will be working. Don't worry about it. You can't change nothing. Don't panic. Yeah, you're all panicky. Don't panic. Just hang on, honey. They're fishing, okay? They're fishing.

[forty-three seconds unintelligible]

RICHARD: I love you. Don't worry about it. Huh?

LILLIAN: Don't write.

RICHARD: Oh, I have to write. Better throw them away, though. Nothing's sacred. Huh? I can't understand what you're saying.

LILLIAN: [unintelligible]

RICHARD: I'll get rid of 'em. [eleven seconds unintelligible] Wait and see. We'll have to wait and see.

[half-minute gap]

LILLIAN: Love you. Hang on.

RICHARD: I am. You just hang on. Hey, you ought to take some of that retirement money and pay off the second. [Citing medical reasons, Ford officially resigned from the LAPD on October 20 so Lillian could collect his pension. He's referring to her paying off the second mortgage on their house.]

LILLIAN: Now?

RICHARD: You're paying sixteen percent for the second, okay? You're only getting eight percent interest. So every month you're losing eight percent. And just in case they try to impound my money. So go pay the second off.

LILLIAN: You're sure?

RICHARD: Yeah.

LILLIAN: All right.

RICHARD: 'Cause I'm not going nowhere.

LILLIAN: I'll see to that right now.

RICHARD: Yeah, pay that second off and that should do it. You don't need that bill hanging over your head.

LILLIAN: All right.

[eleven seconds unintelligible]

RICHARD: [laughter] Hey, when it rains it pours.

LILLIAN: I thought I [unintelligible]. I laid in bed and I said [unintelligible].

RICHARD: Who did? The lady?

LILLIAN: [unintelligible] I didn't hear [unintelligible].

RICHARD: Well, they took everything they could find, I guess.

LILLIAN: Yeah, they went through the whole house. They didn't go through the refrigerator.

RICHARD: Huh?

LILLIAN: I gave her a cup of coffee, sugar. Robbery/Homicide isn't as bad as, uh, Internal Affairs. They're nicer. I gave the man from the pound some lunch. I made him a sandwich.

RICHARD: What they bring him for? Thought my dogs gonna hurt them? How are my kids? They're getting used to it, huh?

LILLIAN: Yeah [?].

RICHARD: [laughter, thirteen seconds unintelligible] Can't imagine it.

LILLIAN: What?

RICHARD: I mean, it's . . . deep.

[ten-second gap]

LILLIAN: Are they gonna come back? Will they come back for the rest of my love letters?

RICHARD: I don't think so. I think they've done it with this. That's it.

LILLIAN: That's what you said the last two times.

RICHARD: Yeah.

LILLIAN: [nineteen seconds unintelligible]

RICHARD: Well, just hang on, babe.

LILLIAN: Okay.

RICHARD: See, they didn't arrest me first, you know. They haven't filed any additional charges.

LILLIAN: Tomorrow is another day.

RICHARD: [laughter] Ah, oh, we'll see, we'll see.

LILLIAN: If I burn the letters will you be upset?

RICHARD: They're your letters, honey. You can do what you want with them, you know.

LILLIAN: Okay.

RICHARD: I hate to get rid of mine. I hate to get rid of my good ones.

LILLIAN: [unintelligible]

RICHARD: They're fishing. They got the idea but they don't have it, I don't think. We'll see.

LILLIAN: [four and a half seconds unintelligible]

RICHARD: He couldn't. He'd go with me. [fifteen seconds unintelligible] I love you. Nah, don't worry about it, Mom. We'll see what they do. They'll try like hell. [twenty-five seconds unintelligible] What month was that, anyway? I don't even remember. March? April?

LILLIAN: Was it after Christmas?

RICHARD: Yeah, it was this year.

LILLIAN: Okay, yeah, that was [nine and a half seconds unintelligible].

RICHARD: They got the wrong dates on there. They have the wrong dates.

LILLIAN: They took my bankbook, for Chris, the savings account at B of A.

RICHARD: Christina's?

LILLIAN: Yeah.

RICHARD: How much was in that? Fifty?

LILLIAN: Fifteen.

RICHARD: Fifteen dollars. Really diggin' the bottom of the barrel, huh? That's why they took the bicycle thing—trying to show money, that I've got more money. [He's referring to an exercise bike.]

LILLIAN: Uh. [twelve seconds unintelligible, including "he called"] That his name? [unintelligible] Name in there?

RICHARD: Yeah. [six-second gap] He's just gone. He's gone. They're trying to find out where he's at. [four seconds unintelligible] We'll see. Game's not over yet. What worries me is the shotgun. The shells. [sixteen seconds unintelligible] I can't imagine it, though. I just [ten seconds unintelligible]. Well, we'll see.

LILLIAN: [unintelligible].

RICHARD: All right.

LILLIAN: I'll see you tomorrow.

The second week of February 1984, the Los Angeles County Grand Jury was convened to hear testimony linking Ford and Von Villas to the disappearance of Thomas Weed. Weed's case had passed from Missing Persons to IAD to Major Crimes, which constructed the case. Robert Jorgensen introduced the testimony of forty-one witnesses at the closed proceedings.

After testifying before the grand jury, Bruce Adams passed a major hurdle on February 10 when his story held up to the scrutiny of an LAPD Board of Rights inquiry into the activities of Geary Cade and the alleged theft of his Honda Accord. Following a three-day hearing before three LAPD captains, Cade was found guilty on three counts: insurance fraud, conspiracy to commit insurance fraud, and filing a false crime report. As a result, Cade was dismissed from the LAPD. The department's case was based almost entirely on Adams's testimony.

Adams appeared even seedier at Cade's hearing than he had at Ford and Von Villas's preliminary hearing. He was wearing a dirty brown sports coat that was two sizes too big, he'd grown a beard, and he wore his hair long. He told his story about "stealing" Geary Cade's car—at Robert Von Villas's direction—and then trashing it and dumping it down a cliff in Pacoima Canyon.

Geary Cade's defense advocate was Jack Stone, who was also Robert Von Villas's defense attorney. Jack Stone, a silver-maned counselor in his forties, had a rep among cops as an ace criminal attorney, a guy who knew all the legal tricks.

His courtroom style, however, was often quite blustery. Stone grilled Adams ruthlessly about his background and various "discrepancies" found in the statements he had given to authorities. He argued that the evidence against Cade was circumstantial and that Bruce Adams simply had no credibility. Citing largely minor inconsistencies in Adams's testimony, Stone claimed that Adams had already lied to everybody—ATF, IAD, Major Crimes, the FBI, and the Treasury Department. Ultimately, he attempted to portray Adams as a sleazy con artist, a stress case, a small-time hood, an escort service driver and chop-shop mechanic who simply couldn't be believed. Jack Stone's contempt for Adams was obvious, searing, and, it seemed, a bit overdone.

After careful review of the evidence, the three presiding police captains found no crucial or substantive discrepancies in the many tellings of Adams's story, but they found the supposedly circumstantial evidence overwhelming. Adams's story was verified by his detailed knowledge of the damage to the car and the location where it was recovered. His story was further verified by a photograph of a Coke machine at California Moving and Storage. Nearly a year after the fact, Cade's address and license plate number were still there, scrawled in Adams's script on the machine where he had written it down after Von Villas had phoned him with the information.

Despite the defense's denials, the evidence also showed that Geary Cade was experiencing financial difficulties and that his car was a lemon. Geary Cade couldn't explain why the make and model of his vehicle, along with his license plate number, was found in Bob Von Villas's personal address book. Nor could he remember the nature of three phone conversations he had with Von Villas, verified by phone records, on the weekend his car disappeared—despite having testified that Von Villas was only a "casual acquaintance" with whom he spoke maybe once a year.

Adams's credibility was strengthened by his volunteering to testify about his involvement in this criminal act without having made a deal with the D.A. for his own immunity. Lieutenant Jack Herman, who served as Department Advocate (prosecutor) at the Cade inquiry, explained it rather simply: "Everything Adams told us checked out."

On February 9, while the Cade hearing and grand jury were in progress, Von Villas officially resigned from the police department so his family could start collecting his pension.

On February 15, a grand jury indictment was unsealed, charging Ford and Von Villas with the killing of Thomas Weed. Also charged in the indictment were

Janie Elmira Ogilvie, Tom Weed's widow, the woman who allegedly hired the cops to do the killing, and Joyce Reynolds. All defendants were arraigned and plead not guilty to the charges of murder and conspiracy to commit murder. Because these charges carried the special circumstance of murder for financial gain, Ford and Von Villas could face the death penalty if convicted.

The *Herald-Examiner* stated, "Prosecutors laid out the case in a fifteen-page indictment often resembling a film noir script, because of its dark, cynical overtones." The *Daily News* described the alleged conversations and negotiations about money drops and the clandestine arrangements of the hit as "something out of a gangster movie."

On March 15, the D.A.'s office announced it would seek the death penalty. "They're bad guys," Robert Jorgensen told the press. "These are police officers who have been granted the highest trust, and the evidence presented indicates a violation of that trust."

In late June 1984, Jan Ogilvie made a deal with Jorgensen, agreeing to testify against Ford and Von Villas in exchange for a reduced sentence. Alleged heavy-handed tactics employed by the D.A., and Ogilvie's credibility, would later become crucial matters for the defense.

On November 18, 1984 Bob Von Villas granted his first and only press interview, with Arnie Friedman and David R. Walker of the *Daily News*. Von Villas told of the depression that had engulfed him after his arrest. "The first three months in here I had nightmares," he stated. "I had a couple of very bad incidents. But after those it settled down." The *Daily News* piece also reported the details of some new civil lawsuits that had been filed against Von Villas:

> Looking pale and thinner than at the time of his arrest, the balding Von Villas, 40, said he decided to end his public silence after news reports last month of two civil lawsuits against him.
>
> In those lawsuits he is accused of defrauding two Santa Monica police officers and bilking a policeman's widow out of her home in Simi Valley. But Von Villas says he never cheated anyone.
>
> His attorney, Jack R. Stone, said the lawsuits upset his client so much he had to allow Von Villas to "let off steam," although he advised Von Villas not to discuss the criminal case.
>
> Although Von Villas has pleaded not guilty and insisted he will not be convicted, he generally heeded his lawyer's advice to refrain from discussing the criminal charges.

But he had plenty to say about the lawsuits.

"To think I would hurt some policeman or a policeman's wife is the greatest insult," he said. "It hurts more than anything else. For sixteen months I haven't said anything. I've had to sit here and say, 'My day will come.' "

Von Villas was accused of defrauding Santa Monica police officers John and Nancy Miehle. The couple and Von Villas traded Simi Valley homes and property in 1982.

Von Villas later sued, claiming breach of payment on a $35,000 promissory note for part of a one acre lot. The Miehles counter-sued, alleging Von Villas led them to believe adjacent property would be developed, thus increasing the value of their land.

Von Villas claims the accusations are unfounded, that it wasn't until six months after the property trade that he learned the adjacent development was falling though.

Von Villas said he was prepared to appear at the upcoming civil trial, "but because I'm in jail, I don't believe at this point anyone is going to care if I'm right or wrong. . . . They'll believe I have no credibility."

The other lawsuit, filed on behalf of Linda Kay Sintic, the cancer stricken widow of a police officer gunned down in the line of duty, accuses Von Villas of tricking her into deeding her home to him.

The suit claims Von Villas knew Sintic, 43, was losing a five-year fight with cancer. Her husband, officer Zlatko "Nick" Sintic was killed by a robber at a Northridge restaurant in 1976.

Von Villas said a fellow officer urged him to see what could be done to save Sintic's home from foreclosure. He discovered she was far behind in her mortgage payments, and that her home, essentially, "was gone in December, 1981." But because of his plan, "she got to keep that house three years longer," he said.

"I was happy with that. I would do it again. But I'm paying a hell of a price because I'm in jail. Since the day I was arrested, 98 percent of the people I dealt with . . . now say I did something wrong.

"Maybe I'm just naive," Von Villas said.

Sintic, who has children 11 and 15, eventually lost title to the house, along with $12,000 Von Villas says he still owes her. He says he'll pay her back someday.

But Sintic was skeptical. "You can't get blood from a turnip," she said.

The pretrial lawyering went on like a masters' chess game where no move was unimportant. The conflict over various motions and evidentiary hearings was taxing and relentless. It also resulted in two casualties: Judge Altman and D.A. Jorgensen.

Originally, "Loguercio" and "Weed" were filed as two separate cases. Bob Jorgensen made a motion to have the cases consolidated into one trial, but it was ruled improper to join a capital charge (Weed) with noncapital charges (Loguercio and the gem robbery). Hence, there would be two trials. Defense attorneys filed motions for separate trials for each defendant in both cases; both motions were denied. During the course of this protracted affair, nine separate motions to dismiss the charges were taken up to the appellate court and then to the state supreme court. All were denied.

The defense also made a motion to dismiss or consolidate the overt acts charged as part of the conspiracy to kill Thomas Weed. Originally, Jorgensen had listed more than eighty overt acts, which the defense viewed as overkill. For example, he would list each component statement made in a single phone call as a separate overt act. Such padding, as the defense saw it, was really just an underhanded way of making an opening statement, of attempting to snowball the jury.

Judge Altman, a graduate of Harvard and former star of the D.A.'s office, was an esteemed legal scholar. He didn't like the way Jorgensen had briefed the law on the matter of the overt acts. He gave the prosecutor ten days to come back with argument to change his mind. Instead, Jorgensen filed an affidavit to have Judge Altman removed from the case. Much speculation ensued as to why he'd made this move. Some observers cited a personality conflict and past history of ill will between Altman and Jorgensen. However, defense attorneys believed that Jorgensen sensed that Altman wouldn't let him have a free hand, that unlike some judges, he wouldn't simply serve as a rubber stamp for the prosecutor.

Defense attorney Richard Lasting was prepared to appeal Jorgensen's move because he felt it was a clear case of judge shopping. But then, Judge Altman announced that he was disqualifying himself, citing what he called the outrageous actions of Deputy D.A. Bob Jorgensen. Basically, Altman said he didn't care what the appellate court might rule, he didn't want to try a case with Bob Jorgensen as the D.A.

Jorgensen had a reputation as a hard-charger, one of the best trial attorneys in the D.A.'s office. Defense attorneys often felt he was a bit heavy-handed, a prosecutor who didn't mind skirting the edge of the law to get results. Richard Lasting thought that this was evident in the way Jorgensen obtained the jailhouse tape of the conversation between Richard and Lillian Ford. Lasting also felt that Jorgensen's concern over Judge Altman's pending ruling on the admissability of that tape, the most crucial evidentiary matter in the Weed case, was a significant factor in Jorgensen's move to oust the judge.

Jorgensen had obtained the warrant to tape, ostensibly, because Von Villas had allegedly made threats against Adams. But even though the tips about those threats had been received at the beginning of October 1983, the warrant hadn't been sought until November and the tape hadn't been made until December 20. If the real concern was public safety, Lasting argued, the D.A.'s office should have acted immediately. A jail commander testified that if the public had indeed needed protection, they would have canceled all visits and denied access to the telephone. Lasting argued that the snitch information and public safety argument were just a ruse employed by Jorgensen so that he could tape jailhouse conversations for the purpose of gathering evidence, which was illegal.

Although fifty Ford conversations were taped, only the one was ever seen as incriminating. And in that one conversation, nothing was really said. It really was a matter of interpretation. Still, without that tape, Lasting argued, the D.A. had no real case against Richard Ford in the Weed killing.

Richard Lasting's frustration was exacerbated by the fact that the informant who had told of threats made by Von Villas, an inmate named Anthony Love, admitted to Lasting, on tape, that he had lied to jailers and to the grand jury in order to receive jailhouse favors. According to Lasting, he was fed information about the case by a sheriffs' deputy and simply regurgitated it, along with his lies, to the LAPD. Love also testified before the grand jury in February 1984 that Bob Von Villas had admitted to the murder of Tom Weed. Since the grand jury is a closed proceeding, defense attorneys were not there to cross-examine him. They didn't learn of the Love testimony until they received transcripts—after the grand jury returned an indictment.

The defense then asked for and was granted a postindictment preliminary hearing, at which they called Anthony Love as a witness. At this proceeding, Love testified to what he had told Lasting and admitted that he had lied to the grand jury.

Lasting made his motion regarding the jailhouse tape to the new judge, Alexander Williams III. Judge Williams chose to accept Love's grand jury testimony and dismiss his preliminary hearing testimony, and he ruled to allow the jailhouse tape into evidence.

Lasting felt as though he were caught between the devil and the deep blue sea. "If the informant testifies for the prosecution, then he's telling the truth," he decried, "but if he says anything other than what the prosecution wants to hear, then he's an ex-felon, a sleaze-bag informant, and how can you accept anything he has to say. It's absolutely a double standard."

Later, lasting commented, "I think the court indulged in some result-oriented reasoning in order to save that tape, and it will be the basis of an appeal. I think there was a recognition that without the tape there was absolutely no chance of a conviction. Von Villas may be convicted, but not Ford."

The only other real evidence against Ford in the Weed case was a wall calendar that had been seized from Ford's home. February 23, 1983, the date of Weed's disappearance, had been blackened out—as though to hide something written underneath.

On March 7, 1985, Municipal Court judge Larry Fidler ordered Ford and Von Villas to stand trial for the murder of Thomas Weed. The ruling capped a two-month preliminary hearing to test the grand jury indictment. About mid-hearing, one of the codefendants, Joyce Reynolds, turned and made a deal with Deputy D.A. Robert Jorgensen. Like Ogilvie, Reynolds agreed to testify against Von Villas. In addition to admitting to acting as liaison between Von Villas and Ogilvie, Reynolds testified that at the Devonshire Division Christmas party in December 1982, Bob Von Villas made this statement to her while they were dancing: "I'm tired of being an honest cop. I get in as much trouble being honest as I would if I were dirty . . . There isn't any job I wouldn't do for money, including murder. I'll do anything for money. Let me know if you know of anything I might do."

The prosecution, meanwhile, didn't escape a few minor setbacks. One piece of evidence disqualified was a scrap of paper found in Von Villas's house bearing a description of Tom Weed's car and his license plate number. This was denied because the court found the seizure of certain bags from Von Villas's house was not within the search warrant.

Judge Williams, who would preside over the "Loguercio" trial, denied a motion by defense attorneys for separate juries for each defendant. This would lead to many conflicts between the defense teams, as they didn't always agree on what was the appropriate way to present evidence to the jury.

Evidentiary hearings went on and on. The van tape was argued over by the defense attorneys, statement by statement, to determine what could be presented to a jury. By the time they were finished, they had a precisely edited version that neither team was entirely happy with. Lasting, for example, would have liked to retain some comments by Ford that were detrimental to Von Villas and showed Ford's disdain for him.

Most of 1986 was taken up with the nine-month-long pretrial hearing. When this finally ended on October 14, Judge Williams read a prepared statement explaining the long delays in the case. "All that is necessary for a case to take forever is for a judge to be willing to let it take forever and that plainly was not my intent," Williams stated. He apologized for the nine months it took just to deal with police searches. "Because both the searches . . . and warrants were overly broad, we ended up going over thousands of documents, including report cards," he said.

He also explained how he had had to retrace the work done by the previous judge, who was disqualified by the prosecutor, and that that prosecutor, Jorgensen, had in turn disqualified himself, making it necessary to appoint a new deputy district attorney to the case, who in turn had had to read many thousands of pages of transcripts, which had caused more delays.

Following Bob Jorgensen's departure, the case had been turned over to Deputy District Attorney Robert O'Neill. A graduate of Southwestern University in Los Angeles, O'Neill had joined the D.A.'s office in 1978 when he was thirty. He'd been assigned to felony trials and the prosecution of career criminals. For the previous five years, he had worked in the organized crime unit. For the next five years, 1984 through 1989, his life would be consumed by one case—*The People vs. Richard Ford and Robert Von Villas.*

21

Killer Cops on Trial

THE FIRST TRIAL OF RICHARD FORD AND ROBERT VON VILLAS—FOR armed robbery and the attempted murder of Joan Loguercio—began on April 1, 1987. Attorneys for Ford and Von Villas confidently predicted acquittal in courthouse-step interviews. This seemed arrogant, even preposterous, in the face of what appeared to be such a conclusive case. How could the defense explain the van tapes?

Ford and Von Villas faced thirteen felony counts each, including two counts of attempted murder, conspiracy to commit murder one, and armed robbery. They were looking down the barrel at hard time—twenty-five years to life at the very least. Because the outcome would affect the future capital trial for the murder of Thomas Weed, each defendant was by law allowed two attorneys, selected by themselves but paid for by the County of Los Angeles. Ford's and Von Villas's personal resources had long been depleted, what with four attorneys and staffs of assistants and private investigators on the clock for almost four years.

Assisting Richard Lasting in the defense of Richard Ford was Rickard Santwier. Donald Feinberg had joined Jack Stone to defend Robert Von Villas.

The trial was presided over by Superior Court judge Alexander H. Williams III in the eleventh-floor courtroom at the Criminal Courts Building in downtown Los Angeles. Williams, a trim, bow-tied Virginia gent, a graduate of Yale and the University of Virginia School of Law, a former Virginia Beach police officer, navy judge, and chief assistant U.S. Attorney, was still boyish-looking at forty-three despite his prematurely graying hair. Williams spruced up the otherwise standard-issue wood-paneled courtroom with fresh flowers that were brought in each week.

Judge Williams, thorough and cool-headed, employed a computer terminal at his bench to keep track of the 140 witnesses and 400 exhibits that would be presented. He set a congenial tone throughout, which was remarkable in view of the case before him. He had just presided over a heated, often bitterly contested nine-month-long preliminary hearing just to determine what evidence and testimony would be allowed at this trial. Four seasoned criminal defense attorneys had examined and questioned his every decision, and he could expect the same at trial. Williams's remarkable tolerance, his willingness to entertain arguments and calmly explain his judgments, seemed to forestall any complaints from counsel. Unfortunately—at least for spectators—it also insured that it would be a long trial.

Jury selection would take two months—longer than most murder trials in other states. Both defense teams employed consulting jury experts to help them question, screen, and select jurors who they felt had not been prejudiced against their clients by pretrial publicity and who harbored no hidden animosity toward police officers. The attorneys also had to find people who had understanding employers, who could set aside their careers and endure the hardship of what was expected to be a year-long trial. By early June, a jury was selected—twelve jurors and three alternates—of eight men and seven women who represented a cross-section of race (five African-Americans, three Hispanics), class, communities, and professions.

Prosecutor Robert O'Neill, thirty-nine, handsome and rail thin in his sharp gray suits, was almost pathologically cool and even-tempered. He began his opening statement on June 8 with a reserved but no-punches-pulled eloquence that would serve him well throughout the trial. "This case will show that the two defendants, police officers at the time, conspired together and formulated a brutal plan to rape, torture, drug, sodomize, and finally murder a woman named Joan Loguercio . . . that they made two attempts on her life . . . and that the motive was money, to collect on an insurance policy. The evidence will also show that, in using the special skill and knowledge they had obtained as police officers, they committed an armed robbery of a jewelry store and terrorized three female employees."

At forty-three, Richard Lasting, chief counsel for Richard Ford, was already a veteran of many high-profile cases. A man of medium height with brown hair, freckles, and a bushy mustache, Lasting's style was warm and compassionate. This highly respected L.A. attorney would prove to be O'Neill's most formidable adversary. "You have just heard a rather grisly and horrible picture painted of Richard Ford," Lasting declared, "but this is the trial of an innocent man." Lasting briefly addressed two key elements of the prosecution's case—the testimony of Bruce Adams and the van tapes. "Evidence will show that Adams is a braggart, a liar, a cheater—and not a very good mechanic." Lasting said he would show that Adams went to authorities with lies about the defendants because his relationship with them had deteriorated and he wanted to take over their business.

As for the tapes: "I know that taped conversation is vulgar. It's profane. It's degrading. It is pornographic. It's disgusting. You may not be pleased at having to listen to it. But that tape does not show Mr. Ford is guilty. It does not show a *real* plan to kill Joan Loguercio. . . . Mr. Adams made incriminating statements on the van tape, but he didn't intend to kill Joan Loguercio. And neither did Mr. Ford."

Jack Stone, fifty-one, chief counsel for Robert Von Villas, boasted, "I am not going to hide behind 'a reasonable doubt.' I am going to prove beyond a reasonable doubt that Mr. Von Villas is innocent." He went on to describe his client as not only a cop but "a businessman . . . an excellent manager, [who is] very attentive to details, who kept meticulous books and records, and probably saved every piece of paper that he ever came across."

Although that last statement would later cause problems for Mr. Stone, his claims were reinforced by the courtroom demeanor of Robert Von Villas, who mothered meticulously over his own defense. Von Villas scrutinized every transcript and exhibit, shuffling through papers at the table throughout the trial. Richard Ford would prove duly attentive; Von Villas, obsessively so.

"Von Villas realized what a terrible mistake had been made," Stone continued. "It turned out that Bruce Adams was not a very good mechanic. Even worse, that he was not a very honest mechanic." Stone, like Lasting, professed that Adams set up Ford and Von Villas.

"You are going to hear testimony that will show this is not an ordinary case," Stone continued. "The police have supplied many teams of officers and thousands of man-hours. . . . Practically every person who ever knew Mr. Von Villas has been interviewed by the police, four or five hundred people easily. . . . Every statement Von Villas has made for probably the last twenty years has been analyzed critically to see if there was any criminal intent—statements that we all make at parties when we've had a drink or two." This last assertion would also come back to haunt Mr. Stone.

Seated at the counsel table with their lawyers were two model defendants—a pair of handsome, well-groomed, middle-aged men in business suits. Ford and Von

Villas seemed pleasant, warm, cordial. They looked like the good guys, like this whole thing was obviously some kind of mistake.

On June 9, prosecutor Bob O'Neill called his first witness, Darlis Chefalo. Identifying Ford and Von Villas in court, the makeup artist described how she had provided the two "undercover cops" with disguises to make them look like dissipated Mexican drug dealers.

On cross-examination, the four defense attorneys spent more than a day questioning Chefalo on minute details: whether she used water- or oil-base makeup, what kind of materials she gave them to take with them, such as adhesives, pencils, brushes, sponges. They had her examine color swatches to determine the exact color of the wigs, questioned her repeatedly about whether it was Dick or Bob who had the most salt in his salt and pepper beard. Was she sure she used dark Egyptian makeup? Could it have been light Egyptian? They also queried her about every discrepancy they could find, no matter how minute, in previous statements she had made to investigating officers.

Such detailed cross-examination would be characteristic of the defense throughout the trial. Rickard Santwier, Ford's second attorney, and Donald Feinberg, second counsel for Von Villas, seemed particularly drawn to such minutia, but from the start, this strategy seemed to backfire. While the defense huffed and puffed over seemingly petty details, the jury seemed to be growing impatient. What they really wanted to know was *why* were these two cops getting professional disguises?

Over the next two months, O'Neill presented a parade of witnesses regarding the November 22, 1982, robbery of the Schaffer and Sons jewelry store in the Northridge shopping mall.

Marilyn Klass, Sue Martin, and Theresa McKinney, the three employees present during the Monday-night robbery, each described their terrifying encounter with the "cordial" armed bandit with salt and pepper hair and beard and unnaturally ruddy complexion. Officers would later testify that "Put your hands behind your back, palms together," the command issued by the gunman, was the command taught to officers at the police academy.

One of the women, Sue Martin, wasn't gagged by the robber. Martin testified that she knew Bob Von Villas and had had dealings with him previously at the store over a period of a few years. Through his questioning, O'Neill established that Martin was a feisty, take-charge type to whom others naturally looked for leadership in times of crisis. O'Neill would later argue that Ford left Sue Martin ungagged—following instructions from Von Villas—knowing that she would keep the other two women calm.

Schaffer and Sons gemologists Eva Wong and Diane Rowbothan testified that some 236 diamonds and 70 rings were taken from the display cases. The cost to the store of the diamonds was $62,361. Their value on the open retail market was at least twice that. The rings had cost Schaffer and Sons $9,888 and had a retail value two or three times that.

Commanding officers from Devonshire Division testified that Von Villas had failed to return his Rover police radio at the end of his watch on the day of the robbery. Lieutenant John Aggas, Von Villas's immediate superior, stated that this was highly unusual and against department procedure. He also explained that Rover radios picked up all deployed police units in Devonshire Division (at forty-four square miles, one of the largest in L.A.) and that the Northridge Fashion Plaza was clearly within the division.

Officer James Dellinger, whose assignment at the time was the Northridge mall, testified that he was off duty on Sunday and Monday, and that it was probably common knowledge at Devonshire that there would be no officers at the mall on those two nights.

Officers who conducted searches of Ford's and Von Villas's homes after their arrest on July 7, 1983, described the evidence they seized. Von Villas's briefcase contained twenty loose diamonds, diamond bindles, and three rings (twelve of these diamonds were described by a Schaffer and Sons gemologist as matching those from the robbery inventory in size, shape, and weight). A pair of boots found in Von Villas's closet were found to contain a pair of surgical gloves. A ring found in his kitchen cabinet was particularly important, because it was from Schaffer and Sons and made of brass, for display only—something not sold to the public. A "cold" 1973 license plate was found under the seat of Von Villas's 1969 Pontiac Grand Prix. Makeup was found in Ford's home.

O'Neill then brought on a series of witnesses to show that after the robbery, Von Villas began selling or trading diamonds "all over town."

Diane Withers and Russell Kafel, members of Von Villas's high school graduating class recalled that in December 1982 Von Villas had told them that he knew where he could get them some quality diamonds at half price. Three different jewelers testified that Von Villas brought diamonds to them for appraisals and offered to sell them. William Justice, a jeweler, stated that he had a number of transactions with Von Villas involving loose diamonds, several of which matched the weight and shape of those in the Schaffer and Sons inventory.

Dan Krowpman, a tool distributor, testified that he traded an air compressor to Von Villas and Bruce Adams for some diamonds and a ring. The ring was submitted as evidence and later identified as having come from Schaffer and Sons. An auto parts supply manager, Charles "Charlie" Beatty, also testified that Adams and Von Villas swapped some diamonds and a ring for auto parts just before Christmas of 1982. The ring, submitted as evidence, again matched the Schaffer and Sons inventory.

Each of these witnesses was grilled by defense attorneys. Again, every detail was scrutinized—time, places, dates, the weight, shape, and size of stones. As the weeks passed, one sensed a growing hunger on the part of the jury for some enlightenment as to how this morass of details would be jig-sawed into a viable defense. But they would have to wait.

By early August, O'Neill now began presenting witnesses related to the attempted murder of Joan Loguercio.

Gayl West, a mortgage broker and financial advisor to Robert Von Villas, testified that she had helped him make arrangements for the refinancing of Loguercio's home. She also stated that in January 1983, while at a party with Von Villas, he had said, "If you know of anybody who wants a contract put out on anybody, let me know and one telephone call and we both make a commission."

Joan Loguercio, the intended victim, had developed cancer—just as she had feared—and died in 1986. Since she was unable to testify, her testimony from the preliminary hearings was read to the jury and entered into the record.

According to Loguercio's testimony, her divorce settlement required her to pay her ex-husband $15,000 in order to keep their house. Her friend Bob Von Villas was helping her arrange a new loan, using his credit. As part of the deal, she agreed to obtain a $100,000 joint mortgage insurance policy.

Loguercio's testimony then ran through the whole sordid tale of her encounters with Dr. Anderson at the Venus Faire and the HollywoodLand Motel. She told how her friend Bob Von Villas "checked out" Dr. Anderson for her and how all the concerns she had mentioned to Von Villas were later addressed by Dr. Anderson.

Answering very specific questions by Richard Lasting during her cross-examination at the prelims, Loguercio stated that she had sexual intercourse with Ford twice. On both occasions she was on her back and he was on top. She also performed oral sex, leaning over with her head in his lap. She also stated that the drugs Dr. Anderson gave her made her more alert.

O'Neill then called Allstate Insurance agent Ray Ossenkop, who testified that he had met with Von Villas on three or four occasions and had also had numerous phone conversations with him regarding the insurance policy. Von Villas had given him the first payment, a check for $117.32, on May 19, 1983. (The prosecution would submit phone records showing a flurry of calls between Ford and Von Villas after this date.) Von Villas took his physical on May 23 and

Loguercio on the twenty-sixth. On several occasions, Ossenkop testified, Von Villas asked him what would be the effective date of the policy, and he told him it was the date of application and first payment—May 19. Mike Udell, another agent in Ossenkop's office, testified that Von Villas called and asked him the effective date of the policy once when Ossenkop wasn't there. Finally, O'Neill established that the close-out date, when a much larger payment of $600 would be due on the policy, was July 21. O'Neill would argue that Von Villas planned to take care of Loguercio before then so he didn't have to make the payment.

During cross-examination, defense attorneys hammered away on what was to be a major point in their case, the issue of "insurable interest." Gayl West had testified that the loan for Loguercio's house had yet to be secured, and that it was her understanding that until this occurred, there would be no insurable interest and the policy would not be in effect. Ossenkop, however, seemed to feel the policy was valid, although he did not seem entirely clear on the issue. If nothing else, detailed questioning by defense attorneys succeeding in obfuscating this issue. Later, in closing arguments, both sides would use testimony by these witnesses to support opposing contentions—that there was a policy in effect and that there was not leaving the jury to decide for themselves. Perhaps what was more important was whether or not Bob Von Villas believed the policy was in effect.

For the first few months of the trial, media coverage was steady but subdued. Like defendants in most high-profile cases, Ford and Von Villas had already been found guilty by the media. Even Chief Daryl Gates, in a very uncharacteristic display of nonsupport for two of his boys, appeared to pronounce judgment on Ford and Von Villas in an early-trial interview with Susan Forrest of the *Daily News*. "It's totally beyond our belief that two of our people could get themselves involved in activities that we fight against every day," said Gates. "Los Angeles police officers don't do those kinds of things. The only thing I can say is that it's a terrible commentary on our life in America today that we can breed these kinds of individuals, who on the surface are supposed to be supporting law and order and yet underneath are completely destroying it."

22

Star Witness

AFTER TWO AND A HALF MONTHS OF TESTIMONY BY SEVENTY-ONE witnesses, Bob O'Neill finally called Bruce Adams to the stand. Adams, who was now living out of state under a new identity, was brought in each day under the protection of Lieutenant Fox. Fox, who had been Sergeant Fox back in 1983, served as the prosecutor's assistant throughout the trial. It was Fox's monumental task to keep track of all of the State's witnesses and coordinate their appearances, as well as keep hundreds of pieces of evidence organized and queued up for submission. Having been one of IAD's principal investigators on the case, Fox was unquestionably the best man for the job.

Adams, now thirty-nine and a few pounds heavier than in 1983, was characteristically nervous. He would have to face down his former buddy Richard Ford in court, as well as undergo what would undoubtedly be a brutal and protracted cross-examination by defense attorneys. He would remain on the stand for three weeks.

For the first week, O'Neill walked Adams through his entire story—his background, service in the marines, treatment for delayed stress, work history, his meeting Richard Ford, the trip to Colorado to buy guns, his partnership with Ford and Von Villas, and the progression of crimes in the case. No mention was made, however, of the alleged Thomas Weed murder, the prostitution service, or other crimes, such as insurance fraud, of which Adams had knowledge. Since there were no charges on these offenses before the court, testimony about them was not permitted.

Prosecutor O'Neill claimed that he wasn't concerned about the missing pieces this restricted testimony might leave in the picture he was presenting to the jury, but one had to wonder. The defense, for example, would make great issue over Adams's "deteriorating business relationship" with the defendants over problems at International Automotive, yet nothing could be submitted by the prosecution to show that those problems had anything to do with Adams and the shop being used as a front. This made it far easier for the defense to paint Adams as a disgruntled business partner.

Adams admitted that he had a stormy relationship with Von Villas, who never paid him what was agreed, kept cutting his salary, generally treated him like an employee instead of a partner, and constantly interfered with his running of the shop. "Von Villas wanted me to overbook, highball prices, gouge customers. Well, not my customers," Adams testified.

Adams had learned of the Schaffer and Sons robbery when Ford and Von Villas got into a loud argument over it at the shop: " 'You weren't doing your job,' Ford says, 'I had to go in, take down the customers, tie them up, take them in back. All you did was stand there by the door and wave at two security officers.' " Adams also testified that Von Villas had later told him some details of the caper that fit the MO of the Northridge jewelry heist.

Adams explained how Von Villas wanted him to go to El Toro marine base to pick up some weapons. When he refused, Von Villas threatened him, and that was when he went to ATF. "I was constantly being threatened by Ford and Von Villas. They told me if I ever talked they would have me killed," Adams testified.

O'Neill then walked Adams through the whole Loguercio scenario—the Greek Gardens dinner and up to the morning of July 7, when he had the broken-wire meeting with Ford and Von Villas at the shop. There, Von Villas told him "the reason the hit had to be made was because Loguercio was calling the insurance companies trying to find out who the agent was and that if she found out and canceled the policy he would be up shit's creek. He said the bitch had to go by midnight."

When O'Neill got to the evening of July 7, 1983, he brought out an edited ninety-minute version of the van tape, which was played in open court. As the jury followed along, reading from transcripts, they listened to the horrible, profane, fox-hole dialogue of the two would-be rapist-killers. The raw intensity of the dialogue was apparently more riveting than anything they'd ever heard either in the movies or real life. Many of the jurors appeared stunned.

As the lurid tape rolled on and on, what was perhaps most chilling was the attitude of the two men, their laughter as they plotted and rehearsed how they would kill Joan Loguercio. They even laughed about the potential consequences of their actions: "What do you call this fucking body, bro?" said Ford. ". . . First fucking degree. You're going to the fucking chair. You're going to be fucking fried!"

"I thought they did away with the death penalty in California," says Adams.

"Not under unusual circumstances," says Ford. What he really meant was "special circumstances" that allow for the death penalty.

"Oh," says Adams.

"Like premeditation," says Ford.

"Planned murder, yeah," says Adams.

"You know," says Ford, "like having some fucking bitch you not only kidnapped but you fucking tortured to fucking death."

Anticipating the onslaught Adams would endure in cross-examination, O'Neill asked Adams if he had ever had sex with Joan Loguercio. "Yes," he answered. O'Neill then asked him why he denied this at a preliminary hearing. "My wife, my kids . . . Things were getting really intense because of all the stuff that had been happening to me. I didn't need any more problems and I didn't want my wife getting any more upset than she was."

Defense attorneys spent nearly two weeks working Adams over on the stand. In addition to poring over his preliminary hearing testimony, they examined all the transcripts of Adams's endless interviews with ATF and the LAPD. Each version of his story was scrutinized.

Prosecutor Bob O'Neill gave Richard Lasting and Jack Stone plenty of leeway, allowing them to ask and re-ask accusatory questions, even to badger the witness to a certain degree. It appeared that O'Neill's strategy was to give the defense all the rope they wanted. By flailing away at Adams, mostly about inconsequential discrepancies, they would only amplify the weakness of their own case. If Adams wasn't totally destroyed by their assaults, he would emerge from the battle an even stronger witness. O'Neill felt confident Bruce could handle it.

Ever the marine, Adams actually seemed to become steadier under fire. By this time, he was an experienced witness. He answered only what was asked, and he rarely dropped the formality that had been drummed into him in the Marine Corps. He must have said "yes sir" and "no sir" a thousand times. Some fifty discrepancies were scrutinized by the defense, most of them so minor they could easily be dismissed—like whether the Colorado gunrunner drove a Dodge or a Ford van. But some were troublesome.

Adams testified that Ford purchased six Mac-10s on their Colorado trip, but Agent Oddo's report stated that Adams had initially told him Ford bought twenty-five automatic weapons. Adams contended that Oddo made a mistake. Adams also stated he didn't know about the guns until they left for Colorado.

Richard Lasting questioned him at length about the gun buy.

"Did you tell ATF about your trip to Colorado?"

"Yes sir, I did."

"Did you lie to them about it?"

"No sir."

"Did you tell Agent Oddo you got twenty-five Mac-tens?"

"No sir."

"When did you find out about the trip to Colorado?"

"A couple of days before . . ."

"Why were you going?"

"To purchase weapons."

"So you knew *before* you left?"

"Yes sir."

With this, Lasting paused. Adams had once again contradicted himself. "Did you ever tell anyone that you *didn't* know?"

"I don't recall."

Later that afternoon, after lunch, as the detailed questioning about Colorado continued, Adams did an about-face. "Didn't you give prior testimony that you didn't know why you were going to Colorado?" Lasting asked. "You gave that testimony at the preliminary hearing, did you not?"

"I believe so," said Adams. "I was confused on the question this morning. I'm having problems with my ears today."

"So the truth was at the preliminary hearing. You *didn't* know until you got there?"

"Yes sir."

Lasting referred to the report from a June 30, 1983, interview with Adams by IAD's Fox and Fruge, which had Adams stating that he had known why they were going to Colorado. "So Fox and Fruge may have misunderstood?" Lasting asked.

"Yes sir, that's possible."

"Did you tell David Jimenez about Colorado?"

"No sir."

"Didn't you tell him when you returned that you didn't get any guns in Colorado?"

"No sir, I did not."

"Didn't *you* tell Ford that you had a contact to get guns in Colorado?"

"No sir."

Lasting accused Adams of setting up the Colorado trip, of telling Ford he had a connection in Colorado, obtained through Adams's father, whom Lasting described as a mercenary. According to Lasting, Adams took money from Ford but then never delivered the promised guns.

Lasting next accused Adams of fabricating lies because he wanted to get Ford and Von Villas arrested and "off his back" at the shop.

Adams claimed he had secured a new partner, William Mayhew, who gave him $2,500, which he in turn gave to Von Villas as payment to buy him out of the shop. He never got a receipt, he said, because Von Villas refused to give him one. The defense charged that this was a lie, that Adams never gave Von Villas the money. Adams weathered heated questions about his problems with employers caused by his argumentativeness, dishonesty, or stress problems. Although Adams issued denial after denial, the sheer weight of all the incidents brought up by defense counsel more than suggested a troubled work history.

"Weren't you concerned that if Von Villas closed down the business you'd be out of a job?" Richard Lasting asked.

"No sir," Adams replied.

"What would happen if he were arrested? Would you still have to pay him his money?"

"Yes sir."

"You didn't like the way Von Villas treated you?"

"No sir."

"Wasn't that your reason for going to ATF?"

"No sir."

"That way you wouldn't have to deal with Von Villas . . ."

"No sir."

Lasting showed Adams the document Adams had drawn up to dissolve the business, a document Von Villas never signed.

"Isn't the reason you never got a receipt from Von Villas because you never gave him Mayhew's money?"

"No sir."

"Isn't it true you never intended Mayhew to be a partner?"

"No sir."

Lasting submitted a bank account Bruce Adams opened for International Automotive on June 21, 1983—after Von Villas had taken away the bankbook and after Adams said he had paid Von Villas the $2,500 he received from Mayhew. Listed as general partners in the business and signatories for the account were Bruce and Shirley Adams.

"Why isn't Mayhew's name on there?" Lasting asked.

"I don't know, sir," answered Adams.

"You met ATF agents for the first time on the very same day you opened that account, on June 21. You made serious accusations to ATF."

"Yes sir, I did."

Lasting also accused Adams of setting up Ford and Von Villas on the morning of July 7, claiming it was Adams who suggested they kill Loguercio.

"Did you break that transmitter?" Lasting asked, referring to the wire that had failed to work properly that morning.

"No sir," Adams replied.

"Wasn't everything you said and did that night designed to convince Ford you wanted to kill Loguercio?" Lasting asked.

"Yes sir," said Adams.

Jack Stone, Bob Von Villas's attorney, picked up the attack. His first question was, "You don't like Bob Von Villas, do you?"

O'Neill objected but was overruled. "Yes sir, that's true," Adams answered.

Stone ran over much the same ground as Lasting, but focused on the arrangements made between Adams and Von Villas regarding the dissolution of their business partnership.

"Did you agree to terminate the partnership as of June 1?"

"I believe so."

Stone submitted as evidence approximately $1,800 worth of checks signed by Adams between June 1 and June 16.

"On June seventeenth, didn't Von Villas become enraged over your having written these checks?" Stone asked.

"No sir."

On redirect, prosecutor O'Neill brought out Richard Ford's briefcase, the homicide kit, which was recovered from the van on the night of the arrest. O'Neill pulled out each item in the bag, holding them up in turn for the jury as he questioned Mr. Adams.

"This dagger, did *you* bring it with you on the night of July seventh?"

"No sir."

"How about this other dagger, did you bring it with you on July seventh?"

"No sir."

"How about these nylon cords, did you bring them with you on July seventh?"

"No sir."

"How about this pill container . . . this K-Y jelly . . ."

The jury had been told of these items before, but as fifteen somber set of eyes rolled up and down, taking it all in, the cold blue steel of the brandished military daggers induced a few shudders.

When he was finally dismissed, Bruce Adams stood in the hall outside the courtroom, looking drained, yet relieved, as he smoked a cigarette. "This was one of the hardest things I ever did in my life," reflected the ex-marine. "Ford and I had really been good friends, but . . . Vietnam was one thing. A lot of terrible things happened over there—the atrocities where phenomenal. But this was different. Killing some broad for money—you just don't do that."

Adams said that just before he left the stand, he and his old buddy Richard Ford engaged in a brief stare-down. "Here I was, getting ready to go home, back to my family. But he was going back to his cell. I felt that realization really hit him hard."

O'Neill headed for the stretch with testimony from the long string of investigators who had worked the case. They all related what they had been told by Adams, how it had checked out, and what evidence they had obtained through other means.

ATF Agent Oddo told of his meetings with Adams and stated that he had no explanation for what had happened to Adams's body wire on the morning of July 7. When he applied it, it was working, but when he checked it later a wire was broken off the transmitter.

Defense attorneys grilled Oddo about the wire, exploring minute technical details. Many observers felt they beat the issue to death, but clearly it was a crucial matter to the defense. They established that there really wasn't any adequate explanation for why the wire worked when Oddo installed it but then failed to work when Ford and Von Villas arrived at International Automotive. Oddo admitted it had never happened to him before.

The defense was obviously alleging that the plot to kill Loguercio was suggested by Adams, and that he had covered this up by purposefully breaking the wire.

Lieutenant Fox of IAD told how he had recovered the three incriminating notes written by Robert Von Villas on the morning of July 7 when Adams was on the phone with Loguercio. These notes, Fox explained, were exactly as Adams had described them.

In addition to the investigators, O'Neill also called Bernard Jack, stepfather of the late Bill Mayhew. Jack testified that he had given his stepson a cashier's check for $2,500 to buy into a partnership with Adams at International Automotive. The money was to be used to pay off Robert Von Villas. The check, endorsed by Mayhew and Adams, was submitted as evidence. While it proved that Adams did indeed receive the $2,500, it did not prove that he had given the money to Bob Von Villas. Bill Mayhew was now dead and couldn't provide testimony in that matter.

On October 12, as O'Neill was wrapping up the State's case, a defense witness was called out of order. David Jimenez, an acquaintance of both Ford and Adams from the Sepulveda V.A., now resided on the East Coast. Since he was in L.A. for other reasons, he had been called as a witness by Jack Stone, attorney for Bob Von Villas.

Before being allowed to testify before the jury Jimenez was questioned in closed court. Judge Williams heard arguments from both sides pertaining to the admissibility of his testimony. Jimenez had been the subject of much pretrial controversy. Defense attorneys claimed that IAD had literally put Jimenez on a bus out of town when they learned he had testimony that would contradict Bruce Adams's story about Colorado. The prosecution scoffed at this assertion and countered that a private investigator who worked for defense attorney Jack Stone, David Boykoff, had told Jimenez that Adams had given the police incriminating information about him, so he needed to discredit Adams for his own good.

Nearly a day was spent arguing over Jimenez's credibility as a witness and to what matters he should be allowed to testify. Jack Stone was particularly determined to get Jimenez's testimony to the jury. During a short break outside the courtroom, Stone exclaimed, "They'll have to slit my throat to keep him off the stand!"

Finally, agreement was reached and the witness was brought to the stand. Jimenez, an overweight bear of a man with dark curly hair and a big bushy mustache, was understandably nervous. He testified that he had been in the delayed stress group with Ford and Adams for about a month and that he had stayed at Adams's house for two or three weeks around the time Ford and Adams had gone to Colorado. He also said that he had met Von Villas once at Adams's house. Asked what he thought of Adams, Jimenez stated, "He was a liar."

Jimenez recalled overhearing a phone conversation at the V.A. in which Adams asked his father about some Mac-10s and got a telephone number of a contact in Colorado. Jimenez subsequently met Adams's father, who told him he was a mercenary. (Adams had testified that his father once applied to *Soldier of Fortune* magazine for a "membership card," but he was hardly a mercenary.) Jimenez also stated that both Ford and Adams had told him, after returning from Colorado, that they missed their contact and had not purchased any guns.

After stating that he "never forgot faces," Jimenez was unable to identify

Lieutenant (formerly Sergeant) Fox, who had previously interviewed him. When asked to identify Richard Ford, he pointed to Bob Von Villas. Told of his mistake, Jimenez said, "Well, he [Ford] doesn't look like he did when I knew him."

In all fairness, this was indeed true. In the four years since his arrest, Richard Ford had lost a good deal of weight and had undergone a dramatic midlife transformation in his appearance. His face was now long and drawn and pale, where it had once been full, robust, and tan. And he no longer wore a mustache.

On cross-examination, O'Neill brought out Jimenez's traumatic medical history. He had served three tours in Vietnam and been wounded four times, receiving four Purple Hearts. Over the years he had been in and out of hospitals. He had made numerous suicide attempts and had suffered from delayed stress, drug dependency, nightmares, flashbacks, depression, blackouts, and, finally, memory loss.

Jimenez appeared sincere, but he was also badly confused. He proved to be such a troublesome witness that it was hard to guess what impact his testimony might have.

23

The Professor

ON OCTOBER 22, RICHARD LASTING AND RICKARD SANTWIER BEGAN
presenting Richard Ford's defense. They started by trying to destroy Bruce
Adams, presenting several witnesses from the V.A., both staff and patients, who
testified to his unstable employment record and his problems with PTSD. He was
described as "argumentative with bosses," some of whom he had physically
assaulted. One former employer called Adams "basically dishonest."

Then, on October 26, Lasting called Richard Ford to the stand, ending five
months of speculation over whether the defendant would testify. After four years
of silence, the man on the infamous van tapes would finally attempt to explain
himself.

Throughout his two weeks of testimony, Ford, now forty-seven, generally
came across as cold and calculating, despite his ever-cordial tone. He occasionally
tried to smile at the jurors, but he seemed uneasy looking at them. His drawn face
and dark, sunken eyes made him appear gloomy and dejected, particularly
during the lawyers' long conferences at the bench, when he would bow his head
and droop his shoulders, as though in a trance. His dark blue suits accentuated
his gloominess; he came off far better in his lighter tans and grays. During his
testimony he would put on a pair of brown-framed glasses whenever he had to
examine evidence or refer to a transcript. The practiced manner in which he
slipped on these spectacles, glanced down his nose at the material before him,
then slipped the glasses off again gave him a professorial air.

Ford's attractive wife, Lillian, sat through some—but not all—of his testimony. They often shared warm exchanges between proceedings. "You look beautiful," Lillian told him once as court broke for lunch. "We should get married," Ford laughed. "Yes," Lillian smiled, "I think I'll marry you."

Under questioning by Richard Lasting, Richard Ford gave his version of the events that led to his arrest. He admitted going to Colorado to purchase some Mac-10s but insisted that the trip was arranged by Adams. He said he was a gun collector and that he had given Adams money up front for some weapons. After hearing a long string of excuses, he had finally told Adams, "We're going to Colorado, we're going to get my guns or the money, one way or another." Once there, however, they never met their contact or purchased any guns. He said he expressed his "disgust" to David Jimenez when they returned.

Ford explained why he had helped Adams open the auto shop in January 1983. "I knew him to be a very good tune-up mechanic. From what I saw he did an excellent job. I felt sorry for him. He was a down and out guy. It's like the old saying, I could have been in the same place."

Von Villas's role in the shop, Ford explained, was to be the financial backer, to handle the books, the business end. "I knew he owned and operated a blacksmith shop and a tile company and was involved in real estate and was in all kinds of businesses. He was the 'division scrounger,' as we call it."

Ford explained that he first went to the V.A. for treatment of delayed stress in June 1981 after being referred there by a police psychiatrist. When Lasting asked about the nature of Ford's problems with delayed stress, O'Neill objected. Judge Williams sent the jury out so this crucial issue could be argued in open court.

"My objection is that this [Ford's problems with PTSD] is irrelevant unless related to specific charges," the prosecutor stated.

"It is offered," countered Lasting, "on specific intent to commit crimes charged and to explain pieces of incriminating evidence—disguises, prostitutes, et cetera. One of the central issues of this case is what was Ford's state of mind on June seventeenth when accused of attempting murder at the motel, and his intent and state of mind on July seventh. His experiences at the V.A. and what led him there play a significant part in the formulation of Mr. Ford's state of mind. Our contention is that Mr. Ford never intended to murder Joan Loguercio. . . . In order for the jury to understand, Mr. Ford's background is crucial."

Judge Williams ruled that Lasting could proceed. When the jury returned, Lasting led the defendant through his tale of woe. "I had a multitude of problems," stated Ford. "Flashbacks to Nam, being shot as a police officer. My mother-in-law was living with us at the time. She had terminal cancer. My wife had been raped and was at home and disabled. I didn't have any kind of sex life

234

because of what happened to my wife, and no personal life. I was drinking excessively. I was popping pills. I was a mess. I couldn't do my work, literally. I would look at a report. I couldn't remember how to make it out, although I had made thousands prior. I went to my lieutenant and I said, 'I need help. My head is not on. I need to get it together.'

"My wife was raped in November of eighty. It happened on the bus at the end of the line by a passenger, and the guy raped her and beat her, tortured her and left her for dead. My wife was hospitalized for five months in a psychiatric hospital, a vegetable case. She wasn't able to take care of herself or do anything, so I took care of her for the most part."

The police never apprehended his wife's rapist, Ford explained, and although he was told not to get involved, he launched his own search for the perpetrator. His wife had a clue to the rapist's identity, a street moniker: Skip. Eventually, he turned up information that Skip hung out around certain dives in Hollywood, and Ford began spending evenings on the streets there searching for him. That was the reason he had acquired a professional disguise: he needed to "penetrate the Hollywood street culture" without being recognized by any of the lowlifes he had encountered in previous years while working as a narcotics and vice officer. Von Villas, who also obtained a wig and disguise, accompanied him on one outing in Hollywood.

Ford explained that he had a number of clues about Skip to pursue on the street. "Skip had a good chance of being scarred. My wife fought and struggled, scratched his face—she lost her fingernails doing it. Sexually, he liked to torture." Ford choked up momentarily, as though holding back tears, but it seemed at least partially orchestrated. A few members of the jury looked disgusted. "I found a pimp who had a girl who had been tortured, a similar assault. He picked her up at a newspaper stand as a trick, by Cahuenga and Hollywood Boulevard. So I spent a lot of time there.... I was concerned about being spotted.... After fifteen years there were a lot of people on the street who knew me. People I'd arrested."

Ford's personal problems escalated as he started hanging out on the streets until the early morning hours. He began to drink heavily and use drugs. "After a while, I used this street thing as an excuse," he admitted. "I was taking amphetamines to stay awake during the day. It became a vicious cycle."

Ford said he first saw Joan Loguercio at the auto shop in January 1983. "Bruce Adams was dating her at the time. He said he was going through a divorce, having problems, thinking about leaving his wife. He was staying at the shop mostly. He said he was in love with her. I thought she was very attractive, a very nice lady." Later, in June 1983, when he learned from Adams and Von Villas that Loguercio was occasionally working as a prostitute, Ford decided to try to start an affair with her. "My relationship with my wife was difficult. I love my wife. She knew I was seeing prostitutes. She said, 'Go ahead, go out.' "

But he was looking for more than just a hooker, somebody he could see regularly, and he thought Loguercio could fit the bill. He didn't really consider her a prostitute. She was a nice lady who had simply fallen on hard times and had resorted to the world's oldest profession out of necessity.

Ford talked to Von Villas about Joany and devised a scenario he thought might work, "something that would make sense to her." He would pose as Dr. Anderson, a high-rolling pharmaceutical executive who came into town occasionally and wanted some sex and companionship. He didn't feel he could get anything going with her if he told her he was a cop.

After approaching her at the Venus Faire, he had arranged to meet her at the HollywoodLand Motel. "When I got there I was looking for a fantasy, a relationship. She was physically similar to my wife. I was trying to develop a relationship. I was playing the big shot. We talked about life, love, mothers, fathers, kids. But after a while I got the message: she didn't want that. When it dawned on me that she wasn't interested in a relationship, [I decided], Let's get on with the show. So I went back to my street self: All right, let's party."

His change of attitude, Ford believed, along with the fact that Loguercio was drinking, smoking dope, and had taken some stimulants he had given her, made her paranoid. It also made her a bit ill. When she said she wasn't feeling well and wanted to leave, he let her. He never had any intentions of killing her. The item he had tried to hide from her on the bed wasn't a choke, it was an elastic cock ring—a sex device used to maintain an erection. He was embarrassed and didn't want her to see it. The story he later told Adams about the motel incident was all a fabrication—as was everything on the van tapes.

As for the alleged second attempt on Loguercio's life on July 7, Ford explained, it was Adams who had brought up the subject of killing Loguercio. After accusing Ford and Von Villas of planning to kill her for the insurance money, Adams offered to do it himself for $25,000. When Ford asked Von Villas what Adams was talking about, Von Villas told him he had made it all up.

What happened next was all an orchestrated mind game they had decided to play with Adams. "I was just pushing Adams, I didn't think he'd go as far as he did. Based on my knowledge of him in the past, I knew he'd back down." While admitting this showed "bad judgment," he insisted he never intended to kill Joan Loguercio. He and Adams were playing a sick game of chicken and he was determined to make Adams blink. "I was calling his bluff. I knew he wasn't going to kill Joan Loguercio. I knew I wasn't going to kill Joan Loguercio. I thought that if he seriously believed Joan Loguercio was going to be killed, he would back down. He always does." Ford called the van tapes "disgusting filth, embarrassing to me and embarrassing to my family."

"What is your frame of mind right now?" Lasting asked.

"Humiliation," said Ford.

Prosecutor Bob O'Neill had a lot to ask Richard Ford. He questioned him about his finances, and, despite the defendant's denials, established that Ford was awash in debt. Despite claims by Ford that he and Von Villas talked on the phone all the time, O'Neill submitted phone records to show that was not the case; most of their conversations occurred during the Loguercio conspiracy. Throughout Bob O'Neill's brutal three-day cross-examination, the press and spectator-packed courtroom was quiet as a tomb. Other than the back and forth parrying between the two men, there was not a sound, not a mutter, not a sigh as one hundred sets of eyes remained glued to their exchanges:

"What was so special about Joan Loguercio that you would pay her three hundred and twenty dollars for her phone number when you could get any prostitute for half of that?"

"She represented something to me at the time that was missing in my life—something I didn't have with pros on the street. Joan was special. It was very personal. Before my wife's rape we had a good relationship. One of the things she would do before the rape was dance for me in an erotic way. Joan reminded me of my wife. I wanted something more than a sexual relationship."

"Did you offer her a thousand dollars?" O'Neill asked.

"Yes, eventually, for the weekend," said Ford.

"What was your salary as a detective in 1982?"

"Forty or fifty thousand, I don't recall. Seven hundred and fifty a week after taxes."

"Did you ever offer to pay a thousand dollars to other prostitutes?"

"No sir."

"Why did you ask her to get the room?"

"Convenience."

"Why was it easier for her to get the room than for you?"

"If she got it, I'd know she was going to be there."

"Wasn't it because you didn't want to be seen?"

"No."

"Isn't it a fact that you were spotted by the Oriental manager?"

"No, that's the story I told Bruce Adams, but it did not actually take place."

Contradicting Loguercio's testimony, Ford claimed he didn't give her any money when he entered the motel room, but that she took it before she left. "What about her testimony?" O'Neill asked. "Was that a lie?"

"Yes," said Ford.

"How long did you work in Vice?"

"Eighteen months."

"Isn't it a fact that the first thing discussed in this kind of situation is money, that the money is always paid up front?"

"In most cases, yes."

"Isn't it a fact that you gave her that much money to have her relax, knowing she would spend some time and not be in a hurry? Isn't it a fact you knew you would get the money back because you were going to kill her?"

"No," answered Ford.

"Didn't you tell Loguercio that you'd pay all her bills, that you'd write her a check?"

"I don't recall going that far."

"Did you keep looking at your watch?"

"Yes, I did."

"Did you keep looking out the window to see if it was light?"

"Yes."

"Because you were concerned that you had to kill her before it got light?"

"No sir. I had problems being there, psychological problems."

O'Neill asked Ford to describe the sex device he had hidden under the covers.

"I only know its street name. It's called a cock ring. It's a rubber, elastic tubing, a locking device that slips over the shaft of the penis and helps maintain an erection. It doesn't allow blood to flow out of the penis." When asked why he hid the device, he said, "Pride, embarrassment, masculinity."

Ford continued to deny O'Neill's accusations. "Didn't you learn when you came back from vacation that Loguercio was trying to cancel the insurance policy?"

"No, there was no insurance policy."

"Is it just a coincidence that all the calls between you and Von Villas were made at the same time of the insurance policy and your sexual encounter with Loguercio at the motel?"

"Yes."

"Don't they reflect your discussion of the plot to collect on the policy?"

"There was no insurance policy."

O'Neill next referred the defendant to statement after lurid statement on the van tapes. Ford remained cool, slipping his glasses on and off to read transcripts placed before him. "None of it makes any sense, it's not logical," he said at one point. "It's just what I told Bruce." Adams had asked him at the shop why he didn't kill Loguercio at the motel, so he made it all up. "A lot of this is just a regurgitation of that." All his sordid statements regarding what he planned to do with Loguercio once they got her in the van were just part of the ruse.

Ford's homicide kit was also part of the deception. He had just tossed some things in his briefcase. O'Neill asked him why he owned "combat gear and commando-style weapons."

"I wasn't playing commando, sir, I was having a problem with delayed stress; part of that I guess you might say was a paranoia toward a war or the enemy." Ford also testified that he had carried his derringer and a knife ever since he was shot and nearly killed in the line of duty in 1969. During that incident, his service revolver had been taken from him by the perpetrator, who was then shot and killed by his partner. "After that I started carrying a knife. I felt if I would have had a knife, I would not have had to kill that person, I could have wounded him."

O'Neill asked Ford about his statement at the end of the van tapes—"That's the end of that caper." "Isn't that an indication of your intent?"

"No, absolutely not."

At times during his cross-examination, Ford displayed a troublesome arrogance. Whenever O'Neill asked him about the insurance policy, Ford always responded with the same dismissal: "There was no insurance policy." His repeated insistence certainly made his opinion clear, but his refusal to address the existence of what some might view as a valid policy was indeed arrogant.

Even worse, when O'Neill asked him on a number of occasions what he would have done if Bruce Adams had returned with Loguercio to the van on the evening of July 7, Ford's repeated response was, "That wasn't going to happen." Again, he expressed his opinion as a matter of irrefutable fact. Surely, even if the question was wildly hypothetical, and even if for the sake of argument he was correct about Adams, he should have realized the jury needed to hear his answer—not a dismissal of the question.

Once Ford was off the stand, Lasting and Santwier began presenting witnesses to support his testimony.

David Lin, the Oriental manager of the HollywoodLand Motel on the night of Ford's tryst with Loguercio, testified that he did not recall having an encounter with a man whom he felt looked suspicious. On cross-examination, however, Lin stated that he had no specific recollections of the evening in question, "because nothing happened." Also, he hadn't begun his shift that night until 9:00 P.M. Loguercio had checked in at 8:39.

Keith Inman, a research criminologist for the coroner's office, explained the battery of tests and evidence-gathering procedures that were routine when a woman is found murdered in a motel room. He described the myriad ways of extracting evidence from fingerprints, hair, fibers, blood, semen, and saliva samples left at a crime scene. Lasting's point was clear: Detective Richard Ford knew all this. If he wanted to kill someone, he would never leave such evidence scattered all over a motel room.

Lasting next called LAPD psychologist Dr. Martin Reiser, who had interviewed Ford in 1981. Reiser, considered a pioneer in the field of police psychology, was a soft-spoken but vital and engaging witness. He confirmed Ford's litany of problems and stated that Ford had told him he "would like to torture his wife's rapist for three or four days." When Lasting probed further about the rape, O'Neill objected, and Judge Williams excused the jury to hear counsel debate over what could be further discussed with the witness.

Lasting argued that he wanted to establish that Ford told Dr. Reiser about his problems long before the criminal charges arose, and that "only if you understand about the torture of Ford's wife could you understand Richard Ford's state of mind, and that information has not been allowed." Without grasping the enormity of what had happened to Mrs. Ford, Lasting insisted, one could not grasp the depth of Richard Ford's pain and despair. Judge Williams was not impressed: "You're trying to turn this into a sympathy trial about Mrs. Ford," he declared. "That is no excuse for the alleged activities of the defendant. I do not like the thrust and focus of the defense." Judge Williams restricted Lasting's line of questioning.

On cross-examination, O'Neill asked Dr. Reiser, "Did Ford tell you he hates people and felt he might blow somebody away?"

"Yes."

"Did he tell you he was an expert in killing and that was kind of sad?"

"Yes."

On redirect, Lasting asked if Ford's remark about being an expert in killing was "in the general context of his involvement with weapons."

"Yes," said Reiser, "and his eleven years with the army and ten with the police."

After a great deal of argument regarding the admissibility of his testimony, Dr. Frederick Hacker, Mrs. Ford's psychiatrist, was called to the stand. Judge Williams again limited the scope of testimony. The jury would not hear all the lurid details of Lillian Ford's torture and rape.

Dr. Frederick Hacker was a distinguished-looking man in his late sixties with a Viennese accent as thick as Sigmund Freud's. Hacker testified to the nightmare of Lillian Ford's rape, providing some, but hardly all, of the lurid details to the court.

From his contacts with Richard Ford, Hacker had discerned that "he was obsessed with finding the rapist; his wife was also obsessed. It seemed to me it was a shared obsession." He also stated that Richard Ford seemed to have "trouble dealing with rage and frustration" over not being able to find the rapist, and this revived his feelings from the Vietnam War, and he had great difficulty dealing with the situation.

Next, Dr. David Lopata, the clinical psychologist who ran the support-group meetings at the Sepulveda V.A., testified to having treated Richard Ford for PTSD and verified Ford's testimony regarding his personal problems. Perhaps most importantly, Dr. Lopata stated that Ford was the kind of guy who liked to play "head games" with people.

By the time Lasting had finished presenting his defense of Richard Ford, many jurors appeared perplexed. Some seemed to have been moved. Were they buying this troubling tale?

24

The Businessman

ON NOVEMBER 9, JACK STONE CALLED HIS FIRST WITNESS—ROBERT Von Villas. Dressed elegantly in deep blue and charcoal pin-striped suits, smiling and confident through most of his two-week testimony, Von Villas looked more like a banker than a cop. Trim and fit, Von Villas, now forty-three and half bald, seemed in good spirits. His wife, Judy, made a few appearances in the gallery.

With Stone leading him through his life story, Von Villas described himself as someone who had always been a businessman as well as a cop. He was originally from Brooklyn but moved to the South Bay area with his parents while still a child. He bought his first house, for his mother, when he was eighteen, while working as a journeyman clerk at a retail union. He had acquired a strong interest in jewelry from his parents. He joined the army in 1964 when he was nineteen and served in Vietnam for seven months. Once, while on R and R in Hong Kong, he used six thousand dollars that he won gambling with other GIs to buy about forty diamonds at the China Fleet Club, "a government-sanctioned place with reputable goods." He bought the diamonds to mail home to his mom because "you weren't allowed to have greenbacks in Vietnam."

He returned to Redondo Beach on December 5, 1969, and six days later applied to the LAPD. He worked patrol in North Hollywood for two years, served as Mayor Sam Yorty's bodyguard for nine months, moved to Devonshire Division in 1974, served thirteen years with LAPD and, at the time of his arrest, was a Policeman 2, making about $30,000 a year—as a cop.

He saved most of the diamonds he bought in Hong Kong as an investment but also traded some over the years. When his mom died in 1970, he inherited

242

a good deal of jewelry from her—rings, stones, antique brooches, and necklaces. Over the years he broke many of these up to create new settings for himself and his wife. He had also been a regular customer of Schaffer and Sons Jewelers since 1973. Jack Stone submitted eight checks as evidence of this, establishing that Von Villas had indeed engaged in much trading and buying of precious stones. The two Schaffer and Son envelopes found in his possession at the time of his arrest had been obtained by him during one of his exchanges at the store.

Von Villas explained that in 1982 he had traded some antique jewelry for some loose diamonds owned by a man named Hal Rosen, who was visiting from New York. He also traded and acquired diamonds at drive-in swap meets, which he had attended regularly since 1971. That was where he got the Schaffer and Sons "display only" brass ring that he had taken to jeweler Bill Justice. Von Villas described the origin of each diamond and ring that had been found in his possession, as well as those he had traded to preceding witnesses like Justice, Dan Krowpman, and Charles Beatty. Although these items were identified as allegedly coming from the Schaffer and Sons inventory, Von Villas insisted they came from Hong Kong, his mother, Hal Rosen, swap meets, or legitimate Schaffer and Sons purchases.

If nothing else, as Jack Stone had his client examine and describe the evidence—gold necklaces, diamond and ruby stick pins, antique brooches, a silver and porcelain rosary, a sunburst brooch—he established that Von Villas certainly knew his jewelry.

Stone then had Von Villas describe his numerous business interests over the years: the Northridge Blacksmith Shop in the Walnut Grove Shopping Center, which had "iron furniture, lighting, stuff like that." He made $60,000 off a real estate deal in Bell Canyon. He had income from the commodities market. He was part owner of three six-unit apartment buildings in downtown Los Angeles. The attorney asked him why he was always engaged in outside businesses. Did he have a great need for money?

"No," Von Villas responded, "I enjoyed being a businessman as well as a policeman."

"Was this within police department rules?"

"Yes."

By the end of the first day, Stone had solidly established his client's business acumen. Yet one couldn't help but wonder how the jury felt about this; it's not a quality most citizens look for in a cop. And Von Villas was coming across as perhaps too smart—a sharpie.

During the next day's testimony, Stone asked Von Villas about Ford's description of him as the "division scrounger."

"Yes, I was," answered Von Villas proudly. "When the division needed something, they'd come to me. It was the same in the army—I had that rep. I once traded a truck of Budweiser for an armed personnel carrier, and I continued trading in the police."

Stone next questioned Von Villas about the ranch he had owned in Simi Valley. Von Villas lit up with a broad smile just talking about the horses. He described how he took care of their minor ailments—treating scrapes with medication, inserting suppositories—and for this purpose he always kept a supply of surgical gloves in the barn. The reason a pair of these gloves had been found in his boot was, when he sold the ranch and moved in 1982, "whatever was on the floor of the closet, I stuffed them in a boot. Those boots hadn't been worn in two years, they were a little bit out of style."

The questioning then turned to his relationship with Richard Ford, whom he first met at Devonshire in 1978. Von Villas said that Ford called him in August 1982 and asked if he could use his contacts from his movie security jobs to find someone who could make him a professional disguise. Von Villas eventually arranged the meeting with Chefalo. "I was aware of what happened to Ford's wife. I asked if it was related and he said yes. He said he was gathering information on his own. I said, Who's helping you? He said no one. I was incensed over what happened to her . . . I'd read the police report . . . I was outraged by the crime—being beaten, raped, tortured. Because of my rage, I decided to help him."

Von Villas recalled paying $246 for his wig. On the evening they received their wigs, he said that they had driven to Hollywood, still in their disguises, to search for Skip. They had walked a wide area on and between Sunset and Santa Monica boulevards. Richard Ford took him to an area he called Grease Alley, which had a number of low-life hangouts. "The entire evening was quite unusual for me," Von Villas explained. "I'd never worked Vice or Narcotics, so the people there were beyond my experience. I felt naive. I'd never dealt with that subculture."

Von Villas recalled seeing people light up marijuana cigarettes and "somebody orally copulating someone in the stairway" at one homosexual pickup joint. "I don't ordinarily see that," he said.

Back in their car, while driving down Sunset between Highland and Cahuenga, Ford suddenly pulled over and jumped out. "Back me up," he yelled at Von Villas as he ran to a footpath that went under a Sunset overpass, apparently chasing two men he had just seen go in that direction. Von Villas tried to follow in the car but he couldn't see where they went. He heard some yelling. When Ford came back he was huffing and puffing and extremely upset.

Von Villas and Ford proceeded to have "a pretty big argument" because

Ford felt that Von Villas had failed to back him up. After that, Von Villas never again helped him look for Skip. He said he returned his beard and, "I had a calico cat that destroyed the wig."

Despite their disagreement, Ford and Von Villas remained on good terms at work. Later, "He asked if I wanted to invest in an auto shop. . . . It was inexpensive to get into; Adams had told Ford that he had the tools. I invested three grand, Ford invested twenty-five hundred dollars, we were one-third partners. I would take care of the books."

He and Ford never became close friends. "There was never a social relationship. It was just business."

That business, however, was trouble from the start. "Adams always had money problems. He started purchasing food out of petty cash, using company money to buy gas, tools, et cetera. Customers were always complaining, no work orders were being signed." Von Villas described Adams as a braggart and a blusterer, a man who never did what he said he was going to do. "Once, a customer took his car without paying. Adams said, 'I'll kill him, I'll get him with a tire iron, fire bomb his car.' . . . This happened at least three times. He was all show, he never did what he said."

Because of friction with Adams, Von Villas decided to get out of the auto shop. "I didn't trust him anymore. I told him on approximately May tenth that as of June first he would be financially responsible for the business. I sent out a letter to that effect [to creditors] on May fifteenth. He said he would buy us out—three grand to me and Ford each. I gave him the checkbook at the end of May, only as a sample to get new ones made, and he agreed he would write no more checks.

"I went there June thirteenth to get my money, but he didn't have it. On my next trip, June fifteenth, I opened the checkbook and he had written eighteen hundred dollars' worth of checks. I was very upset. I told him he had thirty days, that by July fifteenth I would take whatever measures necessary to make good [on what he owed]. On June sixteenth, I closed out that account." Checks were submitted as evidence. Von Villas seemed absolutely convincing—the respectable businessman describing his problems with an errant employee.

Von Villas stated that he let Adams read the police report on the Schaffer and Sons robbery—which he happened to have with him one day—while working with him at the shop. That's how Adams knew the details of the jewelry heist he'd supplied to the police.

Stone next questioned Von Villas about his relationship with Joan Loguercio. Von Villas testified that he befriended the woman after meeting her through his police work. They did not have a sexual relationship. He had helped another friend in the past to refinance her home, and when Loguercio told him of her troubles, he offered to help. "The insurance policy was to protect the mortgage . . . but I was told it would not be valid until there was an insurable interest."

Stone took Von Villas through a long and complex explanation of the Loguercio home loan and insurance policy arrangements that dragged on for most of an afternoon. The deal was so complex that it seemed unlikely that anyone but a financial planner could understand it fully. Von Villas, at least, seemed to know what he was talking about. One could easily see how a vulnerable person like Joan Loguercio would be happy to turn her financial problems over to such a savvy businessman.

At one point while submitting various receipts and records, Jack Stone had trouble finding something, so he walked up to the stand and handed a huge loose-leaf binder crammed with paperwork over to Von Villas. "He's the one who knows where everything is," commented Stone, triggering chuckles through the court. Sure enough, Von Villas fished out the needed papers in a heartbeat.

Von Villas stated that Gayl West had told him that until the Loguercio house loan closed escrow, there wouldn't be an insurable interest and thus the insurance policy would not be in effect. As far as he was concerned, "There was no insurance policy." He would insist on this point repeatedly before he got off the stand.

On the morning of July 7, Von Villas stopped in at a Foster's Donut shop he frequented. Carol De Lisle, the daughter of the owner, complained to him about her car, which she had taken into International Automotive for repairs. It was taking much longer than she had been told. Bruce Adams had told her to rent a car and said he'd take care of the bill, but he hadn't. Now the rental company was upset and calling her for the money. Von Villas wrote out a personal check for $385 to Budget car rental car and gave it to her. "Bruce had done this in the past. She was a friend. I decided I would worry about collecting from him."

When Von Villas arrived at the shop, he was "hot" and bent on having it out with Adams over this and other problems. First, at ten-thirty, he drove with Adams to pick up a Firebird owned by a friend, Marylynn Petretti. When they returned, he lit into Adams. " 'Bruce, I just paid three hundred and eighty-five dollars because of you.' He says, 'I finally got some M-seventy-nine grenade launchers.' I said, 'I don't want any, I want to talk about the checks, problems at the shop.' He said, 'Loguercio thinks you're trying to kill her.' I said, 'Bruce, no more games, I want to talk about the shop.' Adams said, 'If the price is right, I'll do it.' I said, 'OK, great, Bruce, I'll give you twenty-five G's, does that make you happy?' "

When Ford arrived and heard them talking about Loguercio, he asked what was going on, and Von Villas took him outside to talk. Von Villas explained how they then hatched their sick plot: "I wanted to hurt him [Adams] mentally. I'd seen him have panic attacks, go in the john, eyes get red, have to take a Valium. It was a terrible thing to do, but I wanted to hurt him. I told Ford, 'There is no policy, follow my lead.' " The two men then concocted a plan to play a mind game with Adams.

"I told him [Adams], 'It's gotta be done tonight, I'll give you twelve thousand five hundred each, but Dick has to go with you.' I expected him to back down, say he couldn't do it. He always comes up with excuses. There was never any possibility he would kill her, I knew that. Once, he told me he was in love with her and was going to move in with her."

His conversation and the notes he wrote were all intended to make Adams think he wanted to kill Loguercio, but he did not have that intention. "I didn't believe the notes were incriminating, that's why I just left them there." After that, Von Villas explained, "I thought that was the end of it." When Adams called him later at home he played along with him again, briefly, but he still never expected anything to come of it.

As Stone finished his direct examination, he submitted the check Von Villas had made out to Budget car rental, dated July 7, 1983. When he stated, "Nothing further," the entire defense team and Richard Ford were grinning from ear to ear. They obviously felt that Von Villas had proven to be the big gun in getting the defense's version of the story across to the jury.

Despite some of his improbable explanations for the evidence at hand, Von Villas had come across as very sincere and believable. Some of the jury members looked stunned, as though they were suddenly wondering if perhaps things really weren't quite as they had seemed. Perhaps determining the truth wasn't going to be as easy as they had thought.

O'Neill's cross-examination was a full-scale week-long attack. He scrutinized the tangle of Von Villas's businesses and soon established that his profitable ventures had all been confined to the late 1970s. During 1981, 1982, and 1983, he was, in fact, overextended and experiencing financial troubles. He was involved in one business, a tile company, that folded, ending in lawsuits and a judgment against him. Von Villas admitted that in 1982 he had to "trade" his ranch, valued at $200,000, for a house in Simi Valley worth half of that to pay off his debts. He owed people money and had approached friends for loans.

"Is that when you considered crime?" O'Neill asked.

"No, I never did, sir," Von Villas answered calmly.

"Did you ask Detective Ray Romero for a ten-thousand-dollar loan, at twenty-five percent interest over six months?"

"That probably occurred . . ."

"Didn't it in fact occur a month before your arrest? You needed money bad. Wasn't the money to come from the Loguercio insurance policy?"

"No."

"Didn't you ask your friend Joe Reiner if his wife could lend you a hundred thousand dollars?"

"No, I have no recollection of that at all."

"The fact is, in 1982 and 1983, you found yourself in a pretty tight situation."

"No sir, that's not correct."

Asked why he didn't turn in his Rover radio on November 22, 1982, Von Villas stated, "I don't know why." He said the 1973 license plate found in his car was not a "cold plate"—despite DMV testimony that it was untraceable—because it had the wrong color sticker for 1983. The reason it was in the car? He probably put it there when he moved. It was a plate from a 1973 Ford Courier he owned years ago that had been lying around. "I always took the front plate off because it detracted from the look. It's against the law but I do it."

"Didn't you stuff these gloves into your boots after the robbery?"

"I didn't do the robbery."

"Isn't it true you didn't have Richard Ford gag Mrs. Martin because of her outgoing and aggressive personality, that you knew she would calm the others?"

"No."

"Couldn't you have gotten a cashier's check in Hong Kong and sent it home?"

"I don't know. I never thought of it."

"The truth is, all these stones are from Schaffer and Sons. . . ."

"No."

Despite describing himself as a "meticulous bookkeeper," Von Villas admitted he had no records of the diamonds purchased in Hong Kong (lost when he was wounded in Vietnam) or those he got at swap meets or in his transactions with the mysterious Hal Rosen. Von Villas explained that he had met the visiting New Yorker through a notice tacked on a community bulletin board at a supermarket. He traded some jewelry with him for approximately fifteen diamonds. He didn't know how to find him. He claimed that he got receipts from Rosen and implied that they were probably lost by investigating officers, who had recovered eight thousand pieces of paper from his home.

Had he threatened Adams with physical violence? "No." Found him easy to manipulate? "No." Received $2,500 from Adams? "No." Ever talked to Ford about the insurance policy during all those phone calls? "No." Been told by the insurance agent that the policy was effective on May 19? "No, the deal was still in escrow. I felt until escrow closed I had nothing."

"When Loguercio called you on July fifth to get the name of the insurance agent," O'Neill asked, "didn't you tell her the name was in your locker?"

"Yes."

"When Gayl West called on July sixth asking for that name—because Loguercio had called her—did you tell her it was in your car?"

"I don't remember."

"Weren't you in fact stalling for time so you could *kill* Ms. Loguercio before she canceled the policy?"

"No, I couldn't remember the name."

"Didn't Ossenkop tell you several times the policy was effective from the time of signing?"

"That wasn't my understanding. I felt until escrow closed, I had nothing."

"Then why did you give him a check for one hundred seventeen dollars and thirty-two cents on May twentieth?"

"Because I'd get it back if the loan didn't go through escrow."

"How many times did you ask Ossenkop when the policy would be in effect?"

"I don't know."

"More than once?"

"Yes."

"Did you know the HollywoodLand Motel was a hotbed for prostitution?"

"No."

"Did you and Ford pick that motel because it was frequented by prostitutes and a sex murder wouldn't be unusual there?"

Jack Stone objected to this as argumentative and was sustained.

"When you talked to Loguercio, did she express her fear of being killed?"

"No, the word 'kill' was never mentioned."

"Did she express concern about what he tried to do to her, about her physical well-being?"

"Yes."

"Did you try to find out how she felt about going out with him again?"

"Partly."

"Did you discuss this with Ford?"

"He said he didn't want to talk about it."

Returning to the morning of July 7, when Von Villas and Ford allegedly decided to play a mind game with Adams, O'Neill grilled him on his story again. "I came up with an idea to make Bruce suffer, to make him have a panic attack," Von Villas stated. Then, suddenly, Von Villas blew his cool. He rattled away in a burst of emotion. "I blew it professionally. I lost my life. I've spent five years waiting for this day. I lost my house, my wife works sixty-five hours a week. I've been in jail for five years and I've lost everything . . ."

Judge Williams pounded the desk with his gavel. "Mr. Von Villas, you know better than that; I won't have this," he admonished.

Jury and spectators seemed surprised at the crack in Von Villas's steely veneer, but it didn't seem to hurt him. It actually made him appear more human. If he was indeed innocent, his rage was understandable.

Von Villas composed himself quickly. "I was tired of Bruce's games, saying he was going to hurt people. There was no insurance policy. Ford said, 'I'm better at head games, let me handle it.' "

"Did you call anybody at the station and tell them somebody was trying to kill somebody?"

"No."

"Did you ever call Loguercio to tell her Adams was going to kill her?"

"No."

"That her fears about Dr. Anderson were unfounded?"

"No."

"After hearing what Adams told you, you didn't feel any need to ease her mind?"

"No."

Referring to the taped phone conversation with Bruce Adams on the afternoon of July 7, O'Neill fired one ripping accusation after another.

"When you got a call from Bruce on July seventh, did you discuss the plan to kill Loguercio?"

"Yes."

" 'Have you got carpet in the back?' Why did you tell him that?"

"No particular reason. It wasn't supposed to go that far."

" 'You haven't talked to her since, have you?' Why did you ask him that?"

"I don't know."

"Were you worried he would blow it?"

"No."

"Did you tell him the site had to be in Hollywood?"

"No."

"Why were you so concerned that it be south of Mulholland?"

"I wasn't concerned. I just said make it the south side. It didn't really matter."

"Isn't it common knowledge that the homicide rate is higher in Hollywood?" (O'Neill would introduce statistics showing that the homicide rate in Hollywood in 1982–1983 was more than five times that of Devonshire Division.)

"I don't think so."

"Did you talk to Ford about bringing daggers?"

"He might have mentioned them."

"Did you tell him to make it look like a sex-mutilation murder?"

"No."

"Like rape?"

"No."

"Did you tell him to bring K-Y jelly?"

"No. He said, 'He wants to see a homicide kit, so I'll show him one, throw some items in a bag.' "

"Whose idea was it to get a long-stemmed bottle?"

"I have no knowledge of that."

"Did you tell Joyce Reynolds, at the LAPD Christmas party in 1982, that you were tired of being an honest cop, that no job was too big or too small, even murder for hire?"

"No sir. When I said no job was too big or too small I was referring to security jobs."

"Did you tell Gayl West to call you if she ever needed someone taken care of?"

"Yes, as a bodyguard."

"Did you tell Gayl West at Marie Calendar's, that if she ever needed a contract on someone, one call and you'd both make a commission?"

"No sir."

"She's in error?"

"Yes."

"Did you tell Joan Loguercio you could find someone to kill her husband?"

"Yes, it was supposed to be a joke. I was kidding."

O'Neill questioned Von Villas about the Foster's Donuts incident, which had triggered his simmering anger at Bruce Adams. "Carol and Cathy De Lisle were interviewed by police and their statements contradict yours."

"Yes, portions do."

"In fact, *you* told her to rent a car."

"I don't remember it that way."

By the time O'Neill finished with Von Villas, he appeared drawn and weary. The days of denials had taken their toll.

For his next witness, Jack Stone called Michele Von Villas Walker, the defendant's daughter. A pretty blonde with flowing curls, just twenty-one and sweet as could be, Michele testified that her father never put the front license plate on their family cars. He always left them lying around the garage. She also stated that her father never left the house on the day or evening of his arrest. That was it.

The information provided by Michele wasn't as crucial as her very presence. Putting the defendant's daughter on the stand, however briefly, had impact. It wasn't hard to imagine the tremendous pain the conviction of her father would cause this innocent girl. To make his point even more poignantly, Jack Stone then submitted as evidence, for perusal by the jury, a picture of Michele and her little sister, Shannon, bundled in a blanket out at the beach, in front of one of the family's front plate-less vehicles.

Donald Feinberg, cocounsel for Von Villas, pursued another line of defense. He brought on a string of five gemologists and jewelry appraisers, all noted experts in their field, including two of the Schaffer brothers of the Schaffer and Sons jewelry store. Feinberg questioned them exhaustively, spending a few days with these witnesses. He ran them through their long lists of credentials and professional affiliations, then had them explain the detailed intricacies of the examining and grading process of precious gems and the importance of the *Rappaport Guide,* the industry bible, in making appraisals. Some of this testimony became so tedious and obscure it was apparent the jury was lost.

However, Feinberg did get across a crucial point. The diamonds stolen from Schaffer and Sons had not been "plotted," a foolproof process of identification tantamount to taking a gem's fingerprint. The Schaffer and Sons diamonds had merely been identified by size, shape, weight, and high- and low-end appraisal. Hence, there was no way to determine with certainty that the diamonds found in Von Villas's possession were the ones stolen from Schaffer and Sons. Only that they were similar.

Jewelry expert Cosmo Altobelli, a distinguished-looking man in his fifties, testified that six of the stones seized from Von Villas's home might match in size and shape to stones on the Schaffer and Sons robbery inventory, but they were as much as 100 percent off in their listed appraised value. Altobelli pronounced that "in my opinion they are not the same stones."

Under cross-examination by Bob O'Neill, however, Mr. Altobelli admitted that appraisals were subjective and that it was common for appraisers to differ.

He also allowed that the values attached by Schaffer and Sons may have been percentages of lot prices. He also admitted that although it was hypothetically possible for an individual to coincidentally possess twelve stones and a number of rings similar to those taken from a jewelry store, that possibility was "remote."

David Boykoff, a private investigator for Mr. Stone, testified that, at Stone's direction, he had attempted to purchase some brass "display only" rings at three Schaffer and Sons jewelry stores. The first two, in Northridge and Woodland Hills, refused to sell them. But he was able to persuade a salesperson to sell him two of the brass rings at the store in Arcadia.

It was a policy of Schaffer and Sons, as well as most reputable jewelers, not to sell brass rings. When worn, they leave telltale black marks on people's fingers, and, since they look like gold, they can also be sold as such by con men. This no sale policy is what made the brass Schaffer and Sons ring found in Von Villas's home so incriminating. "They told me it was Schaffer and Sons' policy not to sell them," Boykoff testified, "but they did. Obviously, if I can purchase them anyone can."

After Stone had finished presenting his case, O'Neill called a dozen more prosecution witnesses. The most important of these were Carol De Lisle, her sister Cathy, and their mother, Margaret Willis, owner of the doughnut shop Von Villas visited on the morning of July 7. The women all testified that it was Von Villas, not Adams, who had told them to go out and rent a car while they were waiting for theirs to be fixed and that he would pay for it. It wasn't just on July 7 that Bob had learned of the problem with the car company; they had hounded him for the money throughout the month of June. During the last week of June, in fact, they had told him they would take him to small claims court if the problem wasn't resolved.

It seemed that the three women had destroyed the story Von Villas had used to explain his bitterness toward Adams and his actions later on that fateful day.

25

To Rob and to Kill

THE ATTORNEYS SPENT TWO DAYS ARGUING OVER WHAT SHOULD be included in the final instructions to the jury. Then it took another day for Judge Williams to read the instructions in court. Finally, on December 14, after eight and a half months of proceedings, which had resulted in 30,000 transcript pages of testimony and 400 exhibits, the jury was brought back to the van tapes by prosecutor Robert O'Neill as he began what would be a week of closing arguments.

"Ladies and gentlemen," O'Neill calmly intoned to the jury in a courtroom packed with spectators and press, "the words of Richard Ford." He then began to read, slowly and deliberately, without deleting a single expletive: " 'It should be obvious to the fuckin' police what happened. A fuckin' sex fiend doped her up, tortured her, and killed her. They do that all the time. That's why I need a long-stemmed bottle to push her fuckin' mouth open . . . and shove it down her fuckin' throat so that shit gets down her fucking throat. Then about thirty minutes later she'll belong to us.

" 'Now, the next part is, she has to be fucked up, right? So it's gotta look like she's been up there dancing her ass off, as in the past, she's been dating. She made a date tonight with somebody. The guy who picked her up was a fuckin' sex fiend, took her out some fucking place, doped her up, fucked her, tortured her fucking ass, buttfucked her, just fucked her up, okay? . . . Fucked her body up, beat the shit out of her, ended up fucking killing her and dumped her in a fuckin' alley in Hollywood. So the whole thing is supposed to look like it was a sex crime. . . . Wham, bam, thank you, ma'am . . . That'll give us twelve thou each.'

"Ladies and gentlemen," O'Neill continued, "you've heard the overwhelming amount of evidence . . . What you've heard is your worst nightmare come true: two police officers sworn 'To Protect and to Serve' this community who turned that motto and obligation of the Los Angeles Police Department into a personal motto: 'To Rob and to Kill.'

"These crimes were committed by men who were remorseless . . . who had nothing but contempt for society . . . What you've heard over the last eight months is an incredible story of incredible crimes. Unfortunately for all of us, it's true."

O'Neill first addressed the evidence pertaining to the jewelry store robbery. He presented a large cardboard chart titled "Amazing Coincidences." He ran the jury through each item on his list: The salt and pepper wigs and disguises. The physical description of the robbers. The police command given to the victims. The Rover police radio. No officers on duty. Surgical gloves. The cold plate. Bindles, diamonds, and rings recovered from the defendant that matched stolen inventory. The "for display only" brass ring. Von Villas trading diamonds. The mysterious Hal Rosen, Hong Kong, and swap-meet diamonds with no receipts. Adams's knowledge of details of the robbery.

O'Neill tore away at the subjective opinion of expert witnesses who stated it was possible for someone to have in their possession twelve diamonds and a few bindles and rings matching those stolen from the store. "Anything is possible," O'Neill scoffed. He threw some of the evidence presented by the defense right back at them. "Just how unusual it is to have a brass display ring if you're not in the jewelry business was presented by the defense in the person of David Boykoff, defense investigator for Von Villas. Boykoff went to the Northridge Schaffer's. They refused to sell him one. He went to Woodland Hills. They refused. Finally, he went to Arcadia. Initially, they also refused . . . How unusual, how *amazing* that Von Villas happened to have one at his home.

"Look at the testimony of Robert Von Villas. A month after the robbery he was at a swap meet in Simi Valley. He just happened to pick out a gold ring. He paid cash, got no receipt. When he took it to Bill Justice and learned it was brass, he didn't take it back. What an amazing coincidence! His diamonds either came from Hong Kong or the mysterious Harold Rosen, but he has no paperwork. This is not only out of character for a man who 'probably saved every piece of paper he's ever come across in his life,' it's an incredible, amazing story when you consider the total picture of the evidence related to that robbery.

"Von Villas tells us he was working at the shop with Adams. Adams commented on his ring. This leads to a conversation about the Schaffer and Sons robbery. Von Villas just happens to have the police report and he lets Adams read it. That's how Adams knows all the details. That, in and of itself, is one for

Ripley's Believe It or Not. Ladies and gentlemen, all the evidence regarding the Schaffer and Sons robbery is more than an amazing coincidence—it points to the cold hard fact that these men robbed that store.

"Let's talk about Bruce Adams. Bruce Adams is certainly not a parish priest . . . but then you don't go out and recruit the parish priest to help you commit a mutilation sex-type murder. . . . The defense has to attack Adams, and in a lot of ways he's an easy target. He's certainly not a Rhodes scholar by any stretch of the imagination. But the defense attempts to attribute a motive to Adams doesn't make sense, because if there's no truth about his statements to ATF, there's no way they are going to do anything to Ford and Von Villas. If they were all lies, it would only bring authorities down on him. It doesn't get Ford and Von Villas off his back, it brings ATF down on Adams: 'This guy is accusing two brother police officers of being gunrunners. Let's investigate *him*.'

"They tell you William Mayhew was a fiction, but Mayhew wasn't a fiction—the check was submitted, endorsed by Mayhew and Adams. They can attack Bruce Adams all they want. The bottom line is that what he tells the police is corroborated right down the line. By property, witnesses, by Joan Loguercio's testimony, the taped telephone conversations, the van tapes. . . .

"In the end of your analysis of his testimony I think you will come to the conclusion that, rather than attacking Bruce Adams, what we should truly do—despite all his shortcomings—is thank Bruce Adams. Because of Bruce Adams, Joan Loguercio didn't die July seventh in that van, at the hands of Richard Ford and direction of Robert Von Villas."

O'Neill addressed Ford's and Von Villas's money problems. He described how Von Villas was overextended, asking around for loans. "Mr. Ford tells us on the van ride, 'I got too fucking far in the hole, man, and I need the fucking money. Twelve grand will make it better. It won't make it right, but it will make it fucking better. . . . By the time I get done paying my bills, I don't eat.'"

O'Neill then turned to Ford's explanation of Dr. Anderson. "Why does he need a cover in the first place? Why concoct this? Anywhere in the city he can gain the sexual favors of a prostitute for considerably less than three hundred and twenty dollars. Then he hands her two thousand dollars in the motel on June seventeenth. On the phone, he promised her a check for twenty thousand dollars to pay her husband off. He knows, from his coconspirator, that her Achilles's heel is money. Ford is a former narcotics officer, he has expertise in narcotics, so he pretends to be a pharmaceutical doctor. Joan Loguercio calls Von Villas to have him check him out. He calls her back, tells her he has all kinds of money. Are these the actions of a man helping a buddy get laid?

"Ford tells her to get the room. Ford says he did it for convenience. Logic tells us it was so he wouldn't be seen. The HollywoodLand Motel is a perfect location: easy access to the freeway, a sleazy motel, a sex murder wouldn't be out of the ordinary. Ford used to be a vice cop. He knows this. His plan was to kill her right away. He gives her two thousand dollars. This is a cop with a family, with mortgages on his home, and he's giving away all this money! Why is he doing this? I'll tell you why—because he expects to get it back. That two thousand dollars he's not gonna even be out, because he's going to *kill* Joan Loguercio and get it back."

O'Neill ran through Ford's lengthy van tape description of his motel encounter with Loguercio—wig, drugs, sex acts, the thousand dollars, hiding something under the covers. "This story is all consistent with Joan Loguercio's testimony," O'Neill concluded.

"After she sees him, he's got to let her go. The element of surprise is gone. She could start screaming. Later on, he can't say it wasn't him, because she identified him when she testified in court. She also identified the tattoo on his arm, shown in People's [exhibit] forty-two, Ford's skull and crossbones tattoo."

O'Neill summarized the entire July 7 plot, Adams's conversations with Ford and Von Villas by phone—the discussion of carpet, location of dump site, payment. "Richard Ford was around cops all day, yet he doesn't tell one soul [about the plot to kill Loguercio]. Von Villas does not call Loguercio. If he did not intend to kill her, wouldn't it be most logical for him to call her and say, 'Hey, this is not true'?"

O'Neill presented another chart, titled "Statements that We All Make at Parties When We've Had a Drink or Two"—a sly reference to a comment made by Jack Stone in the opening arguments. The chart listed four statements that four different witnesses had attributed to Robert Von Villas:

1. "I'm tired of being an honest cop. . . . There isn't any job I wouldn't do for money, including murder."
2. "If you know of anybody who wants a contract put out on anybody, let me know and one telephone call and we both make a commission."
3. "If you want, I know someone who would kill your husband for $10,000."
4. "I can have people killed if you feel they're doing the wrong thing, I can arrange things like that."

"I ask you to consider each of these statements and see if there's ever been an occasion at a party when you've had a drink or two, or any time in your life, where you have made even one of these statements.

"These provide a clear indication of where his mind was at—a willingness to kill for money. Joan Loguercio presented him a perfect target—a nude dancer at a sleazy club. What better way than to make it look like a sex maniac killed her. Maybe it's more than money for Mr. Ford, maybe it's just the thrill. He tells us on the van tape: 'I'd do it for a fuckin' grand, let alone twelve.' . . .

"Above and beyond all the other evidence presented to you in this case, there is nothing more convincing than the unrehearsed, spontaneous, candid, free-flowing, secretly taped recorded statements of Richard Ford made on July seventh, 1983, expressing his intent and the intent of his coconspirator Robert Von Villas. . . . If you have the slightest doubt . . . relisten to those tapes, listen to the calm conviction in the voices of both of them. . . . Listen to Richard Ford as he says, 'As a matter of fact, we should probably get a reward for getting rid of this bitch.' Ladies and gentlemen, in and by your verdicts, tell these men what their reward will be."

Jack Stone, in his closing argument, insisted that nothing but circumstantial evidence had been presented to link Robert Von Villas to the Northridge robbery. He also declared that the defense had clearly established there was no valid insurance policy, and hence there was no motive for the attempted murder of Joan Loguercio. Ultimately, he charged, the prosecution's case rested on the testimony of a witness who had no credibility—Bruce Adams.

"If you believe Mr. Adams, that's the end of this case. . . . He admitted he perjured himself. Mr. O'Neill says that's despicable—but it's more than that. Your instructions say to watch for that when evaluating the credibility of a witness. Mr. Adams has a strange inability to tell the truth. . . . I believe for some reason he could not tell the truth even if he wanted to."

Jack Stone pointed out that the people who testified about statements made by Von Villas did so after his client had been arrested and subjected to intense publicity. Such media scrutiny always causes people to reexamine a person's past statements, making new and sinister interpretations they never previously considered. That was why he referred to these as "statements we all make at parties when we've had a drink or two."

Stone served up an illustration: "When I'm at parties and people ask me about their divorce, I always tell them to kill their spouse—that way I can defend them. That could later be brought up against me."

The statements attributed to Von Villas, Stone argued, were made in much the same vein. Later, they were misconstrued. "Gayl West admitted she had a bad memory. Maybe he didn't use the word 'contract,' maybe he said 'taken care of.' That's what Von Villas did, he took care of people—as a bodyguard."

Donald Feinberg spent a day making closing statements about the jewelry store robbery. He insisted that nothing but circumstantial evidence linked Von Villas to the crime. By the time he ran through his examination of evidence and testimony pertaining to carats and shapes and high- and low-end appraisals, of the probability of possessing particular bindles and rings, of varying testimonies regarding the appearance of the perpetrators, of Darlis Chefalo's makeup shades and color swatches, he had succeeded, at least, in befuddling the jury. Whether this would prove beneficial to the defense remained to be seen.

Richard Lasting, who delivered the most impassioned and inspired argument for the defense, addressed the jury on December 21. "While examining the district attorney's case, I'm reminded of a scene from a movie, *The Cincinnati Kid*," Lasting began. "Ann-Margret is doing a jigsaw puzzle, and a piece doesn't fit. So she takes a pair of scissors, cuts it, and makes it fit. In some sense, that's what you're being asked to do in this case. You're being asked to find the true picture of what the puzzle is all about by trimming and omitting certain evidence."

Lasting insisted that the evidence did not show Ford committed the Schaffer and Sons robbery. No positive identification was made. He was only "circumstantially identified," and by descriptions rife with discrepancies. One witness described a dark plaid suit and a small black leather briefcase. "Look what the prosecutor brings you—not a dark plaid suit, because Ford didn't have one. He brings you a dark overcoat and a large black vinyl briefcase.

"The finding of guilt to any crime may not be based on circumstantial evidence," Lasting reminded the jury, "unless the proved circumstances are not only one, consistent with the theory that the defendant is guilty of the crime, and two, cannot be reconciled in any other fashion." Lasting argued that all the circumstantial evidence was easily reconcilable. "Possession of property, bartering and trading diamonds . . . Is that the evidence? In March of 1983, Ford and his wife went to Ira Kaplan at Goldrush Jewelry. He measured a stone, a point eight three marquise. Look at the inventory of diamonds stolen from Schaffer and Sons. There's no point eight three marquise. The only diamond the prosecution puts in the possession of Richard Ford is clearly not a stolen diamond."

Then, Lasting went after Bruce Adams. He presented a chart, titled "Lies by Mr. Adams" and ran down his list to the jury—Adams's friends from the V.A., former employers, psychologists, investigating officers, all of whom stated or "showed through their testimony" that Adams was dishonest.

"One of the things you look at when judging credibility is an individual's ability to remember and communicate the facts. Adams told you Mayhew was part of the business, but his name was not on the bank account. Adams says he didn't write checks on the company account after May of 1983, but he did, and he had no idea how they would clear. Adams told Agent Oddo they bought twenty-five guns in Colorado; he tells you it was six. He tells one person he didn't know about the guns, another that he did. It's not an 'ear' problem. It's a total problem. He can't keep his story straight. Why? Because he's *lying*.

"If you were telling the truth, would you have discrepancies? Mr. O'Neill says Adams is an easy target, and yes, he is—not because he isn't a Rhodes scholar, but because he's a liar."

Continuing his impassioned plea, Lasting presented a masterful summary, a grand picture that—perhaps for the first time—seemed at least plausible. Crucial to this picture was his portrayal of Bruce Adams. Rather than attempting to present Adams as a man with some diabolical master plan, Lasting drew a portrait of a simple but desperate man who got caught up in a progressive web of lies. "You can't understand this case without understanding Bruce Adams. He wants to take care of Ford and Von Villas. He doesn't want to worry about them. He's scrambling, going from moment to moment. . . . He wanted to frame Ford and Von Villas with guns to get the shop, so he built half-truths into lies. . . . But Adams couldn't find any weapons, ATF couldn't corroborate his story. . . . Then, he gets a call from Loguercio—and he sees another chance.

"Loguercio is paranoid, she thinks everybody is out to get her. Her paranoia at the motel is understandable—she's drinking alcohol, taking stimulants, smoking marijuana, she's with a strange man wearing a wig—she gets paranoid. . . . Why didn't Ford kill Loguercio at the motel? He had army experience, police experience—he could control her. He didn't kill her because he didn't want to. There were times he was on top of her, times she had her head in his lap. He had five hours to kill her."

Lasting presented another chart, titled "Motive." It read: "If Joan Loguercio died July 7, 1983. 1. House to husband. 2. Insurance payoff $00.00."

"Gayl West said there was no insurable interest," Lasting declared.

The van ride, Lasting explained, was a grand production for which Ford even threw together props—the Tuinals, the homicide kit—to heighten the drama. "Adams knew Ford liked to play head games. Dr. Lopata told you Ford was the kind of guy who plays head games to find out about people. It was stupid, disgusting—but he didn't intend to kill."

It was all for the benefit of Bruce Adams, Lasting explained, and it was Adams's idea, his suggestion to kill Loguercio—something that would be very clear if the transmitter on his body wire hadn't mysteriously malfunctioned on the morning of July 7. "Agent Oddo told you the transmitter was destroyed at the shop and he couldn't understand why. Ford and Von Villas did the same thing Oddo told Adams to do. They played along, drew him out."

As for Ford's dialogue on the van tapes, Lasting declared, "It was cheap talk for which Mr. Ford has paid a heavy price. But that tape is consistent with Ford's plan to make Adams back down. Mr. Ford is guilty of stupidity, of lack of judgment. He stands before this court humiliated. But he is not guilty of attempting murder because he never had the intent to kill."

One sensed that Richard Lasting had invested far more than his time and expertise in this case. He had given it his heart as well. Either he genuinely believed in his client's innocence or he was an exceptional actor.

Court adjourned for the Christmas holidays, so the jury didn't begin deliberations until Monday, January 4. On Tuesday, they requested another playing of the van tapes. Court was readjourned and they again heard the lurid and seemingly damnable admissions of Richard Ford, only perhaps this time from a new perspective. One could only speculate.

On Thursday, January 7, after only three and half days, the jury announced they had reached a verdict. All involved in the case were surprised by how quickly they had arrived at their decision.

The courtroom was packed with spectators and the press. Just before the jury arrived, a procession of about fifteen LAPD officers filed in. They stood in a line, stoically, like sentinels, at the back of the court. These officers came from all over the city to hear the verdict in person. They made a show of their presence, as though performing some hallowed ritual of the LAPD brotherhood. Whether there to show support for the defendants or witness an LAPD housecleaning, it seemed somehow very important, perhaps essential, that they make this united appearance.

"You've given us all an experience we'll never forget," the jury foreman told Judge Williams as he handed over the decisions. It took the clerk half an hour to read through the verdicts. Ford and Von Villas were each found guilty of conspiracy to commit murder in the first degree; guilty of attempted murder (June 17); guilty of attempted murder (July 7); guilty of conspiracy to commit robbery, guilty of robbery, false imprisonment, and assault with a firearm of the three jewelry store employees (a total of thirteen counts each). Richard Ford was also found guilty of attempted administration of stupefying drugs—Von Villas was found not guilty on this count. Asking for a poll of the jury, the defendants again listened to the word "guilty," recited to them 324 times, as each jury member gave his or her verdict on each of the twenty-seven counts.

It was a devastating defeat. Richard Ford hung his head, a brooding portrait of gloom. His attorneys, registering shock and dismay, leaned in to offer support. Von Villas registered little emotion.

The jury declined to meet or speak with the press. They apparently felt the verdicts had said it all.

The police officers in the back marched out of the courtroom in single file, as stoically as they had entered.

Judge Williams praised the assemblage before him. "This has not been a carnival," he proclaimed. "This has been a real trial, with dignity brought to it by both the jury and the attorneys." He set sentencing for March 11. By that time, Ford and Von Villas's next trial—in which they would face the death penalty— would likely be under way.

"I think it's a fantastic verdict," said Bob O'Neill. "It was based on the overwhelming evidence of their guilt."

"They looked for the truth," said Richard Lasting. "They tried real hard to find it, but they didn't."

"I'm shocked at how fast they came back," said Jack Stone. "I had thought they would spend a lot more time going over the evidence. I think they [the jury] couldn't get over the fact that these were police officers who perhaps had gone wrong. And I think that colored the decision. They just decided they were dirty cops, so they didn't spend a lot of time going over the evidence." He indicated they would consider an appeal.

Citizen Bruce Adams, alias unknown, whereabouts unknown, called in to make a statement: "The wheels of justice move slowly," Adams said, "but they move very finely. I want to thank the jury. They did a wonderful job of seeing the truth. I also want to thank Mr. O'Neill, who did a fabulous job, and all the guys at IAD and RHD [Robbery/Homicide]. I don't know what I would have done without them, if somebody hadn't believed me . . . This nightmare still isn't over for me, and it probably never will be . . . But at least now, the truth is known."

On March 11, 1988, the two convicted men returned to Judge Williams's courtroom for sentencing. Deputy District Attorney Robert O'Neill argued for the maximum sentence. He told Williams that Ford and Von Villas had "abandoned their oath for two reasons—greed, and the pure love of violence. Our society should never be subjected to the freedom of either of these two men."

Defense attorneys submitted briefs and argued for leniency. Despite the verdicts, they maintained that their clients were innocent. They submitted packages containing the military and police records of both men and cited before the court their many acts of heroism, actions above and beyond the call of duty, multiple commendations, and lifetimes of exemplary service to their country and community. They also cited the punishment Ford and Von Villas had already endured, having each been incarcerated for nearly five years in Los Angeles

County Jail—something knowledgeable guardians of the court knew to be cruel and unusual punishment.

L.A. County Jail is not designed to accommodate prisoners for extended stays. Ford and Von Villas had gone five years without sun or exercise or radio or TV or any of the "comforts" provided to penitentiary inmates. Von Villas once stated that he could write a book about the inhumane and ungodly things he had seen and experienced in County. As one of its longest, and certainly most articulate, residents, nobody doubted this.

The defense attorneys knew Ford and Von Villas would get twenty-five years to life on the murder conspiracy charges. Ultimately, what the lawyers were arguing for was that any sentences given on the other charges would run concurrently with the murder sentence so their clients would have a better chance for parole. Since Ford and Von Villas were model inmates, they'd probably only have to do twenty-five years. With time already served and their good behavior and the overflowing condition of the state penal system, they could probably get out in ten to fifteen years—if they got concurrent sentences on the other counts.

Both defendants asked to address the court.

Richard Ford made a rambling, tearful speech. He insisted that he was innocent of the crimes he had been convicted of. "I'm devastated," he said. "I don't know why I feel guilty about having been found guilty when I'm not guilty."

Reading from notes on a yellow legal pad, Ford described his past four and a half years in jail as "virtual hell." He said he had been spit on, kicked, punched, and had urine poured on him "because of my prior occupation." He also complained that he had been deprived of sunshine and an opportunity to attend mass.

Although professing his innocence, Ford admitted to his own stupidity and bad judgment. He expressed regret over his behavior following his wife's attack, "for taking the law into my own hands" by trying to find her assailant on the Hollywood streets. "Instead, I wound up becoming part of it. I got out there and acted like a fool. I took a few drinks, took a few pills, smoked a little dope. As I got deeper into the quagmire of Hollywood, I lost my morality. This is where I ended up."

He called his discussions of the murder plot with Adams on the van tapes "asinine" and said there was no excuse for it. Although proclaiming his innocence, he blamed only himself for his predicament.

Despite the substantial investigative role played by IAD in his conviction, Ford expressed his loyalty to the police department. "They break their neck to get a call where they might die at in order to keep someone from getting hurt. If you print anything," he said, addressing a bank of reporters, "please, I want them to see that.

"I loved my country and I served it. I watched men die," said a weeping

Ford. "I took another oath and swore to protect and serve you, the public. I didn't do a very good job of that either. We lost the war in Vietnam and we lost the war in the streets too.

"I tarnished the badge and I let down the community, but it's wrong to blame them [the LAPD] for what I did."

Wiping tears from his eyes, Richard Ford pleaded with Judge Williams. "I don't want to die in some hole, I want to die in my wife's arms. I've never asked for anything in my life. I'm asking you now for a break. I'm an old man. I'm forty-seven, but I feel like a hundred and seven."

When it was his turn to address the court, Von Villas likewise proclaimed his innocence. "After nine months of trial, it took the jury only three and a half days to return a verdict. It just tears my guts out. In less than sixteen hours, a jury could be so sure of itself when a man's life is at stake. I was mad. I wanted to scream and yell, The jury's wrong!"

Calling himself "a proud cop," Von Villas apologized to his former colleagues for "that garbage they're taking right now about cops gone bad. I've watched the press take apart the Los Angeles Police Department. That's wrong. They didn't do anything. I tarnished the badge." He also apologized to all the kids he had counseled. "I want those kids to know I didn't lie to them. I always told them we are accountable for what we do."

Like Ford, Von Villas didn't place blame on anyone but himself. And like Ford, he also pleaded for a break. "I need to know I have something to go for," he told Williams.

It was an emotional three-hour hearing, and Judge Williams appeared to be genuinely moved. He marveled at the defendants' exceptional military and police records and noted "the personal tragedy that is inherent in their fall from grace." It appeared that Williams, a naval officer during the Vietnam War, was leaning toward leniency. He personally read into the record the commendation Von Villas had received with his Bronze Star, which described how he had risked his life to help save members of his platoon from a burning helicopter. He mentioned again and again their years of exemplary service.

"They grew up as all American kids. Both of them did what Americans were supposed to do and what about fifty thousand of them didn't come back from doing in Vietnam. They volunteered to serve their country and volunteered almost immediately to serve this community as police officers. I have nothing but highest respect and personal pain for what these gentlemen went through and their fall from grace."

But despite these sentiments, despite the anguished pleas by the defendants, Judge Williams proclaimed that mitigating factors were outweighed "by one overwhelming factor . . . and that is they were in fact police officers.

"There is another victim here," said Williams. "That victim is represented by the seven thousand men and women who protect the city wearing badges that these men sullied. I cannot overlook that these were men sworn to uphold the law."

Judge Williams imposed maximum terms of ten years plus twenty-five years to life for Von Villas and eleven years plus twenty-five years to life for Ford, who got the extra year for the one extra guilty count. And he made the sentences run consecutively.

They each had thirty-five years to life. With luck, they could be eligible for parole in about twenty-five years.

Judge Williams's decision proved an old saw: A convicted cop gets no mercy. Ford and Von Villas were both devastated. Hearing the pronouncement of sentence was too much for the two ex-supercops. They both broke down and sobbed.

But their ordeal was far from over. Ford and Von Villas now faced a possible date with the gas chamber.

26

Capital Case

"EX-OFFICERS' MURDER CASE GOES TO TRIAL" ANNOUNCED THE April 12, 1988, headline in the *Los Angeles Times*. The capital case against L.A.'s killer cops would serve up material for yet another nine months of newscasts and headlines. Once again, those who anticipated an open and shut case were in for a dizzying ride.

Standing before the glare of TV lights at Van Nuys Superior Court, defense attorneys expressed confidence that their clients would be proven innocent. They claimed that the State's case was built on circumstantial evidence and unreliable witnesses who had received immunity for their testimony. "They will testify because it is to their advantage to cooperate with the prosecution," Donald Feinberg stated. "Everybody has got something to sell."

Ford and Von Villas were charged with murder one with special circumstances (murder for financial gain) and conspiracy to commit murder. For the first time in history, two LAPD cops faced the death penalty.

A motion for change of vicinage had been granted, so the trial landed in the Van Nuys court of Judge Darlene E. Schempp. A diminutive woman with short blond hair and glasses that she often gazed over while reviewing briefs, Schempp was low-key, mild-mannered, patient, and cordial—qualities that would be sorely tested for the next nine months. A former court clerk and prosecutor, Schempp was a no-nonsense jurist. She would receive the highest marks from both sides of the aisle.

Assisting Deputy District Attorney Robert O'Neill in this trial was LAPD

266

detective Harry Eddo. Eddo had spent the past three years working due diligence—the ongoing attempt to locate Thomas Weed. Also assisting O'Neill was LAPD detective William Gailey, who had been working the case since its inception.

Richard Ford was again represented by Richard Lasting and Rickard Santwier, Von Villas by Jack Stone and Donald Feinberg. Defense counsels had motioned to sever the trials, but Judge Schempp ruled that Ford and Von Villas would be tried together but judged by separate juries. Jury selection took almost three months—once again, longer than entire murder trials in most states. Judge Schempp explained to the thirty-four chosen jurors (twenty-four sitting jurors plus ten alternates) that some testimony presented would apply only to Ford, some only to Von Villas, and some to both. Hence, throughout the trial, they would be shuffled in and out of court. She directed the jurors not to talk to members of the other jury and admonished them to avoid all media coverage of the trial.

Opening arguments began on July 5. Richard Ford, now forty-seven, looked smart in his light gray suit, his hair freshly cut. His wife, Lillian, sitting in the gallery with their twelve-year-old daughter, Christina, looked vibrant and upbeat. Von Villas, sharp as ever in dark pinstripes, smiled broadly at his wife, Judy, and his two daughters, Michele and Shannon. He became all business, however, as soon as Robert O'Neill rose to make his opening statement. Von Villas eyed O'Neill like a hawk throughout his opening address, as though determined to stare down his accuser.

O'Neill began by displaying to the jury a large color photograph of Thomas Weed, the alleged victim in this case of murder for hire. He explained that Jan Ogilvie, Weed's wife, had "a seething hatred" for Weed and was involved in bitter legal disputes with him. After a series of negotiations with Von Villas, who used the alias Mr. Ory, Ogilvie agreed to pay him $20,000 to have her husband killed. On February 23, 1983, Weed vanished without a trace. Von Villas later told Ogilvie, "Let's just say there's a lot of desert between here and Las Vegas."

In addition to crucial testimony by Ogilvie, O'Neill told the jury they would also hear from Joyce Reynolds and Julie Rabold, the two women who connected Ogilvie with Von Villas. O'Neill also previewed some of the corroborating evidence for his accusations: bank and phone records, the calendar seized from the Ford home with the square for February 23 blacked out, notes seized from Von Villas's car and Judy Von Villas's purse, and the December 20 conversation between Richard and Lillian Ford recorded at L.A. County Jail.

Richard Lasting presented the opening statement in defense of Richard Ford. Although not conceding that Weed was in fact dead, Lasting insisted "the evidence will not show that Richard Ford killed Thomas Weed." Rather, he explained, it would show that Bob Von Villas allegedly offered to kill Tom Weed. It would also show that Julie Rabold offered to get some Hell's Angels to kill Tom Weed; that Jan Ogilvie's attorney, Ron Brot, offered to get a mob hit man to kill Tom Weed; and that Jan Ogilvie had repeatedly threatened to kill Tom Weed herself. It would also show that two "mob types" from Vegas had come looking for Weed to collect on gambling debts.

Lasting presented a chart titled "Deals" and explained how the three major witnesses for the prosecution had all made deals with the D.A. Jan Ogilvie had pled to second-degree murder and would get only fifteen years—and would perhaps serve only eight—instead of the death penalty or life without parole. Joyce Reynolds, in exchange for her testimony, was given probation and the promise that her daughter Julie would be spared prosecution. Julie, in turn, was given full immunity. These witnesses, Lasting contended, all told the D.A. what he wanted to hear simply to save their own necks.

Lasting also told the jury he would prove that Jan Ogilvie was "a pathological liar" who had deceived everybody—friends, family, police—and had even perjured herself under oath. She was a woman with psychiatric problems who had her own agenda.

Jack Stone, attorney for Bob Von Villas, covered much the same ground. He called Ogilvie a woman with "an unparalleled ability to lie" and a "warped notion of what the real world was like. . . . The evidence you'll be hearing will be out of the mouths of convicted felons . . . admitted perjurers, and basically that's it. That, and a lot of suspicion and smoke."

July 6, the first day of testimony, began with Ford and Von Villas being introduced to the assembled juries. The two men stood, faced the thirty-four men and women, nodded hello, and smiled. Many jurors returned a warm smile, others seemed startled; these guys sure didn't look like criminals.

O'Neill began by presenting the prosecution's foundation witnesses. Lieutenant Vernon Higbee testified that Richard Ford had taken a five-day vacation over the Presidents' Day holiday, February 19 through 23, 1983, returning on the twenty-fourth. Von Villas, meanwhile, worked his regular day shift, 7:30 A.M. to 4:00 P.M., on February 22, 23, and 24. Darlis Chefalo again testified about making wigs and giving makeup lessons to "undercover narcs" Ford and Von Villas.

O'Neill also introduced evidence seized by IAD investigators, from notes to phone bills and the Ford family calendar. Easily the most dramatic, of course, was the jailhouse recording between Richard and Lillian Ford. While the tape was played in court, the jury was given transcripts so they could better follow the garbled conversation. They heard Ford making statements like:

"No way to tie me to it. . . . Is that the right dates? . . . We didn't put any money in the bank, did we? . . . What the hell did we do with it? . . . Good, there's no connection to me there. There's nothing there that connects me. . . . Don't worry about it. . . . They're fishing . . . it's just one more charge. . . . How you gonna prove it? . . . There's nooooo body. . . . The Shell credit card . . . I don't know if I got gas. . . . They got the idea but they don't have it, I don't think. . . . He's just gone. He's gone. They're trying to find out where he's at. . . . Game's not over yet. What worries me is the shotgun. The shells."

Although these excerpts seemed damning, Richard Lasting was able to soften their impact somewhat. He established, through cross-examination of Detective Jack Holder, the tape technician, that there were eight minutes and nine seconds of gaps on the twenty-five-minute tape, nearly as much unrecorded as recorded, and that it offered mostly a one-sided version of the conversation "so you have to guess, speculate, to know what is being said."

But the defense's full explanation of the tape would have to wait.

Jan Ogilvie, now forty-five, had already pled guilty to second-degree murder and conspiracy and could be sentenced to fifteen years to life; she was to be sentenced at the end of the trial. She had spent her last four years in custody at the Sybil Brand Institute for Women in downtown Los Angeles.

A plump, pear-shaped black woman, Dr. Ogilvie favored floral print dresses and wore her hair up in a bun. She glided slowly into the courtroom each day with the smooth movement of a ghost. She proved to be soft-spoken, with a calm and pleasant demeanor, almost sweet at times. But from the moment she began to testify, it was apparent that she was uncommonly intelligent and articulate— and carried a lot of heavy baggage. Knowing she had admitted to hiring someone to kill her husband gave her sweetness a sinister edge. Indeed, before her three weeks of testimony came to an end, the portrait that would emerge of Dr. Jan Ogilvie would be cause for some troubled deliberation in the jury rooms.

LAPD investigators, court hounds, and reporters had all come to refer to her as "The Black Widow." Remarkably, this handle never made it into the press, perhaps because editors considered it politically incorrect. During less delicate times, when papers didn't blanch at the sensational, headlines over the trial coverage would have screamed with this reference.

Under questioning by Robert O'Neill, Dr. Ogilvie told the story of her troubled marriage to Thomas Weed, of being physically and verbally abused, of how her divorce and partnership became legally tangled, of suits and counter-suits, and of how she cried on the shoulders of her employees at the Ford/Kennedy Medical Laboratory. At a lunch in the fall of 1982, Julie Rabold had told her, "Why don't you just hire a hit man and get rid of him?" She also indicated to Ogilvie that she knew someone who could "take care of" Weed for her. At the time, Ogilvie didn't take the suggestions seriously.

Later, as her problems with Weed escalated, Julie Rabold again suggested that Ogilvie hire a hit man. She told Ogilvie she knew some Hell's Angels who could do it. She also told her she had friends at Devonshire Division who could take care of Weed. In mid-December, at a restaurant called Wolfies in Reseda, Joyce Reynolds made the same suggestion.

On New Year's Day, 1983, at 8:00 A.M., two men came to the door of Ogilvie's home. She noticed they were driving a Lincoln Continental with Nevada plates. They told her they were looking for Tom Weed. They had some "business" with him. Ogilvie assumed it was about some gambling debts because people had come looking for Tom a few times before. Weed, she said, played the horses, football, cards—anything.

Later, Ogilvie told police these two men identified themselves as "Vic and Charlie." Now, however, she testified that she had been lying. "There was an investigation at the time about Tom [Weed's disappearance], and I was nervous about it." The significance of the names Vic and Charlie would be made apparent later in her testimony.

At a lunch meeting in mid-January 1983, Joyce Reynolds again suggested that she have Weed "taken care of." It was then that Reynolds first mentioned the name of her friend, Bob.

"I thought about it," Ogilvie testified, as she broke down in tears on the stand. "I was just tired." The tears seemed genuine, as did Ogilvie's remorse. The jury appeared to buy her tale of an abused woman reaching the end of her rope. Judge Schempp called a fifteen-minute recess so Ogilvie could compose herself.

When Ogilvie resumed her tale, she told of going to court for a divorce hearing in January. Tom Weed had filed a suit contesting funds taken out of the lab and the court ordered Ogilvie to put $50,000 of these disputed funds in a trust fund, pending resolution. It also ordered both of them to stay away from each other. A few days after that hearing, at about 6:00 P.M., two men showed up unexpectedly at Ogilvie's home on Justice Street in Canoga Park. They told her their names were Vic and Charlie and that they were Devonshire Division police officers. Although they were wearing disguises, Ogilvie identified them as Von Villas (Vic) and Ford (Charlie), to whom she pointed in turn in the courtroom.

Vic did most of the talking. He told Ogilvie he had heard she was having trouble with her husband. He told her that they had some mutual friends, Joyce Reynolds and Julie Rabold, and that he and Charlie could help her with her problem.

"What do you mean?" Ogilvie asked.

"We can take care of the guy for you," said Vic.

"What do you mean?" Ogilvie asked again.

"Well, we can either hurt him real bad or he can just disappear," Vic answered as Charlie paced around the room. "You're looking at anywhere from seventy-five hundred to thirty thousand dollars."

Ogilvie said she was stunned and didn't know what to say. She told them she'd have to think about it. Vic told her that if she decided to take them up on it she should get hold of Joyce.

Ogilvie explained that the two men didn't look at all the way Ford and Von Villas looked now. She said she could tell Vic was wearing a wig because it was a little too busy and puffed up. It was brown with some gray in it. He had a mustache but no beard. His complexion was dark, but it looked like makeup. His face was darker than his hands. He wore an olive drab fatigue jacket and a khaki green army shirt. O'Neill produced two such items that had been seized from Von Villas's closet. Ogilvie didn't give a positive ID, just a maybe.

Charlie also had gray hair that "didn't look like it fit the man." He also had dark skin, but no facial hair. He wore a tweed jacket with a white turtleneck sweater. "Yeah, that looks like the sweater," Ogilvie said when O'Neill produced a white turtleneck. But she couldn't say it was definitely *the* sweater.

The next day Ogilvie talked about this visit with three of her employees— Diane Shamis, Elzo Perkins, and Pat Smart—whose versions of these conversations were all later picked apart. Ogilvie said she received four or five calls from Vic after that first meeting, although he never identified himself. He just said, "I'm calling about our meeting the other night."

One evening at the end of January, Ogilvie met Joyce Reynolds at Darby's restaurant off Sherman Way. After they left they drove around in the rain. Ogilvie told Joyce that Tom was still threatening her, that she was fed up. She told Joyce she wanted to get in touch with her friends, but she was concerned about their being cops. Could they be trusted? Reynolds told her yes, but she would have to pay them well. Ogilvie told her all she had available was $20,000. Reynolds told her she'd get in touch with Bob and give him Ogilvie's home number.

Reynolds called Ogilvie back the next night and told her that Bob would call, but that he would use the name Mr. Ory. He called the next night. "I understand from Joyce you want to go ahead with the plan to take care of Tom," he said. He told her he would need a dossier on Tom—a physical description, his address, phone, his schedule and work habits, places he frequented, description and license number of his car. Ogilvie put the information together and gave it to Mr. Ory when he called back a few days later. Ory told her he had to determine how difficult the job would be before he could get back to her with the price. Four days later he called and told her it would cost $20,000. He said he worked with guys from out of town, that a guy named Dickie would call her back. But she never got a call from Dickie.

Instead, Mr. Ory called back and told her that she would have to make three payments—$7,500, $5,000, and a final $7,500 when the job was done. He gave her instructions on how to make the drop for the first payment during the first week of February. Mr. Ory told her to get the money in fifties and hundreds, put it in an envelope, and drop it through the driver's window of a red car parked behind a Standard gas station at the corner of Roscoe and Reseda boulevards in Northridge. He told her someone would be watching her. Ogilvie found a "burgundy Chevy or Pontiac" parked along the wall behind the station and did as instructed. O'Neill entered pictures of Von Villas's red Chevy Camaro as evidence. "That looks like the car," Ogilvie stated.

Mr. Ory contacted her the night of the first drop and told her he had received the money and would let her know when to make the second payment. A few days later, around the middle of February, he gave her an address on the 6000 block of Reseda Boulevard and told her to drop the five thousand dollars through the open window of a white van. Ogilvie asked him what would happen to Weed. "Well, they're never going to find him," Mr. Ory said. "Let's just say there's a lot of desert between here and Las Vegas."

Ogilvie, however, didn't make that drop. Instead, she gave the money to her attorney, Ron Brot, whom she met at Charley Brown's, a restaurant in Marina Del Ray near Brot's office. Ogilvie said she was tired and also had a previous commitment, so she asked him to drop it off for her. She told Brot what the money was for and "he didn't try to encourage me or discourage me. He was neutral." Brot took the money from her, but instead of dropping it in the van, he used it to buy cocaine.

Ogilvie got a call from Mr. Ory late that night. He was upset because the money drop hadn't been made. Ogilvie called her attorney and yelled at him but she never got the money back. She put together another five thousand dollars and made new arrangements with Mr. Ory. On February 20 or 21, she dropped the money into a different car at the same gas station as the first drop.

On February 22, Ogilvie and Weed attended a city attorney's OSC (order to show cause) hearing regarding assault charges the couple had filed against each other. The city attorney declined to pursue criminal charges in either complaint, telling them they could take it up in civil court. Weed called Ogilvie that evening and gloated over the decision, which enraged her. She talked to Mr. Ory later that night and told him to "do it."

On February 23, Ogilvie talked to Tom Weed again to tell him that both of their signatures were needed on some insurance forms. Her son T.J.'s car had been wrecked and repaired, but the auto shop wouldn't release the car until they had both signed the papers. She never spoke to Weed again. Ogilvie went to the auto shop at four o'clock and signed a check and the papers.

On February 25, Ogilvie received a call from Mr. Ory. "You owe me seventy-five hundred dollars," he said. He gave her the location of the final drop—a white van parked at Oxnard and Reseda boulevards. "It's all been taken care of," he said. He told her not to let anything happen to the last drop. "He said he knew where my son went to school and he knew his route home." Ogilvie dropped off the last payment as directed.

Bank officials would later testify that Von Villas deposited eight thousand dollars in fifty and hundred dollar bills into his account on February 22, 25, and 28. To explain this damning evidence, the Von Villas defense presented testimony from Bill Justice, a jeweler, who stated that he bought sixty-six diamonds from Bob Von Villas in late 1982, paying him a total of $6,800 in cash.

During the ensuing investigation to locate Thomas Weed, Ogilvie had avoided talking to police as much as possible, often canceling interviews with detectives at the last minute. When she did talk, she told them Weed was probably living with his ex-wife in Fresno, or with his sister in Canada, or somewhere in Mexico, where he once owned a home. She told them Weed had often used the names Michael White and Roy Stevens when he worked as a bill collector—which was true—and could be traveling under an assumed name. She claimed, erroneously, that she had received calls from Weed after his disappearance and even forged his name on some documents. "I wanted to make it appear he was still alive." Later, she contacted a detective agency and asked them to look for Weed. "It was a smoke screen," explained Ogilvie. "That way I could say I looked for him."

Police obtained a search warrant in December 1983 to search the Ford/Kennedy Medical Laboratory and Ogilvie's home. Tucked away in a drawer of her desk at the lab, they found a newspaper clipping of a September 30, 1983, *Los Angeles Times* article about Ford and Von Villas. The headline read "2 Officers Reportedly Got Disguises." Attached to the clipping was a note from an employee, Diane Shamis, which read, "Hope you're sleeping well."

On January 9, 1984, Ogilvie sent an anonymous letter to LAPD detective

William Gailey, who was heading the investigation into Weed's disappearance. In this rambling, unsigned, four-page diatribe, Ogilvie sought to remove suspicion from herself and focus it on two of her former employees, Diane Shamis and Elzo Perkins, with whom she was involved in a legal dispute over her Phoenix lab.

Ogilvie testified that following a car accident in 1978, in which she suffered a mild concussion, she experienced problems with headaches, blurred vision and memory loss. She was treated at UCLA Medical Center, however, and had experienced no problems with her memory after the time she met Tom Weed. She also testified that after her arrest, in February 1984, she saw a jailhouse therapist and was treated for depression and anxiety. She was prescribed Haldol, a tranquilizer similar to lithium, but she had an allergic reaction to it and was then given Mellaril.

She decided to cooperate with authorities while in jail because she was overcome by guilt. "I had reviewed some of the evidence, which was basically true, and I was feeling very guilty. I was feeling terrible." She said she signed her final agreement with the D.A. of her own volition and with no reservations.

Ogilvie was subjected to a brutal cross-examination that went on for two weeks. This time around, Donald Feinberg and Rickard Santwier did the honors. Both attorneys tried to lead and browbeat Dr. Ogilvie. As during Adams's cross-examination in the first trial, Bob O'Neill showed remarkable restraint, demonstrating confidence in the fortitude of his witness. Throughout the questioning, Ford and Von Villas busily paged through transcripts, highlighting sections with yellow markers, then passing them along to their attorneys. Most of these transcripts were of interviews between Ogilvie and Robert Jorgensen, the original D.A. on the case.

Donald Feinberg, counsel for Bob Von Villas, a short, bespectacled man in his forties, first focused on the deal Ogilvie had made with Jorgensen, questioning her about the many interviews she had had. He frequently tried to lead Ogilvie, saying things like, "So you decided you had something of value the prosecution wanted." His premise was that Ogilvie, over many months of questioning by investigators, was "auditioning" for a deal—tailoring her testimony from interview to interview to meet the needs of the D.A.

"Isn't it true that your getting a deal all depended on what you had to say and its value in the eyes of the prosecution?"

"I suppose that's true," answered Ogilvie. "But I understand the deal was made when I agreed to tell the truth."

"Isn't it a fact that your sentence depends on your performance in this case? Suppose you said now that you made this all up—pulled out of the deal—what would be the effect?"

"I suppose I would probably go to trial."

"Did Jorgensen suggest the way the answers should go?"

"I never felt that."

Feinberg examined numerous "changes" in the evolution of Ogilvie's story, huffing and puffing with righteous indignation over each and every one. Was it really such a problem that Ogilvie described the money drop car as "burgundy" in one interview and "red" in another? Feinberg's reaction came off as a bit histrionic, yet the combined weight of these "adjustments" in her story was troublesome. Under a similar grilling later by Rickard Santwier, Ogilvie would flatly admit that she "had not been consistent" in relating the turn of events. Both attorneys charged that Ogilvie had been led by police, that she was told before viewing photos which car belonged to Von Villas, that she learned about wigs and disguises from the *Los Angeles Times* clip found in her desk and added that to her story after it was first suggested by D.A. Jorgensen.

It was hard to determine just how troubling all this would be to the jury. Was Ogilvie lying, as the defense would insist, or just having trouble recalling details?

At one point, Ogilvie admitted that she had no proof Weed was dead, but she stated, "I don't think he just disappeared. I paid to have him killed."

"Nobody sent you an ear or a finger?" Feinberg asked.

"No."

Feinberg asked if she had ever told anyone that she was "capable of committing the perfect crime; you just make them disappear."

"No."

"Did you ever tell Ruth Caplan [Tom Weed's sister], 'Don't let anyone push you around in this world. It's easy to scatter their bones. I'm just the gal that can do it'?"

"No, I'd never call myself a gal. I think Ruth Caplan is lying."

Feinberg asked if she wrote a letter to Ruth Caplan in which she stated, "I have taken a lot of abuse [from Weed] and it has made me angrier than I thought possible. It is deep. I frequently shudder when I think my rage is sufficient to rip the flesh off his bones."

"It was a figure of speech I used, yes."

Feinberg questioned her about her volatile moods. "One minute you want to kill him, the next you'd have sex with him? Isn't that true?"

"No."

"That quote about the desert, you made that up, didn't you?" Feinberg charged, raising his voice. "That came from your own murderous rage!"

Ogilvie remained cool. "No," she said.

"Didn't you tell him [Weed] you would kill him and plead to a lesser charge and walk away? Wasn't he worried about you taking gun lessons, didn't he write that?"

"No."

Feinberg questioned her at length about Vic and Charlie. She had testified that the shorter one was Vic (Von Villas), about five foot seven, and the taller one was Charlie (Ford), at five foot ten to six feet tall.

Feinberg asked both defendants to rise, had them remove their shoes, and stand together. As Ford grinned, Feinberg measured with a tape measure. Both proved to be about five foot ten.

"Could you be mistaken about their heights?"

"Yes."

"Could you be mistaken about them coming to your home?"

"No. I'm not mistaken about that."

"The whole business about Vic and Charlie was made up by you, wasn't it?"

"No."

Feinberg questioned her about medications she was taking and problems in the past with memory loss, about a psychiatric history that included reports of delusions of grandeur, an inability to separate fact from fantasy, of hearing voices and having hallucinations. He asked about wild statements she had made in the past, like telling people her son T.J. was really the son of her sister, who'd been raped by an uncle. He questioned her about an incident in 1977 when she "found herself" in Nashville without knowing how she got there. He asked about her suffering from "pernicious amnesia" following a car accident. Ogilvie admitted to past problems with memory but claimed she had had none since 1978. She also stated that she had not been taking Mellaril on days she testified at the preliminary hearings.

Feinberg next turned his attention to Ron Brot, Ogilvie's attorney. Ogilvie admitted that she paid $32,000 to Brot and his firm ($20,000 solely to Brot) and talked with him repeatedly on the phone around the time of Weed's disappearance. She once mentioned Julie's hit man suggestion and Brot commented that "it was done all the time." He told her he knew someone named No Neck who could do it. She admitted she knew he was doing drugs and had left his firm under a cloud and she was concerned about him handling her affairs. On the evening she gave him $5,000 to make a drop for Mr. Ory, she was tired and had a meeting to go to, she believed in Palos Verdes. It was some professional group, but she couldn't remember which.

"You gave him five thousand dollars for a drop and he put it up his nose?"

"Correct."

"You drove thirty miles [from the Valley to Marina Del Rey] to give the money to somebody else to drive thirty miles all the way back to Reseda, which was five minutes away from you?"

"Brot had a commitment in the Valley and he said he could do it. I just wasn't in any shape to drive or make the arrangement."

"Did you fire him?"

"No. The next day, we screamed and yelled."

"And you paid him another four thousand dollars in March—after he'd taken that five thousand dollars?"

"I was convinced the case was complicated and I didn't want to switch attorneys."

Feinberg asked why Brot never sent her bills. She had no paperwork to show for all the money she paid him.

"He always told me verbally what I owed him."

"What did Brot get out of this? Nothing? You're just friends?"

"Yes."

Feinberg presented a chart of checks Ogilvie had given to Brot between January 26 and March 17, 1983. "Ms. Ogilvie, do you think it's just a coincidence that you claim that you paid twenty thousand dollars for the murder of your husband and you paid Mr. Brot almost that exact figure?" Feinberg asked.

"I think that's a coincidence," Ogilvie responded. "It has to be a coincidence." She said the $20,000 was to cover Brot's fees for representing her in divorce and civil proceedings against Weed.

Presenting phone records, Feinberg showed that Ogilvie had made an 85-minute call to Brot the day before Weed's disappearance and a 77-minute call on the day of his disappearance. Asked about these, Ogilvie said she couldn't remember what she and Brot had talked about on those two occasions. She also had a conversation with Brot for 242 minutes—4 hours—on February 14, which she said was about the OSC hearing. "We had lots of conversations," she said.

Feinberg opened up a broadside attack. "Isn't it a fact, Ms. Ogilvie, that you and Mr. Brot conceived of a plan to take care of your husband—to permanently eliminate your husband?" Feinberg asked.

"That's not true," said Ogilvie.

"Isn't it true that Mr. Brot told you he had a person named No Neck who was involved with organized crime who could do the killing?" Feinberg asked.

"Yes, at one time," Ogilvie stated.

"And isn't it a fact that as you sit here you are still afraid, still fearful of drawing any connection between Mr. Brot and what happened to your husband because of what could happen to you?"

"No."

"Isn't it a fact that you have lied from the beginning, that you have accused people who are innocent of committing crimes of which you and perhaps your attorney, Mr. Brot, committed?"

"That is not true," Ogilvie replied.

Feinberg stated that he planned to subpoena Ron Brot later in the trial.

It was now time for Rickard Santwier, Ford's attorney, to take up the attack. He began by reviewing Ogilvie's background: a PhD in public administration from USC in 1972; master's degree in labor management relations from Michigan State in 1968; BS in social science from Tennessee State in 1964. Then Santwier recited a list of false statements Ogilvie had allegedly made about her past—that she had terminal cancer, that she'd been raped by an older uncle, that T.J. was adopted, that she had taught at UCLA and worked for the coroner's office. She denied ever having made such claims.

Santwier also probed her apparent duplicitousness. Despite her bitter war with Weed, Ogilvie admitted to twice spending the night with him over the 1982 Christmas holidays. She also claimed that in late January she was pulled over on the street by two gambling-debt collectors, to whom she later paid five thousand dollars. "So, while you were negotiating his killing," Santwier asked, "you paid off his gambling debt to keep him from getting hurt?"

"No. It was to keep them from hurting me," Ogilvie said.

On redirect, Bob O'Neill asked Ogilvie if she had in fact pled guilty to second-degree murder, accepted a sentence of fifteen years to life, and if she knew that Tom Weed's family could speak at her parole hearings. Ogilvie broke down and cried as she answered in the affirmative. Under additional questioning, she displayed even more guilt as she sobbed, "It's the same thing, paying to kill and doing the killing."

O'Neill ran through a number of details in an effort to rehabilitate his witness. Ogilvie explained that Weed was abusive only when he drank. Later, he would tell her he didn't remember doing it and she believed him. That's why she temporarily reconciled with him on a few occasions. O'Neill also had her go through a long list of professional groups she belonged to, like Women in Management and the National Institute of Health Advisory Council. Obviously, she couldn't be expected to remember which meeting was when.

O'Neill also established that Ogilvie was used to paying excessive fees to attorneys. Before hiring Ron Brot, she had paid famed divorce attorney Marvin Mitchelson a nonrefundable $10,000 retainer. A month later she dropped him and paid another $10,000 to Brot's firm. The picture O'Neill presented was of a woman who required a lot of hand-holding by her attorney and was willing to pay for it. He presented a chart showing fifteen phone calls made to Mitchelson's office in one month, forty-one calls to Brot in November 1982, forty-three calls in December—and that did not include return calls. O'Neill's point—that she spent a lot of time talking with attorneys—was a point well made.

"If you give false statements, you could be prosecuted for perjury, couldn't you?" O'Neill asked.

"Yes."

"Do you have any doubt that these men are Vic and Charlie?" O'Neill asked, pointing to Von Villas and Ford.

"No."

Donald Feinberg took a few more shots on recross. "The question is, who did you pay to have him killed?" Feinberg cried. "It doesn't make a difference to you who you accuse, does it?"

"No, it does make a difference."

"What does an oath mean to you? Which is more important to you, telling the truth or getting out of jail?"

"Telling the truth."

"Doesn't your getting out depend on what the prosecutor says at your parole hearing?"

"Yes."

"You started out auditioning for Jorgensen. Aren't you still auditioning for the D.A.?"

"No."

"Do you think you would have had a deal if you said Brot did it?" he asked. O'Neill objected; it was sustained.

"If you said it wasn't these two men," Feinberg cried, pointing at Ford and Von Villas, "you wouldn't get your deal, isn't that true?"

O'Neill objected and the objection was again sustained.

"You knew Ford and Von Villas had been arrested on some other charges?"

"Yes."

"You felt you'd still have a deal if you identified someone else?"

"Yes."

"You're not telling us everything about your relationship with Brot, isn't that true?"

"No."

It was hard to tell whether the grillings by defense counsel had weakened Ogilvie in the eyes of the jury. Some observers felt the attacks had actually made her more sympathetic—a sobbing, guilt-ridden woman being browbeaten while trying to tell the truth. Others felt the attacks had inflicted critical damage to her story.

27

Pathological

BOB O'NEILL'S NEXT WITNESS WAS THE VICTIM'S FIRST WIFE, BETTY Weed. A slight blond woman with glasses, Ms. Weed proved to be an effective witness. She came equipped with notes and was very precise with dates and details.

Betty and Tom Weed had been married for twenty-eight years, from 1952 until 1980. They had lived in Toronto, Canada, until they moved to San Diego in 1977, primarily for a change of weather.

Tom Weed changed after they got to California. He went out and got a curly blond wig and new clothes—white pants and shoes and loud shirts—and spent a lot of time out in the sun. He owned a soda shop in San Diego for two years, then sold recreational vehicles, and eventually became a bill collector. He frequently used aliases in this occupation.

The couple separated in February 1980 because Tom wanted a different lifestyle. He was forty-eight and going through a major midlife crisis. When the couple broke up, Betty moved to Fresno and Tom moved to L.A.

After their divorce, Betty and Tom remained close friends and talked to each other frequently. The last days she talked to him were February 14, 15, and 21 of 1983. "I could never get him after the twenty-first. I tried every day between the twenty-first and twenty-eighth [Tom's birthday], but there was no answer." Betty finally called Tom's sister in Canada and then Donald Slayton, Tom Weed's attorney in L.A., who in turn eventually went to the police.

"Tom was not the type who ran from his problems. He stood up to his problems," Betty insisted. "He would definitely contact me if he were alive." She also stated he would never just disappear, even for a few days.

Betty Weed had never met Jan Ogilvie but had spoken to her three times on the phone. They were bitter exchanges. Ogilvie resented that Tom kept in touch with his ex-wife. On one occasion, Ogilvie sent Betty a scathing eleven-page letter.

Under cross-examination by defense attorneys, Betty presented a picture of Tom Weed that was entirely different from the one painted by Jan Ogilvie. Tom Weed had a duodenal ulcer and was not a drinker. He was an athlete who jogged five miles a day, and he never took drugs. Although they had belonged to a turf club in Toronto, Tom was never a heavy gambler or a deadbeat who had bill collectors chasing him, and he was not a woman hater. During her twenty-eight years of marriage to him, he had never hit her or treated her badly, never driven her to a "murderous rage."

Donald Feinberg read Ogilvie's words from the letter she sent her: "Tom is a thoroughly ruthless and conniving person, a woman hater."

"That's her opinion," Betty scoffed. Asked her opinion of Ogilvie's truthfulness: "She was not one-hundred-percent honest."

On redirect by O'Neill, Betty did allow that she wasn't entirely familiar with Tom's lifestyle after 1980.

Betty Weed's testimony was supported by additional witnesses, including Ruth Caplan, Tom Weed's sister. Caplan testified that "Tom would never run away and disappear. When he said he would call, he'd call." She talked to her brother on the February 20 and he told her he was going to call on the twenty-fourth. She never heard from him again.

Caplan testified that an angry Ogilvie once told her on the phone, "I could have him [Weed] run down. People down here will do that for five hundred dollars." Once, while Caplan was visiting in L.A., Ogilvie told her, "Don't let anyone push you around in this world. It's easy to scatter their bones." She also said that "she knew how to commit the perfect crime . . . I know the law. It's a challenge to outsmart people. I can get away with anything. Just chop them up in little pieces and scatter them all around."

"It was just words, mouthing off," said Caplan. "She was in a bad mood . . . We were talking about the feminist movement and our attitudes toward men."

Caplan testified that later, when going through Weed's papers, she had found a note in which Weed had written, "Jan threatened to kill me today," but it was not dated. "Tom said he was scared [Ogilvie might try to kill him] but he was careful. He said he didn't run in the morning anymore. He didn't open the doors unless he knew who was there." (Nonetheless, the manager of Weed's apartment complex would later testify that the parking garage under the building had no security.)

After Caplan was dismissed, witnesses were called to testify to Weed's last sightings. Warden Black of Grand Prix Autobody in Canoga Park testified that Tom Weed came to sign an insurance form for his stepson's car sometime between three-thirty and four-thirty on the afternoon of February 23. Black was the last person who ever saw Tom Weed.

Donald Slayton, Tom Weed's attorney, described the break up of the Weed-Ogilvie partnership and marriage as "a legal quagmire" of filings, actions, and counteractions, battery charges, and civil suits. Four actions were still pending at the time of Weed's disappearance. "My opinion was that Weed was entitled to thirty-five percent of the business, which was worth six hundred thousand dollars. We offered to settle for a hundred and fifty thousand. They offered fifty thousand."

Slayton last saw Weed at the hearing on February 22, when the city attorney decided not to pursue either battery charge criminally, telling the couple to take it up in civil court. Weed and Ogilvie hollered and screamed at each other and both lawyers had to quiet their clients. Slayton stated that Weed had no intention of leaving, that he was planning to set up his own lab. After not hearing from him for over two weeks, Slayton finally filed a missing persons report on his client on March 12.

Questioned by Jack Stone, Slayton said that his total billings to Weed were less than $10,000. He also stated, "More than once, Weed told me if we didn't settle the case, Jan might put him away. He told me she said friends could handle it. If there's no body, there's no murder charge. He was very upset, nervous, shook up most of the time I talked to him. He said he was afraid she would carry it out, that maybe we should settle." Slayton also stated that he never saw Tom drunk and had no knowledge of any gambling debts.

Detective James Lewis, who handled the missing persons report, described Weed's apartment when he and Donald Slayton had gone there on March 16. "It looked like he [Weed] walked out to get a paper and didn't return."

Lewis also examined Weed's car when it was recovered. It was extremely dusty, as if it had been driven in the desert. There were some buttons and heavy twine in the backseat. Several different brands of cigarette butts were in the ashtray. Lying on the dashboard was a map of Wyoming. Also found was a small box of matches from Hamburger Hamlet. (Defense attorneys claimed this incriminated Ron Brot, who frequently met with Ogilvie at Hamburger Hamlet.) Police criminologists later testified that they couldn't derive any blood types from saliva on the two Benson and Hedges, three Marlboro, and two unidentified cigarette butts in Weed's car ashtray. No prints were found on or in the car—it had been wiped down. The print guys found one latent print on the Wyoming map. It was unmatched and unknown, belonging to neither Weed, Ford, nor Von Villas.

Lewis testified that he contacted Jan Ogilvie and she told him that Weed was "voluntarily missing" and that Ruth Caplan would know where he was. She told him that Weed was an alcoholic and a drug abuser. Donald Slayton later alerted the detective that Ogilvie might be involved in Weed's disappearance. Lewis tried to have a face-to-face meeting with Ogilvie, calling her about thirty times. She kept making appointments to see him and then canceling. She evaded him until July 1983, when the case was reassigned to Sergeant Fox at IAD.

On cross-examination, Lewis testified that some of the cigarette butts found in Weed's car had lipstick prints. Also, evidence-gathering specialists had not been brought to Weed's apartment because there was no indication of foul play. And, although Ogilvie had told him Weed was an alcoholic, Lewis found no bottles at his apartment.

O'Neill next presented witnesses to show that Weed had left money ($1,600) in his bank account and safe deposit box, that his credit cards had gone unused, payments had been missed, and projects abandoned since February 23, 1983.

Detective Harry Eddo, O'Neill's assistant in this case, then spent most of a day on the stand describing his exhaustive due diligence search for the missing Thomas Weed. A husky, good-looking guy in his early thirties, Eddo had spent the last three years of his life attempting to find Tom Weed.

A due diligence investigation was essential in this case, since the prosecution bore the burden of disproving, or at least dismissing as unreasonable, any claims by the defense that Weed was still alive. This was crucial in any murder trial where no body has been found. One could not expect a jury to convict unless they were convinced, beyond a reasonable doubt, that the victim was in fact dead, rather than just missing.

O'Neill walked Eddo through everything he had checked, category by category. Eddo had called every single number in Weed's personal phone book and had contacted everyone he could find who had ever known the man. He had checked all possible means of escape from L.A.—airlines, travel agencies, buses, boats, trains, taxis. He'd checked hospitals, the coroner's, city agencies, utilities, social services, land records. Anything a human could use or buy that required taxes, permits, licenses, registration, contact with a state, county, or city agency, he explored. Churches. Dating services. Credit bureaus and unions. Banks. Eddo's thoroughness was impressive. The jury looked convinced when he was only about a quarter of the way through his testimony. It didn't seem likely that Tom Weed could still be alive.

On cross-examination, defense attorneys picked away at Eddo, finding stones here and there that had been left unturned. Although the defense would not argue strongly that Weed was still alive, neither would they concede he was dead. As long as there was no body, Weed could be among the living. They made sure to impress upon the jury that, however remote, this was always a possibility.

On July 27, O'Neill called Julie Rabold Kanoske to the stand. A petite and attractive girl in her mid-twenties, Julie described how she had known Bob Von Villas and his family since 1970, having met him through the DAPs program when she was nine. Von Villas was "like a father figure." She worked for Ogilvie as a medical technician, drawing blood from clients and examining it under a microscope. Tom Weed was rude to her, mean, abusive. "I hated him," she testified.

"Beyond hate?" O'Neill asked.

"Yes."

"You wanted harm to come to him?"

"Yes."

Weed was drinking almost every day, Julie claimed. He yelled at Jan Ogilvie all the time. Julie also was a target for his verbal abuse, and she had told both her mother and Bob Von Villas how much she hated him. One day at lunch she suggested to Ogilvie that she hire a hit man and "blow the bastard away," but Jan hadn't taken her seriously.

"Did you love Jan Ogilvie?" O'Neill asked.

"Yes."

"Did you lie to the grand jury?"

"Yes, to protect my mom and I."

Neither defense team chose to cross-examine the witness. Courtroom observers were shocked, as were Judge Schempp and Bob O'Neill. Apparently the defense was stockpiling all its ammo for the next witness, who was far more crucial.

Joyce Aleta Reynolds, Julie's mother, testified that Bob Von Villas was like a brother. Reynolds worked as an administrator in a doctor's office. She had met Jan Ogilvie through Julie and they had become good friends. Jan became emotionally agitated and cried a lot when talking about Weed. "I told her she should get a hit man, for the first time, in September or October, and she laughed."

Joyce suggested it again later and Jan took her seriously. Finally, at a rainy-night meeting at Darby's restaurant, Jan was in Joyce's car, crying. She said she was tired and wanted Tom out of her life forever. She said Tom Weed threatened to tell her son T.J. about his true origins. "Jan said that a young girl had been raped by an older uncle. The vivid way she talked, I was under the impression it was her. I told her Bob did work for money. She said she had twenty thousand dollars available."

"You mentioned the name Bob Von Villas to her?"

"Yes."

Reynolds explained what happened next: "I went home and called Von Villas. I asked him if he remembered Jan Ogilvie, the one having problems with her husband. I told him she wanted him killed. He said he could do it. He started giving me a list of things I should ask her for—a picture, a description of his car. Then he changed his mind. He said he would talk to Jan and ask her himself. He didn't want me involved. I gave him her numbers. He told me to tell her that he'd call and use the name Mr. Ory."

Some time later, while talking to Von Villas, she inquired about Tom Weed. "He said, 'The only thing I can tell you is that there's a lot of desert between here and Las Vegas. Julie doesn't have to worry about Tom Weed anymore.' He told me Tom Weed was dead."

Reynolds explained that she had lied to the grand jury in February 1984 to protect herself and Julie. She had been arrested on July 16, 1984 (a year after Ford and Von Villas) and had spent seven months in jail before making a deal to testify for the D.A.

O'Neill asked Reynolds about the statement Von Villas had made to her at the 1982 Christmas party. "He said he was tired of being an honest cop, that he got in as much trouble being an honest cop as he would if he were a dishonest cop. He asked me to keep him in mind if I heard of any jobs, anything people wanted done—prostitution, murder for hire, nothing was too big or too small. He would do anything for money."

Reynolds also testified that in August 1983, Von Villas had called her from the county jail and asked her to borrow $30,000 from Jan Ogilvie as a loan for his wife and kids. Reynolds, however, hadn't called Jan Ogilvie.

During cross examination, Ford's attorney, Richard Lasting, had one important question: "Did you ever hear of Richard Ford before your arrest?"

"No," Reynolds answered.

When it was his turn to question the witness, Jack Stone zeroed in on Reynolds's deal with the D.A. He walked her through her own personal nightmare—being arrested, imprisoned at Sybil Brand, where she had undergone a painful and traumatic radical mastectomy for breast cancer. Until the preliminary hearing, she had been a defendant along with Ford and Von Villas.

"You sat there at the table with Ford and Von Villas, didn't you?" Stone asked, pointing at the defendants.

"Yes."

"You were aware that Ogilvie had made a deal."

"Yes, I heard her tell lies about me."

Stone charged that Joyce knew what prosecutors were looking for and decided that she had better give it to them because she was facing hard time—maybe even the death penalty. "On January fourteenth, 1985, Jan Ogilvie testified at the preliminary hearing. She testified for eight days. Shortly thereafter your attorney approached Jorgensen. . . . At first, you told the police that you asked Von Villas if he could 'help' Jan Ogilvie, not kill Tom Weed. Sergeant Gailey said, 'Come on, Joyce, you're not telling us the whole truth.' Later, you realized they were interested in Von Villas and you could help them. . . . So you changed your story on January twenty-fifth, 1985. That's the first time you told about the 'anything for money' statement at the Christmas party. On July sixteenth, when you were arrested, Officers Gailey and Theiss asked you, 'What made you think Bob would do it? Bob had to say something in the past to give you the impression he wasn't an honest cop.' That's why you later had to make up that statement."

"No."

"You heard Jan Ogilvie say, 'Lots of desert between here and Las Vegas,' so you said the same thing."

"No."

Defense attorneys would later grill Detective Gailey and Lieutenant Roger Fox about their early interviews with Julie Rabold and Joyce Reynolds in July and August 1983. They would argue that Rabold and Reynolds later constructed their stories partly from information gathered during their questioning.

Stone suggested that the Christmas party conversation had been taken out of context. Von Villas had just learned he was being suspended and was expressing his frustration and disillusionment through facetious exaggeration. Stone questioned Reynolds as to whether the word "kill" was ever used in her conversations with Von Villas, as opposed to "help" or "take care of."

"No, 'kill' was used," said Reynolds.

"That party conversation is what got you your deal, isn't it?"

"No."

When the defense attorneys had finished with Joyce Reynolds, O'Neill called a half-dozen employees from the Ford/Kennedy Medical Laboratory, who all told their versions of the war between Weed and Ogilvie. They described a lot of screaming and yelling, slamming phones, statements by Ogilvie about how she'd like to get rid of Weed. On cross-examination, however, Weed was not portrayed so villainously as he had been by Ogilvie. Some did not recall seeing him drink. Meanwhile, the witnesses described Ogilvie as the type of woman who made so many outlandish statements that it was difficult to know when to believe her.

Lab administrator Diane Shamis Perkins stated that Ogilvie had told her she was having an affair with Brot and Brot confirmed this to her. When questioned about her relationship with Ogilvie, Perkins described how she and her husband, Elzo, had opened a new lab with Ogilvie in Phoenix but they had a bitter falling out and the business had closed because Ogilvie falsely accused Perkins of forging $40,000 in checks.

After O'Neill rested his case, defense attorneys brought forward many of their own witnesses to weaken Ogilvie's credibility. Debbie Schroeder, the lab's receptionist, testified to wild tales told by Ogilvie, such as the time she claimed Tom Weed "beat her into signing the papers" granting him 35 percent of the business, leaving her bloody and unconscious for a couple of days. Schroeder never observed any drinking by Tom Weed. Asked her opinion of Ogilvie's honesty, Schroeder stated, "I thought she was a pathological liar—but very charming, sophisticated, and intelligent. She could charm your socks off. She could make some people believe anything."

Ronald Franzman, a handsome blond, mid-fifties cowboy from Tucson, had become Jan Ogilvie's husband after Thomas Weed. Franzman, wearing cowboy boots and hat on the stand, testified that he met Jan Ogilvie on February 24 or 25, 1983—the day after Weed's disappearance—while he was selling cars at a Woodland Hills Porsche-Audi dealership. Jan Ogilvie had come in to cosign for a vehicle he sold to one of her employees, Diane Shamis. They started a relationship and he moved in with her during the first week of March. They were married in November 1983.

Ogilvie told Franzman her divorce was final and that Weed was either in Canada or Mexico. She told him that T.J. was her sister's boy, that she had been a pathologist with the L.A. coroner's office and taught at UCLA, that she had a PhD in biology. Basically, Ogilvie had lied repeatedly to him about her personal and professional background. She also claimed to have spoken to Weed months after he disappeared. Asked his opinion of Ogilvie's honesty, Franzman stated unequivocally, "She's a pathological liar."

Richard Ford, sitting at the counsel table, smiled broadly when he heard Ogilvie's own husband characterize her this way.

During cross-examination by O'Neill, Franzman explained that, about two months after they met, Ogilvie had set him up in his own business in Tucson—the Flying F Ranch—where he raised racehorses. This operation cost Ogilvie about $10,000 a month. They stayed together until she was arrested in February 1984. He had had their marriage annulled in January 1985. She never confided to him that she had had Weed killed.

Richard Shepard, Jan Ogilvie's first husband (before Weed) was a man in his forties with a black mustache and wire-rimmed glasses. Shepard explained that he had met Ogilvie at Tennessee State University in Nashville in 1960, and that he had married her in late 1963. "T.J. is my son," he stated. "There is no question about it. He was born in 1964 on February 14. We lived at UCLA at the time. Janie was working on her master's."

Their relationship had deteriorated soon thereafter, and they had fought bitterly. Ogilvie occasionally became "hysterical" and would "rip drapes off the walls." They had separated in June 1964 after Ogilvie threatened to kill him with his own pistol during a fight. They later had a bitter dispute over the raising of their son, during which Ogilvie threatened Shepard again. "I will get even with you no matter what I have to do," Ogilvie once told him. "Even if I have to kill myself and put my body in a trash can behind your business."

Shepard had gotten a call from Tom Weed shortly after Weed married Ogilvie. Weed wanted to find out more about Ogilvie's background. The two men spent a long evening commiserating in the lounge at the LAX Marriott Hotel. "He was a nice guy," said Shepard. When Weed told Shepard that he had been threatened by Ogilvie, Shepard told him he'd had the same experience; that's why he'd left her. "My advice to him was to just give her the business. Janie is crazy. I said, 'You can start another business, but you can't start another life.' "

Asked his opinion of Ogilvie's character, Shepard stated, "She's what the psychiatrists would call a sociopath; she can look you in the eye and make you think she's telling the truth."

Dr. David Conney, an expert witness in the field of neuropsychiatry and psychopharmacology, testified about Jan Ogilvie's past medical and psychiatric problems. He described delusions, voices, disorientation. "She showed indications of schizophrenia, but not enough to be so diagnosed." He characterized some statements made by Ogilvie in the past—threatening to throw her own body in a trash can, saying T.J. was adopted—as "bizarre" and indicative of "something wrong with her thinking." Dr. Conney also described the tranquilizing effects of some of Ogilvie's medications, like Mellaril.

On cross, O'Neill asked if it was bizarre to hate and kill, in view of the fact that hundreds of spousal killings occur annually in L.A. alone. "Emotion of hatred is not bizarre," said Dr. Conney. "It can be bizarre. You have to know the whole picture." O'Neill also established that Dr. Conney hadn't talked to doctors who had treated Jan Ogilvie, that he was an expert witness who had been asked by the defense only to review her records to interpret and clarify them. Dr. Conney also stated that the drugs Ogilvie had taken would not keep her from telling the truth—nor would they prevent her from lying.

*   *   *

Richard Ford's lawyers had decided that Ronald Brot, fearing disbarment or possibly worse, would only plead the Fifth if they subpoenaed him and put him on the stand. Instead, they had Brot's grand jury testimony, from February 15, 1984, read into the record. Under questioning by then-D.A. Robert Jorgensen, Brot had described his involvement in Ogilvie's "bitterly contested" divorce and business dissolution.

"Did Miss Ogilvie ever suggest to you the possibility of the disappearance of Thomas Weed?" Jorgensen asked.

"Yes. I indicated to her that intentions to commit future criminal acts might not be privileged," answered Brot.

Brot explained that it would be difficult to relate what Ogilvie told him in chronological sequence because there were "simply too many conversations on too many subjects."

"I acted first as a lawyer in a divorce action, then quickly became enmeshed in three different actions, thereafter became Dr. Ogilvie's personal lawyer and general counsel to the Ford/Kennedy Lab. I believe that, from mid-November through February, I probably spoke with her three or four times a day on a variety of subjects. Since Thomas Weed was always on her mind, I'm sure that he came into virtually every conversation. This was as emotionally charged a matter as I have engaged in my practice of law over ten years."

Ogilvie indicated to Brot that her father, a Colonel Ogilvie of Tennessee, was going to intercede if she didn't take care of things herself. "She was extremely concerned that her dirty laundry was being aired, and that wasn't the way their family did things." Brot stated that he wouldn't be surprised if Ogilvie had in fact said all the things attributed to her by her employees. "The telephone calls were flying back and forth and the rumor mill still continues."

At one point, Ogilvie mentioned the figure of $50,000, a payment to be made to someone in an official position back east, like a councilman. Brot explained that this was not an outrageous claim for Ogilvie. "Those who knew Dr. Ogilvie knew that she seemed to know everybody and was on a first-name basis with anyone and everyone."

There was a point during the proceedings where Ogilvie told Brot she needed to know if it was going to be settled "because there was a point beyond which she would have no control of the other matter. I think the implication was clear." But then, Brot also said that Ogilvie engaged in a lot of "puffing," or "talk which really had no basis."

Brot recalled that Ogilvie told him an officer named Von Villas had come to her home one night. "As I recall the story, I was not told that a deal was struck but rather that Von Villas had said, 'If you ever need any help with Weed, let us know.' Now, the implication there was, I hasten to add, not what we are talking about—at least not as I took it."

Later, when he read about Ford and Von Villas in the papers, he didn't even recognize the officer's name until it was brought to his attention by Diane Shamis. "Even at that juncture I didn't draw any connection between Von Villas and the disappearance of Thomas Weed. In fact, to this day I don't have any reason to connect the two, although I don't have any reason not to."

Jorgensen: "Did Jan Ogilvie ever say anything about Von Villas actually offering to kill Thomas Weed for a sum of money?"

Brot: "No, I don't believe so. What Ogilvie told me was he would help if Weed got to be too much of a problem if she wanted him to. That could mean anything, I suppose."

According to Brot, Ogilvie had poisoned the minds of everyone at the lab about Thomas Weed. "It was a militant laboratory. That man couldn't walk in there without hatred just reeking from the walls. I mean, it was a real job that had been done. Everyone in there just couldn't stand him. When I came in there—foolishly or not—I felt that I was a knight in shining armor, rescuing all these people from this horrible man."

When Brot interviewed the lab employees, everyone told the same stories about Weed. He realized that most of what they were saying had come from Ogilvie. "When you actually got down to it, most of the things happened privately between Jan Ogilvie and Thomas Weed."

Later, when Ogilvie told Brot that she had nothing to do with Weed's disappearance, she had had a smile on her face. Brot never pressed her for details because, "I didn't know if he had really disappeared or not. For all I knew, it was a scheme between the two of them to collect insurance proceeds. The whole affair was so absolutely bizarre that in my mind absolutely anything was possible. And I don't mean to be tongue in cheek. If the man walked in here today, I'd be surprised but not shocked."

Although divorce and other litigation was still pending, Ogilvie cut off her relationship with Brot after about March 1, when she "suddenly became absolutely convinced that she had been overcharged. Perhaps coincidentally that was the same time she had begun her relationship with Mr. Franzman. I don't mean to be indelicate, but perhaps the most charitable word that she had for me was, quote, asshole, end quote, which she used repeatedly, screaming on the telephone, and it was impossible to carry on any conversation with her in any respect over anything."

Brot ended his testimony by declaring that Ogilvie had not paid all his fees. No questions had been asked about his cocaine use or alleged involvement with the money drop to Mr. Ory.

Unlike their colleagues at the defense table, Jack Stone and Donald Feinberg, attorneys for Bob Von Villas, decided to subpoena Ron Brot to testify at trial. The lawyer was first brought to the stand for a hearing outside the presence of the jury. Brot was in his forties, dark-haired and bespectacled, and sported a diamond ring and gold bracelet with his pin-striped business suit. He stated that he lived in Woodland Hills. Then, when asked if he knew Jan Ogilvie, Brot cited the Fifth Amendment. That was all they would get from Ron Brot, at least for now.

Timothy Chang, an attorney for the downtown L.A. law firm of Evans, Harte and Brot, testified that he had assisted Ron Brot on the Ogilvie case. After Ron Brot left the firm, Chang stated, Brot repeatedly stalled and delayed in signing a substitution of attorney form until February 23, 1983, the day Weed disappeared.

Normally, before attorneys sign such substitution papers, they must reexamine all the standing and pending agreements. This might include having to confer with the opposing party—in this case, Weed and Weed's attorney; it would have been a lot of work. The defense would later argue that Brot knew Weed was going to be killed and waited until he knew Weed was dead before he signed the form. Weed wouldn't be around to contest the many agreements, and Brot wouldn't have anything to do but collect his fees.

Chang also testified that Brot often spoke about thugs and hit men. Once, shortly after he began working on the Ogilvie divorce, Brot asked him to look up the number of an individual he called "his muscle."

On cross by O'Neill, Chang testified that Brot had a problem with alcohol and cocaine, that he acted less than professionally. He had a big mouth and liked to talk a lot, always trying to make an impression. Chang also testified that Brot left the firm when he was fired by the other partners because of his alcohol and drug use. After he left, the other partners wanted to be rid of the Ogilvie case, to have it "substituted out," but Brot delayed signing the necessary forms.

Next, Donald Feinberg re-called Jan Ogilvie to the stand for further cross-examination. She again glided into the courtroom as though floating on air. This time she wore a bright floral print dress and had her hair done in a wild Afro.

Feinberg questioned her about statements made by other witnesses, about her misrepresenting her education and work background, her claims to have had cancer or suffered a miscarriage, and her additional wild statements, all of which Ogilvie denied or somehow explained away.

Then Feinberg moved to the subject of Ronald Brot. Ogilvie reiterated Brot's alleged statement regarding hit men, that "it's done all the time."

"Did you tell Brot that Weed's car would be found far away?"

"No."

"Did you tell him Weed would disappear without a trace?"

"No."

"Did you tell him fifty thousand dollars had been paid to people in the East for the killing?"

"No."

"Did you tell him a councilman would be involved?"

"No."

Then a rather peculiar procedure took place, the result of protracted legal arguments that had occurred earlier outside the presence of the jury. The court bailiff went out into the hall and brought in Ronald Brot, who sat down in the gallery next to his attorney. Brot, still a practicing attorney himself, was concerned about having to make statements that could potentially be used to have him disbarred. Judge Schempp had ruled that the court could not make Brot testify if he chose to cite his Fifth Amendment right. However, a compromise of sorts was arranged whereby the Von Villas defense would be allowed to present Ron Brot to the jury while Ogilvie testified.

"Do you see someone here you recognize whom you can identify for us?" Feinberg asked.

"Yes, that's Ron Brot," Ogilvie answered, pointing at her former attorney.

Feinberg asked Brot to stand. Then, while pointing dramatically at Brot, he spewed a litany of questions at Ogilvie, his tone of voice suggesting that each inquiry and answer were utterly damning.

"Is this the man you gave five thousand dollars to to help you get rid of your husband?"

"Yes."

"Is this the man who took the five thousand dollars to to make the drop?"

"Yes."

"Is this the same man you met at your home and at restaurants to talk about killing your husband?"

"Yes."

"Is this the same man you gave twenty thousand dollars to?"

"Yes."

"Is this the same man who offered to help you find a hit man?"

"Yes."

"The man who said he knew a man named No Neck?"

"That's a man he said he used."

"Your attorney did all these things for you?"

"Yes, that's correct."

After this brief exchange, Ron Brot was excused. The Von Villas defense obviously wanted to present Ronald Brot as a viable alternative suspect in the conspiracy. No explanation was made to the jury, however, of this unusual proceeding. They weren't told that Brot had pled the Fifth and refused to testify. Why Brot had been brought into court for them to see but not to testify was a mystery. It wasn't the first time—nor would it be the last—that members of the jury would appear bewildered.

28

Lillian

ASIDE FROM OGILVIE'S TESTIMONY, PROSECUTOR BOB O'NEILL HAD only two pieces of evidence that would link Richard Ford to the alleged conspiracy to kill Tom Weed. Both of these—the calendar and the jailhouse tape—were circumstantial at best. But O'Neill had to make the best of them.

O'Neill first introduced as evidence a Norman Rockwell wall calendar that had been seized from the Ford home after Richard Ford's arrest. The February 1983 page had one square that had been totally obliterated with black ink. That square was for Wednesday, February 23—the day of Tom Weed's disappearance.

Six different experts testified about their attempts to determine what, if anything, had been written beneath the markings. An infrared photographer, ultraviolet lab expert, and FBI technician all failed to find anything. A documents expert who used an electrostatic apparatus to detect writing on the next page with "graphite beads that adhere to indentations" also struck out. A computer specialist brought in from British Columbia explained how he fed a photo of the calendar into his computer to enhance the image through "binary thresholding and density slicing, processes by which you try to make things discernible to the human eye." He also came up with nothing. Finally, Bruce Greenwood, LAPD's senior examiner of documents, testified that he pulled a few strings and got some of the boys over at the Jet Propulsion Lab in Pasadena to stick the page under a high-tech device called a Doyer J-Infrared Microscope. Even they could make out nothing under the ink.

In the end, the experts could only collectively conclude what the cops had figured out when they first looked at the calendar: somebody had taken a felt tip pen and blackened the space out so thoroughly that you couldn't tell what had been written underneath.

Richard Ford, Jr., the defendant's adopted nineteen-year-old son, was called to the stand by the defense to provide the explanation. Richard Junior was dark-haired, handsome, and very nervous. Under careful coaxing by Lasting, he related how the Ford family always kept a calendar in the kitchen by the phone. Everybody in the family used it, himself in particular.

Lasting paged through the calendar and Richard explained many of the stars, slashes, and other markings he had made on it. The only date on the entire calendar that was completely blackened out was Wednesday, February 23. "It was some social function," Richard insisted. "A barbecue or maybe a dance. She [my girlfriend] kept saying, 'Don't forget it.' It was something where I *had* to be there." Because of his girlfriend's insistence, he said that he kept writing on the date until he had completely filled it in. Lasting later entered evidence into the record that there had been an afternoon dance at Granada Hills High on February 23rd.

During Richard Junior's testimony before the Von Villas jury, he stated that he had improved his memory of the February 23 blackout. "I've been trying to remember exactly. It was something recreational. She [his girlfriend] kept saying, 'Remember, remember.' I thought it was a school dance; now I know it was. I even have a picture." Richard Junior stated he was "positive" that he made the mark to remember the semiformal Vice Versa Dance, where the girl asks the boy.

On cross-examination, O'Neill asked Richard Junior if his school had noon dances. "Yes," he said. Were they big social events? "No," he answered. Richard also recalled for O'Neill that he wore a gray and black tux to the Vice Versa Dance and that he and his girlfriend were driven there and picked up by their two moms.

On redirect, Jack Stone tried to prevent the impending disaster. At first, Richard Junior stuck to his story that the blackened February 23 marked the date of the Vice Versa Dance. Then Jack Stone asked, "If I told you there was a dance at noon on February twenty-third, would that cause you to reconsider? Is it possible you could be confused?"

"Yes," Richard allowed.

"But you crossed off that date on the calendar."

"Yes, definitely," said Richard.

"You wouldn't be lying, would you?"

"No."

The next witness called by Jack Stone was Janice Jacobson, Ford's former girlfriend. An attractive twenty-year-old college coed, Miss Jacobson explained that, as a fifteen-year-old high school sophomore at Granada Hills High, she had gone steady with Richard Ford, Jr., for seven months. They attended the Vice Versa Dance, where the girl asks the boy. It was semiformal. She wore a pink dress and he wore a white tux. She even had a picture, which showed heart decorations in the background. It took place around Valentine's Day. She and Richard broke up later, "a mutual thing."

"Did you ever tell Richard not to forget certain things?" asked Jack Stone.

"Yes."

"Did you ever have to tell him several times not to forget something?"

"Not that I remember," the Valley girl replied. "Unless I made an absolute fit about something, which I can't remember absolutely doing."

"Did you and Richard ever go to a daytime dance?"

"I don't think so. I vaguely remember walking in and walking out of one with Richard."

On cross-examination, Miss Jacobson stated that the Vice Versa Dance "was definitely on a weekend, most likely a Saturday." She also said, "I believe my folks took us and his mother picked us up." Asked if there were occasions when they went out during the week, Jacobson said, "I can't say we never went out during the week, but they were few, except in the summer."

"Were there a lot of barbecues in the middle of winter?" O'Neill asked.

"I don't remember," answered Jacobson.

Jack Stone gave it another try on redirect. "How about picnics?" he asked. "Did you and Richard attend any of those?"

"I can't remember."

Later, prosecutor Bob O'Neill would enter evidence into the record that the Vice Versa Dance at Granada Hills High in 1983 was held on Saturday, February 5—not on February 23.

Considering all the attention paid to minute details by the defense throughout the trial, it was puzzling how they had apparently allowed Richard Ford, Jr., to testify about the Vice Versa Dance without first checking when it had taken place.

On September 15, Richard Lasting called Lillian Ford to the stand, ending many long months of speculation as to whether Richard Ford would testify. If Ford had planned to speak for himself, he wouldn't need Lillian to do it for him. But if he wasn't going to take the stand, somebody had to explain that jailhouse tape.

The jury had heard Ford say things on the tape that sounded incriminating: "No way to tie me to it. . . . There's nooooo body. . . . I don't know if I got gas. . . . What worries me is the shotgun. The shells."

Lasting and Santwier felt they couldn't put Ford on the stand. If they did, the prosecution could ask about his previous conviction in the Loguercio case. Even worse, O'Neill could bring in the van tapes. Lasting commented, "Our feeling was after hearing that, the jury would believe anything about him. They would convict him of selling atomic secrets to the Russians after they heard that conversation."

Despite her voluptuous figure, Lillian looked almost girlish in her beige skirt and brown blouse. Her delicate features and beautiful dark complexion matched those of her son, with whom she also seemed to share a high-strung, emotional intensity. Occasionally, between questions or during the attorneys' conferences at the bench, she would get a faraway look in her eyes, like the thousand-mile stare of someone in shell shock.

Questioned by Rickard Santwier, Lillian described how her life had become a hellish nightmare after she was brutally beaten and raped on that Thanksgiving night in 1980. The event changed her life completely, and she was still undergoing psychiatric treatment. Lillian explained that her obsession with finding the rapist, a man named Skip, virtually destroyed her relationship with her husband.

"Did you blame your husband because the LAPD couldn't find Skip?" Santwier asked.

"Yes."

Because of her obsession, Richard Ford had frequently gone out searching for Skip. For that reason he had obtained a wig and makeup for a disguise. Lillian described the cosmetics and applicators that had been seized as evidence from their home, explaining that she often helped him apply the makeup and even accompanied him on a few occasions.

Lillian then gave her explanation of the jailhouse tape. She had just been served with a search warrant. Officers had come into her home to seize records and all sorts of things, including her personal letters and those of her daughter. She was very upset and confused. She didn't even know who Tom Weed and Jan Ogilvie were. She immediately went to visit her husband at the county jail. The phones were half-dead. They had trouble conversing. Richard was trying to explain to her—as best he could—what the police were looking for. He was trying to reassure her that there was nothing to worry about, that Ogilvie was a friend of Bob's and that's why they were looking into the disappearance of her husband. Statements made by Richard Ford like "there's no way to tie me to it" were not the statements of a guilty man trying to cover up, but simply those of a man trying to reassure his wife that he was not involved and could not be framed.

Lillian denied they ever discussed his involvement in the alleged murder. They were only discussing the search warrant. "He was trying to figure out what the police were doing. I told him I was worried they were going to frame him with this."

Lillian went through each of the seemingly incriminating statements and explained what they were about. It clearly caused her a great deal of stress.

Richard Ford: "Did we pay anything off? . . . What the hell did we do with it?"

"That was a reference to our tax refund," Lillian explained. The investigators had seized all their bank records and she was afraid they were going to try to find something they could use to frame her husband. She said she told him, "I probably cashed it and put it in the closet, like I usually do"—a statement the tape had not recorded—to which he had replied, "Good, there's no connection to me there."

Ford: "How you gonna prove it? . . . There's nooooo body."

According to Lillian, Richard was explaining that they were trying to pin a charge on Bob, a missing persons case, but that no body had been found.

Ford: "The only thing that worries me is the gas. . . . The Shell credit card."

Her husband was trying to figure out what the police were doing, what they were looking for. They had seized some gas cards that neither of them had ever even used.

Lillian also testified that she asked her husband if Bob Von Villas was involved. "I asked him, 'You don't think Bob would try to incriminate you, do you?' "

His answer, which was recorded, was, "Can't imagine it." He also said, "It's . . . deep." Lillian said he was referring to the investigation, to all the things the police were looking into.

Ford: "They got the idea but they don't have it, I don't think."

According to Lillian, he was referring to the idea to incriminating him.

Ford: "What worries me is the shotgun. The shells."

Lillian was worried they were going to try to frame him. On two earlier warrants, they had taken his shotgun and some shells. Now they had taken some more shells. Richard was trying to figure out what they were up to.

Lillian had done her best to explain away the incriminating statements on the jailhouse tape. But with the start of Bob O'Neill's cross-examination, the fireworks began.

Any notion that the prosecutor might go easy on her were quickly dispelled.

The courtroom had filled in anticipation of this showdown, and the spectators would not be disappointed. The exchanges between Lillian Ford and Bob O'Neill made for high-voltage melodrama.

Questioned by O'Neill, Lillian explained that Bob Von Villas was a business associate, not a friend. O'Neill showed her a phone bill and asked if she recalled two telephone calls to her home from Von Villas at five and seven o'clock on the evening of February 22. She did not. Asked if she knew where her husband was on February 23, Lillian said, "No, I don't." She also could not remember his taking off work between the nineteenth and twenty-third of February.

O'Neill began going through the jailhouse conversation, one statement at a time. "The words 'twenty to thirty'—wasn't that a reference to the money paid for the killing of Tom Weed?" O'Neill charged.

"No, no," Lillian shot back.

"Didn't he discuss the killing of Tom Weed with you?"

"No!" Lillian exclaimed. She would spend half a day making vehement denials. O'Neill's charges clearly upset her to the point of breakdown, but they also seemed to ignite her fiery temper. It was a chilling exchange, a no-holds-barred mortal combat.

Richard Lasting placed his arm around Richard Ford at the counsel table, comforting him as they watched his wife battle valiantly for his life.

"Did your husband tell you that Bob did the negotiating with Jan Ogilvie?"

"No! No!" Lillian exclaimed.

"On this tape, aren't you talking about the money your husband got for killing Tom Weed?"

"No! That's not true!" Lillian fired back. "We were talking about income tax."

"When he said, 'There's no connection to me there,' was he talking about the Ford/Kennedy Lab?"

"No!"

"About Jan Ogilvie?"

"No!"

"About Julie Rabold?"

"No!" Lillian spat with unrelenting intensity. Her denials came almost too quickly, as though she wasn't bothering to listen to the prosecutor's charges.

" 'There's nooooo body.' What did you ask your husband right before he said that?"

"I asked him if he knew anything about the case, if he knew what was going on."

"Did you ask him if the police could have found Weed?"

"No."

"If they might be able to find him in the future?"

"No!"

" 'I don't know if I got gas.... Don't remember.' Does that refer to his driving Weed out to the desert?"

"No!"

"Why is he concerned about the gas?"

"We were trying to compare the two credit cards, why they [the police] took credit cards both times [they searched their home]."

"Getting gas doesn't relate to any specific incident?"

"No."

" 'Can't imagine it.... It's ... deep.' What was the context of that?"

"I was asking him about the investigation. He said it was deep."

"In fact, wasn't he telling you about the body, that it was buried deep, that he couldn't imagine them finding it?"

"No! No!" Lillian shouted. " 'Heavy, deep, hot, large'—those are cop words! He was referring to the investigation."

" 'They're fishing. They got the idea but they don't have it, I don't think.' What preceded that statement?"

"I asked him if Bob knew anything about it."

"Isn't he telling you the police have got the right guy, but—"

"No! No!" Lillian shot back before he could finish. "I was fearful that Bob might try to connect my husband."

"You were fearful he would roll over?"

"No!"

" 'He'd go with me.' Isn't he saying Von Villas will never roll over because he'd go with me?"

"No!"

" 'What month was that, anyway? ... They have the wrong dates,' your husband asks. And you say, 'Was it after Christmas?' What were you referring to?"

"I don't know."

"Weren't you referring to the Weed killing?"

"No I wasn't!"

" 'What worries me is the shotgun.' Why did he say that?"

"They [IAD] took some shells on the third trip. He was trying to figure out why they took something they already took before."

"Wasn't he concerned about having used it in killing Weed."

"No!"

"That he had left some shells at the murder site?"

"Oh, pleeeease, no!"

"That the shotgun would connect him to Weed?"

"No!"

O'Neill finished his cross-examination by commenting on the numerous expressions of love between Lillian and Richard on the tape. "Do you still feel that?" he asked.

"Yes," said Lillian.

It was the only question asked by O'Neill that Lillian Ford answered in the affirmative.

29

Judy

LIKE FORD, VON VILLAS WOULD NEED SOME HELP FROM HIS FAMILY
to explain the State's evidence. Jack Stone first called Michele Von Villas Walker.
Von Villas's daughter appeared even more radiant than she had at the first trial,
her long sun-bleached blond tresses cascading down her back. Bob Von Villas
beamed at his daughter as she took the stand; he looked like a man feasting on
sun after years of imprisonment in the dark. A few brief conferences at the bench
were called in the course of Michele's testimony, during which father and daughter chatted delightedly back and forth between witness stand and counsel table.
It was touching.

Michele testified that her family had a red Camaro that was used exclusively
by herself and her mom. She turned sixteen in June 1982 and got the car in
January 1983. Her father used the Pontiac Grand Prix. Her sister Shannon was
ten in 1983. "I had soccer practice and drove home at four-thirty. My sister had
swimming. She swam two hours a night, Monday through Friday, all year round.
She was on the Simi Valley swim team. Mom would drive her and sit through
practice from five to seven. Dad usually got home around six. Mom always used
the Camaro. She never switched cars with Dad." Michele recalled only one day
her dad ever took the Camaro—to have it serviced at the shop.

The defense obviously intended this testimony to refute the prosecution's
contention that Von Villas used this red Camaro as the money drop car.

Bob O'Neill only had one question for the witness. "Did you have a family
cat?" he asked.

"Yes."

This last question puzzled all but the keenest observers. Over a year ago, back at the first trial, Bob Von Villas had testified that his cat had eaten his wig. O'Neill was just checking. The canny prosecutor didn't let anything slip through the cracks.

On Monday, October 17, the gallery was swarming with courtbirds. They knew they were in for a show.

The first witness called to the stand was Judy Von Villas. Once again, a cop's wife was being led to the arena to battle for her husband's life.

Until this point in the trial, defense attorneys Jack Stone and Donald Feinberg had told reporters that they were undecided as to whether Bob or Judy Von Villas would take the stand. They knew that one of them had to get up there and do some explaining. Apparently, it was a matter of heated debate. The defendant wanted badly to testify, but his attorneys didn't feel he should take the stand.

Judy wore her black hair in a short, new-wave style, her nails long, varnished a dead white. Compared to Lillian Ford, Judy seemed calm, remarkably unstressed. She didn't act the part of a distraught woman bearing up under a great ordeal. She remained composed throughout her day-long testimony—even during the inevitable grilling from Bob O'Neill.

Under questioning by Jack Stone, Judy explained that she had been married to Bob Von Villas for twenty-two years and they had two daughters. She then reaffirmed Michele's statements about the Camaro, about how only she and her daughter ever drove it.

Judy then related how she and Joyce Reynolds, wife of another police officer, had become close friends. They spent time at each other's houses and went out socially. Judy and Bob attended the department Christmas party every year, and after her husband was killed, Joyce Reynolds always went with them and sat at the same table. Others joined them as well, including Linda Sintic, another police widow.

Judy stated that at the 1982 Christmas party on December 9 at the Granada Hills Country Club, "I drank white wine. So did Joyce. We both had more than one. Joyce drank more than me. I had three, usually." Basically, her testimony was that Joyce Reynolds had gotten a little high at the party.

Judy explained that Bob was suspended by the LAPD from January 11 to 31 for "improper use of his position to do off-duty work." Her husband had often applied for and received permits to do outside security and bodyguard work. He had even once been Mayor Yorty's personal bodyguard. Jack Stone introduced a summary of Von Villas's numerous work permits as verification. Apparently, however, the department felt he had acted improperly in soliciting outside work from one particular woman. Hence the two-week suspension.

Sometime in early February 1983, Joyce Reynolds called Bob at home late at night when they were both in bed asleep. The phone was on Bob's side of their king-size bed and he answered it. Judy overheard some of the conversation. She heard Bob say, "How do I get a hold of her" and "When's the best time to call?" She also saw him jot down some phone numbers and heard him say something about Roscoe and Reseda. When she asked her husband what the call was all about, he told her Joyce might have some work for him as a bodyguard—that the lady Julie worked for was having some trouble with her husband. This explained when and why Bob wrote "Ros Res" and Ogilvie's phone numbers on the back of a bank deposit slip.

Later, after talking to Ogilvie, Bob decided not to work for her. "He didn't feel comfortable with it. He didn't like some of the things she said."

After Bob was arrested in July 1983, Judy visited him regularly at L.A. County Jail. She often made notes, particularly of his instructions regarding the family finances, which he had always handled. She also took notes during their phone conversations. Jack Stone showed her the yellow loose-leaf sheets that had been seized by investigators. These included her notes: "Close friend, Mr. Ory in jail, *emergency,* police might have #, don't worry, need loan $30,000, will be paid back, no blackmail. Pay phone. Joyce."

Stone walked her through her explanation of these notes. At that time, Judy said, they believed they might soon be able to post bail for Bob's release, so they were trying to raise money. They owned a property that they offered to sell to a firm called Rice Construction. The property was initially valued at $40,000. They expected to soon receive enough money to repay a $30,000 loan.

While discussing this matter with her husband, Judy told him that Rice Construction had made an offer of $20,000. This made Bob very angry. "He said they were taking advantage of the fact that he was in jail and needed the money. He said it was just like extortion, like blackmail." Judy was writing while he was talking and, she explained, "I couldn't spell extortion, so I wrote down 'no blackmail.' "

To provide verification, Jack Stone submitted as evidence a $40,000 trust deed on the property, as well as a signed mutual release covenant and a signed document accepting a cashier's check for $27,000—the amount for which they finally sold the property two weeks later, on July 26, 1983.

The words "Jan," "Lab," and Ogilvie's phone number were also written on the paper. Judy Von Villas explained: "I was supposed to borrow money from Jan, the lady who owned the lab. He had dealings with her before." Besides talking to her about bodyguard work, Judy explained that Bob had once spoken with her on the phone about the possibility of investing in her lab.

Her husband had used the name Mr. Ory because "when he talked to her about being a bodyguard, he used a different name because he'd already been suspended [for soliciting bodyguard work]." Mr. Ory, an old friend of Bob's, had been the best man at their wedding.

Judy also explained that, because investigators had seized Bob's phone book, Bob had instructed her to call numerous people and tell them not to worry, that police had their number and might be calling.

Despite the "I couldn't spell extortion" alibi, Judy's story seemed to make sense. She came across as sincere, believable. While pundits would later mock her bad speller defense, they would have to admit that it was a rather poor choice for someone concocting a premeditated lie.

After Stone's sympathetic questioning, Judy braced herself for cross-examination by Bob O'Neill.

One of the first areas O'Neill directed his attention to was the department Christmas party. Mrs. Von Villas testified that Bob danced with Joyce Reynolds, and she had no idea what they said to each other. "Wasn't his suspension the culmination of an investigation into his activities?" O'Neill asked.

"I assume so," Judy responded.

"On December first, 1983, wasn't he notified they were taking administrative action?"

"I don't recall."

"At the Christmas party of December ninth, was your husband upset about the suspension?"

"No."

"He never discussed his possible suspension?"

"No."

"Did he discuss work with you?"

"Not much."

"Did you know a lot about your husband's business?"

"No."

"How many times did you discuss these notes in jail?"

"We didn't."

"He never mentioned in your conversations that 'Ros Res' appeared on a note found in his car?"

"No."

"Do you know where your husband was on February twenty-third?"

"At work and at home."

"Were you having financial difficulties at the time?"

"No," Judy answered. Under further questioning by O'Neill, however, she admitted they had an outstanding debt of $20,000 at the time and a judgment against them for $6,000 over a tile business. A year earlier they had found it necessary to swap their $200,000 Simi Valley ranch for a house worth half as much.

Then it was back to the notes. Her explanation of "Close friend, Mr. Ory in jail"?

"He said to say a friend *of* Mr. Ory."

" 'Emergency,' underlined. What did he tell you in regard to that?"

"I don't remember."

" 'Police might have #'?"

"He wanted me to tell her not to worry. She might not want to lend money if involved with a police investigation."

"Why were the words 'Pay phone' written on the left side?"

"I don't know why."

"Von Villas didn't tell you to use a pay phone?"

"No. It's a nervous habit. I was doodling."

" 'Joyce'?"

"He told me it was better to call Joyce and have her do it. He told me to have her call the lady at the lab."

"You wrote 'no blackmail' because you couldn't spell 'extortion,' is that right?" O'Neill asked.

"Yes."

"Did you try to hide this note from the police?" O'Neill asked. Now that Judy had taken the stand, he was free to bring this out.

"Yes."

"You stuffed it in your purse?"

"Yes."

"Because it was incriminating?"

"No."

"Incriminating because it had Jan Ogilvie's phone number and the words 'no blackmail'?"

"No, no. I thought it was something private between us."

Judy stuck to her guns, issuing nearly a dozen more denials regarding the note and the reason she had stuffed it in her purse. She remained unruffled throughout O'Neill's long string of accusations.

On redirect, Jack Stone had Mrs. Von Villas list a number of other people her husband had directed her to call—friends, business partners, actors David Soul and Robert Fuller. She had also stuffed notes regarding these instructions into her purse.

Then, apparently hoping to bail Judy out on another troubling matter, Stone asked, "Does the auto garage have a pay phone?"

"No," Judy answered.

Reviews of Judy's performance were mixed. Some observers thought her lame explanations, like "I was doodling" and "I couldn't spell 'extortion,' " were devastating. Others thought she came across just fine, quite believable despite these clumsy excuses. The defense attorneys acted as though they were pleased—but then, so did prosecutor Robert O'Neill.

O'Neill later expressed shock that Bob Von Villas hadn't taken the stand. Most observers of the case were similarly surprised. Von Villas was a man with keen communication skills, an extraordinary salesman with an upbeat and engaging personality—provided he kept his arrogance in check. He made a very good witness. And everybody knew he wanted to take the stand and speak his piece.

Because of evidence like the jailhouse tape, Judy's jailhouse notes, and the *Times* clipping found in Ogilvie's desk, the jury already knew that Von Villas had been arrested for some other crime. Some believed that it might be best for him to get on the stand and explain everything, including his previous conviction. His attorneys, however, were convinced that if the jury learned he had been convicted of attempted murder and armed robbery they would automatically conclude he was also guilty of killing Tom Weed, no matter how good a witness he might be. Despite Von Villas's burning desire to testify, he had apparently chosen to listen to his attorneys.

30

Killers Behind the Badge

PROSECUTOR BOB O'NEILL GAVE TWO CLOSING ARGUMENTS, EACH basically the same. He walked each jury through the case, summarizing testimony and detailing the importance of each piece of evidence—notes, phone records, bank deposits, the Von Villas deposit slip with "Ros Res" and Ogilvie's phone numbers, the notes from Judy's purse, the newsclip and "Hope you're sleeping well" note found in Ogilvie's desk, the Ford calendar with the blackened-out box for February 23, the Ford jailhouse tape, the due diligence work on Weed, and most importantly, the testimony of Janie Elmira Ogilvie, Joyce Reynolds, and Julie Rabold.

Robert O'Neill's uncommon restraint, his ability to keep his intensity perfectly adjusted at all times, was something to behold—and appreciate—at the end of such a long trial. O'Neill had mastered the delicate art of presenting argument without sounding like he was arguing, void of any troublesome additudinal baggage.

At the start of both trials, many observers had described O'Neill as perhaps too cool and aloof, even wooden in his performance. But after a few months trapped in a courtroom with a bunch of arguing trial attorneys, those same observers became O'Neill's die-hard fans. Histrionics work just fine in a thirty-second scene on "L.A. Law." But in a year-long trial, you really want someone who'll just cut the crap and present the facts. O'Neill had it down.

"That's the most thorough prosecutor I ever heard," remarked one courtbird. "He's the best." Another commented, "If O'Neill had tried that *Twilight Zone* case,

John Landis would be directing license plates." This last reference was to movie director John Landis, who had recently been acquitted on charges involving the death of actor Vic Morrow and two children during the filming of *Twilight Zone*. Pundits claimed the case against Landis was strong but was "lost" due to overkill by a grandstanding prosecutor.

While reviewing the evidence in his summation, O'Neill pointed to Von Villas's phone records of February 22: a call at 5:15 to the Ford/Kennedy Medical Laboratory, a three-minute call to Ford's home at 5:37, and another twenty-nine-minute call to Ford at 7:04. O'Neill also pointed out that Von Villas's February 22, 25, and 28 bank deposits of $8,000 in hundred dollar bills were made two and a half months after he had allegedly sold $6,800 in diamonds to Bill Justice.

O'Neill also ripped into Judy Von Villas. "I recall her testimony and I sure hope you do. Her explanation of 'Pay phone'? 'I was doodling'! Remember that! How about 'no blackmail'? It goes from the incredible to the absurd. She couldn't spell 'extortion' so, she says, 'I wrote "no blackmail." ' Did you want to laugh?"

Anticipating the attack on Jan Ogilvie, O'Neill told the jury, "Jan Ogilvie is not Mother Teresa. Distasteful as it may be, compromise was made with a murderer . . . so that all the people responsible for the murder of Thomas Weed could be brought to justice. Society can't excuse a woman like Jan Ogilvie, nor can society excuse a couple of cops who became contract killers behind the badge."

O'Neill challenged the primary defense contention, stating, "She had no incentive to lie." He said Ogilvie would still have gotten a deal if she had accused someone else, like Ron Brot.

"Richard Ford and Robert Von Villas became the very enemy they swore to protect us against," Bob O'Neill declared. "They used our trust as the perfect cover. Who'd ever suspect police officers? They became professional contract killers, masquerading as police officers." O'Neill also stated that the jailhouse conversation between Ford and his wife revealed "the mind of an assassin at work."

Rickard Santwier and Richard Lasting both gave closing arguments for Richard Ford. Santwier presented a chart titled "Ogilvie" and then reviewed each item on the list for the jury:

- At times been truthful at times a liar
- Treated for memory loss
- Wanted a deal

- Inconsistencies
- Who is first? In this case, Me.
- Lied under oath? Yes I have.
- Plead guilty to felony? Yes.

He presented another chart listing seven people whom Ogilvie said had all been "mistaken" or lied about her on the stand.

As at the first trial, Richard Lasting made an impassioned plea for a man he had come to consider his dear friend as well as a client. "Ogilvie lied to avoid a possible death sentence," he told the jurors. "Without Ogilvie there is no evidence—none—that proves Richard Ford was a member of a conspiracy to murder Thomas Weed or that he murdered Thomas Weed."

In addition to arguing that Ogilvie had auditioned for a deal to get a lenient sentence, Lasting also emphasized that conjecture—such as that over what was said on the eight minutes of gaps in the jailhouse tape recording—did not constitute proof.

Lasting argued that if Weed was dead, all the evidence linked Von Villas to the murder, not Ford. Ford was just Von Villas's business partner, guilty only by association. "To convict Richard Ford, you must believe Jan Ogilvie has told you the truth. She says that he came to her house as Charlie of Vic and Charlie. Her credibility is crucial, because she alone says Ford was involved. Julie Rabold Kanoske and Joyce Reynolds didn't know Richard Ford.

"Depending on what she says, the D.A. is going to decide how good a deal she gets. She knew the D.A. was trying to connect Von Villas and Ford. She knows what the D.A. wants and what she needs to do to make a deal. She lied because her goal was a lenient sentence. She wanted community service, to be a negative example for battered women, and she didn't want to go to the state penitentiary."

Lasting pointed to all the problems with Ogilvie's story, the most glaring being her tale about the missed drop. "First, she says she was too tired to make the drop. So she drives all the way from the Valley to Marina Del Rey and asks Ron Brot to drive back to the Valley to do it for her. Does this make sense? No! So she comes up with a new story. She had a business meeting—but she can't remember what it was."

Lasting asked many troubling questions. Why all the calls to Ron Brot? Why did Ogilvie pay him such excessive fees, and without receiving any billing invoices? Why did Ogilvie tell some people that only one cop had come to her house? Why did her story change? How could a "professional killer" forget whether or not he used his credit card to get gas? Why didn't Ogilvie say anything in court about her love affair with Brot, which she mentioned to Perkins and others? Why all the other apparent lies by Ogilvie—to which seven different witnesses had testified?

"The evidence suggests Ron Brot was involved as much as Richard Ford—the money, phone calls, matches, lovers, lies—but it was insufficient to charge him."

Lasting stated, "The D.A. would have you believe that he [Richard Ford] drove Weed's car to the airport wearing gloves, but left his cigarette butts; that he got someone else's fingerprint on the map and left it with the matchbook; that he left shotgun shells; that he can't remember whether he got gas or when the murder occurred or what he did with the money!" Lasting's exasperation with this scenario did seem justified.

Now it was Stone's and Feinberg's turns to give closing arguments in Von Villas's defense. Jack Stone first contended that the prosecution had not conclusively proved that Weed was dead. "They have only proven that he can't be found," said Jack Stone. "Are you so sure he's dead you're willing to take another man's life?"

But the main crux of his defense was that Ogilvie was emotionally and mentally unstable, a pathological liar, and had given her testimony to get a sweet deal for herself with the D.A. "The prosecution chose not to say one word about whether this woman is sane," said Jack Stone. "They knew in 1985 [when her deal had been made] that she had been treated for psychiatric problems, but they ignored it. They did worse than that. They put her on drugs because she was anxious and depressed. You have to be able to sleep at night. If I were a juror I'd want to know if she was sane."

Stone insisted there was as much evidence pointing to Ron Brot as her coconspirator. The long phone conversations, her excessive payments to him, her affair with him, their conversations about hit men. Why didn't they indict him?

"Why did Brot put off signing the substitution of attorney form until February twenty third? Now this *is* an amazing coincidence. Is it because he now knows that Weed will never be heard from again and he has no fear of legal consequences?"

Stone also suggested that Ogilvie could have murdered Weed herself. "Jan Ogilvie had a pattern of using men. Soon as she didn't need them anymore, away they go. Jan Ogilvie was a crafty lady, but a sick one. Did she lure Weed away from his apartment? Did she say, 'Let's go to Las Vegas' or whatever? Yes, she's the type who could easily lure him away . . . If she was the one who alone killed her husband—and I maintain it eminently reasonable in this case—she couldn't make a 'deal' with that.

"Jan Ogilvie has a need to bring people into this. She's not just crazy, but arranging avenues of escape if she gets caught. She has the guys from Vegas, Ron Brot, or Von Villas—three people to point the finger at. I maintain that the first time she ever saw Ford and Von Villas was at the arraignment.

"Joyce Reynolds is arrested in July of 1984, spends six months in jail, has cancer of the breast, a mastectomy, and she fears spending her life in prison. But she sees at the preliminary hearing that Ogilvie has made a deal and will do only nine years. So she comes up with this statement about being an honest cop at the Christmas party. That's the power of the D.A., to force them to testify by granting immunity. The D.A. won't believe her if she tells the truth!"

According to Stone, Ogilvie had been rebuffed by Von Villas, who declined to work for her, "and hell hath no fury like a woman scorned, and that's twice the case with a woman like Ogilvie. Von Villas became a way out for Ogilvie, something to keep in reserve."

Stone then turned his attention to the testimony of the defendant's wife. "Judy Von Villas is a victim. She's been married seventeen years [at the time of her husband's arrest], has two kids, her husband is in jail, she's having to deal with the lawyers. Should we laugh at her? She had to drive all the way downtown to see her husband. She's not sophisticated, just an average housewife. Her husband ran the finances, he was the head of the family, so she took notes when he told her to contact people she didn't know."

As for Judy's hiding papers from the police, Stone claimed she hid six personal papers, including a letter from their eleven-year-old daughter to her father. Stone read some of it: "All my friends know you didn't do something like that. We will get you out. I love you. You are my dad." Von Villas, sitting at the counsel table, visibly choked up as he listened. "These are the types of things she is trying to keep from the police," Stone concluded.

"The red Camaro. That was police work at its worst. The first step in a fair trial is the initial investigation of a witness by police. What they did was reprehensible and it denied Von Villas a fair trial forever. They shoved a picture of a red Camaro in front of her [Ogilvie]."

Stone presented a chart showing the progression of Ogilvie's testimony on a number of details. Did Vic and Charlie have makeup? Her response to that in her first interview was, "It could have [been makeup]." Later it changed to, "It looked like makeup to me." Did it look like a wig? First: "It could have been." Later: "It was a wig. I can tell a wig when I see it."

"This is rare, but it could happen to anyone," Jack Stone charged. "All our rights can be trampled on. They made up their minds too soon that Von Villas was guilty and structured the case to make it fit. All of our freedom rests on them doing their job properly.

"This is a case based on circumstantial evidence," Stone concluded, "and you can't convict on circumstantial evidence unless there is no other rational explanation of the evidence, no other reasonable conclusion—and that is not the case."

While Jack Stone at times seemed to bluster and overstate his case, Donald Feinberg, in turn, put too much effort into his examination of minutia and fine discrepancies. By spending fifteen minutes reviewing Ogilvie's various descriptions of Vic's and Charlie's facial hair, he succeeded in putting some jurors to sleep.

But Feinberg picked up steam and began to shine when he told the jury: "Let me take you on a bizarre journey into the mind of Jan Ogilvie."

The detailed profile Feinberg presented of Janie Elmira Ogilvie sounded like it was lifted from a psychology textbook. He described her as a megalomaniacal schizophrenic charmer, a self-willed, vindictive paranoid, a woman who blamed everybody, accused everybody, and needed no motive to lie. She was a delusional sociopath with a self-destructiveness that wouldn't allow her to enjoy her own success, a woman who exaggerated and made up stories of beatings, who married a man she claimed hated and humiliated her, who turned her entire staff against her husband, who believed her own stories about having miscarriages and being beaten unconscious, a woman who was very alluring, manipulative, and dangerous.

"Ultimately, she's alone in the world," said Feinberg, "like an animal in a cage, pitted against everyone. She's either lying or crazy or both. And this is the witness you must believe. Poor Jan Ogilvie, a battered woman who cries at lunch to her employees. Come on! She was setting up her employees, setting them up as her escape route, to blame someone else."

Feinberg argued that Ogilvie knew she was going to kill Tom Weed and that drawing her employees into the plot was her way of finding and arranging to have someone else to blame. "She got her employees to suggest a hit man, and her employees have a connection to Von Villas. This is her way out."

Feinberg described how Ogilvie developed her story, how the story changed and grew over time as she added bits and pieces, like the details about the wigs and disguises she picked up from the Los Angeles Times clipping. He described how she was a master of taking small truths and transforming them into grand lies.

Placed in the context of Feinberg's portrait, the weight of all the minute inconsistencies in her story proved troubling. He concluded, "How do you spell reasonable doubt? O-G-I-L-V-I-E."

Then Feinberg turned his attention to Ron Brot. "When you get to the Brot connection, you step right into the twilight zone. She spent an hour and a half on the phone with Brot on the day of decision, February 22, and she can't remember what they talked about. You are asked to believe this. Why bring Brot in? To bring him down. No one involved in her life escapes unscathed. All she has to do is implicate Brot in solicitation to make him lose his license. When she wrote that letter to the police, she's not just throwing them off, she's trying to hurt people. It's a psychiatric problem. She has to hurt these people for real or imagined hurts she felt at their hands . . . Ogilvie's motivation is self-preservation. She really believes herself to be harmed or threatened by those around her.

"The missed drop is so bizarre it could only be concocted in someone's imagination. The last thing you would ever do in such a situation is bring in an outsider. She had a commitment? She couldn't break it? A life and death matter isn't more important? And if this commitment was so crucial, wouldn't she remember what it was? And the prosecution can't provide any evidence to corroborate this meeting commitment!

"It's our contention those drops never took place. The prosecution hasn't proven they have. There's absolutely no corroboration.

"To convict Von Villas you have to believe witnesses who bartered for their freedom," said Feinberg. "They admit they lied to police before they made their deal with the prosecutor. Now, after they've made their deal, they're cleansed. Now they're telling the truth. If you believe that, I have a bridge in Brooklyn I'd like to sell you."

On redirect, Bob O'Neill stated, "The defense strategy is to point the finger anywhere but at your client. Jan Ogilvie is guilty of lying, inconsistencies, emotional problems, but her testimony is corroborated by others and by evidence. Their first theory is that she's nuts, from the twilight zone. The second is that she's smart and devious. You're asked to pick whichever one you want."

O'Neill denied that he had ignored Ogilvie's mental state, pointing out that he had presented testimony from her doctors. " 'Doctor' Feinberg says she's paranoid," stated O'Neill, demonstrating a rare snappishness, "but her two doctors say she's been stable the entire time and shows no signs of mental illness. She was diagnosed with hysterical neurosis years ago at UCLA, and with residual schizophrenia while in jail. She may in the past have suffered some symptoms, but she is 'nuts' only according to Doctors Feinberg and Stone—not her real doctors.

"They say the D.A. was overzealous, unethical, that he programmed Jan Ogilvie with his questions. When all else fails, attack everybody. Everybody in this case is either sick, lying, has a hidden agenda, is overzealous, devious, and they are all conspiring to get their client, Mr. Ory.

"Judy Von Villas. It's sad. I don't want you to laugh at her. It was panic time,

Stone says. You bet it was panic time. He says I was insinuating that she was lying. No I'm not. I'm *telling* you that she was lying."

The verdict came in first on the matter of Richard Ford, on October 11, 1988, after the jury had deliberated for seven days. Richard Ford was brought into a courtroom packed with spectators, press, friends, and family. A solemn jury filed in to pronounce its judgment.

Winston B. Peterson, the jury's elderly black foreman, presented the verdicts. Richard Herman Ford was found guilty on both counts—conspiracy to commit murder and murder in the first degree. The jury, which was then individually polled, also found him guilty of the special circumstances allegation—killing for monetary gain— which qualified Ford for the death penalty.

Richard Ford lowered his head and shook it from side to side in disbelief as the verdict was read. Before being led from the court, he shook hands with his lawyers, flashed a thumbs-up sign, and blew his wife a kiss. The penalty phase of Ford's trial, during which the jury would decide whether he would go to the gas chamber, was slated to begin on November 7.

"He's getting what he deserves," pronounced LAPD spokesperson Commander William Booth, quoted in front-page articles in both the *Times* and *Daily News*. It was also the top story on radio and TV news.

The next day, October 12, Jack Stone asked that the Von Villas jury, which was still hearing trial testimony, be polled as to whether they had seen or heard any of the substantial media coverage on the Ford verdict. Judge Schempp declined. Instead, she questioned the jury at large. None admitted to having heard the verdict, and the Von Villas trial resumed.

After deliberating for five days, the Von Villas jury returned on November 3 with their verdict. Von Villas was found guilty of both murder and conspiracy to commit murder, as well as the special circumstance allegation of murder for financial gain.

Von Villas displayed no emotion as the verdicts were read. But as the jurors were polled one by one, Von Villas stared at them unbelievingly, defiantly. He finally turned and hung his head, staring down at the counsel table.

"We put a lot of energy, resources and time into getting this conviction, so we're pleased that it's been a very successful prosecution," said LAPD spokesperson Booth in a front-page story in the *Daily News*. A large accompanying photo showed Von Villas, staring down at the counsel table as he listened to the verdicts. The headline read "Guilty of Contract Killing. Ex-Policeman Could Receive Death Penalty."

While speculation as to why the defendants had been convicted could fill volumes, both defense teams felt a significant factor was the juries' ability to figure out that Ford and Von Villas had been arrested, and perhaps already convicted, of another serious crime. The taped conversation between Dick and Lillian Ford had taken place in county jail. The jury couldn't help but wonder why he was there. The *Los Angeles Times* clipping found in Ogilvie's drawer stated "Officers Got Wigs and Disguises." Why was the *Times* running a story about Ford and Von Villas getting disguises, before Ogilvie had been arrested and fingered them in the Weed murder? Obviously because they'd been arrested for something else as well. Which meant they were probably just plain dirty cops.

There was also a widespread belief that some of the jurors, who had not been sequestered, had probably learned about the previous trial and conviction. Every newspaper, radio, and TV account of the Weed trial invariably mentioned that Ford and Von Villas had previously been convicted of attempting to murder nude dancer Joan Loguercio. The feeling among defense attorneys was that sometime during this long trial, one or more of the jurors must have heard something.

"I think that the other case working in the background led to the conviction," said Richard Lasting after the trial. "When it came time to analyze the tape recording between Richard Ford and Lillian Ford, that [the obvious other case] was a major influence. I think both convictions were erroneous, and each served to reinforce the other."

Lasting felt the jailhouse tape was virtually the whole case against Richard Ford in the Weed trial and that it should never have been allowed as evidence because of the underhanded way in which it had been obtained. He blamed an overzealous D.A. "Bob Jorgensen made a determination in his mind that they were both guilty. He felt that if a guy's a criminal, then why shouldn't he do anything and everything to get him. So what if you trample his rights."

Both defendants and their defense teams felt there would be adequate grounds for appeal. But at the moment, they had a far more pressing concern: the gas chamber. The appeal could take years and was most uncertain. The effect of cyanide gas was not.

31

Total Package

THE ENSUING PENALTY PHASES EACH RAN LIKE MONTH-LONG MINI-trials. In many ways, they provided the most dramatic moments in Ford and Von Villas's five-and-a-half-year trip through the courts. For one, they were historic, because Ford and Von Villas were the first LAPD officers ever to face the death penalty. Second, the range and scope of the testimony was unprecedented. Family, friends, cops, psychologists, clergymen, and celebrities all took the stand. Most death-trial defendants are unable to present any testimony on their behalf, other than that of paid expert witnesses. This case was something else entirely.

What proved most remarkable, however, were the revelations offered in the testimony. If truth be stranger than fiction, here was proof. The court learned of trauma and terrible dark childhood secrets, and of dedicated lifelong public service. Before now, no one had known what pieces of work Ford and Von Villas really were. Nor did they really have a clue as to how these two seemingly good cops turned bad. The press had presented this case largely as one of simple greed. They were not even close. Suddenly, a torrent of complex and troubling issues spilled out: psychological damage from child abuse, the shattering impact of war horrors and PTSD, job stress, disillusionment, racism, the police/military mentality—and the apparent failure of the LAPD to recognize and deal with any of these problems.

Few convicted killers have lives that warrant close examination. The same empty hole lies at the core of most sociopaths. But the evidence and testimony in this case would show that Ford and Von Villas did not fit that mold. They weren't Ted Bundy–type monsters who simply acted like nice guys. They weren't animals who felt no empathy for their fellow human beings. The record would in fact show that they were extraordinarily good men who had devoted their whole lives to the service of others. But something had happened. While their case would in some ways remain inexplicable, the penalty phases revealed some compelling clues to the baffling puzzle that was Richard Ford and Robert Von Villas.

Prosecutor Robert O'Neill began each proceeding by recounting the lurid details of the plot to kidnap, rape, torture, and murder Joan Loguercio. Many of the jurors were aghast. Others appeared relieved, as though this horrible tale put to rest any niggling doubts about their own decision. As part of his presentation, O'Neill displayed Ford's homicide kit, including the fearsome military combat daggers. Even a pair of empty brown Michelob Light bottles looked somehow sinister when displayed inside a clear plastic evidence bag.

O'Neill also called Bruce Adams to the stand. O'Neill hadn't called Adams during the Weed trial because he felt he would have been a problematic witness. Bruce had contradicted some parts of Jan Ogilvie's story. He remembered Ogilvie calling the shop to talk to Von Villas, but Ogilvie claimed that Von Villas only called her. And when Adams was played a selection of tapes by investigators, he identified one voice as Ogilvie when it was actually Joyce Reynolds. This, along with the inevitable full-scale assault on his character, could have rendered him a less than credible witness. Fortunately, O'Neill hadn't needed him to get a conviction.

But he needed him now. O'Neill made a deal with defense counsel not to play the van tapes; in turn, they agreed not to attack Adams. Most concurred this was a point in favor of the defense. After all, the van tapes were abominable, two men talking and joking while they rehearsed a sex-torture-mutilation killing.

Bruce Adams traveled from parts unknown to have this final face to face with his old partner Richard Ford. He told an abridged version of the same tale he told at the first trial: "Mr. Ford would grab her by the neck, drag her in, flip her over, tie her hands and legs . . . She was supposed to be tortured, raped, sodomized, burnt with cigarettes, and then murdered . . . to make it look like a sex crime."

The Ford defense was aided by Casey Cohen, a renowned penalty phase consultant, one of two such experts in the country. A former probation officer, Cohen, fifty-two, had previously assisted in more than fifty death penalty cases. His job was to locate relatives, coworkers, friends, and experts, persuade them to testify, and then package their testimony into a sympathetic biography of the defendant. Most often this was a difficult, even futile task—but not so with Richard Ford. Cohen's extraordinary case on behalf of Richard Ford was captured by the British Broadcasting Company in an acclaimed documentary produced for their "Everyman" series. Many intimate details about Ford were revealed. Richard Lasting explained the defense's philosophy: "Ultimately, a juror might say, 'I don't care.' But he should never say, 'I didn't know.' "

The defense teams were concerned that the juries might prove merciless because the defendants were cops. "It's a very real aspect of this case and the reason it has gotten publicity," Rickard Santwier said. "But I don't think Ford should be held to a higher standard because he's a policeman. We are all more human than we are anything, and that is true of Richard Ford."

As a man with twenty-five years of public service in the army and the LAPD, Ford was presented as "an anomaly in our criminal justice system." He had a home in the suburbs, a wife and two kids, and was regarded in the community as kind, loving, caring, and selfless. Yet behind this exterior, he was a man with problems. "We don't intend to offer you justification," stated Santwier, "but we will tell you this: he told both the police and the V.A. psychiatrist that he had problems—long before the insinuation of any illegality. Not little problems. Major problems."

The most stunning revelations were those about the former detective's childhood, which had always been a mystery even to those who knew him well. The defendant's father and stepmother, Donald and Mary Ford, had sat quietly through nearly two years of trials. Now, along with Richard Ford's sister, Donna Sue, and his half brother, James Neel, they took the stand to reconstruct the defendant's early years.

Donald Ford, a thin, wiry man in his seventies, explained how he had married Dick's mom, Lorine Hunt, in June 1937 in Evansville, Indiana. Lorine was a wild one, just sixteen at the time, and Don suspected that she married him "just to get out of the house." Back then Don was a trucker, hauling coal for a dollar a day and room and board. Dick's older sister, Donna Sue, was born in 1938, but Lorine, who waitressed at night, continued running around. The couple got divorced, then reconciled and remarried. Lorine had another baby, Richard, on May 21, 1940.

Don and Lorine moved to California, and Don went to work with his brother as a sheet metal mechanic. Before long, Lorine fell back to her old ways. One night Don came home from work and caught her with another man, named Jim Neel. Lorine said, "So what? What are you going to do about it?" Don left and moved in with his brother. Lorine took off for San Francisco with Jim Neel. Later, she returned and took Donna Sue.

When the war broke out in 1942, Don Ford enlisted in the navy and Dick was sent back east to his grandmother. Don returned after two years at sea and married his current wife, Mary. They could only afford a small one-room apartment in Glendale, so they boarded four-year-old Dick with another family until they got a larger place in 1947. Even then, Dick continued to be shuttled back and forth to his mother, who was now living in Bakersfield with Jim Neel. Don wanted Dick and Donna to have a chance to grow up as brother and sister, but that never worked out.

Ford's older sister, Donna Sue Whiteman, a plump, fifty-year-old woman with curly light brown hair, described how Dick was continually rejected by their mother. Lorine always promised Dick he could come live with her but she never kept her promises. Once, when Donna was six and Dick was four and they were living with Don Ford, Lorine came to see them. "She pulled up alongside the curb and reached out and grabbed me and yanked me into the car. She drove off and left Dick standing on the sidewalk."

According to Donna, Dick was boarded with another family because Mary Ford, Dick's stepmother, "didn't want him." Dick received little love or nurturing from either Don or Mary Ford. "My dad's a sweet little man, but he is not capable of feeling or showing that type of thing. And Mary was always extremely resentful because Dick and I resembled my mother. So much so that when you look at Dick or I you see our mother. And Mary and Mother never got along. Never." Her little brother's life with the Fords was harsh. She described how Mary once forced Dick to fight it out with a much older neighborhood bully. "This other boy pulverized Dick . . . and Dick became literally hysterical with fear. That was the type of treatment he received at home."

Dick's real mother, meanwhile, was voluptuous, sensuous, with long dark hair. She was also hell on wheels—a manipulative drug-addicted whore. When Dick was eight, he spent the summer with Lorine and Jim Neel while they were living at an army base outside Bakersfield called Minter Field. During that time, Lorine molested her son, Richard Ford, orally copulating him. "James Neel was molesting me," Donna Sue explained. "He had been since I was seven and continued till I was fifteen. Mother knew about it. Mother liked to recount her sexual activities to the children. She used sex as a means of power and control, absolutely, either by guilt or by the enjoyment of the association. She would start out with you as your partner and pretty soon you were her victim." Later, when Donna was fifteen, Lorine forced her into prostitution.

Lorine was an alcoholic who later turned to drugs—Demerol, Seconal, Tuinal—anything she could dissolve into a liquid and inject. Neighborhood kids rarely came around because of her addiction. During that same summer at Minter Field, some high school boys broke in the house while the kids were home alone.

"They wanted to have sex with me because they had seen my mother having sex with some army guys," Donna related. "They thought I was like her. Dick, who was even littler than I was, fought the boys off. He protected me."

Lorine and Jim were "rounders," and it was not uncommon for them to be gone for two or three days at a time. Sometimes they were gone so long Donna nearly went to the police to report them missing. And they didn't always leave enough food for the kids. Donna recalled that one time all they had was dried bread and some lard, so she made her two brothers lard sandwiches.

Don and Mary Ford bought a house in Pico Rivera in 1951, and eleven-year-old Dick finally got his own room. According to Don, Dick got along with his stepmother, but he missed his real mom and liked to visit her. One time he and another boy from the neighborhood ran away. They were headed for Bakersfield to see Lorine, but they only got as far as the bus station in El Monte, where they ran out of money and got picked up by the Sheriff.

Dick wanted to join the navy when he was sixteen, but the Fords wouldn't let him. He won the lead in the school play at El Rancho High in Pico Rivera at the end of his junior year in 1957, when he was seventeen. He joined the army soon after. The Fords didn't hear from him too much after he broke for boot camp. Several years later, Dick called and said he was getting married in Virginia, where he was serving in the President's honor guard. The Fords didn't go to the wedding. They would hardly see Dick for the next twelve years as he went off to serve in Europe, Japan, and finally Vietnam.

When Dick returned in 1969, he met with Donna Sue and related some of the horrors he had experienced in Vietnam. "One time he went into a village they had blown up. There was a pregnant woman lying on the ground, still alive, and the baby was kicking. His commanding officer told him to kill the woman and Dick couldn't do it. So the officer shoved him aside and killed her. Dick went off to the side and cried and threw up. Another time, one of his best buddies was right beside him when he had his head blown off."

Dick returned to L.A. and went right into the LAPD. Mary Ford, Dick's stepmother, a petite, gravel-voiced pixy who waved her hands expressively as she spoke, recalled that Dick and his first wife, Sue, stayed with them for a few weeks. Dick was a "pretty nice guy, proud of his accomplishments," Mary stated, but his marriage was on the rocks. "She [Sue] told me he mistreated her. She called him a woman hater." Asked if she loved Richard Ford, Mary responded, "Yes, as much as I can get close to him." The problem with Dick, she said, was his mother. "I think he always resented the fact that he couldn't live with her. It made it tough on me 'cause I knew he wasn't too happy."

Lorine never changed. After divorcing Jim Neel in 1956, she married an air force sergeant in Las Vegas, with whom she also drank, caroused, and fought. When Lorine died in 1985, Jim Neel, Jr., received all her belongings, which included personal effects such as letters, journals, and pictures. Among these papers were many of Dick's things, from report cards to military citations. Jim Neel showed the court some of the old letters he found written by Dick Ford to his mom. "When growing up Dick wanted to be part of our family. He wanted to be a Neel or a Hunt." One letter written by Dick to his mom in 1956, when he was sixteen, was signed, "Your loving son, Dick (Neel)" with an arrow drawn to it and the words "I wish." Another letter, sent while he was in the service, was signed, "Your loving Son, Dick Hunt (I'd like it better than Ford)."

Neel displayed numerous photos from his mom's files: Dick in uniform being awarded the Purple Heart, another of him receiving the Bronze Star. On the back of that one he had written: "P.S. I won the war, so they gave me a medal and sent me out to win another one." Another picture showed him recuperating in a hospital in Japan. There was also his graduation photo from the Los Angeles Police Academy. All of these had been sent by Dick to the mother who could never be bothered with him.

Jim Neel met with Dick right after he returned from Vietnam. It was a joyous reunion for both, as they had a lot in common. "I left home the day I turned sixteen and could drive on my own," Neel explained. "Dick did basically the same thing. We both had to pave our own road and our goals seemed to be the same: family, security, happiness, and a feeling of self-esteem that we were both able to achieve."

Neel later moved to Las Vegas, where he joined the fire department and started his own construction business. Dick and Lillian got married at his Las Vegas home in June 1973. Afterward, the Neels and the Fords "spent as much time together as possible." They both had children. Neel showed a picture of Dick holding his newborn daughter, Chris. "He was absolutely thrilled. When we went to see him he was a different man."

The marriage of Dick and Lillian, many testified, was made in heaven. The couple was "head over heels in love" and "very sweet to watch." Dick loved Lillian's son, Richard, as his own, adopted him, and gave him his name. Richard Ford became the model of a loving husband and father, "a homeboy who didn't go out a lot," a man who always wanted the best for his kids—a good education, a nice neighborhood—and he provided it from day one. His family meant "everything" to him. Many close to him sensed that his "obsession" with family was the result of his own deprived childhood.

Jacquie Arends, a longtime neighbor and friend, explained that while Richard Ford was not materialistic, a simple thing like food was very important to him. "He always liked to have lots of food around. It was part of the whole completion of the family picture as far as what was important to him."

The domestic bliss in the Ford household was shattered by Lillian's rape. "It changed their lives totally. Lillian was not herself, she was hanging on by a thread," Jacquie Arends explained. The resulting destruction of his family destroyed Richard Ford.

Jacquie's husband, James Arends, described how he often dug shrapnel out of Richard Ford's back while they sat around Ford's backyard swimming pool. He and Jacquie later moved to Washington, and the Fords visited them after Lillian's rape. Dick was distraught, worried about Lillian. "I don't think he ever really worried about himself. Dick's family meant everything to him." Like many witnesses, Arends expressed his undying faith in Richard Ford. He explained that he and Jacquie had asked the Fords to be godparents to their youngest child—who was born after Ford had been arrested and was residing in Los Angeles County Jail facing a capital murder trial.

During the 1970s, Dick Ford and his mother had reconciled somewhat, and Lorine had visited Dick and Lillian occasionally. Then, sometime over the 1980 Christmas holiday—one month after the rape of Lillian Ford—Lorine dropped a bomb that rocked the family. According to Donna and Jim, it virtually destroyed Richard Ford. Donald Ford had dropped in to visit Dick in Northridge over the holidays while Lorine was there. After Don left, Lorine began to belittle him, and Dick stood up for his father. Then Lorine told Dick, "He's not your goddam father." Later, Dick confronted Don Ford. "It just hit me like a ton," Don explained. "I said, 'Well, Dick, I have raised you as my son. I have loved you as my son. Why don't we just leave it there?' "

Donna Sue said, "Mom had told me Don was not Dick's father, that his real father was a man named Holbrook. She never liked Don. She thought it was very fitting that he should raise another man's child. She swore me to secrecy." Lorine later wrote Dick an angry letter and sent him a photo she had kept over the years of his real father. "It was a photo button and it shows an absolute resemblance. I think he [Dick] was forty, forty-one. This happened right after Lillian had been raped." Don Ford subsequently admitted to Dick that he had once chased a man named Holbrook out of their house back in Indiana.

Dick visited Donna in Montana in 1981 and unburdened his soul. "His reaction was total confusion and a lot of pain and anger because of what Mom did to him. He couldn't figure out why she told him after keeping it secret all those years. We were both feeling a great deal of hatred. But Dick had always loved his mother. He worshiped her. We both did. She did that kind of magnetism thing to you. We felt confusion, feelings of conflict. We discussed it, trying to figure out how in the world somebody could make you love them so much, then turn around and do these things she always did to us."

Donna and Dick also discussed, for the first time, the sexual abuse they had endured as kids. "I thought Dick was in a bad way. I took him out to the backyard and said, 'Dick, I need to tell you what happened to me.' And he said, 'Wow, it wasn't my imagination.' He told me that he came to my room once and saw what Jim Neel was doing to me. He thought he had been dreaming it. He said, 'Oh my God, I thought I had been crazy all these years. I thought I was sick, that I had been imagining those things.' I said, 'No, you weren't crazy. It wasn't dreams. These things really did happen to us as children.'

"I could see that things were coming unglued for him . . . I talked to him about discussing his pain and the things that had happened. I told him we ought to come out and tell everybody, to try and get some help. He told me to forget it. 'People don't really give a damn. Just keep it inside yourself and do the best you can, because people don't really care.' "

Donna explained that she had moved to Montana after learning that Lorine was molesting her son—Lorine's own grandson. Donna concluded by saying, "Nobody can begin to imagine what our lives were really like," and she described her mother as "the most evil woman I ever had the disopportunity to meet."

Jim Neel described the impact of the Holbrook revelation on his half brother as "devastating, as it would be on anyone." Neel showed a series of torn photographs he had pulled from his mother's files. One picture was of Dick and his Mom standing by Dick's pool—only it was torn in half, so that they were separated. There were numerous other photos of her and Dick, also torn in half. "My mother's way of handling herself when she felt hurt or deceived was to tear pictures. I have many pictures I received upon her death which are torn or have a head cut out. That was mother's way of separating people. There's another picture with little Richard Junior torn out."

Richard Ford apparently developed the same predilection. Later, Lorine had regrets and wanted to make amends with her son, but Dick Ford never forgave her. Lorine sent him pictures and some poetry she wrote, but Dick returned them, torn up in pieces. "Mom tried to reconcile with Dick and Lillian many times. It was never resolved until her death. Never." Despite Dick Ford's bitter hatred for his mother, however, Dick's half brother, Jim Neel, nonetheless stated that there was also "no question" that he loved her very much.

Patricia Neel explained how she and Jim were interested in genealogy. After she compiled a family history book on the Hunts, she sent a copy to Dick and Lillian. It was returned a few weeks later. "The pictures of Dick's mother had been defaced. Her face had been x'd out and next to her pictures were written the words 'Evil, devil, witch, whore.' In the back of the book there was a note stating that they didn't want anything further to do with the family. Dick had signed it and so had Lillian.

"I think this [the Holbrook revelation] really backfired on Lorine. I think she intended for it to endear Dick more to her and turn him away from his father. Instead, Dick became enraged, filled with hatred. Many times he discussed how he couldn't understand why his mom had raised Donna Sue and left him with Don Ford. And then, finding out that Don was not even his father. . . . I'm sure Dick still loves Don Ford, but it was like a double rejection from his mother, and I think a very great source of betrayal. The break caused a bitterness in Dick, a bitterness that far outreached his mom. He extended it."

A parade of witnesses testified to Richard Ford's stellar twenty-five years of service with the U.S. Army and the LAPD. Peter Gravett, a former U.S. Army colonel, as well as an LAPD officer for twenty-two years, had been one of Ford's training officers in 1969. Gravett spent most of an afternoon explaining all the medals that had been awarded to Staff Sergeant (E6) Richard Ford: a National Defense Service Medal with an oak-leaf cluster, representing reenlistment; a Vietnam Campaign Medal with three clusters, indicating four combat campaigns; a Vietnam Service Medal, representing fifty hours of aerial combat; the Purple Heart, with cluster, received twice for injuries sustained in combat; the Army Good Conduct Medal with clusters indicating four awards; the Army Commendation Medal, received for valor.

Gravett also described Ford as "a good, conscientious police officer. I was glad to have Richard Ford. He was a staff sergeant, had been a leader in combat, he was decorated. All combined, it made him a good NCO for the unit." Gravett implied that Ford's exceptional military record literally enabled him to walk right into the paramilitary LAPD. Any other considerations of Ford's suitability were secondary.

Sam Banks, a retired army lieutenant colonel, flew the command helicopter for First Infantry Brigadier General James Hollingsworth in Vietnam. Ford was the door gunner on his crew. The drift of Banks's testimony was that Hollingsworth, an army legend, wouldn't fly with anything but the best. One reason Ford was selected was that he had previously served with the Honor Guard Brigade at the Tomb of the Unknown Soldier at Arlington National Cemetery, which entailed protecting visiting dignitaries and heads of state—a prestige assignment granted only to the most outstanding candidates.

The testimony of General James Hollingsworth was introduced on videotape. The feisty sixty-eight-year-old retired Texas general stood with a pointer before a map of Vietnam and declared, "Richard Ford was a soldier of mine and I feel an obligation to support him to the last." Hollingsworth described how they were forced to fly eighteen hours straight under terrifying conditions in a chopper "honeycombed with holes." Ford held up under extreme stress. Hollingsworth concluded by saying, "Staff Sergeant Richard Ford was the epitome of the young American male serving his country with devotion and great loyalty to crew and country. I know of no man who better exemplifies the highest honor, duty to country, of the millions who served under me."

Robert Hickey, Ford's LAPD field supervisor on the night he was shot in 1969, explained that Officer Ford could have easily left the police department with a tax-free pension for the rest of his life. "Officers have gone off for less," Hickey stated, "but he didn't choose that path. It amazed me that he came back so fast. My impression at the time was that he was one of the finest officers ever to work under me." Hickey went through fifteen years of Ford's rating reports for the jury; the evaluations were all good to excellent.

Officer James Cypert was trained by Richard Ford at Central Division. "He was outstanding. He was very concerned about the public, the safety of citizens. He continually stressed that we were public servants . . . He loved the LAPD, and that's what he instilled in me." Cypert also stated, "Ford was unable to talk about his personal life, but if someone was having a problem, he was the type of senior lead you could talk to." Cypert described a harrowing incident involving a flaming car wreck. Ford pounded feverishly on the car with his baton, attempting to remove the injured driver, but the car exploded into flames and the driver was killed. "Ford was very distraught. Later, he said, 'Life goes on and things like that happen and that's the job. Maybe next time we'll be able to save a life.' "

The defense next called a battery of five psychologists and psychiatrists, all of whom had counseled the defendant, to present their profiles and attempt to explain what had happened to Richard Ford. These experts included LAPD psychologist Dr. Martin Reiser; Dr. Gerald Motis and Dr. David Lopata from the V.A.; Lillian Ford's therapist, Dr. Frederick Hacker; and expert witness Dr. Berton Chertock, who had been seeing Ford since his incarceration. The conclusions of each member of this august group fell along similar lines.

Richard Ford's early environment was "deprived," and he had "poor internalized parent figures." (In other words, his role models were not good.) All contact with his mother, "that supposed parental figure," was highly traumatic. He was a "severely abused child" whose early years were filled with pain, rejection, and bizarre experiences. Although this was "extremely stressful and damaging," he never received any treatment or therapy.

Denied a real family as a child, he had hoped to find one in the service. "In my experience," Dr. Lopata explained, "anybody who was in Vietnam for two tours was really trying to make something go for themselves. And then he jumps right into the police force; again, it's a family to him."

By the late 1970s, Ford was suffering from an "intense, exacerbated case of PTSD" as a result of his experiences in Vietnam. Symptoms included "a reexperiencing of traumatic events through nightmares or intrusive thoughts, which are like ruminations or daydreams." He also suffered from "police stress" and "PTSD from the occupational arena as well," the result of his near-fatal shooting while on duty. He suffered from depression, anxiety, and isolated himself from everyone except people at work and his family. His "no problem" attitude masked a state of denial, which kept him from facing his problems.

According to Dr. Motis, people who had psychological problems before a traumatic event sometimes experience more difficulty with posttraumatic stress. "Someone victimized by child abuse goes into the military. He has to shoot children—as we did in Vietnam, because they came running after us with grenades and could blow up a whole squad. This, layered onto a background of child abuse, would make the manifestations worse and I think more noticeable."

After Ford's transfer to Club Dev his PTSD had gotten "progressively better" and was under control. He had "reached an equilibrium" and was "functioning satisfactorily." Then Lillian Ford was raped.

Dr. Frederick Hacker, presented on videotape, provided the gruesome details of Lillian's sexual torture that weren't allowed at the first trial. He also described Lillian's pitiful regression, her needy condition following the attack. Dr. Hacker described the stress this placed on Richard Ford and how his being "carried away with rage" served to greatly reinforce his PTSD, his nightmares of violence, and his dissatisfaction with the LAPD. Nevertheless, Dr. Hacker stated that Richard treated his wife with unwavering patience and compassion.

The other doctors concurred that Lillian's rape had sent Richard Ford over the deep end. It was a "tremendous traumatic event" that "stirred up the underpinnings of a lot of previous traumatic events"—his childhood problems, feelings of deprivation and disjunction from the family, reaction to violence in Vietnam and the LAPD. All these "tended to coalesce." And Ford had new problems to cope with as well: a son experimenting with narcotics, a terminally ill mother-in-law, a growing problem with excessive drinking and pill popping, all of which further exacerbated his condition. Symptoms that were apparently manageable before the rape became unmanageable. "These things layer," Dr. Motis explained.

"We live in a continuum, and every traumatic event we come upon has the same ingredients: threat to life and limb and feelings of helplessness. With his life history, there's always the last straw that could just strain the camel's back a little more."

Dr. Chertock described Lillian's rape as "more than overwhelming" to Richard Ford. "The human being can't separate or compartmentalize them [traumatic or stressful events] in any way. Altogether, it was a total package and a huge burden he was attempting to deal with. . . . I think it was like he had five or six cases of posttraumatic stress going on at the same time." Dr. Chertock allowed that many people who suffer from severe stress are capable of going about their everyday lives, but, he stated, "Some will perform better than others."

Ford felt that his family had in some measure been destroyed when his wife was raped. "Vietnam and the rape were two extremely stressful events," Lopata explained, "and I don't know if you can say where one started and one ended. When his wife got raped, that could have essentially blown his cover. All of a sudden he had a lot of feelings of anger, rage and detachment. . . ." One symptom of prolonged stress, Lopata explained, was that values often got "scrambled," that victims of such stress could become "a little loose in their thinking."

Dr. Chertock commented, "His marriage was the most positive thing he had ever experienced. Hence, the rape was the most devastating thing that ever happened to him."

Dr. Chertock explained that Ford's family remained his greatest concern in life. "He's concerned about their day-to-day adjustments with his situation. I see him as the father figure, as the man of the house, in spite of the fact that he hasn't been home in five years. The family looks to him for direction and guidance. He's concerned about his daughter, her grades. He's concerned about his son; he's been acting out, seems to be on drugs. He's been concerned about his wife, her suicidal manners and her inability to stay in contact with her family and take care of the kids. I still see him as the one who keeps the family together, in spite of where he is. And I see him as the one that will continue to provide guidance and hopefully help them to adjust and to get some kind of meaningful lives for themselves. Because, in a sense, they're all failing right now. He knows it, and he would like to help them through this."

As for the impact of a death sentence on the Ford family, Dr. Chertock stated, "They would never recover. Especially the children. This would be a stress and trauma to them indefinitely."

Outside the courtroom, some observers would question whether the LAPD bore any blame for Detective Ford's situation. Basically, Ford had been turned over to the care of the V.A. While most agreed this was appropriate and sufficient action, others would contend that the LAPD had allowed Richard Ford to fall through the cracks. Some friends and relatives, in particular, felt that the LAPD should have done more than just "stick him behind a desk." This went to the very heart of a seemingly irresolvable catch-22. Was a police department responsible for treating stress cases or for getting rid of them? If a department allowed for stress by treating it, they might encourage people who have difficulties with stress to become police officers. But the idea is to get people with the right stuff, people who can handle it. On the other hand, if a department were intolerant toward stress cases, officers would never seek help because they'd be afraid of losing their jobs.

Defenders of the LAPD would argue that the department had done all that could be expected. They hadn't tried to ignore Richard Ford's problems, and they hadn't tried to drum him out of the LAPD. They had sent him to competent people to get help. It was all they could do.

The defense then brought in another cavalcade of witnesses to testify to the ongoing good works of Richard Ford—a presentation that left many jurors struggling to reconcile the picture of Richard Ford, good citizen, with that of Richard Ford, killer cop. Francis Isaman, Ford's neighbor in Northridge and a born-again Christian like Richard Ford, described how Dick had "several ministries" in the jailhouse and had spent the past five years counseling other inmates. Christopher Mazurek, a former county jail inmate in his twenties, explained that counseling from Richard Ford had prevented him from committing suicide. "He introduced me to Jesus. He took me under his wing. He said one of the men on the cross next to Jesus was a murderer, and if He could forgive him, He could forgive me. He gave me a reason to live."

John Salas, twenty-four, Ford's nephew, a technical illustrator for Hughes Aircraft, explained that after his parents had divorced when he was in the fourth grade, he had always sought counsel and advice from Dick Ford. "I attribute where I am today almost entirely to my uncle. He was there during those very important years when I was making important decisions about the future. We discussed school, he couldn't stress how important it was. That, and the importance of family. My uncle was always there for me." Salas stated that he would continue to seek guidance from Richard Ford, even if he were locked up in prison for the rest of his life. "I not only would like it, but I need the opportunity. He always said that everybody needs somebody to turn to, even men, you know. He also said that men don't always do that. Today, the only person I can really turn to, who I can open up to and say personal things to, would be my uncle."

Three deputy sheriffs who had come to know Richard Ford over the past five years testified that Richard Ford was a model inmate who had been made a trustee at the L.A. County Jail. The deputies all stated that they had never before testified on behalf of an inmate. They described Ford as a warm man whose sole concern was always for his family and who had never expressed any bitterness toward the judicial system.

Louis Nelson, a former warden of San Quentin prison, described the life that awaited Richard Ford if he were given life without parole. Defense attorneys were concerned that, due to the media, many jurors had the opinion that prisons were all miniature resorts. They used Nelson to dispel any such notions. Nelson explained that an individual loses all control over his life when he's confined in state prison. "Every decision is made for him. What time to get up. What time to eat. What time to go to work . . . Every aspect of their life is regulated and controlled."

Nelson spoke of the need for good inmates. "No warden can run an institution without the cooperation of a portion of the inmate body. In many cases they take the place of personnel who would cost the state a great deal of money." Nelson also pointed out that a person serving a life sentence could contribute to the proper functioning of a prison far more than somebody doing three years. "This is their home. They want to make the best of it, make the climate as good as they can, because they know full well they have to live there."

On the final day of the trial's penalty phase, November 22, many of Richard Ford's family and friends were in attendance. Jim and Jacquie Arends, with their two children, sat in the packed spectators' area with Lillian and Christina Ford. Lillian, looking drawn and distraught, wore dark sunglasses to cover her eyes.

The first witness was Sister Janet Harris. A nun in her early forties, she had stylishly cut gray hair, large round glasses, and wore a smartly tailored skirt and blue blazer. She appeared very hip, more like a Hollywood agent or studio executive than a nun.

Harris was in fact a woman of the world. She had taught high school and worked with inner-city juvenile delinquents. Believing youths could be positively motivated by the media, Sister Harris had obtained a master's degree in screenwriting and filmmaking. She had made a documentary about L.A. street gangs that was widely acclaimed and had brought her to the attention of L.A. County officials, who hired her as a street gang counselor. It was while working in that capacity, visiting young inmates at L.A. County Jail, that she happened to meet Richard Ford. She eventually had a number of lengthy visits with the defendant.

"The thing that really struck me was that he would never really talk about himself," Harris stated. "He always talked about his wife, who he thought was very fragile for all that she had suffered, and about his daughter. He was very concerned about her schoolwork and so forth. He knew that I had taught high school girls, so he asked me if I would talk to his daughter and, you know, see how she was doing. And I promised I would do that. He also felt that with all the stress his wife had been going through, that she had disconnected from her faith. So he wanted me to tell her that she needed to come back to her faith because she needed it to sustain her."

Sister Harris subsequently developed a close relationship with both Lillian and Christina Ford. "Lillian is a remarkable woman. If I had gone through what she's gone through I don't know if I would be that strong. Chris, well, Chris has somewhat neglected her studies, which is a concern of mine. But other than that I find her very mature. For someone her age I think she's coping well."

The final witness to take the stand in the matter of Detective Richard Ford was his daughter, Christina. A tall, slightly plump thirteen-year-old with a dark complexion and dark hair done up in a ponytail, Christina had a sweet smile that still exuded little-girl innocence. She and her father beamed broad smiles at each other as she walked to the witness stand. Christina's very appearance on the stand—which brought home to the jury all she had endured over the past five years—was heart-rending. The silence in the courtroom was somehow heavier than it had been before.

"Chris, how old are you?" Richard Lasting asked.

"Thirteen."

"Do you visit your dad in county jail?"

"Yes."

"Do you talk with your dad on the telephone?"

"Whenever I can, yes."

"Does he try to call your house every night?"

"Yes."

"Does he ask you how you're doing and talk about your problems with you?"

"Yeah, he acts like a dad."

"Does he try to help you with the problems that you have?"

"He tries."

"Is your dad still special to you, Chris?"

"Yes. I love him very much."

Lasting paused a moment. Then he said, "I have no further questions."

"No questions, Your Honor," said Bob O'Neill.

Lillian Ford's face was streaked with tears as she draped her arm around her daughter and walked her directly out through the large courtroom doors. Many in the courtroom wept as well.

Prosecutor Robert O'Neill wisely called for a brief recess before he began his closing argument. He wouldn't plead for the execution by cyanide gas of Richard Ford while members of the jury still had tears in their eyes.

"You've been presented over the past few weeks with the tragedy that befell Richard Ford," O'Neill stated in his closing remarks. "I don't in any way want to diminish the significance of that. . . . But you've also been presented with the tragedy that befell Thomas Weed. . . . You don't see him cry, and you don't see his pain and suffering. Thomas Weed isn't with us because of that man, Richard Ford . . . Thomas Weed had family and friends that loved him and continue to cry for him."

O'Neill described the Loguercio caper. "The plan was to make it look like a sex fiend killed her. His words were, 'They'll never suspect a cop of that.' He was a cop, a police officer, and he made that part of his cover. And that, ladies and gentlemen, is frightening. We place our trust, our lives, our families' lives, our safety in the hands of police officers. Perfect cover! Consider that when you consider Richard Ford's career as a police officer and how he served the citizens of Los Angeles.

"The horrors of war have touched many people's lives . . . but they don't go out as a result of that experience and turn to violent crime. There are many people in our society that are victims of violent, unjust, traumatic assaults. That doesn't drive them to violent crime. . . . It doesn't turn them to planned and premeditated contract murder. Richard Ford is more than a cop who fell from grace. Richard Ford is more than a man with emotional problems. Richard Ford, ladies and gentlemen, is a cold-blooded killer.

"Occasionally, ladies and gentlemen, the magnitude of certain criminal conduct warrants the death penalty. It's not revenge. It's not vengeance. It's justice—recognizing the sanctity of life. It's the appropriate punishment for Richard Ford, a punishment he has imposed on himself as a result of his own conscious actions. As he told Bruce Adams that night on July seventh, he knew better than anyone the consequences of his actions. He knew that someday he'd be facing a jury like you."

Richard Lasting then rose to address the jury. "The responsibility to present a case when a man's life is at stake, a man that I care about very deeply, is an awesome responsibility." Lasting then pointed out that Ford's alleged criminal activities had all occurred during the final six months of his career. "This was not a person utterly without redeeming qualities," Lasting stated, "but a human being who finally unraveled under continual stress and tragedy more than many of us could bear. Donna Whiteman told you that Dick said, 'Just keep it inside yourself and do the best you can, because people don't really care.' I hope he was wrong about that, ladies and gentlemen. I believe you care."

Lasting addressed Ford's PTSD and his reaction to Lillian's rape. "You learned of its devastating impact on Richard Ford. He again cried out for help. He asked the police department for help. He wasn't hiding his problems. He wasn't hiding behind the police badge. He wasn't a man looking for the best cover to commit crimes. What kind of cold-blooded killer turns a spotlight on himself and says, 'Look at me. I'm suicidal. I'm homicidal. I can't cope. Help me!' Sadly tragic, the help he got didn't solve his problems. It didn't end his confusion or his mental deterioration."

Lasting addressed the public's perception of the death penalty. "You know, there hasn't been an execution in California since 1967. But one morning in the near future it will happen. The current supreme court upholds death sentences daily. You must understand that if you set the punishment at death, Richard Ford *will die* in the gas chamber. This is not an intellectual exercise."

Indeed, the public had become so cynical about the justice system's inability to implement the death penalty, to override the barrage of ACLU-type appeals, that most people simply didn't believe there would ever be another execution in California. And they generally believed that the death penalty was the only sentence that really insured life without parole.

"Life without possibility of parole is not a lenient sentence," Lasting declared. "Richard Ford does not get away with anything. Unlike Jan Ogilvie, he will never be eligible for parole. He will spend the rest of his life in a man-made hell of concrete and iron. . . . He will never again smell the night-blooming jasmine . . . plant a garden or enjoy the pleasures of his home. . . . You may wonder if he wouldn't be better off dead. But I tell you, ladies and gentlemen, Richard Ford wants to live. He wants to see his family. He wants to give them advice and share in their lives. Jim Neel said that Dick wanted a family, security, happiness, a sense of self-esteem. Is prison for life punishment for a man who wants those things? It is severe punishment! It is continuing punishment! It is punishment forever! But at least Richard Ford will be able to communicate with the people he loves. He will be able to share their lives, their joys, and their accomplishments. And they will be able to share them with him.

"Many people came into this courtroom who love and care about Richard Ford. You could feel it. They came to testify for a man convicted of murder.

Oftentimes, a lawyer can't get a person to say a good word about someone convicted of petty theft. . . . Many people came because they see the decency that is in Richard Ford. And I'd like to close by telling you that over the past five and one half years, I too have seen that decency." Richard Lasting's voice began to crack. Tears flowed from his eyes. "He's not just a client. He's a friend that I care about. I have seen his warmth, his love and concern for his family. I have seen his day-to-day concern for the people in the world around him. I don't understand how he got where he is today, but I know that life is precious, and I know that his life is precious. It's worth saving. I beg you to spare his life."

After thirteen hours of deliberation, the jury returned on November 29 and informed Judge Schempp that they were deadlocked, 11 to 1 in favor of life in prison, and had exhausted any hope of reaching an agreement. This penalty phase "mistrial" left the prosecution with the option of continuing to seek the death sentence in a second penalty phase before a new jury or accepting the lesser sentence of life without parole. This would be decided later.

The sole juror who held out for death later explained his feelings. "The people of California voted overwhelmingly for the death penalty. They removed a state supreme court justice because she wouldn't enforce the death penalty. That's a very decisive vote in my opinion." Basically, the juror implied that others on the jury were simply opposed to the death penalty.

The juror, the elderly black foreman of the jury, Winston Peterson, identified himself as a former military police officer. He stated that Ford "not only disgraced the police department, he also disgraced the military." Having closely reviewed Ford's police record, he found something terribly amiss, something with broad and frightening implications. "According to the police department, Ford had a perfect record as a policeman. All this mishmash about being under strain is a lot of hogwash, because the police department said he was top-notch. My strong thinking is we should have civilian review of the police department, because he was not a very good police officer. We need a civilian review board! That should be impressed upon the people of this great city of Los Angeles. That's what we need and we need it very badly."

This strident plea came three years before the Rodney King incident. But in this case, there was no sensational videotape of the worst crime ever committed by an LAPD officer. Nobody listened. The juror's sentiments didn't even appear in press accounts.

32

The Cop Who Cared Too Much

"YOU WILL LEARN THAT ROBERT VON VILLAS, IN SPITE OF LOVE being denied him as a child, became a loving man himself," Jack Stone declared at the start of the Von Villas penalty phase. "And you will be absolutely astounded at what this man did for the community." While Stone would deliver on this promise, the most illuminating revelations would come in testimony about the defendant's hidden childhood. This was presented by Von Villas's cousin, Ronald Willis, a tall, handsome, Daytona Beach lawyer, and Ronald's mother, Louella Willis, Bob Von Villas's aunt.

Louella Willis, a feisty woman in her seventies with a thick Brooklyn accent, was the youngest of three sisters—herself, Isabelle (Bunny), and Bob's mother, Frances (Franny). They grew up in Brooklyn during the Depression, when "Franny just ran out and got married." Franny's husband, Alexander Von Villas, was a store manager for W. T. Grant, first in Pittsfield, Massachusetts, then in Connecticut. Franny was very beautiful, with long blond hair and a great figure. Her marriage was a battlefield from day one. "She thought no man could resist her," Louella recalled, "and I think she ran around. Alex told me that Franny had several abortions. They fought a lot—not just words, but pushing and hitting. Bob's father was a jealous man. My sister flirted and they would get in fights. Sometimes they'd go out for dinner and he'd come home with a black eye. And she drank. One time around Christmas she was in bed passed out and I found Robert, who was about five, all alone putting tinsel on the tree."

Ronald Willis, who was two years older than Bob, had "unpleasant" recol-

335

lections of visiting the Von Villases in Connecticut. He recalled an incident when Robert was eight. Franny picked up a large mirror off a dresser and "clobbered" Alex over the head. "His father had blood pouring down his face and was picking out the glass while Robert was crying." During another fight Alex picked up a kitten and threw it against a tree, killing it while Robert and his older brother Al Junior watched.

Little Al and Robert lived in constant fear of their father, who beat them regularly and with little provocation. "Little Al was so frightened when we visited," Louella recalled. "When that little boy did something, he [Al Senior] took him in the bathroom and beat him with a brush." When Bob was about six he had "screaming nightmares" while staying overnight with the Willises in Brooklyn. "It was terrible. They should never have had children. Some people have so much love to give—but they didn't. Bob never got love as a child. He [Alex] was an abusive, uncaring father who never took time with them or showed them any affection."

Bob's big brother, Al, was killed when he was about nine. He was learning to ride a bike. He rode out into the street in front of a cement truck and was run over.

After this tragic accident, the fighting between Franny and Alex escalated. Finally, they got divorced. Alex moved to California and Franny returned to Brooklyn, taking an apartment above her sister Bunny on Sixtieth Street between Third and Fourth avenues. Bob, who was about eight, was taken under the wing of Ronald Willis, who became his new big brother. "He was a shy kid and gravitated toward me. I was his hero because I was a little older and pretty streetwise. He was a good, gentle kid and I had a deep love for him. I had to protect him on the streets from some of the rougher kids. We played stick ball—things like that."

Franny's apartment was two blocks from the Brooklyn army base, several blocks from Fort Hamilton, and close to the Brooklyn Navy Yard. "It was a party apartment," Ron Willis recalled. "She treated us good, but she was a party girl. There was a lot of whiskey flowing and a lot of music on the stereo—and a procession of soldiers and sailors and marines in and out."

These servicemen treated the boys pretty well. One sailor took them to the Armed Forces Day parade in New York, lifting them over the crowd so they could see. A marine gave them a record of all the military songs, like "Anchors Aweigh." "Franny took Robert and I to a pizza parlor once with a guy who was just back from the Korean War, and she was all over this guy. That's the kind of relationships she had. Most of the time Robert stayed at my house because she would be gone for four or five days at a time. As I got a little bit older . . . I came to my own conclusion that what she had been doing was probably prostitution."

According to Ron, Robert worshiped his mother. "She was fun to be around, but she pursued her own fun most of the time. He was neglected. Absolutely." Louella took care of Bobby whenever Franny disappeared. "He was an affectionate child. He loved us and hugged us. He did what we told him. He was such a good boy. He always got along. He gave his friends everything. He always shared. Robert was a nice kid, popular. He was a happy child with us, but he wanted his mother. He would cry for her. He loved his mother so much, but she was always gone."

One time, Franny was supposed to take Bobby with her to Coney Island, but she went with a boyfriend instead. So Louella and her sister Bunny took Ronnie and Bobby. They found Franny in the barroom at Coney Island having a drink. "After little Al died, Franny became an alcoholic, a run-around—different men, sailors. She took men home. Once she was buying toys for a sailor's kids. She used her money for that kid but didn't get Robert any toys. She never worked. She could have gotten money from the men she brought home—that was my impression."

Although no one ever knew why, Franny suddenly decided to move to Redondo Beach, California. Her ex-husband was in Fresno, but they didn't see each other. She remarried, but it was another bad coupling. "Robert was very frail when he was about twelve or thirteen," Louella recalled, "and his stepfather beat him up. One time while I was visiting her in California, she left me in a parked car at two A.M. while she went into a bar looking for the stepfather."

Alex and Franny both died of cancer. Bob was twenty-six when his mother passed away. "She was terribly vain," Louella explained. "She had a lump on her breast but wouldn't go for a mastectomy, so it traveled through her body."

Ron Willis cried when Bob moved away to California because "we were really like the two musketeers." He didn't see him again for ten years, until after he'd finished college. One day Bob showed up on their doorstep in Brooklyn. "He was there in his airborne uniform. He had just completed training, I guess at Fort Benning, and hitched to New York out of the blue to see us. We were really pleased to see him. He spent four or five days with us and our relationship was like he'd never left."

Bob Von Villas served as one of the ushers at Ron's wedding in September 1965. A few years later, he went to Vietnam. Willis described a letter he received from Bob. "He was a sergeant and it was pretty horrible. In his opinion they were sending in a bunch of young kids who were not properly trained. His job was to keep them alive, and it was pretty difficult. He was losing a lot of them. It was a very emotional letter. I wrote back and told him I was going to Florida, but I never heard from him again. I was contacted and told about this [Bob's arrest] in 1985. I was shocked. He was such a good, gentle kid."

Louella visited Bob Von Villas in California after he returned from Vietnam. "He took me on my first trip to Las Vegas, along with his wife, who was pregnant. He was just as sweet as could be, a real gentleman. I never saw any change in him. Even when he came back from the paratroopers, he was all sweet and smiling. I still can't believe he did all that stuff [the crimes]. In Vietnam he was always helping somebody. He had a good heart. He was so happy and proud about having a baby. He was very different from his father. He showed love and affection. Bob was always such a sweet boy, a gentle boy. I can't believe this is him. I can't believe anything would change him, as good as he was."

This sentiment was echoed by the defendant's wife, Judith Von Villas. Judy had her jet black hair cut in a short, new-wave style, and she wore her long fingernails painted bright red. On the day she testified, she sported a black blouse and dark eye shadow and large gold hoop earrings. She looked attractive, but tough. This aura was dispelled, however, as she unveiled a sweet, cheerful disposition. She smiled warmly as she described her twenty-two-year marriage.

Judy met Bob in 1963 at a dance club in Long Beach when they were in their late teens. They dated for three years—movies, dancing, parties. Bob was always nice, well-mannered, a gentleman, and very straight. He drank little and never did drugs or smoked. "We used to go look at model homes together," Judy recalled. Bob went into the army for about a year, but then got released on a hardship discharge because his mother was ill. Judy never met his stepfather. They married and had their first child, Michele, in 1966. Then, when Michele was two, Bob went back into the service. "He volunteered to be recalled. He hadn't really finished his tour of duty and he felt he should go back in and complete it. Because of the war, he felt that serving his country was something he should do. He figured he would probably go to Vietnam. He was willing to do that."

Bob wrote to her three times a week. "Not things I want to repeat—love letters, you know. He said the war was very difficult because the Vietcong could fight wherever they wanted, but the American soldiers could only fight up to a certain point. A lot of his friends died. One died the day before his tour ended. He was part of Bob's patrol. Bob won a decoration for that operation. It was the Purple Heart or the Bronze Star—he got both."

Judy read the citation for Bob's Bronze Star for valor as it was submitted as evidence: "Sergeant Von Villas distinguished himself by exceptional heroism in connection with military operations . . . in the Republic of Vietnam on twelve July, 1969, while assigned to Company B, Fifth Battalion, Twelfth Infantry, One hundred and ninety-ninth Infantry Brigade. On that day Sergeant Von Villas was participating in sweep operations when a helicopter was hit by enemy fire and crashed near the company's position. With complete disregard for his own personal safety, Sergeant Von Villas exposed himself to withering enemy fire in order to evacuate the injured personnel. He then went back into the wreckage and succeeded in blocking the flow of explosive fuel while another soldier pulled the last injured man to safety."

Von Villas also received a Purple Heart, awarded for wounds received in action on April 25, 1969. "He often wrote to me in letters about his fear of booby traps," Judy explained. "Once, someone did step on one, and he was killed. Bob was wounded."

Her husband had "changed a little" when he came back. "He was a little quieter, more serious. But you can't go to war and not change somewhat. He'd grown up more. He had bad dreams once in a while, but he didn't go into details." Still, Bob was always a gentle person. "I never saw him violent. He doesn't even have a temper. That would make me mad. It's very hard to argue by yourself." He was always meticulous, neat, organized—and a great dad. Judy recalled how she went back to work when Michele was just six weeks old. "A lot of men don't help with babies, they think it's a woman's job. Bob took care of her. He fed her, bathed her, everything. In fact, she could have cared less if I was even there, because she was always daddy's girl. Even at two."

Bob joined the LAPD in 1970, shortly after returning from Vietnam, "because he liked helping people." He always loved police work but really hit his stride when he got assigned to the school car in 1976. Judy spent a few hours describing all the work he'd done with kids. "Bob loved all of that."

Judy read the inscription from a plaque, a special award given to Bob Von Villas: "To Officer Bob, the greatest leader the DAPs ever had or ever will have. Good luck in the future and we love you. [signed] The Devonshire DAPs. June first, 1978." She read another plaque from the Devonshire Police Athletic League Supporters. She explained various framed photos of Bob with celebrities at important functions. Before Judy left the stand, every inch of a long banquet table placed in front of the jury box was completely covered with plaques, certificates, medals, commendations, and tokens of appreciation to Bob Von Villas for his untiring service. This evidence of a lifetime of altruism was more than impressive; it was overwhelming. Many of the jurors—who had just convicted Von Villas of first-degree murder—looked bewildered.

"Bob never expressed dissatisfaction. He loved his job. It's what he was," Judy stated. And although Bob worked off-duty jobs and was involved in many businesses, she explained, "He never neglected me or the kids. We always found time to go out. He never forgot a birthday or anniversary. He always surprised me. He was very much a good husband and father."

Judy stated she was still in love with her husband but could no longer bear to visit him at L.A. County Jail. "It's dirty, the food is lousy, the deputies are not nice, and it's not the safest place. Bob spends his time trying to help other inmates. He'd probably loan them money if he had it. I don't write because I know they [jail authorities] would read my letters. I visited a lot in the beginning, but money is short now and sometimes I don't have enough for gas to go downtown. And I'm working two jobs now. I have to sleep. I've visited him a few times on New Year's Eve. He calls almost every day. He talks to Shannon, who is sixteen now. She was eleven when he was arrested. If she has any problems, she knows she can still talk to him. Shannon is on the swim team, and Bob always went to her meets. That's one of the worse things for him. He was always there for the kids. He missed their graduations and Michele's wedding two years ago. He couldn't give the bride away. His main concern has always been for me and the kids."

Judy described the impact of Bob's arrest on the family. "You can't explain it to anybody, especially if your husband was a police officer. It's like he went from the good guy to the bad guy. Some friends just disappeared. They never called again. There were a few who wouldn't let their children play with Shannon because her father is in jail. One time the yard duty teacher at school accused Shannon of chewing gum. Shannon said, 'No I'm not.' The teacher said, 'You're probably lying; after all, your father is in jail.'

"I got behind in the house payments and we had to rent out part of our house to meet expenses. The insurance company canceled our homeowner's insurance because he was in jail. Shannon is sixteen and she has a job." At this point, Judy started to cry. "Eventually we lost the house. We left the day before the sheriff came for the auction. I had to sell a lot of items, tools, furniture.

"It's still a solace and a comfort when he calls," Judy sobbed. "It makes our life easier. He still contributes to mine and the children's well-being. The children still love him. He's their father."

A parade of San Fernando Valley educators arrived to heap praise upon L.A.'s convicted killer cop. Shirley Hess, the Chatsworth High social studies teacher who had barged into Lieutenant Higbee's office, read the letter she sent Chief Gates just two months before Bob's arrest: "Officer Von Villas is intelligent, articulate, dynamic and has a keen sense of humor. . . . He is the personification of a competent, concerned, caring human being who honors the community with his service as a police officer. He has opened minds and hearts to the role of the police. . . . No one can replace him." Hess explained that the students had been "outraged" by Von Villas's removal from the J car and had begun circulating a petition. They had obtained six hundred signatures by the time of Officer Bob's arrest. Another educator described Von Villas as being "like The Pied Piper.

Whenever he was on campus, you could always be assured of seeing at least ten kids around him."

Joe Reiner, Bob's good friend, business partner, and former CO, took the stand and described Von Villas as "a very spirited policeman, what we call a hard-charger. He's very dedicated. He got *lost* in his work. He wasn't a nine to five man. . . . I relied on him for his ability to get things done through people. He had an uncanny ability. He was a salesman, he was street smart, he knew what to do to prevent crime."

Reiner reviewed thirteen years of Von Villas's semiannual LAPD personnel rating reports, nearly all of which were outstanding. "Usually, only the top ten percent get outstanding. Bob was the cream of the crop." After spending most of a day going through all of Von Villas's commendations, Reiner concluded, "Bob Von Villas was dedicated and multitalented, tops in every category. He was in the upper one percent."

Once again, the jury appeared baffled. The big question was etched across their faces: what had gone wrong?

Dr. Bebe Johnson, an LAPD staff psychologist, explained to the jury that she had met with Von Villas approximately ten times in 1981. "He was having stress problems related to a possible reassignment. He loved what he was doing as a juvenile officer. But talk at the station was that he had done that enough . . . His interest in kids was genuine. One of his problems was that he overextended himself with kids outside of work. He was also very involved with his daughter's swim team. He had probably taken on more than he should have. He left me one time and went straight to the hospital because I believe he had an esophageal ulcer. He was in a great deal of pain."

Expert witness Dr. Mark J. Mills, a psychiatrist at the UCLA School of Medicine, had recently spent ten hours with Von Villas to make an evaluation. His conclusion was that Von Villas had "no major psychiatric disturbances or antisocial disorders." He then presented his psychological profile. "The man I found is so different from the man who apparently committed those crimes," Dr. Mills stated. "In some ways his childhood was unremarkable. Most of us don't grow up under ideal circumstances. Whether by virtue of genetics, a lack of his mother's affections, or shyness, early on he became more responsible than most." Stating that he had previously interviewed "thousands of vets," Dr. Mills observed, "Bob Von Villas has one of the most distinguished records I have seen. He risked his life for others, yet he came out relatively unscarred. He is still very compassionate and caring."

341

According to Dr. Mills, Von Villas's thirteen years of distinction as a cop were largely the result of his psychological makeup. "His keen ability to ease domestic situations goes back to his own mom and dad. He has that ability to tell a joke at the right moment, to give people a new slant on looking at themselves. He's very compassionate." Von Villas's vocation for aiding neglected youths was also rooted in his own neglected childhood. "His gift is in part an ability to perceive their hurt and calm the situation."

Dr. Mills pointed to incidents in the army and LAPD where Von Villas had placed himself in harm's way to save others. This compassion for others, he stated, was real. "There are so many little aspects of this nature. He has a history of genuine caring. You can fake this for a few days or a month, but it's very hard to put on a posture for life."

Perhaps the best clue to the undoing of Bob Von Villas was provided by Christine Lund, the veteran KABC Channel 7 news anchor. Platinum blond, gorgeous, in her mid-thirties, one of the most popular TV news personalities in Los Angeles, Lund proved to be cerebral and insightful—a side of her not usually shown on the nightly news.

Lund explained that after she met Von Villas in 1980, "he became a regular feature in my life." Bob stopped by her house regularly to talk and she called him to get information. "In my business, we try to have connections—but that was not the reason I had a relationship with Bob. But that's how it started." Bob would talk about the police department, she about the news. "We would both grumble. And we'd talk about our families. Bob would talk my ear off about his family."

Their bond grew stronger from their mutual concern for the plight of children. Aside from being a newscaster, Lund is also a certified marriage and family counselor. As Lund described it, she and Bob were both activists. "Children and their lot in life is a passion to me. Children are not taken seriously in our society. They still have the status of chattel, of third-class citizens, and that's reflected in the way they are treated. People don't generally have respect or empathy for them or a sense of what their needs are. It's a rare person who understands that they are sacred, that their nature is different from adults, that they deserve not only equal but special status.

"Bob is a man who has given this a great deal of thought, who is very alive to children, not in just the hearts and valentines sense, but in the fact that they have rights that are not understood. On a day-to-day basis, he saw the way things went wrong for kids because they were not taken seriously. He's a unique

342

person. . . . He was smart and loving about kids, and he *worked* for them. In my business I run into an awful lot of people, some who have notions that are real, some not so real. Bob always had plans for something that was going to work for kids in the community. It was realistic. . . . All his plans with the Devonshire PALs and the DAPs weren't just talk; those were real things he was working on."

Lund tried to put a finger on Von Villas's special gift. "He has a wonderful thing that is so rare, that sense of timing, that sense of assurance—and that comes from knowledge—of when to make a move to reach out to somebody at the right time in a crisis. He always had that sense of some heroic deed. He knew that if somebody just did the right thing at the right time they could change a kid's life. It maddened him, drove him crazy, knowing that things were terribly wrong but nothing was done about it. And he had a sense that 'I'm the only one who knows this kind of thing.' He was one of those unusual people who would actually make the decision to reach out and help."

Lund also attempted to explain the flip side. "He had a sense of isolation and an obsessive quality about him, that passionate quality. It could go a couple of different ways, evidently. In my heart I know his disappointment with the police department was a crisis for him. He was crushed and broken by his experience. He talked a lot about how if you are not prepared to operate in a political way, you were going to be in the backwater. This was a crusher for him. He was constantly going to be pulled off his job to do almost anything else. . . . He felt good people were getting stepped on. He felt he would never get anyplace through politics, and he felt broken. I sensed a growing, deepening crisis—the obsession over all the good he could do, and the disappointment at having the rug pulled from beneath him. His view of the world narrowed quite a bit. It became quite black and white for him because of this passionate, idealized sense of the police department."

That idealized view ultimately came undone. "He felt the department's priorities extremely poor—a lot of paper moving around, a lot of back-stabbing, a lot of misrepresentation. Maybe he had a childish idea of the police department, but I don't think so. I think he was perhaps too passionate and it led him to a certain kind of crisis. . . . He said things like, 'I don't know how much longer I can go on with this. I don't know if I can stand this any longer.' He felt so low and desolate. I didn't understand it. He needed to talk, and I didn't have that much to offer. As he started talking more openly about the byzantine quality of the police department, how hard it was to do things in a simple, straightforward way in the community, vis-à-vis helping the kids, the conversations got deeper and darker."

Although his removal from the J car "hurt him terribly," Von Villas's love for the LAPD never wavered. "Never. I think part of his despair over this was because he was torn. If he didn't care anymore, I think that he would have gone on. But he couldn't. He couldn't. This was so critical to him. It was so much a central feature of his life. I've known lots of policemen, and I have not encountered one who placed police work—its nature, appearance, its function in society—so centrally in his life. I think it was because he cared so deeply that he was so disappointed. He never would have experienced that despair if he hadn't cared so much."

David Soul, the handsome blond actor who first came to fame by playing a cop on TV, took the stand dressed California casual in jeans, sports coat, and open-necked shirt. He related how he had met Von Villas in 1977 while doing "Starsky and Hutch," for which Bob had served as a location traffic cop. "He was very warm, open, friendly. He'd stand around while we were waiting to shoot and we would talk. Of all the police I'd worked with on sets, he struck me as the most accessible, the most open. . . . There was a genuineness that was undeniable. . . . He came to my home on several occasions. He was always welcome. He'd mostly pick up the phone, give me a call, and say, 'I'm in the neighborhood.' That kind of thing. As a friend."

Soul, like Lund, was taken by Bob's passion for young people, since children's issues were also one of his concerns. "He invited me to PAL luncheons on several occasions. I attended one. It was a first-class affair. He was as proud as the father of a newborn baby. It meant a great deal to him, to share with people in the community this important work being done with children."

During the fall of 1982, Soul was arrested on a battery charge after an altercation with his estranged wife. Bob Von Villas stopped by, "quite unsolicited," to offer his help. "He just wanted to let me know somebody cared. That was a time when there were very few phone calls or visitors, except for the press, people who wanted to monger a story. Friends in the industry had turned their backs on me. Bob saw a need and he responded to that need as a human being. He didn't come with accusations or judgment . . . [He's] the kind of person I like to know, and the kind of person I wish there were more of, actually."

Soul's testimony for L.A.'s killer cop was trumpeted in the local press and in one of the national tabloids. Nevertheless, he later expressed no regrets about having publicly supported his friend Bob Von Villas.

Robert Fuller, the cowboy TV veteran, felt the same way. Fuller described all the work he'd done for the Police Athletic League and Von Villas's passion for neglected kids. "At PAL luncheons he was sort of like the mother hen. All these kids flocked around him. They all knew him and he knew all of them. He really wanted more help for his programs. He was genuine, a gentleman, a good police officer. A good friend."

Fuller also recalled an occasion when Von Villas had helped him cope with a personal crisis. It was in the early 1980s, when a man attempted to molest his youngest child. "I was pretty upset. Like any father, I wanted to take this man apart. And I came very close to doing that. But before I did, I called Bob and told him what I was going to do. He became very upset with me. He calmed me down and told me I was absolutely wrong, that I should not take the law into my own hands. He counseled me quite well on how to behave myself. I believe it's because of Bob I'm probably not in jail today."

Outside the courtroom, Fuller admitted he was still "dumbfounded" over what had transpired with his friend Bob Von Villas. "I'll never get over it." He said he was still having a hard time trying to "resign myself to the fact that it's him, that he did it."

Several witnesses testified to Von Villas's ongoing philanthropy, despite his incarceration. Michael Lee, a young skinhead, taunt and lean, with tattoos on both his arms and a Fu Manchu mustache, was brought into court in chains by deputies. Lee explained that he was serving forty years to life for first degree murder. While being housed at "high power" in county jail, he had developed a relationship with Bob Von Villas that had changed his life. "I was a skinhead—a violent racist type person. Von Villas made me see the error of my ways." Lee had once hated all the blacks and Mexicans he encountered in jail, but now he'd learned to live with them. "I feel a lot less violent. I'm not as aggressive." Von Villas had also saved him from committing suicide after his girlfriend was killed. "I've never had a father in my life, and Bob has taken on that role. I feel I have that love for him like he's my father—something that I've never had."

Lee described the setup at high power at L.A. County Jail, where Von Villas had resided for the past five and a half years. High power is for the sick and people who need protection—like cops, gays, celebrities, and inmates who are "marked." Lee's racist views were well known, so he'd been placed there for his own protection. There were twenty-four one-man cells, twelve on each side of an aisle. Each man was allowed one half-hour a day of runway time outside his cell, when he could make phone calls and talk to other inmates. As Lee described it, Von Villas had become the godfather of high power. He supplied other inmates—who had no friends, family, or money—with necessities like toothpaste, pencils, and stamps. Von Villas spent his runway time on the phone in their behalf, communicating for them with attorneys, family, "whoever they want him to call. He'll explain the situation to them."

Stephen Benwell, twenty, who was awaiting trial for murder at high power, or "Fish Row" as he called it, testified that Von Villas saved him from committing suicide, had given him a reason to live, and had become a father figure to him. Benwell explained that he was a homosexual, which had caused problems for him with other inmates. The influence of the row's "leader" became his salvation. "Bob came out and said that he didn't care what I was or who I was. He just liked me for being me, and [after that] everybody on the row kind of followed suit."

Jack Anderson, the L.A. County Jail watch sergeant, explained that Von Villas had "taken it upon himself, more or less, to monitor the floor." He was extremely helpful and had helped solve many problems. "In order to simulate riot conditions for the Deputy Training Program, Von Villas came up with the idea of having inmates throw water balloons. He and Mr. Ford filled thousands of water balloons. It took quite a few days. It was quite successful. It was great fun."

Next, James Park, a former warden of San Quentin prison, described prison life. "It's like living in a bathroom. . . . And each thirty days is the same as the last. It's the same, same, same." Boredom, Park explained, was the biggest problem in prison. "The youngsters break the boredom with fights and riots. The average prisoner is twenty-five years old, with less than seventh-grade-level schooling, and has never really held a job." Von Villas, forty-four, the antithesis of the typical inmate, could help defuse dangerous situations and prevent riots. "Age is the biggest factor with regard to misbehavior. A twenty-one-year-old is wild and dangerous. He thinks he's king of the world. But young prisoners look to older ones for guidance and help. A prison is like a small city. It has to be run properly. Older prisoners have a stabilizing effect."

Dr. Mills, in his earlier testimony about Von Villas's psychiatric profile, had also stated that Von Villas would be particularly useful to the penal system. "He has a unique ability to pour oil on troubled waters, to make situations better. He's known as a cop in jail and he wears his past with dignity and uses it instructively. He is a man who has shown a lot of compassion and bravery, and I'm sure this will continue."

On the final day of the proceedings, while everyone waited for court to come to order, Judy, Michele, and Shannon Von Villas engaged in some cross-courtroom dialogue with the defendant. Bob Von Villas repeatedly rubbed his hands together, relishing the opportunity to chat with his family without the Plexiglas barricades of the county jail.

Michele Von Villas Walker, twenty-two, radiant, and beautiful with long blond hair, wore a colorful dress that was like the breath of spring in the stuffy courtroom. Michele's short, tearful testimony softened all but the most calloused hearts. "I was seventeen when my dad was arrested. Everything changed. My mom lost the house, we had to move. We still speak on the phone a lot. He wants to know everything. I still listen to his advice. There's a feeling of comfort and security, knowing I'll always have someone to talk to. We've been very close. My whole life, I was Daddy's little girl. I don't like to visit him in prison, to see him there." At this point, Michele's tears welled up. "I hope he'll be around when I have kids. I love him very much. I still think he's a good person and doesn't deserve to die."

Shannon Von Villas, sixteen, had the same long blond hair, the same radiant innocence. She too was choked up throughout her brief testimony, which was perhaps too obviously led by Jack Stone. Shannon explained that she was eleven when her dad was arrested, that he was always a loving father, then and now. "He was always there for me. Now, if I have something to do in school or a problem with a boyfriend he's always there to help. He's still a big part of my life. We write a lot and talk on the phone." Shannon described her father as "strict sometimes. He taught us right and wrong. He was always fair. If he yelled at me I deserved it. Now, I have a job and swimming, and he asks all the time if I'm studying."

Shannon's pain spilled over in a giant wave. "Every kid wants a father and I haven't had one for five years. People walk up to me at school and tell me my dad's a murderer. Some parents won't let their kids hang out with me 'cause they think the whole family must be like that." The sobbing teenager ended by saying: "I don't want you guys to take away my dad."

Following a brief recess, Bob O'Neill ran through much the same drill he had with the closing arguments in Ford's trial, adding a few choice remarks. "Recall the testimony of Shirley Hess, the sociology teacher," O'Neill suggested. "She said that after Robert Von Villas would speak to her students, they would say in admiration, 'Are all policemen like him?' You have to wonder what those students would say today. I can tell you what they would say: 'God, I hope not!'

"Dr. Anderson and Mr. Ory! Now, at the police academy they issue you a uniform and they issue you a badge. Symbols of trust. They don't issue you aliases like Dr. Anderson or Mr. Ory."

Donald Feinberg made an unabashed appeal for sympathy. "If there is anything that connects this man to the world it is his family. That's the umbilical cord you sever if you condemn this man to death. Is there a purpose to be served by killing him? Do you send a message to the schoolchildren that Mr. O'Neill referred to? This man touched the lives of those children. Whatever you have convicted him of, that doesn't take away from that. Do you benefit the people that he saved in combat? Do you benefit the people in county jail that he saved? ... You are not faced here with a psychopathic killer, an animal, a person beyond the pale of society who can do no good."

When it was his turn, Jack Stone asked the jury, "Could this be the same man the district attorney calls a cold-blooded killer?" Indeed, this question truly did seem to have the jury puzzled. "Why did we go through Mr. Von Villas's background? To show that he was a poor unfortunate person and therefore we can excuse what he did? Absolutely not. We put it on to show that Mr. Von Villas is an unusual man in that he rose above what he was denied to find a tremendous capacity in himself to help other people. ... If you could erase just for a moment from your mind the latter part of his life that led to his problems, this is ... an extraordinary man. Absolutely extraordinary."

On December 14, after one day of deliberation, the jury sent an inquiry to Judge Schempp. Their question: "Does 'life without parole' really mean life without parole? We've all heard of cases of people sentenced to life who had their sentences commuted and were later released."

As defense attorneys had feared, the jury, like many in California, was cynical about the integrity of the system. They didn't believe "death" really meant death or that "life" really meant life. Californians saw regular signs of the system's failure on the nightly news. Jails released more prisoners because of overcrowding. Charlie Manson, who was sentenced to death, was shown standing before yet another *parole* hearing. Ditto for Sirhan Sirhan. Who could blame citizens for being cynical? Although no death or life sentence had been commuted in at least five years, since Jerry Brown was governor, citizens still believed it happened all the time.

Jack Stone argued what was apparent: the jury wanted to give Von Villas life but they wanted assurances that it would mean life. He asked that the jury not be told that the sentence could be commuted. It would be ludicrous, he argued, if the court told them the truth—that the sentence could in fact be commuted by the governor, but that they were not allowed to consider that fact in their decision. Judge Schempp, however, did not agree. She admonished the jury, explaining that reports they'd heard about prisoners being let out early were about county jail, not state prisons. She told them that the governor, under certain circumstances, had the power to commute both death and life sentences. However, they would violate their oath to consider this. "You must assume he will be executed and you must assume he will serve life without parole."

As the jury filed out, one couldn't help but feel that Jack Stone's argument had merit, that despite the judge's admonishment, the jurors weren't really buying it. The system had been subverted so long that civic cynicism couldn't be dispelled with a simple speech. But apparently it worked. The jury returned the next day, December 15, and recommended that Von Villas be sentenced to life without the possibility of parole.

Outside the courtroom, many jurors frankly admitted that they felt sympathy for Von Villas. "It's better this way for his kids, not to have their father put to death," said one. "Under controlled circumstances, maybe he can do a little good." Another woman identified herself as the final holdout for capital punishment. "If there was any case that dictated the death penalty, this was it," she said. "This man scares me to death. Unfortunately, there was no argument I could present that would sway eleven other jurors to my way of thinking. I think the crime was heinous and this man was a tremendous menace to society. . . . But I think justice will be served as long as he is in prison for the rest of his life." Von Villas, she stated, "seemed to have two drastically opposite personalities; one who did wonderful things for kids and another who did horrendous, sickening acts. It's almost impossible to reconcile the two."

This commonly expressed view was one that some longtime observers of the case found unsettling. Many people didn't feel any *need* to reconcile the two. Public cynicism was so deep that citizens could easily—even readily—accept the existence of a police officer's hidden dark side. Three years later, when the officers who beat Rodney King were acquitted by a jury in Simi Valley, many would speculate that juries don't like to convict police officers, that because juries generally believe police officers, it was hard to win cases against them. If anything, *The People vs. Richard Ford and Robert Von Villas* showed the very opposite. The juries had no trouble accepting that the two men were rogue police officers; in fact, they seemed predisposed to believe it. It appeared more difficult for them to accept that they might have also once been good men.

As to the trial itself, most jurors agreed that they had found the testimony of Jan Ogilvie highly suspect. "I thought she was a dirty rotten liar," said one middle-aged juror. Still, he and the others concluded that the charges were supported by other evidence.

After sentencing, prosecutor Robert O'Neill stated, "I'd have preferred the death penalty, but I'm not disappointed. They [the jury] did what they were asked to do, and that's the way the system works."

On the day of the trials' conclusion, O'Neill was appointed to a judgeship in the Los Angeles Judicial District. "It was overwhelming," said O'Neill, describing the double whammy of having a four-year project conclude within moments of receiving the new appointment. "He'll make an outstanding judge," commented

Judge Schempp when she was told of the news. Indeed, just two years later, O'Neill would be promoted to a superior court appointment.

The trials had been a long haul for Bob O'Neill. "I lived with it seven days a week. Sleeping at night, I was thinking about it." He noted that, prior to the trials, it had taken many months of twelve-hour days just to read all the reports at least once. "I was fortunate, because my then-fiancée was studying for the CPA exam. So we got along." The case so dominated his life that it served as the sole backdrop for his romance and marriage to his wife Linda. "We were dating when I got this case [in 1985]. Since then we got engaged, got married, had our first child, and now we're expecting our second. She's obviously relieved it's over."

At a later hearing before Judge Schempp, prosecutors ruled out the death penalty for Richard Ford, announcing they would not retry the penalty phase of his trial. Deputy District Attorney Lonnie Felker, who had taken over for Robert O'Neill, cited the almost unanimous decision by the jury and the considerable expense of launching a new trial. Superior court trials generally cost about five thousand dollars a day, not including defense attorneys' fees. While a new jury wouldn't have to determine guilt or innocence, prosecutors would in effect practically need to retry the entire case in order to present a foundation for sentencing. "We tried our best case," Felker told reporters outside the courtroom. "Trials don't get better the second time around."

The two trials of *The People vs. Richard Ford and Robert Von Villas* had cost around $1 million apiece. The four years of hearings before that had probably cost another $2 million—not counting four sets of (high-priced) attorneys' fees and attendant private investigators' fees and exorbitant expert witness fees, which, over the six-year haul, probably clocked in at another $5 million. At least. So the taxpayers were already looking at a tab somewhere around $10 million. No one raised any objections to the D.A.'s decision not to try Ford's penalty phase again.

Ford smiled when the decision was announced, but Rickard Santwier commented, "It's hard to have a good feeling when your client is going to spend the rest of his life in jail."

33

Urban Legends

DESPITE THE SENSATIONAL REVELATIONS OF THE PENALTY phases, media coverage was remarkably subdued. City editors ignored protests by court reporters that the testimony was beyond the pale of standard-issue "he's-really-a-nice-guy" death trial testimony. Editors, apparently, and perhaps the public alike, were jaded, cynical, or just tired of the case. Even the headlines displayed this cynicism: "Stars Praise Hired Killer's 'Loving' Side." News directors simply assumed that Ford and Von Villas were sociopaths and that all the mitigating testimony was so much hogwash.

But those who had been in court knew otherwise. As Dr. Mills had testified, one can fake being a good guy for a few days or a month, "but it's very hard to put on a posture for life."

Another factor that perhaps subdued the media was that the case had just gone on too long. Hundreds of stories on Ford and Von Villas had appeared in the papers and on TV. Most of these, however, were updates on what had occurred at the latest court proceedings. Few attempts were made to present a comprehensive account of the case, and those had appeared *before* the trials had begun.

Now, after the second set of convictions, there was a rush by the media to drop the lid on the story. Short shrift was given to the penalty phase revelations. Nobody did any postmortems or wrapups. Splashy page-one and top-of-the-evening-news stories announced the verdicts—and that was it. Two greedy killer cops had finally gotten their just desserts. End of story.

Meanwhile, however, the corridors and bars and coffee shops outside the courtroom rang with passionate debate over ramifications the media never bothered to explore. What, if any, was the LAPD's responsibility in all this? Hadn't Richard Ford made two deliberate cries for help to his supervising officers and the LAPD psychologist? Some of Ford's staunch supporters claimed he was a victim of the LAPD's archaic method of stress treatment, the old "stick him behind a desk" syndrome. Certainly there was no excuse for his crimes, but wasn't the LAPD perhaps negligent?

Some felt so. A few years later, following the beating of Rodney King, pundits in the national media would decry the woefully inadequate system of psychological testing, stress-detection, and misfit winnowing practiced by the LAPD. A virtual national consensus agreed that police departments everywhere had to do more to identify out-of-control cops. Many cities would revamp their training and supervisory practices as a result.

And what about the racist excuse Richard Ford had given Dr. Reiser to get himself sent to Club Dev? Ford had told Reiser he was going to "end up shooting a coon" because he was so fed up with the black criminals he encountered working Central Division. Later, Ford was heard bragging about how he had used that story to get himself transferred. Most people who knew Richard Ford, cops and citizens alike, say he was not a racist, that this was really just a scam.

The implication is that Ford's story to Dr. Reiser was such standard issue that every cop knew about it. If you wanted to get off the streets really bad, you just told the department shrink you were going to shoot an African-American. Years before Rodney King, didn't this serve as a clear indication that an us versus them mentality was in fact endemic in the LAPD? Why was it necessary to see a videotape of four white cops beating a black man before anything was done?

At the very least, wasn't there something to be learned from this case about the impact of stress, disillusionment, and greed on LAPD officers? And what about the arrogance they showed once they turned to crime? Wasn't this in part the result of a mentality fostered by the LAPD? Hadn't these men felt shielded by their badges, protected, beyond suspicion, and above the law? Wasn't it painfully obvious that the enabling power and security of the badge had been crucial to their capering?

Detective Ford often spoke of badging interloping members of the blue brotherhood, of how the shield protected him from the scrutiny given to average citizens. Wasn't this the same attitude that would later terrify citizens most about the Rodney King affair—that the policemen who did the beating were not afraid of being reported by their fellow officers? Wasn't it a result of cops being taught that carrying a badge made them different, that they were cops before they were citizens? Before they were even human? Wouldn't it be far better at the end of watch if cops checked their badges and walked away from headquarters as citizens?

This us versus them mentality is very similar to that fostered by the military. Perhaps soldiers need to dehumanize their enemy during wartime so they can kill gooks or jerrys or japs or commies without concern. But should police be encouraged to develop the same mentality? Should cops be trained to think of themselves first and foremost as cops—a separate species—as opposed to citizens who do police work? The LAPD had long boasted of its paramilitary style. But what about that paramilitary mentality?

Chief Daryl F. Gates was quoted in a 1984 *Los Angeles Magazine* story on LAPD's Internal Affairs Division as saying, "One of the reasons that we've built the reputation of being the finest police department in the country is that we've always been willing to critically examine everything that we do. The investigations of Internal Affairs are some of the most detailed you will find anywhere."

What Gates said was true. The LAPD was fearless when it came to investigating crimes or misconduct by its police officers. But unfortunately, that did not include examining the root causes of the crimes or misconduct. And one of these was the mentality Gates fostered in the department from the top—something he would steadfastly refuse to acknowledge. Locked in denial, he would refuse to own up to any responsibility for his officers' attitudes even as he was finally pushed, kicking and screaming, from his post as chief.

And what about Vietnam? Some observers viewed the metamorphosis of Ford and Von Villas into L.A.'s killer cops as an inevitable legacy of that war. Men have difficulty adjusting to civilian life following any war, but the arbitrary "morality" of Vietnam, the lack of clear purpose or tangible objectives, served to compound the problems. If one could kill to help Uncle Sam's "business," without any clear sense of moral purpose, then why not kill for one's own personal business? This very attitude was expressed by Richard Ford on the van tapes. For him, like a mafioso, violence had simply become a matter of business.

But issues such as these would remain unexplored. Ford and Von Villas were forgotten by the media—as though cast into a deep black hole—once they were sent off to the joint.

The most startling silence came from the city's "paper of record," the *Los Angeles Times*. Wags joked about how Ford and Von Villas would have been a *Times Sunday Magazine* cover story, or the subject of one of those 80,000-word, five-part, page-one series, if they had only been cops somewhere exotic—like Bangkok or Cincinnati. "There's a rumor the *L.A. Times* is opening a bureau in

Los Angeles," critics often joked about this great "global" paper. Indeed, this did appear to be just a rumor.

But then, Chief Gates would prove even more hypermetropic and video-propelled than the *Times*. His 1992 autobiography, *Chief,* doesn't even mention, much less examine, the case of Richard Ford and Robert Von Villas—the most corrupt cops, the worst criminals, the only convicted killers ever to have worn the LAPD badge during his or anyone else's reign as chief.

The public, meanwhile, would not so easily forget L.A.'s killer cops. Reporters always hear plenty of cafeteria and courthouse-steps chatter at big-story trials. But normally it's just a regurgitation of what's been printed in the papers or stated on the stand. That was not the case with Ford and Von Villas. Everybody, it seemed, had heard some story about them. In the wake of their convictions, speculation ran wild, and unfounded tales became rife, particularly in the San Fernando Valley. Many stories about Dick and Bob began to take on the aura of urban legend—those unlikely yarns that everyone hears but no one can verify.

The most commonly heard tale was that of the pretty Latina RTD bus driver who was brutally raped. Little did her assailant know that her husband was "that killer cop out in the Valley," who tracked him down and killed him. The gory details made it seem as though the teller had just seen it on one of those made-for-TV movies. Yet nothing of its kind ever appeared in the media. It was simply passed around by word of mouth.

Richard Ford had in fact mentioned to a few cops at Club Dev that he had located the perpetrator and "the problem had been taken care of." But no one knew if this was truth or puffery. And no one has ever verified that Ford in fact found or killed the assailant. But perhaps speculative chatter by officers at Club Dev spread out into the community and gave rise to what has now become Valley folklore.

Whenever one asks a teller of this tale about his source, the answer invariably is "my brother-in-law's cousin has a friend whose hairdresser knows somebody at Devonshire Division." Either that or they heard it from somebody on an RTD bus.

Dope-dealing lowlifes and burglars told stories, none corroborated, about how they'd been "shaken down" by a vociferous shark of a burglary detective named Richard Ford. Von Villas was said to be the mastermind of numerous heists. The fact is Ford and Von Villas eventually got blamed for, or at least suspected of, committing every unsolved crime in the history of the San Fernando Valley. Everything they had ever done was scrutinized. While many of the two cops' friends and cohorts remain loyal believers of their innocence, others "turned" and began to suspect evil in everything the pair had ever said or done. In many ways, it was frightening how *easily* some people could accept that these "great guys" had such a dark side.

Many people said that the cop played by Richard Gere in the movie *Internal Affairs* was really Bob Von Villas. Indeed, many fictional cops were said to be inspired by Bob. The Gere character suggested a complexity that included outside business interests and some weird macho thing about screwing other cops' wives. The Gere character also lived in the Valley. But he was a creep— hardly as charming, intelligent, or likable as Von Villas and nowhere near as interesting and multifaceted. And while Bob was a ladies' man and he did have a "godfather" thing about taking care of women (suggested in the Gere character), there's no evidence that he targeted his buddies' wives.

For a while, popular opinion had Ford and Von Villas as the ringleaders of a large gang of rogue Valley cops who were operating like Murder Incorporated. This rumor was surely just an outgrowth of uncommon civic cynicism. One had to wonder whether the escalating tale of L.A.'s killer cops was somehow emblematic of the Valley's decline.

British reporters were for a while exploring a connection between Ford and Von Villas and an alleged Brit killer named Harvey Raider. Raider, who lived in the Valley and was a partner in a Valley auto shop that served as a front for an international smuggling operation, was suspected of being responsible for the disappearance of an entire Valley family, the Solomons. No connection was ever found.

Rumors arose concerning connections to William Leasure, an L.A. traffic cop who was indicted for murder and yacht theft. Perhaps this tale came about because Lillian Ford became friends with Leasure's wife, Betsy Mogul, after meeting her at L.A. County Jail while they were both visiting their husbands.

If there was an unsolved crime, sooner or later somebody tried to blame it on "those killer cops out in the Valley." People wanted to believe Ford and Von Villas were the baddest desperadoes the Valley had seen since Kit Carson rode the pony express over Cahuenga Pass. And it wasn't the media, which actually showed restraint and stuck to the facts. The stories got around the old-fashioned way: by word of mouth. Something about these guys fired the public's imagination.

34

The People's Wish

SENTENCING FOR RICHARD FORD WAS HELD ON FEBRUARY 22, 1989. Following motions for a new trial, all denied, Richard Lasting asked the court to strike the special circumstances on Ford's conviction. This would have the effect of making him eligible for parole, probably when he reached his late seventies. In his plea for leniency, Lasting cited Richard Ford's years of public service and his tragic personal problems. "A rogue cop, a desperado hiding behind a badge, wouldn't go to a police psychiatrist seeking help and shine a light on himself. He would seek anonymity."

Then Richard Ford addressed the court. Speaking in his smooth voice, reminiscent of a TV newscaster, often gesturing with the glasses he held in his hand, Ford tried to maintain a cool veneer during his thirty-minute speech, but he was obviously tense with emotion. His address was puzzling, and not just because it was rambling and jumbled. The basic message was hard to swallow. He claimed he was innocent, but he didn't blame anybody. He was about to spend the rest of his life in prison for crimes he didn't commit, but he wasn't bitter toward the people or the system that was unjustly sending him there. He kept rearguing evidence from the trial, yet he didn't want to blame anybody for misinterpreting that evidence. It was strange.

"Your Honor . . . number one and foremost I am innocent. I did not kill Thomas Weed . . . I believe I was convicted because I was a police detective. . . . It was a shock to be convicted. I didn't think it was humanly possible. . . . How can you find someone guilty based on evidence that doesn't exist? I am just completely baffled! What it consisted of was the tape. That's what the case consisted of against me."

Ford explained the jailhouse tape. "I knew about the investigation on Mr. Weed through Mr. Von Villas. I was also aware the police department was investigating every unsolved homicide in the San Fernando Valley and I was the subject of at least ten or fifteen detectives running around town on a fishing expedition. And that's exactly the perspective from which I viewed it. I wasn't a civilian. I'm a cop, a detective." His statements, he said, were simply those of one detective trying to figure out what other detectives were up to. "The main thing I said was, 'There's no way to connect me.' I don't find that so mystifying. I didn't do it; therefore, I cannot be connected to a crime I didn't do. The jury seemed to think that I didn't say I was innocent, therefore I was guilty."

The fact that he thought and talked like a detective, Ford claimed, was his undoing. The jury was unable to hear the tape from that perspective. "That was the hardest thing. There was no way to get this to the jury. I'm a detective. They take my shotgun and they take my shells. . . . All right. They do my house four more times. . . . What I'm concerned about is I have four or five different kinds of ammunition. Well, I know as a police officer you can't get ballistics from a shotgun. In rare exceptions, if the cartridge is left at the scene of a crime, then you might be able to run a lot number and determine if my lot matched this lot. What concerned me was the police department now had themselves a body someplace. The body had been shot with, say, birdshot. They want to lay this at my doorstep, but they don't have any birdshot. So they come back to my house on the fishing expedition and they take the birdshot. So I'm concerned with why are they doing this."

Everything else could be similarly explained. The gas credit card—he couldn't figure out why they took a card he never used. "Can you be so damned dumb if you went out and killed somebody you don't even know if you bought gas?" Ford exclaimed.

He also expressed his bafflement at claims that he was a greedy individual. "I supposedly robbed a jewelry store for a hundred and eighty thousand dollars worth of jewelry. They found no rings in my house, no diamonds in my house, and not a damn nickel . . . I didn't have any money. I lived like every other cop, from payday to payday. I go to Puerto Vallarta and I take the special for two hundred and ninety bucks. And I have twenty thousand dollars laying around? I can't understand it!"

Regarding the whole case against him, Ford said, "It doesn't fit. It's a round peg in a square hole. You beat it long enough you make it fit. That's exactly what happened to me. I don't feel I deserve this. My wife has been through a lot. I'm not going to stand here and tell you I'm a little virgin, an innocent person, because I wasn't. What they are saying did happen to me. My wife was raped and I did go out on the streets of Los Angeles and Hollywood and I was acting foolish and I did get involved in drugs and I did a lot of things out there I had no right doing. And I put myself here. I don't blame the system. The police department didn't do it. They did their job. I don't agree with some of their tactics, but nonetheless they did the job."

Ford asked that the partial fingerprint found on the Wyoming map be preserved, so that it could someday be used to prove his innocence, "when technology catches up some way in the labs." He asked the same of the jailhouse tape, stating that he felt it had been tampered with. "It just seems amazing to me that things my wife and I talked about that would prove my innocence are not there.

"I defy the police department or the district attorney's office to give me a scenario of what happened to Thomas Weed. I can't tell you how many sleepless nights I've spent trying to figure out what happened to Weed. I'm going to spend the rest of my life at a wall trying to figure it out . . . The police department can't even tell you what happened to the money. You know why? Because there is no money. You know why? Because I didn't kill him. You know why? Because *Ogilvie* killed him. I don't know how she did it, but that's where all the fingers point and that's what I believe.

"I have no problem with the system. I think everybody in this courtroom did their job. My attorneys were great, okay? I think the district attorney was absolutely brilliant. He did a fantastic job. He convicted me, you know, and with any other district attorney—that probably would have never happened. My qualms would only be this. As I tarnished the badge—and I agree I did, there's no doubt about that—I would say to the district attorney, You are the seeker of truth, sir, and you have a responsibility to do that. You don't put a witness on that stand when you know that she's perjured herself over and over again." Ford's logic had some people shaking their heads: The D.A. "did a fantastic job"—but he was unscrupulous?

"In closing, I'd like to say that I don't blame the system, and nothing's changed in my life. It doesn't matter. I would like to have the privilege of holding my wife . . . I have served and I will continue to serve. It doesn't matter what this court does to me. It doesn't matter what anybody does to me. The only reason I exposed the things that happened to me in the past was so I might spare my daughter and my wife the agony of having to live with my possibility of death. If I would have had my druthers, give me a gun, send me out back, and I'd just kill myself and we would all be much happier about it. But I'm living for the purpose of my wife and my children and maybe I can help somebody. And I served God first and my country second. And that's not changed and it's not going to change now. And if you think about it, Your Honor, how the hell is it a guy who spends his entire life serving doesn't have something coming? I mean, I just don't believe that. But it doesn't change anything because I served in the county jail and . . . when I go to prison and I die in prison, I will have every intention of doing the very best job on whatever I'm assigned. I don't care if that's picking up cigarette butts. And I'll try to help inmates and I intend to help the establishment. It doesn't make any difference. I have served my entire life. I'm a soldier. I'm a policeman. And I will die the same and I can't change that."

Ford implored the court to do something about conditions at L.A. County Jail. "No one pays any attention to me. I'm going to say it again. I have gone five years without any sunshine or fresh air. I don't think that's right. I've gone five and a half years without TV and radio. I don't think that's right. And most of all, what concerns me the most, I've gone five and a half years without being allowed to go to a religious service. I think that's absolutely criminal. I think that's absurd. I think that's ridiculous. Now I'm not a Bible thumper, but I'd like to go once in a while. Once a year would have been nice . . .

"The last thing I'd like to say, Your Honor, is would you at least order me out of that county jail forthwith and send me to wherever they are going to send me? And, I would dare to say, that I love justice. Like Socrates—I can understand what he must have went through, the feelings that he had. I've been condemned, but the district attorney said—and I agree with the district attorney—it is the people's wish. And I will live by that wish. I will live by it. I have served them. It is the law. And there is nothing more sacred in this world, nothing more sacred than truth and justice, and I love it. And even though I am a victim of it, it's not the system's fault. It is not the system. That's all. Thank you."

Judge Schempp then responded to Ford's speech. "The abuse you were subjected to caused you to have a very sad and troubled childhood. However, you managed to rise above that and distinguished yourself in your military career, for which you received honors, and with the Los Angeles Police Department, where you enjoyed an outstanding reputation and service record. Then something happened. Perhaps this was due to frustration over the police department's failure to capture your wife's brutal attacker, after one of the most aggravated and violent rapes I have ever heard of in my long criminal career. This left your wife with extreme emotional problems and was also very difficult for you to cope with.

"Despite the tragedies in your background, I cannot find any reason to be lenient with you in regards to your taking the life of another in such a meaningless and cheap way . . . for the sole reward of getting a few dollars to pay some bills. You have brought disgrace to the Los Angeles Police Department that you once so proudly and honorably served. I'm sorry for your family, but at least through the outstanding lawyers that you have given credit to, they have certainly saved your life. And I think that is all that you can ask from this justice system."

And that's all he got: life without possibility of parole. No striking of the special circumstance. No Parole.

Robert Von Villas was sentenced on March 8, 1989. First motioning for a new trial, Von Villas's attorneys argued that the jurors had learned of his previous convictions. They presented testimony to support their claim. Defense investigator David Boykoff testified that jurors he interviewed stated that other jurors had made comments during their deliberations that indicated such knowledge. Judge Schempp ruled that while the jurors may have learned of the previous convictions, they were not influenced by that knowledge. Three years later, this issue of jury misconduct would be a key subject of appeal.

Jack Stone also argued for the commutation of the special circumstances, which was denied. This would have made parole possible in about thirty-two years and would have made it possible for Von Villas to have physical contact with his family during visits. Sentences of life without parole don't allow for it. "It's an irony that a man who has risen so high has that much further to fall," said Jack Stone. He argued that all those years his client spent as an exemplary police officer, as someone who cared for young people, should mean something.

With no family or friends in attendance—likely at his own request—Von Villas stood to address the court for the last time. Wearing his banker's navy pinstripes, his wavy brown hair flowing back at the sides of his bald dome, his blue eyes red with tears, he too issued a rambling monologue. Although Bob Von Villas was now forty-four years old, his high-pitched voice and ebullient personality still gave him a boyish quality.

Von Villas denied participating in the Weed killing. He said he was convicted "based on the fact that I was a policeman and not on the evidence. I have never met Mrs. Ogilvie," he said. "I have not met Mr. Weed. This is a mockery of the system. A lot of things didn't come out in the trial. I definitely wanted to testify. My attorneys didn't want me to.

"I was a professional. I was very good at what I did. I worked on fifty murder cases, fifteen in my first two years. I knew and studied crime for years. I would not go up and knock on a door with an Afro wig on my head and makeup on my face and hands and say, 'Hi, I'm a Los Angeles police officer and I'm here to discuss the murder of your husband.' "

Von Villas told Judge Schempp that when she asked the jurors if they had discussed or heard anything about the proceedings outside the courtroom, no juror raised a hand, but "I saw no less than four jury members look down or look away. I knew they knew something. You don't spend thirteen years as a cop without knowing when people are lying." He said he believed the jurors knew about his previous convictions. Again, he added, "I don't believe if I was a civilian I would have been found guilty."

As for Joyce Reynolds and Julie Rabold: "The witnesses corroborated what Ogilvie said, not what happened. This was never properly brought out to the jury." Von Villas looked down at the counsel table, twisting a pencil as he spoke. "Mr. Jorgensen had no right to give people the answers when he interviewed them." He charged that Assistant D.A. Jorgensen had stopped making tapes of police interviews with witnesses after August 1983 because he didn't want to be "haunted" by them later, and that many crucial phone calls had never been discussed with the jury. He described a call from Joyce Reynolds, who told him: "Bob, I love you with all my heart, but I'll do anything I have to to protect Julie." Later, Von Villas stated, "She would in fact and did in fact do anything to protect her family."

Judge Schempp told Von Villas: "You were a very hard-working man. You have a good background. . . . Greed overtook you. . . . Sometimes, the more money one makes the more one wants to acquire. I don't know what triggered your change . . . but your conduct was so outrageous to take another's life for profit that you deserve the maximum sentence." Like Ford, Robert Von Villas received life without possibility of parole.

Bruce Adams, calling later from parts unknown, launched into a vitriolic diatribe when asked for his opinion of the sentences. "It's played a heavy trip on my head," he said, admitting that the life or death question had kept him up more than a few nights. "But I say *gas* the motherfuckers. After five years, those motherfuckers didn't have the balls to say one fucking word to atone for their fucking crimes. All through the penalty phase, it's been a whole sympathy routine, which is a crock of shit, a fucking masquerade. Ford has no remorse for taking Weed's life or attempting to take Loguercio's life. . . . It never seemed to bother him. He wasn't remorseful when he got that ten grand from Von Villas in the office for doing Weed. I mean, he was laughing. And now all of a sudden, I guess we should just have a fucking lonely hearts club, a sympathy club for

Ford. And Von Villas, he's despicable. I mean, you have over three million Vietnam veterans in this country. I'd say forty-eight percent of them suffer from posttraumatic stress. You don't see them out in the street killing innocent people. Furthermore, you don't see them as police officers, sworn to serve and protect the people of Los Angeles, out killing people for fucking money. So I can't see this sympathy routine. And this bit about the kids. If they cared so much about their fucking families they would have never started this shit. And you can tell me all about this 'born-again Christian' religion Ford suddenly found, but I don't buy it. I really don't, because *I've* become a born-again Christian. I was baptized a Christian two years ago on Easter Sunday."

Adams went on to explain that his newfound faith had finally helped him to overcome his problems with PTSD.

Epilogue

Where Sunset Ends

BRUCE ADAMS AND HIS FAMILY ARE LIVING IN PARTS UNKNOWN. Adams remains fearful of possible attempts on his life by Ford and Von Villas. Unlike protected witnesses in federal programs, he has received no additional financial assistance or aid in relocating and starting a new life.

Jan Elmira Ogilvie is serving fifteen years to life in the Frontera Institution for Women. She will become eligible for parole in 1993. Currently, however, the California Parole Board is extremely conservative with regard to indeterminate sentences, so it is likely that she will serve a full fifteen years—at least.

Subsequent to her incarceration, Ogilvie has expressed her dissatisfaction in a string of legal actions, most notably a $760 million lawsuit filed on November 30, 1992. That action lists former Deputy D.A. Robert O'Neill as chief defendant, enjoined by a long list of codefendants, including the State of California and the County of Los Angeles. Ogilvie claims that she was forcibly drugged and beaten by jail authorities and that her confession was coerced by "unlawful plea bargining" that was "induced by drugging and false representations and false evidence, suborned testimony from drugged plaintiff in regard thereto, and other 'tricks' and deceptions used by prosecution and defense counsel to manipulate drugged plaintiff witness."

During the Weed trial, a Sybil Brand psychiatrist testified that Ogilvie has been diagnosed as "residual schizophrenic" and was on tranquilizers during the time she testified against Ford and Von Villas at the preliminary hearings.

It should be noted, however, that Ogilvie's action details forty-three claims.

These involve almost everyone—her own attorneys, former husbands, employees, Ford and Von Villas's defense counsel—in an entangled "conspiratorial cover-up" of the "alleged disappearance" of Tom Weed. The entirety of the suit, at the very least, is bizarre. Its disposition is pending.

Robert Von Villas is serving life without parole at New Folsom prison (California State Prison at Folsom), a modern high-security facility adjacent to "old" Folsom prison. Von Villas has worked in the prison infirmary's medical lab, and since April 1991 has been assigned as a clerk in the prison law library, where he helps other inmates prepare appeals. His rating reports have all been excellent.

On November 16, 1992, the California State Court of Appeals ruled to vacate Von Villas's first-degree murder conviction in the Weed case. The court cited jury misconduct—the fact that two jurors apparently knew of Von Villas's previous convictions. Rather than ordering a reversal, however, the court ordered that the trial judge Darlene Schempp conduct a hearing to "test the credibility" of the jurors to determine if Von Villas should be afforded a new trial. As of January 1993, that hearing is still pending. Von Villas has additional appeals pending as well. Those close to him say he is committed to pursuing all possible appeals if these should fail—in federal court, before the Supreme Court, and through writs of habeas corpus.

Von Villas is now a happy grandfather. Judy has divorced him and remarried. According to Jack Stone, Bob remains remarkably upbeat. "If I were in his position I'd be terribly depressed, but Bob's an amazing individual. Throughout my five years of dealing with him, I rarely ever saw him depressed. Even now, when I talk to him, there are times when he has tremendous ups."

Richard Ford is also serving life without parole at New Folsom prison and resides in the same cell block as Von Villas. Ford works as the cell block clerk, performing administrative duties such as maintaining supply lists. His rating reports have all been excellent, and he has had no disciplinary actions against him. He is also involved in shepherding numerous appeals. Lillian Ford has divorced Richard and remarried.

Richard Ford was quoted in a story about the death penalty written by Tim Rutten in the *Los Angeles Times* on March 19, 1992. "The gas chamber is a nice quick death," Ford stated. "Life without the possibility of parole is a slow death. That's what it amounts to. This is no paradise. You know in every situation that confronts you here that there is no light at the end of the tunnel. There is no light, period. You're going to die in prison—alone, by yourself, and that's the way it is. There is nothing you can do about that. So, to say you're getting off easy is an absurdity."

Notes and Acknowledgments

THE MAKING OF THIS BOOK HAS BEEN A LONG, ARDUOUS ADVEN-
ture, and I am indebted to many people for help along the way. Foremost among
these is my agent, Mike Hamilburg, who stuck with me through the whole
bumpy ride.

My research on this case began in 1984 while I was writing a story on
LAPD's Internal Affairs Division for *Los Angeles Magazine*. Later, in March 1988,
I wrote a piece on Ford and Von Villas for that magazine. (My thanks to editors
Bill Braunstein, Lew Harris, Roger Claire, Jean Penn, and the whole *L.A. Mag*
crew.)

I met Bruce Adams in 1984 at the Geary Cade Board of Rights Hearing.
Adams later granted me an exclusive interview and provided me with a transcript of the van tapes, which had been supplied to him to refresh his memory
before the preliminary and grand jury hearings. Using this document, in March
1985 I wrote for *Hustler* magazine an unexpurgated (NC-17 rated) story on the
case and Adams's ongoing plight as a protected witness. (My thanks to editors
Glenn Hunter and Richard Warren Lewis.)

Later, in July of 1986, I was subpoenaed by Von Villas's defense attorneys
to appear at an evidentiary hearing in superior court. The court demanded that
I hand over the tapes of my interview with Adams so the defense attorneys could
examine them for "discrepancies" with testimony Adams had given to IAD
investigators, the grand jury, and at various hearings. I refused, believing I was
protected by the First Amendment "shield" law.

Notes and Acknowledgments

I was informed that freelance writers were not covered by this law and was threatened with immediate incarceration. My attorney argued in court on my behalf for nearly a week. Lengthy briefs were filed on both sides. Following an "in camera inspection" (a private hearing of the tapes in chambers), Judge Williams finally ruled that I did not have to release my tapes.

I would like to thank Larry Flynt for supplying me with an excellent attorney, Edwin McPherson, then of Cooper, Epstein and Hurewitz, and for paying my (substantial) legal fees in this matter. The publishing community can say what it likes about Mr. Flynt; few publishers would have so nobly come to my rescue.

Mr. Flynt has reason to be proud, as the decision regarding these tapes eventually resulted in a landmark ruling. After Ford and Von Villas were convicted, my tapes became the principle subject of an appeal. On October 9, 1992, the California appellate court upheld Judge Williams's decision. The California Supreme Court further upheld this decision on January 14, 1993. As a result of these rulings in *The People vs. Von Villas,* rights granted under the First Amendant shield law have been expanded to protect all freelance writers in California.

Many of the 140 witnesses called during the first (Loguercio) trial did not prove crucial enough to mandate inclusion in this book. However, propriety calls for mention of one of these—me. I was subpoenaed by Jack Stone and questioned about my relationship with Bruce Adams. I testified that I had written one magazine article on the case, was working on another, and had signed an agreement with Adams for the exclusive rights to his story. I was then pursuing book and film deals, from which Adams could potentially gain financial compensation. Defense attorneys would argue that this constituted additional motive for Adams to lie. On cross-examination, I stated something I now wish to reiterate: my purpose and intent was to write a nonfiction, unbiased account of the case based on multiple sources. My agreement with Adams specifically called for him to tell me only the truth.

In exchange for his cooperation, I have granted Adams a percentage of the royalties from this book. This arrangement did not preclude me from employing additional sources or questioning his version of events. Bruce Adams is at the center of the story, but I have not endeavored to tell it solely from his point of view.

From my personal experience, certain aspects of Adams's character are problematic—primarily a trustworthiness in regard to finances. Bruce is not someone to whom you want to lend money. However, in his relating to me the events of this case, I found no substantive discrepancies with what he told authorities or testified to in court. Perhaps the only grievous exception is this:

Bruce testified at the first trial that he never told Von Villas about his sexual relationship with Loguercio. He later told me that he had. In fact, he told me he enjoyed rubbing it in Bob's face.

I'd like to thank Bob O'Neill, Richard Lasting, Jack Stone, Rickard Santwier, Donald Feinberg, Judge Alexander Williams III, and Judge Darlene Schempp for helping me make sense of the legal morass of this case; Harry Eddo, Roger Fox, Sam Oddo (ATF), and Commander William Booth (LAPD spokesperson) for helping me understand the investigation and Bob Sojquist (unofficial LAPD historian) for supplying me with historical data. I would also like to thank all of those in the LAPD, as well as family and personal acquaintances, who spoke with me about Ford and Von Villas. My thanks to reporters Tom Mallory, Patricia Kline Lerner, Claudia Puig, Susan Forrest, and Arnie Friedman for aid, commiseration, and encouragement.

Richard Ford and Robert Von Villas declined to be interviewed for this book. To my knowledge, they have yet to grant interviews to anyone in the media, aside from one *Daily News* story.

I met with Von Villas on one occasion at L.A. County Jail shortly after the first trial. I did not interview him; he interviewed me. He sought to learn whether I believed he was guilty. I told him I was keeping an open mind. Apparently, that wasn't good enough for Bob. He also said he would have to be compensated before he would talk. I told him that couldn't be arranged. (At the time, the Son of Sam law forbade convicted felons to profit from their stories. This law has since been overturned.) He suggested that there were ways around the law. He didn't want anything for himself; he wanted money for his family. He implied that if I were to cut a deal with his wife, Judy, he would talk. "I have a trunk somewhere. And inside that trunk are all my diaries from Vietnam, everything I saved from my years with the LAPD," Von Villas teased. Of course, since I'd sat through the first trial, he knew I was aware of his reputation for being a pack rat and a meticulous record keeper. "And perhaps that trunk could be made available to you," he said.

I told him that such an arrangement would violate the spirit, if not the letter, of the Son of Sam law, and neither I nor any reputable writer or publisher would agree to do that.

Although chained to a bench and dressed in prison blues, Von Villas was very charming. He smiled broadly, and I felt a genuine warmth, even through the plexiglass partition that separated us as we spoke over telephones. But I was more than charmed. I was flabbergasted by his moxie. He not only insisted on speaking to a writer who would champion his innocence, but he wanted that writer to pay him for the privilege. Tom Sawyer, who demanded payment from friends for the privilege of whitewashing his fence, was a piker compared with Bob Von Villas. Of course, from what I've learned about Bob's gift for hustle, I wouldn't be surprised if he someday made such a sale. Richard Ford, through his attorneys, also indicated to me that he would not talk unless there was "something in it for his family."

However noble the concern for family, this reasoning always struck me as preposterous. Ford and Von Villas didn't really have a story to sell—unless they admitted their guilt and agreed to relate how they had descended into a life of crime. They wanted to sell the story of their innocence—a tale they'd already told at the trials. If they had new (previously undisclosed) information to show their innocence, would they make someone pay them to reveal it? I couldn't help but think that if they were truly innocent, they would talk to anyone willing to listen.

Some peripheral research for this book was done by Kathleen O. Ryan, to whom I am most grateful. I'd like to thank Morgan Entrekin and Anton Mueller at Atlantic Monthly Press for enduring some rough seas with this often-crazed gonzo (okay, difficult) author. Finally, my thanks to a treasured collection of inspirators, mentors, benefactors, and friends: Cliff Yudell, Paul Stevens, Rick Cramer, Stewart Weiner, Alan Williams, James Dalessandro, Terry Corey, Rick Profita, Val Comsa, Ted Nugent, Lori Behren DeStefino, Carol and Edward Plocha, Michael Graham, Michael Tennesen, members of the Monday night writer's group in Santa Monica (founded by Michael Lally), and, of course, Helen Golab (Mom).